African Traditions Meeting Islam

A Case of Luo-Muslim Funerals in Kendu Bay, Kenya

I0091983

Lawrence Oseje

Langham

MONOGRAPHS

© 2018 Lawrence Oseje

Published 2018 by Langham Monographs
An imprint of Langham Publishing
www.langhampublishing.org

Langham Publishing and its imprints are a ministry of Langham Partnership

Langham Partnership
PO Box 296, Carlisle, Cumbria, CA3 9WZ, UK
www.langham.org

ISBNs:
978-1-78368-543-1 Print
978-1-78368-555-4 ePub
978-1-78368-556-1 Mobi
978-1-78368-557-8 PDF

Lawrence Oseje has asserted his right under the Copyright, Designs and Patents Act, 1988 to be identified as the Author of this work.

All rights reserved. No part of this publication may be reproduced, stored in a retrieval system or transmitted, in any form or by any means, electronic, mechanical, photocopying, recording or otherwise, without the prior written permission of the publisher or the Copyright Licensing Agency.

British Library Cataloguing-in-Publication Data
A catalogue record for this book is available from the British Library

ISBN: 978-1-78368-543-1

Cover & Book Design: projectluz.com

Langham Partnership actively supports theological dialogue and an author's right to publish but does not necessarily endorse the views and opinions set forth here or in works referenced within this publication, nor can we guarantee technical and grammatical correctness. Langham Partnership does not accept any responsibility or liability to persons or property as a consequence of the reading, use or interpretation of its published content.

To:
My lovely wife Dorcas, and our beautiful, handsome, and wonderful children – Jael, Rosebell and Emmanuel.

Contents

Dr Lawrence Oseje has carried out an unusual phenomenological research into a local Muslim culture. His descriptions and analyses of Luo-Muslim funeral practices in Kendu Bay, located in the western part of Kenya, reveal the complex nature of religio-cultural expressions of Islam in Africa. The kind of Islam that Luo Muslims uphold is a result of the integrative synthesis of two human realities: Luo traditions and Islamic ideas. Dr Oseje takes painstaking effort to present the insider's religio-cultural perspective of life and death among the Luo Muslims. His work provides us with many insights into intriguing realities of ordinary Muslims. I am certain that this book will be a source of invaluable information on cultural features that have been missing in the field of Islamic studies. I recommend this rare volume on Muslim culture to cross-cultural missionaries, inter-religious academicians, and organizational leaders, who intend to understand cultural concepts and values that ordinary Muslims hold, particularly in Africa.

Caleb Kim, PhD
Director, Institute for the Study of African Realities
Coordinator, Centre for the Study of Religions
Africa International University, Nairobi, Kenya

A study into cultural issues of death such as this is indeed a milestone into seeing the very fabrics that hold, guide and inform the day-to-day experiences of the life of ordinary Muslims in Africa. From the beginning of his writing to the very end, Dr Oseje has demonstrated that the real fear that faces ordinary Muslims is not mainly found in the major issues of life, such as joblessness, economic deprivation and national governance, but mostly in the very basics of life, such as disease, sickness, natural disasters and death. The funeral, as he has discussed it, is the converging point where both tradition and Islam meet. The similarities and the differences between Luo traditions and Islam thus define the kind of identity to which these ordinary Muslims ascribe. His research has no doubt demonstrated the need to understand every culture from its own context. By so doing, the temptation to generalize cultures will be avoided.

Josephine Mutuku, PhD
Senior Lecturer, Africa International University, Nairobi, Kenya

This study on the impact of Luo traditional views on the contemporary Luo-Muslim conceptualization of death is simultaneously relevant and articulate.

Part of the strength of this work is the manner in which it utilizes religio-cultural images to clarify important theological justifications. The story of the late S. M. Otieno that Dr Lawrence Oseje writes about exemplifies this reality. His focus on Luo-Muslim funerals narrows the larger conversation to one ethnic extraction's point of view in respect to the question of death. The solidarity and the unity that the Luo Muslims demonstrate when one of their own or any other member in the Luo community dies, is itself very insightful. The Luo-Muslim community discussed here not only presents the significance of the place in which one should be buried, but it also provides meaning and value attached to one's ethnic identity. Oseje has thus reminded us that our traditions affect our religious beliefs, our practices and ultimately our theology.

James Kombo, DTh
Deputy Vice-Chancellor of Academic Affairs
Associate Professor of Systematic Theology,
Daystar University, Nairobi, Kenya

List of Diagrams

List of Tables

Acknowledgements

First and foremost, my deepest gratitude and sincere appreciation go to the almighty God who has enabled me to come this far. I am indebted to my family for their prayers and encouragement. My lecturers, colleagues with whom we have toiled together in our doctoral studies, and my students whom I have taught in various colleges, seminaries and universities, have all been a blessing to me and my family. A very special appreciation goes to African Scholarship Exchange (ASE), Langham Scholars Programme, and friends to Prof Caleb Kim in South Korea and USA. They have overwhelmingly supported me financially and with their prayers. In 2014, Langham Scholars Programme through Dr Ian Shaw gave me the opportunity to travel and do library research in Oxford University in England. While there, I made new friends with people like Drs Ida Glaser and John Chesworth, both from Centre for Muslim-Christian Studies (Oxford), CMCS. Dr Chesworth in particular took his time to introduce me to different libraries in Oxford. He also helped me get the books and other resources that were very helpful for my research. Rev Victor Ayuko and his family were also very resoureful to me during my stay in England. I spent most of the nights in their home while doing research in the SOAS library in London. My special appreciation also goes to Liz McGregor for her motherly care and love. As the Langham representative in charge of pastoral care to Langham scholars in Europe, she travelled all the way from Edinburgh in Scotland just to come and encourage me in Oxford. She has kept writing and encouraging me ever since I left Oxford University.

My deep-felt appreciation goes to my supervisor Prof Kim and his wife. He has not only been my academic mentor but also a father and a friend. He has worked and nurtured me in this academic journey for over twelve years. His love and dedication to his students is quite outstanding. He has shown us through his life that it is possible to integrate academic life and the Christian faith. His wife has been a mother and a role model to many of us. Amidst challenges of health, she is ever smiling and ever welcoming. I have enjoyed her hospitality for the many years I have been in AIU. I owe a lot of gratitude to my brother, Rev Charles and his family for their generosity. Special thanks also go to Rev Walter Andhoga, Dr Oliver Wala, and Prof Alex Mekonnen. They too have overwhelmingly offered me financial supports. I cannot forget to thank Mrs Susie Mercer, Edwin Maina, and Dr Broadhead for their editorial work on my dissertation.

Abstract

This study has attempted to investigate the impact of the Luo traditional view on the Luo-Muslim conceptualization of death in Kendu Bay. The study consists of eight chapters. In the introductory chapter 1, a discovery is made on how the triple religions (Christianity, Islam and ATR) have interacted with each other in Africa. A specific reference touching on the origin and the spread of the Luos from their homeland in South Sudan to Kenya and in Kendu Bay in particular has been made. The contact of the Luos in Kendu Bay with Islam has also been shown. In chapter 2, a review has been made on the exisiting literature. The center of focus is on how different communities view death and the practices accompanying it. This review has been done with the view of seeing how different communities that have become Muslims in Africa cope with the changes. A special reference in the study of the Luos has been made in the light of the event of death of S. M. Otieno that occurred in 1986.

In chapter 3, data was collected from a group of sixty-five Luo Muslims residing in the town of Kendu Bay. Ethnographic research method was used. Data was analyzed using Kim's Synthetic Triangular Approach, STA. From this approach, a theoretical approach that provides a description of Luo traditional elements in Luo-Muslim perception of death was developed. Chapters 4 to 8 address the findings of the research. Chapter 4 explains how Islamic teachings have influenced the Luo-Muslim traditional view of death. These teachings are centered on the meanings and causes that Luo Muslims ascribe to death, and the rituals that they follow right from the time somebody dies to the time of burial and after. The chapter has also sought to explain the outcome that Islamic teachings bring on the Luo-Muslim view of death. In chapter 5, it has been argued that despite the influence of Islam, the elements of Luo tradition in the Luo-Muslim perception of death are still evident. In looking at these Luo traditional elements, the Luo-Muslim funeral was first divided into three stages: initial, middle and later stage. The three domains that emerged from those three stages are the total, partial and non-Islamic domains. In each stage also, similarities and differences between Islamic and Luo traditional elements have been described.

Chapter 6 analyzes the effects of Luo traditional elements on Luo-Muslim understanding of death and its related practices. These influences were approached in each stage of the Luo-Muslim funeral. In each stage also, the elements of continuity and discontinuity of the Luo-Muslim view of death and its related rituals were analyzed. Chapter 7 discusses the synthetic nature of Luo-Muslim conceptualization of death in Kendu Bay. This chapter has been divided into two. In the first part, the religio-cultural characteristics and themes underlying Luo-Muslim views of death have been described. The second part highlights the Luo-Muslim conceptualization of death as reflected in the funerals of the Luo Muslims. Chapter 8 gives a summary of the findings, and recommendations. In general, the finding chapters reveal two fundamental truths about the Luo Muslims in Kendu Bay. First, the Luo Muslims have kept due diligence to their past Luo traditional funeral practices. The findings have also revealed that the Islam that Luo-Muslim practice is contextual.

Arabic Transliteration

The table below contains some Arabic words, their transliteration and meanings as used in this book. All of them except Allah have been italicized in the text.

Arabic	Transliteration	Meaning
الله	Allah	This denotes the name of God.
الذكر	Dhikri	It is a practice mostly by Sufis in which death is remembered continously.
الغسل	Ghusl	This is used to refer to the ritual of ablution performed on the deceased body. It is meant to purify the person from any obstacle that could hinder his or her "journey" to paradise
الفقه	Fiqh	This is the jurisprudence that is part of the Islamic law. It is the Islamic philosophy and science that is established based upon the teachings of both the Qur'an and the Ḥadīth.
وضُوء	Wuḍū'	It is another Islamic procedure in which every part of the body of the deceased is washed using water. This is done in the belief that Allah loves those that have been kept pure and clean.

CHAPTER 1

Introduction

A lot has been written about Christianity and Islam. Such writings have included the kind of relationship which for many centuries has existed between these two major religions of the world. Armour in a more specific way provides the timeframe by which Christians and Muslims have related with each other in history: "This interaction between Christendom, East and West, and Islam has gone on for the better part of fourteen centuries as the two civilizations have lived side by side, their land borders coterminous."[1] While expressing similar views in respect to the period that both Christianity and Islam have engaged and interacted with each other in history, Bennett in his book, *Understanding Christian-Muslim Relations: Past and Present*, also points out the various dynamics which have characterized the relationship of those two religions: "Confrontation versus conciliation, debate versus dialogue."[2] In other words, and as Goddard puts it, Christians and Muslims have encountered both moments of peace as well as conflicts in their existence with each other.[3]

Whereas the focus depicted above has mainly revolved around the historical development of both Christianity and Islam in terms of their relationship, both religions have also been seen to have had contact with traditional religions in Africa. In fact, Ali Mazrui, in his article, "African Islam and Competitive Religion: Between Revivalism and Expansion," refers

---

1. Rollin Armour, *Islam, Christianity, and the West: A Troubled History*, Faith Meets Faith Series (Maryknoll, NY: Orbis Books, 2002), 1.

2. Clinton Bennett, *Understanding Christian-Muslim Relations* (London; New York: Continuum, 2008).

3. Hugh Goddard, *A History of Christian-Muslim Relations* (Chicago, IL: New Amsterdam Books, 2000).

to African indigenous religion, Christianity and Islam as "Africa's Triple Heritage" or "Africa's Trinity of Cultures."[4] On the one hand Mazrui describes both Christianity and Islam as highly competitive and universalists in their quest for conversion of all humankind. But on the other hand he describes indigenous tradition as very tolerant.[5] Mazrui further notes that "The indigenous toleration today has often mitigated the competitiveness of the imported Semitic religions (Christianity and Islam)."[6]

Tolerance by African traditional religion and the competition by the two Semitic religions greatly help to explain the widespread influence that both Christianity and Islam have made in the continent of Africa. But does it mean that such impact by these two faiths into the African society has replaced the African traditional beliefs and practices? If this is so, how should Mbiti's argument that "Africans are notoriously religious"[7] be viewed? Does the African religiosity exhibit a mixture of some Christian or Islamic elements with the African traditions? Do the African Christians or African Muslims still perform their traditional rituals or have the two faiths have completely transformed and replaced their old practices? Such questions are also posed by Mazrui in his writing about the Nigerian context: "Can one be both a Christian and a follower of an African indigenous religion? Can one be both a Muslim and a follower of an African indigenous religion?"[8] In answering these questions, Mazrui argues that Muslims in countries like Guinea, Algeria and Somalia have produced hybrids in which traditional religion is practiced alongside Islam. The late Kwame Nkrumah is also reported to have declared that he was a Marxist-Leninist and a non-denominational Christian.[9] Although Nkrumah's case is a bit different, it nevertheless illustrates the kind of religious hybrid that is commonly adopted in many parts of Africa.

---

4. Ali A. Mazrui, "African Islam and Competitive Religion: Bewteen Revivalism and Expansion," *Third World Quarterly* 10, no. 2 (1988): 503.

5. Mazrui, "African Islam," 500.

6. Mazuri, 500.

7. John S. Mbiti, *African Religions and Philosophy* (New York: Praeger, 1969), 1.

8. Mazrui, "African Islam," 504.

9. Mazuri, 504.

Apart from those countries mentioned above, Senegalese, despite being predominantly Muslims, are also still viewed as clinging to their African cultural practices. This is proven by the writings of both Diene and Burrell who, observe that "90 percent of the people in Senegal are Muslims, 10 percent are Christians but 100 percent are 'animists.'"[10] This trend brings into question the kind of influence both Christianity and Islam have had over the African traditional worldview. Has this influence ever permeated all aspects of African life in terms of religious tradition and practice? If so, why is it that the majority of African Muslims or African Christians still fall back to their traditional customs when death strikes? Does African traditional religion offer better answers than either Christianity or Islam?

The first clue in responding to the above questions is found in what Diene and Burrell write about the African culture: "There is an African 'core culture' that basically decides the forms of expression of these religions [Christianity and Islam], as well as the dynamics of their progress or decline, on the continent of Africa."[11] The understanding that may be derived from the above statement is that it is the indigenous culture that dictates the kind of Christianity or Islam being practiced in a given context. At the same time the above sentiment also carries the very idea that Christianity and Islam as practiced by the Africans are basically "African" and not so much of Western or Eastern as it is usually perceived.

This study examines the African traditional practice in relation to Islam. However, the inclusion of Christianity in this section is due to the many similarities but also dissimilarities it shares with Islam in the way they have interacted with African traditional religion. Both religions have had great influence in the lives of the African people, yet both religions have also been affected in a similar way by the African traditional religions. There is, therefore, a lot in common between these three religions. In the light of such understanding, it is only vital that the discussions revolving around African traditional religion, Christianity and Islam be examined further.

---

10. Doudou Diene and Jean Burrell, "A Dynamic Continuity between Traditions," *Diogenes* 47, no. 187 (1999): 16.

11. Diene and Burrell, "Dynamic Continuity."

Relationships in the Triple Religions

A study focusing on the interactions of Christianity and Islam with the African traditional religions is a development which has been widely discussed by various scholars in their different academic disciplines. In the field of world Christianity, some renowned scholars such as Andrew Walls,[12] and Philip Jenkins[13] have in their respective books written about the shift of Christianity to the Majority World. While mainly focusing on world Christianity, the two argue that Africa in the past was mainly a field for mission but has now become a missionary sending agency to other parts of the world. Jenkins and Walls further highlight the fact that Christianity was not brought to Africa by foreign missionaries as is usually claimed but rather Africans were practicing it long before the coming of the missionaries from the West. Unlike Jenkins whose writing covers very little about Islam in relation to African traditional religion, Walls candidly writes about "Africa as the theatre of Christian engagement with Islam in the nineteenth century."[14] In his discourse, Walls describes how Africa, more specifically West Africa, had become highly competitive in the search for converts to Christianity and Islam. He also narrates the kind of influence that the two religions have brought into the continent of Africa such as social, political and economic.

In both anthropological and theological circles, the influence of Christianity and Islam on Africa has also been captured by such scholars as Olupona, and Kato.[15] Olupona who in particular focuses on both Christianity and Islam, argues that the presence of those two religions in Africa has completely transformed the African way of worship and their lifestyle.[16] In other words, this view lays an emphasis on the fact that the

12. Andrew F. Walls, *The Missionary Movement in Christian History Studies in the Transmission of Faith* (Maryknoll, NY: Orbis Books, 1996); Andrew F. Walls, *The Cross-Cultural Process in Christian History Studies in the Transmission and Appropriation of Faith* (Maryknoll, NY: Orbis Books, 2002).

13. Philip Jenkins, *The Lost History of Christianity: The Thousand-Year Golden Age of the Church in the Middle East, Africa, and Asia – and How it Died* (New York: HarperOne, 2011).

14. Walls, *Cross-Cultural Process*, 136–154.

15. Jacob K. Olupona, "Major Issues in the Study of African Traditional Religion," in *African Traditional Religions in Contemporary Society* (St. Paul, MN: Paragon House, 1991), 25–33; B. H. Kato, *Theological Pitfalls in Africa* (Kisumu, Kenya: Evangel, 1975); B. H. Kato, *African Cultural Revolution and the Christian Faith* (Jos, Nigeria: Challenge, 1976).

16. Olupona, "Major Issues in the Study."

African traditional way of life has been transformed by those values found in Christianity or Islam. This sentiment is echoed by Kato who in both of his books, *African Cultural Revolution and the Christian Faith*[17] and *Theological Pitfalls*,[18] sees Christianity as having produced change in African religion.

But although Kato does not speak in the same way of Islam as an agent of change, his claim reflects how Islam may be engaging the African customs. This is based on the fact that both Christianity and Islam are similar in their mode of operation towards African traditional religion. Kato's conviction on the absolute transformation in African Christianity to become devoid of any traditional practices is portrayed in the manner he raises a serious warning against the danger of universalizing Christianity. This, in his view, can easily lead to syncretism and proselytism.[19] However, such views as presented by Olupona and Kato, which basically advocate discontinuity of the African traditional view as a result of the impact of Christianity and Islam, have been disputed by several scholars. Among them are Oduyoye,[20] and Bediako[21] who have referred to such claims and positions as the "rejectionism" or "radical discontinuity."

The transformation of African traditional religion as a result of its interaction with Christianity and Islam has been the subject of discussion for several decades. On one side as outlined above is the position of discontinuity argued by both Olupona and Kato, among other scholars. On the other side is the argument advocated mainly by Bediako[22] and Oduyoye.[23] They contend that the coming of Christianity, and in Mbiti's case, Islam[24] as well, did not in any way erase or replace the African traditional practices. Their argument strongly emphasizes the very concept of continuity. Whereas these concepts of continuity and discontinuity may only be viewed to represent

---

17. Kato, *African Cultural Revolution*.

18. Kato, *Theological Pitfalls in Africa*.

19. Kato, 94.

20. Mercy Amba Oduyoye, *Hearing and Knowing: Theological Reflections on Christianity in Africa* (Eugene, OR: Wipf & Stock, 1986), 62.

21. Kwame Bediako, *Theology and Identity: The Impact of Culture upon Christian Thought in the Second Century and in Modern Africa* (Oxford: Regnum Books, 1992), 386.

22. Bediako, *Theology and Identity*.

23. Oduyoye, *Hearing and Knowing*.

24. Mbiti, *African Religions and Philosophy*; John S. Mbiti, *Introduction to African Religion*, 2nd ed. (Nairobi, Kenya: East African Educational Publishers, 1975).

extreme ends of the spectrum in their respective capacity, there is a sense in which, another perspective has been brought into the discussion. This has been reflected in the writings of some scholars such as Conn,[25] Musk,[26] and Kim.[27] Their view tends to merge both sides of the issue in a term they refer to as synthesization of culture. While mainly focusing on Islam, the above scholars have argued in their respective writings that since Islam is a cultural religion, its interaction with an African traditional worldview has brought about the element of cultural synthesis. Viewed from their perspective, the idea of dichotomizing or segmenting into either continuity or discontinuity for both Islam and the African culture becomes insignificant.

The Challenges of African Traditional Religion

The researcher has previously outlined the three main areas namely, continuity, discontinuity and synthesis under which the outcome of interaction between African traditional religions and Christianity or Islam is usually categorized. But while the influence of Christianity and Islam on the African customs and traditions is undisputable, very little effort has been made to study the level of the impact African traditional practices have caused to those major religious traditions. The wide acclaim to African traditional forms of rituals and practices by those who have already converted into Christianity or Islam in our contemporary society is something worth exploring. But unlike in Christianity where many of its African followers are still generally known to be following and participating in the traditional ceremonies, Islam for a long time has generally been regarded as an exception. This was not until recent anthropologists have ventured into this particularly area of study. Lamin Sanneh, I. M. Lewis, Gilliland Stewart, Bill Musk, Hiebert, Shaw and Tienou, and Caleb Kim, have ventured into this research and have

---

25. Harvie M. Conn, "Islam in East Africa: An Overview," *Islamic Studies* 17, no. 2 (1978): 75–91.

26. Bill A. Musk, *The Unseen Face of Islam: Sharing the Gospel with Ordinary Muslims at Street Level.* (London: Monarch, 2004).

27. Caleb Chul-Soo Kim, "Considering 'Ordinariness' in Studing Muslim Cultural and Discipleship," in *Discipleship in the 21st Century Mission*, eds. Timothy Park and Steve K. Eom (Kyunggi, Korea: East West Center for MRD, 2014), 177–192; Caleb Chul-soo Kim, *Islam among the Swahili in East Africa*, 2nd ed. (Nairobi: Acton, 2016).

provided quite substantial information on the kind and shape that Islam is taking as a result of its contact with the indigenous society.[28]

Their writings are contextual in the sense that each one of them has focused on an area within the local setting that has given Islam an identity in line with the local context. The local expression which gives Islam its very identity by which it manifests itself significantly points to the fact that the kind of Islam practiced by the local communities vary from one setting to the other. Areas in Islamic practice which have been compatible with the African traditional customs, and to which the above scholars have pointed at in their respective writings mainly include; the view of supernaturalism, religious leaders and institutions, ancestral veneration, relationships between human beings and divinities, and the interpretation of life and death and their accompanying rituals.

Several communities in Africa, particularly in areas where Islam has taken root, can easily identify themselves with those areas of cultural life as mentioned above. Whereas it is an interesting venture to explore such areas in their respective contexts, the researcher limits himself to a study surrounding death among the Luo Muslims in Kendu Bay. The focus in this area of study has been motivated by a couple of reasons. First, even though the Luo community is generally known to have been following many of its traditional customs for over several decades, the area that has received a considerable amount of publicity is its practices surrounding the aspect of death. The death of S. M. Otieno in 1986 brought into public domain the intense and elaborate rituals that usually accompany the Luo traditional death ceremonies. If the discussions by missiologists such as Paul Hiebert and Charles Kraft on "culture change" are anything to go by, then it may

---

28. Lamin O. Sanneh, *The Crown and the Turban: Muslims and West African Pluralism* (Boulder, CO: Westview, 1997); I. M. Lewis, *Islam in Tropical Africa*, 2nd ed. (London: International African Institute, 1980); Dean S. Gilliland, *African Traditional Religion in Transition: The Influence of Islam on African Traditional Religion in North Nigeria* (Ann Arbor, MI: Univ. Microfilms, 1972); Dean S. Gilliland, *African Religion Meets Islam: Religious Change in Northern Nigeria* (Lanham; London: University Press of America, 1986); Musk, *Unseen Face of Islam*; Paul G. Hiebert, Robert Daniel Shaw, and Tite Tiénou, *Understanding Folk Religion a Christian Response to Popular Beliefs and Practices* (Grand Rapids, MI: Baker Books, 1999); Kim, "Considering 'Ordinariness'"; Kim, *Islam among the Swahili*.

be argued that some Luo traditional practices are slowly fading.[29] However, traditional customs pertaining to the death of loved ones, mourning and burial processes are still found to be commonly followed not only among Christians but also among the Luos who have converted to Islam.

Another factor that has motivated the researcher in carrying out this area of study has to do with the practice of Islam by the Luo people. As it is elaborated in different sections of this study, it is interesting that although the Luo Muslims are scattered in different towns and cities, the majority of them are mainly found in Kendu Bay. Even though it may not be necessary to construed that the presence of many Muslims in Kendu Bay is as a result of some mysterious "powers" in the area, their large concentration in that particular environment still elicits some kind of interest in the subject. In the first place, this interest provides the need to look into the factors that are responsible for the Luo conversion into Islam. Second, this interest emerges due to the fact that both the Luo community and Islam are cultural entities that are usually viewed as representing opposite sides in matters to do with obsequies or funeral rites.

Looking at the two cultures from both surface level and from a historical perspective, Muslims tend to bury their dead ones almost immediately. On the other extreme end, the Luo people tend to take many days with the dead body before burying it (such as with the case of S. M. Otieno). Such a reflection obviously provides the need to bring into perspective various concepts such as the view of time and the understanding of the human body. These aspects have been incorporated into this study. This study further examines other core areas in the Luo-Muslim practices of death, mourning and burial that are fundamentally relevant to the Luo people in Kendu Bay. These areas as explored will go a long way in providing the answer to the question concerning the cultural identity of the Luo Muslims, whether they are Luo or Muslim or both. But apart from exploring the factors that have significantly contributed to Luo conversion into Islam, another area that forms the basis of interest for the researcher in carrying out this study is the fact that whereas a lot has been written on both the influence of Islam and

---

29. Paul G. Hiebert, *Anthropological Insights for Missionaries* (Grand Rapids, MI: Baker Books, 1985); Charles H. Kraft, *Anthropology for Christian Witness* (Maryknoll, NY: Orbis, 1996).

the traditional customs of the Luo people, as far as their practices of ritual at funeral services are concerned, there is very little that has been written in providing specific description into the kind of life that the Luo Muslims follow in their day-to-day living.

The focus of this whole study is on the cultural aspect of Islam in relation to the Luo customs which have been in existence for many decades. Special emphasis is on those customs revolving around death. As it shall be noted in the preceding sections, many scholars such as Shiino,[30] Ocholla-Ayayo[31] and Kisiara,[32] are very categorical that the Luo people put a lot of emphasis on rituals such as those surrounding the passing on of their loved ones. The demise of S. M. Otieno in 1986 has widely been used to illustrate the rigor by which customs of bereavements are strongly upheld by the Luo community. Shiino for instance, in her writing on *Death and Rituals among the Luo in South Nyanza*, observes that: "Luo, a Western Nilotic people, perform a series of rituals feasts for the dead because of their strong fear and respect for the dead."[33] Shiino's thesis is very relevant in this study since her writing is within the context of the Luo in South Nyanza to which Kendu Bay is part of. This by extension may imply that the customs being carried out following the passing on of a member of the community may not be new to both Luo Muslims and non Luo Muslims. But if it is true that the Luo Muslims are fully aware of these rituals and do practice them, then the question as to what extent Islam has permeated the lives of these Muslims out of their traditional customs is a very valid one. The interest of this study partly emanates on the need to respond to the above concern.

Apart from investigating the area mentioned above, it is also in the interest of the researcher to examine ways by which the Luo Muslims have conceptualized Luo traditional practices regarding death. The intention of this is to bring to surface those aspects of Luo funeral customs that have

---

30. Wakana Shiino, "Death and Rituals among the Luo in South Nyanza," *African Study Monographs* 18, no. 3/4 (1997): 213–228.

31. A. B. C. Ocholla-Ayayo, "Death and Burial: An Anthropological Perspective," in *The S.M. Otieno Case: Death and Burial in Modern Kenya*, eds. J. B. Ojwang and J. N. K. Mugambi (Nairobi: Nairobi University Press, 1989), 30–39.

32. Richard Kisiara, "Some Sociopolitical Aspects of Luo Funerals," *Anthropos* 93, no. 1/3 (1998): 127–136.

33. Shiino, "Death and Rituals among the Luo," 213.

been incorporated into the Luo-Muslim practice. The other areas of traditions which have not been infused into Luo-Muslim system have also been explored in this study. Reasons that seek to explain the continuing or discontinuing aspects of the Luo customs in Luo-Muslim funerary procedures are also provided. Ways in which the life of an ordinary Luo Muslim is affected by the change and continuity of culture have also been discussed. In summary, this study aims to establish the emerging trends revolving around Luo and Muslim customs within the Luo-Muslim funeral practices. However, since this study is one that involves interactions between Islam and African traditions that are generally assumed to be different and far from each other, especially when it comes to funeral practices, it is necessary first to provide a brief history about the Luo Muslims. Such a background outlines certain historical facts that help to explain the very existence of the Luo Muslims. It also identifies various fabrics of the individual culture in the context of Luo Muslim that defines its identity.

The Luo People in Islam

The way Islam has gained ground among the Luos in Kendu Bay, despite the belief that they are deeply rooted in their traditional practices, may obviousy be a surprise to many people. A cultural phenomenon in the Luo customs that over the years has been quite perplexing and has been followed with a lot of interest in different parts of the world is funeral practices. On the other hand, Islam, as a cultural religion, has been tenacious in many of its practices. Both Luo and Muslim customs seem to pull in the opposite direction. Investigating this tension between them is therefore necessary in order to understand the kind of Luo Muslims who are residing in Kendu Bay. But in order for such to be undertaken, it is first necessary to understand both Luo and Muslim cultures separately. It is against such analysis that the Luo-Muslim perspectives on issues surrounding death can be weighed. This impacts the question of whether or not the individual cultures from both Luo and Islam inform their worldview.

The Perception of Luo on Death: A Case Study of S. M. Otieno

The perception of Luo on death is best illustrated by the incident of S. M. Otieno, who died in 1986. Several scholars have widely written on this subject. Most of their writings tend to portray the Luo as culturally inclined to their funeral traditions. Van Doren, for instance, while writing in *Death African Style: The Case of S. M. Otieno*, points out that: "A funeral is a very important social event that is believed to be vital in keeping touch with the spirits of ancestors of the ethnic group."[34] The importance being referred to in the above should not be construed to mean that death is something that the Luo people usually look forward to, but rather when it happens, relatives and other community members get involved in providing various rituals as required by the culture. Such importance may also imply the urgency by which matters pertaining to death are handled among the Luo people.

In the above statement, van Doren has also pointed out a belief in ancestors. This religious sensation was very common in most African traditional religions. Such a belief in the ancestors, found among many African communities, is very significant for two reasons. First, it points to the fact that there is a belief in life after death. As it is pointed out elsewhere in this study, several rituals were carried out in respect and in honor of the dead. Such rituals were also meant to appease the dead so that they could actively protect the living from various calamities including premature deaths. But also, the whole notion about ancestors especially among the Luo was a matter that was not only religious but also carried with it social, economic and political meaning to the community. Apart from van Doren,[35] Stamp in her article, "Burying Otieno: The Politics of Gender and Ethnicity in Kenya," also highlights on the social aspect of a Luo funeral. She states that a "Funeral is an occasion to affirm kinship ties and reify the social order, which encompasses the living, the dead, and the unborn."[36] Although it is possible to argue that this social aspect of a funeral is something common

34. John W. van Doren, "Death African Style: The Case of S. M. Otieno," *The American Journal of Comparative Law* 36, no. 2 (1988): 337.

35. van Doren, "Death African Style."

36. Patricia Stamp, "Burying Otieno: The Politics of Gender and Ethnicity in Kenya," *Journal of Women in Culture and Society* 16, no. 4 (1991): 833.

in many communities, Stamp's comment that "the burial site affirms and testifies to the inviolable connection between a lineage and its land,"[37] draws a sharp contrast with the view that is apparent in orthodox Islam. He seems to suggest that traditionally, the Luos are attached to their ancestral land. It is therefore unimaginable to bury the deceased outside their ancestral land.

The land of one's birth which is commonly referred to as the "ancestral land" was the place where the remains of a Luo adult were expected to be buried. It was due to this expectation that the body of S. M. Otieno took such a long time before being buried. Stamp captures on the incidences which followed after the death of Otieno.[38] The battle between the widow of the deceased and his clan revolved around what can be referred to as "house" and "home" concepts. As Stamp reports, "Clans argument was that Otieno's matrimonial residence in Nairobi was his 'house' but not his 'home.'"[39] The "house" concept means that wherever any Luo person resides apart from their own ancestral land, they are there temporarily. This means that after death, the body is supposed to be transported "home," to the ancestral land. Religious, social and political dimensions were all displayed in this death saga of S. M. Otieno. Religiously in the sense of the widow, Wambui argued in court through her lawyer that her late husband was a Christian and therefore could not wish to be subjected to the traditional customs of burial.[40] But on the other hand, the clan argued that "Mr Otieno having been born and bred a Luo remained a member of the Luo tribe and subject to the customary law of the Luo people."[41] The fact that ruling was made in court in favor of the customary law helps to affirm the perception by many concerning the Luo as Shiino points out: "The Luo are generally known in Kenya as a people who are seriously concerned with their burial place, more than any other ethnic group."[42] While Shiino has helped to provide a general understanding that many people have towards the Luo as far as their

---

37. Stamp, "Burying Otieno," 833.
38. Stamp.
39. Stamp, 823–824.
40. Stamp, 809.
41. Stamp, 825.
42. Shiino, "Death and Rituals among the Luo," 213.

practices of funeral rituals are concerned, she has not attempted to explain why the concern for the burial place is a very serious issue among the Luo.

The concern over funeral matters is essentially cultural. The researcher therefore addresses this subject by looking at the concept of worldview and how it affects the life of the community. This topic of worldview has been discussed by both Kraft[43] and Hiebert.[44] In using the two sources, the researcher explains how things displayed on the surface of a given culture such as insistence on burial in the ancestral land and widow inheritance have deep assumptions. In other words, the main concern here is that it is useful to explore and get the deeper meaning of the practice being undertaken. This subject on death has many rituals that go with it such as mourning and burial, forms, and meaning. They have been explored.

Both religious and political dimensions also played out over the death of S. M. Otieno. This was well demonstrated by the presence of many politicians and the presiding bishop, Henry Okullu. Stamp, reports: "Members of parliament praised Okullu for highlighting the compatibility of Christianity and African traditions."[45] Okullu's statement was in reference to the fact that Otieno's body had finally been returned "home." He is quoted as speaking in aphorism: "Even a bull, no matter how ferocious, is always tethered in the homestead."[46] Such a statement coming from a religious clergy is further proof of the seriousness that the Luo attach to their funeral customs. In fact, the circumstances that emerged as a result of the demise of S. M. Otieno highlight the manner in which the Luo community handles death related matters. It is in this sense that Stamp further concludes: "Otieno had a more vivid presence in Kenyan politics and society in death than he did in life."[47] What Stamp implies is that there are a lot of Luo traditions that are followed when someone dies than in any other ceremony. The evidence to this can presently be observed in a funeral situation of a Luo person. Irrespective of where one has died, every effort is made to transport the body in order to be

---

43. Kraft, *Anthropology for Christian Witness.*

44. Hiebert, *Anthropological Insights for Missionaries.*

45. Stamp, "Burying Otieno," 835.

46. Gisesa Nyambega, "Controversy Stalks Wambui Otieno Even in Death," *Standard Newspaper Kenya,* 19 May 2013, https://www.standardmedia.co.ke/article/2000083940/controversy-stalks-wambui-otieno-even-in-death.

47. Stamp, "Burying Otieno," 835.

buried in the ancestral land. This may prove to be economically expensive since it is not only the body that is transported but also the coffin and food must be bought.

The above incidences which include the story of the death of S. M. Otieno are issues that have happened in the recent past. Observing old customs is a matter that is still in place today. All these are indications that there has been very little change as far as the perception of death is concerned among the Luo. Due to this minimal change, the term "tradition" had been used in this study to refer not only to the old customs that are no longer being practiced in the modern world but also to the on-going practices among the Luos and other African communities. The fact that the Luo traditions are still being followed in a religious community and in particular Islam raises some critical questions. One of these critical concerns has to do with the role of religion (Islam) as a transforming agent to the existing Luo traditional practices. The question as to whether there is a concrete distinction between a Luo and a Luo Muslim is also a very valid one. In most of the anthropological circles, especially among cross-cultural missionaries, the issue of bi-culture is very common. According to Hiebert, a bi-culture is established when missionaries interact with the people in their local context.[48] But the level of this interaction is very hard to tell bearing in mind that both missionaries and the local people have their own cultures which do not always disappear. It is in this sense of the matter that Hiebert firmly puts it that: "No matter how hard they [missionaries] try, they cannot completely 'go native,' since the earlier culture of their childhood can never be fully erased. While the bi-culture borrows from different cultures of its participants, it is more than the sum or synthesis of those cultures."[49] Although Hiebert is less particular on what exactly becomes of the two cultures as a result of their interaction with each other, he has nevertheless helped us to understand that the outcome might be more than the mixing of the two cultures.

In applying what Hiebert shares above in the light of this study, the researcher proposes that the Arab Muslims (missionaries) who brought Islam to the Luo people may not have completely gone "native" in the manner

---

48. Hiebert, *Anthropological Insights for Missionaries*, 228.
49. Hiebert, 228.

they bury and conduct other rituals of death. This same truth has also been noted among the Luo who despite being Muslims are not necessarily practicing Islamic traditions in matters to do with funerals. If the situation on the ground is as it has been described, then it is valid to ask why the Luo Muslims still revert to their traditional practices especially whenever somebody dies. Could it be said that traditions never die? Or has religion (Christianity or Islam) lost its effort to make a complete difference in the lives of the local people? In responding to the above concerns, the researcher has attempted to show that whereas Islam, just like Christianity has had a great influence in the lives of the Luo people, the Luo traditional worldview has equally affected the Luo-Muslims' view of death. Both Luo and Islam as cultural entities have each affected the perception of the Luo Muslims in regard to the manner in which they carry out funeral practices.

Luo Muslims in Kenya

The study in the previous section has mainly dealt with the broader picture of the Luo as a whole. A fair presentation has been made showing different dimensions of the Luo customs on death. In this section, the researcher highlights how the Luo came into contact with Islam. This is very vital since knowing a people's past helps to understand their present situation. It is from this study that the current Luo Muslim residents in Kendu Bay may be understood. Luos are said to be the largest group of the Nilotes.[50] Their contact with Islam stretches back to the time the Nilotes were migrating from South Sudan.[51] The history of South Sudan and how the Nilotes got in touch with Islam in that region is a very interesting one (see appendix B). This contact came about as a result of fighting. As Adede puts it:

> Conflict ensued as the Nilotes pushed their way to enter Southern Sudan. As they managed to enter Sudan they named

---

50. Bethwell A. Ogot, *History of the Southern Luo* (Nairobi: East African Publishing House, 1967), 127; Jude J. Ongong'a, *Life and Death: A Christian–Luo Dialogue* (Eldoret, Kenya: Gaba Publications, AMECEA Pastoral Institute, 1983), 6.

51. George W. Otieno Adede, *Luo Origins and Politics: Emergence of Nilotic Luo in 1000 AD and After* (Nairobi: Gramowa, 2010); Marie France Perrin-Jassy, *Basic Community in the African Churches* (Maryknoll, NY: Orbis Books, 1973); Ogot, *History of the Southern Luo*, 41; Pasquale Crazzolara, *The Lwoo. Part I,* (Verona: Instituto Missioni Africane, 1950), 31–32.

it "Kasudna." This might have come from the Luo speakers word *Sudna* which means "move out." This is the word the Nilotes might have used to drive away the Northern Egyptian Muslims during their expeditions; hence it became the name of the modern Sudan as a country.[52]

The name "Sudan" is also used to mean "black" in Arabic. This name might have come from the northern Egyptian Muslims who originally occupied the place. If the above facts are accurate, then it is possible to conclude that the Nilotes had some understanding of Islam before migrating into the places they presently occupy. The Luo migration into Kenya came about from three main areas through Uganda: Joka-Jok (presently occupy western Kenya), Joka-Owiny (occupy Alego land) and Joka-Omolo Ochielo. It was this third group that, after coming slightly later in the middle of the sixteenth century or so, migrated into western Kenya spreading into Ugenya, Gem and later to South Nyanza.[53] It is these Luo people who moved to South Nyanza who are of interest to this study. This as it has been pointed out previously, is due to the fact that Kendu Bay is located in South Nyanza.

Luo Muslims in Kendu Bay

In two of his books, *History of the Southern Luo*[54] and *A History of the Luo-Speaking Peoples of Eastern Africa*,[55] Ogot provides in detail the history of the Luo people in South Nyanza. He claims that "the Luo migration into South Nyanza came as a result of clan feuds in which a section of the Luo decided to adopt the remedy their forefathers had always employed in such circumstances – they migrated, to South Nyanza."[56] The fact that these Luos in South Nyanza were able to incorporate that which their forefathers had always been doing literally describes what the term "Luo" signifies. It comes from the literal word, *luwo* which, in Luo, means to "follow." In providing

---

52. Adede, *Luo Origins*, 10–11.

53. Adede.

54. Ogot, *History of the Southern Luo*.

55. Bethwell A. Ogot, *A History of the Luo-Speaking Peoples of Eastern Africa* (Kisumu: Anyange, 2009).

56. Ogot, *History of the Southern Luo*, 159.

the meaning, Ongong'a states that, "the name 'Luo' was derived from the fact that the members of this group of Nilotes were constantly following one another in groups in search of better pasturage."[57] But as Ogot also puts, this "following" was not only limited to the search for pastures but it also applies on customs of burial. He shows this through an example of the Padhola group in whom he classifies the Luo as part of the group.[58]

Concerning burial of the dead, Ogot states that: "According to Padhola custom, all the dead are buried with their heads facing the direction from which the clan of the deceased entered the country."[59] If as Ogot argues, the Luo are part of the Padhola, then the "father-son" relationship is likely to have played out between the two communities. But relationships are always changing. It might therefore not be surprising to see that the same *luwo* concept is still being reflected in the customs that the Luo people are practicing. This conclusion may be true considering the kind of experiences that the Luo society has had in the past. One such area is politics, where the majority of the Luos are widely perceived to be "following" in the footsteps of their leaders whenever important decisions are to be made. Such decisions seem not only to be limited to politics but also other areas of life as well. The issue of opinion leaders and the act of "following" after them are also fundamental in the Luo society. It is in this light that the researcher seeks to establish in this study whether or not this aspect of "following" has contributed to the Luo conversion into Islam.

As it has previously been noted, Luos are part of the wider Nilotic group that moved into Kenya. Other groups include; the Highland Nilotes, Plain Nilotes and River-Lake Nilotes. Ogot cites Luo as the group with the highest population among those Nilotes who migrated to Kenya. He also adds that Luos are "the second largest tribe in Kenya."[60] However, this truth might only be as accurate as the census that was taken in 1962. In the last demographic study,[61] it was revealed that the Luo community comes fourth. One

57. Ongong'a, *Life and Death*, 7.
58. Ogot, *History of the Southern Luo*, 108–112.
59. Ogot, 108.
60. Ogot, 127.
61. Peter Greste, "Kenya Defends Tribal Census Figures," *BBC News, Africa*, 31 August 2010, https://www.bbc.co.uk/news/world-africa-11143914.

of the communities that now is ahead of the Luos in number according to the last census taken is the Kalenjin that now stands as the second largest tribe in Kenya (2009 Census). This is paradoxical considering the fact that Ogot has placed the population of Kalenjin below that of the Luos. If the current statistics are correct, then the most probable conclusion that can be made to justify the decrease in the Luo population as compared to those of other communities that are now ahead of them is that many of their members have been dying. This is due to the wars that Luo people faced during their migration with the other communities – first, with the Abyssinians of Ethiopia and then with the Muslims of Sudan in their attempt to occupy the area.[62] Another justification is that the other communities have been multiplying much faster.

But in a religious system such as that of the Luos, there are obviously questions that strike people's minds whenever somebody dies. Does their traditional religion offer any explanation about the existence of death? Where do the dead go? Who is responsible for death? What should be done to restrain it? These are just but a few questions that seem to imply that the Luo people must have been concerned with matters surrounding death. But since this reality of death is obviously disturbing, could it be that Islam came into Kendu Bay as an answer to this quest? This question about the coming of Islam with a view to responding to the needs of the Luo regarding their religious inquiry is very valid. It's valid in the sense that Islam was not the only religion that was being practiced in Kendu Bay. Christianity had also been spread in this region. In fact, according to Adede, the Seventh Day Adventist (SDA) church was established in Kendu Bay in 1906. Islam came and was established six years later by the Arab Muslims.[63] The above evidence shows that Christianity was established in the region much earlier than Islam.

If the arguement that Christianity came much earlier than Islam into Kendu Bay is accurate, then it is expected that the majority of the Luo people in this region should have converted into Christianity. Although this might have been the case in the early periods of Christianity in Kendu Bay, the current trends show that majority of the population in Kendu Bay

---

62. Adede, *Luo Origins*.
63. Adede.

are basically Muslims.[64] Many of these Luos have adopted the Islamic faith despite the tremendous efforts that various Christian organizations have put in place in transforming the lives of the people in the area. This is evidenced by the presence of many NGOs (Non-governmental Organizations) and other faith-based institutions such as health centers, schools, HIV testing and counseling services and orphanages in Kendu Bay town and its neighboring environs. Although the said organizations are mostly run by Christians, some of them are also been operated by the Muslims. Apart from the other NGOs which are not faith related, the organizations that are run by both Christians and Muslims have the sole purpose of converting as many people as possible to their side. But whereas this goal of conversion is something that both faiths have strived to achieve through such various institutions as have been pointed out above, it cannot be said for certain whether these Luo converts to Christianity or to Islam are Christians or Muslims.

Several evidences abound that raise this uncertainty for both Luo-Christian and Luo-Muslim identity particularly in the area of death rituals. The question is commonly asked and indeed not easily answered, is why the Luo people tend to revert to their traditional cultural practices whenever they are faced with death? A number of practices that are carried out in the event of death seem not to auger well especially from the Christian traditional standpoint. As it has been pointed out in the previous section, many of these Luos who mixed their traditions with their Christian faith are usually described as having forsaken the true faith. In some places, they are not allowed to participate in the Holy Communion while in other places they are even excommunicated from the church. This problem becomes worse among the widows who in most cases are the ones expected traditionally to undergo many rituals when their husbands die. The most common of these rituals is wife inheritance. The issue of wife inheritance is viewed differently from Christian and Luo traditional perspectives. The researcher in various sections of this study has attempted to provide the different perspectives as they are understood.

Although this research is centered on the Luo Muslims, the idea of discussing Christianity alongside Islam has three main reasons. First, as it has

---

64. Kenya National Bureau of Statistics, *The 2009 Kenya Population and Housing Census* (Nairobi: Kenya National Bureau of Statistics, 2010).

been discussed before, both Christianity and Islam have a long common history. In this sense, it is not easy to understand the involvement of one without the other. Second, both faiths have also had a common interest in Africa. They have moved in almost every country in Africa with a similar zeal of making converts into their religions. Christianity and Islam have also made some significant contributions as far as spiritual, political, social and economic development is concerned in the African region. All these aspects, though in different measures, have in turn impacted the cultural hegemony of the African societies. Lastly, such cultural influence has caused various African groups to react differently to both Christianity and Islam. It is therefore common to find in some areas like Nigeria and other places that different communities are embracing either the Christian or the Muslim faith. Within the Luo community, some people follow Christianity while others are Muslims.

But while it is commonly perceived as normal in following different religions, what has been found to be quite interesting is the manner in which these very people who are known to be followers of either Christianity or Islam are still reverting to their traditional beliefs and practices. The argument here is that once a person has become a Christian or a Muslim, their traditional beliefs and practices should not only give way to the new religion but the new religion should influence their life. People, who mix their religious faith with traditions especially as evident in funeral ceremonies, are perceived as not true followers of their new found religion. But interestingly, this suspicious thinking is mostly common in Christianity. Islam has generally been perceived as a religion whose cultural practices are similar to those of African traditions. It is also regarded as an influential religion. To those who have converted to Islam, this could mean to them that every bit of practice is completely Islamic. A number of examples are cited showing the kind of change that has taken place in those Muslim converts such as their style of worship, their use of Arabic language in prayer, and their lifestyle in general. The impression that this brings is that Islam is a transforming religion compared to Christianity.

Even though this research is not about comparing the two religions, this kind of thinking about dominance and superiority between Christianity and Islam has helped in understanding the historical developmental of the two religions. Such a wealth of history is very significant since it helps both individual Christians and Muslims to understand and to appreciate the kind and the evolvement of the religion that they are practicing. Generally, history is an appealing subject even to the Africans themselves. It is all about the past in which African cultures are deeply rooted in. This current study is partly historical since it looks into the past traditions and how they have shaped the experiences of the contemporary Luo Muslims on death and its surrounding rituals. There is therefore nothing wrong with a historical study such as the one advanced between Christianity and Islam.

But while appreciating the various writings on both the historical and the advancement of Christianity and Islam, very little focus has been made into the kind of impact that the traditional African practices is having especially towards Islam. The aspects of continuity and discontinuity have mostly been understood to be as a result of the contact between Christianity and African traditional beliefs and practices. The contact between Islam and African worldview particularly that which touches on death and burial practices seems to have been ignored. But in areas where both Islam and African traditions are mentioned as interacting with each other, the focus seems to center on the kind of influence that Islam has brought to the African practices. Such evidence that emanates only from the surface level has provided very little help in understanding how African Muslims contend with their traditional beliefs and practices in their religion of Islam. Little or no understanding on the impact of local traditions has caused the thinking that Islam is a more superior to the traditional religion. Little knowledge has also minimized the need to study and understand the values that African communities attach to their cultural beliefs and practices such as the ones followed when a person dies.

This issue of reverting to traditions as is common among the Luo Muslims should elicit some throbbing questions by any serious seeker as to the kind of impact that such reverting has caused. Asking questions should be necessary considering that there has been interest in exploring how Islam has interacted with different African traditions and the results that have been produced by being in contact with each other. Even though it is important to recognize that the presence of Islam in Kendu Bay has changed the cultural life of its Luo Muslims in many significant ways, reverting to their

Luo traditions is an indication that this change is very minimal. Just like other communities around the world, funeral proceedings among the Luos are usually characterized by numerous rituals. Interestingly, and just like in Christianity, this area of death and its accompanying rituals is the point to which most reverting occurs among the Luo Muslims. This being the trend, there are certainly many questions that require some answers. Among such questions are: How were the Luos converted to Islam? What kind of teachings do the Luo Muslims follow? How does the mixing of Islam and Luo traditions inform the Luo-Muslim understanding of death and its rituals?

This research has been done with a view to providing the answers to those questions. In so doing, the researcher seeks to establish matters involving Muslim conversion, the teachings provided by Islam and its influence. The kind of relationship and experiences that have emerged as a result of the interaction between Luo traditional customs and Islam in the area of death is also addressed with a view to understanding how Luo Muslims identify themselves. Understanding their identity not only minimizes the idea of generalizing Muslims but also would play a very crucial role among the anthropologists, missionaries working in cross-cultural contexts, theologians in seminaries, institutions of higher learning, and other mission organizations in putting in place viable structures and systems that address the felt-needs of the people.

Problem Statement

The central research issue being addressed is how the Luo traditional view has affected the understanding of death among the contemporary Luo Muslims living in Kendu Bay, Homa Bay County of Kenya.

Research Questions

From the above problem statement, the following research questions have been raised:

(1) How has Islam influenced the contemporary Luo-Muslim view of death?

    (a) What is the Islamic teaching on death that Luo Muslims in Kendu Bay follow?

(b) How does the Islamic teaching in Kendu Bay inform the
contemporary Luo-Muslim view of death?

(2) What are the elements of the Luo traditional view that still exist
in the contemporary Luo-Muslim perception of death?

(a) How do the contemporary Luo Muslims explain the
existence of the Luo traditional view in their cultural
perception of death?

(b) How does the Luo traditional view affect the Luo-Muslim
understanding of death and its related practices?

(c) What determines continuity or discontinuity of the Luo
traditional view of death among Luo Muslims in the Kendu
Bay context?

(3) How can we best describe the synthetic conceptualization of
death among contemporary Luo Muslims in Kendu Bay?

(a) What are the religio-cultural characteristics and themes
underlying Luo-Muslim view of death?

(b) How do the Luo Muslims conceptualize death in their
funeral rituals?

Objectives of the Study

This study has three main objectives. First, it seeks to assess the extent to
which Islam has affected the contemporary Luo-Muslim view of death.
Under this objective, the study identifies the Islamic teachings on death
which are being followed by the Luo Muslims in Kendu Bay. It also describes
how the Islamic teaching informs the contemporary Luo-Muslim view of
death in Kendu Bay. Second, the study identifies the elements of Luo traditional views that are still in existence in the contemporary Luo-Muslim
perception of death. This objective further gives a description on how the
contemporary Luo Muslims explain the existence of Luo traditional view in
their cultural perception of death. It explains how the Luo traditional views
affects the Luo-Muslim understanding of death and its related practices.

It also identifies what determines continuity or discontinuity of the Luo
traditional view of death among the Luo Muslims in Kendu Bay. Finally,
the description to the synthetic conceptualization of death among the contemporary Luo Muslims in Kendu Bay is offered in the best way possible. In

order to achieve this, the experiences that the contemporary Luo Muslims have in their understanding of death, and its related practices, as a result of mixing both Luo and Muslim cultures are have been explored. A description on how the experiences of the Luo Muslims explain their conceptualization of death has also been sought.

Significance of the Research

A lot of studies have centered mainly on Christianity and Islam as the two major religions impacting many societies around the world. While this is true, very little has been said concerning the increasing influence that the African traditional religion has in some parts of Africa. One such area and community where traditional practices seem to dominate is in the death of a loved one among the Luo community in Kendu Bay. It is increasingly becoming common to find Luo Christians or Luo Muslims especially in Kendu Bay reverting back to their former customs whenever there is a funeral. The Christian community in particular, has been quick to term such reversion as "backsliding." Some of the so called "backsliders" have found their way into Islam although still hanging on to their Luo traditions. This study provides a window to the understanding of the experiences of the Luo Muslims that make them easily revert to their Luo traditions even after converting Islam. Comprehending these experiences is insightful in two ways. First, it helps pastors, cross-cultural missionaries and other church workers devise meaningful approaches and programs that not only appreciate local culture but also respond to the felt-needs of the people. Second, creating a positive approach and view to culture would also encourage the local people to appreciate their cultural heritage.

In the academic world, a lot has been written that tend to confine Islam only to beliefs and ideologies such as politics, law and philosophy. While these are necessary areas to be investigated, very little has been said in regard to the person (Muslim) who holds and is influenced by these beliefs. This in turn has produced a chasm between orthodox or classical Islam and popular or ordinary Islam. A lack of understanding about the existence of this chasm has partly led to a widespread claim that Muslims throughout the world are identical in their religious beliefs and practices. This generalization has minimized the need to adopt relevant approaches and methodologies that are necessary for the understanding of Islam in its cultural context. Training church workers and doing ministry in a cross-cultural context such as Africa require the understanding of the local culture. This study has therefore put into focus the need to do contextualization among the Luo Muslims. This requires that new meanings and forms are provided especially on funeral practices as they apply in Luo-Muslim context.

Last, this study poses a challenge to the theologians over the need to provide curricula that will seek to address and promote cultural values that traditional religion holds. This challenge is also expected to raise interest among missionaries and other Christian bodies that are involved in cross-cultural ministry and interfaith dialogue to give priority to the studying of courses related to phenomenological synthesis of Islam and the local traditions.

Delimitations

Apart from Islam, Christianity has also brought about some significant influences on the Luo traditional view of death. But on the other hand, it is also a fact that the Luo traditional view has also affected the way Christians view death and other related practices such as mourning and burial. But even though these are valid areas that could have been necessary to explore, the researcher has not undertaken to study them but instead has focused on the way Luo Muslims understand death and practices related to it.

Limitations

Death being a very unpredictable incidence, the researcher did not have the opportunity to attend many funerals and to observe the many activities that take place as he would have wished. The two funerals he attended had also some limitations. For instance, he was not able to observe very closely the washing and the shrouding of a deceased female. This was due to the fact that Luo Muslims do not encourage male persons to mix with female persons. Even the male deceased that he had the opportunity to observe more closely had still some restrictions. One of the restrictions was that he was not allowed to take pictures during the process of washing and shrouding the body. The door where the body of the deceased was being washed remained closed most of the time. He was given very little access to observe those ritual activities of washing and shrouding. Many people also preferred not to talk freely about death when they were at the funeral. The researcher had to wait to a later time. With many people in the funeral and the busy schedule they had, the researcher was limited by time to interview as many as he would have wished.

Assumptions

In this research, it was assumed that both Luos who are not yet converted to Islam and the Luo Muslims alike believe in the existence of one God who has manifested himself to people in different ways. It was also assumed that religio-cultural beliefs and practices of the Luo Muslims on death can be used as a source of contextualizing the gospel.

Definition of Terms

Certain terms (that are italicized) which are used in this study have been defined based on different writings by some scholars. The term *view* as used in Luo traditional view is derived from the term *worldview*. According to Geertz, a people's worldview is their picture of the way things in sheer actuality are, their concept of nature, of self, of society.[65] Rapport and Overing also define a worldview as "representing fundamental conceptions of the world, conceptions which ramify into all other thoughts and feelings about the world, and conceptions which directly influence how people behave in the world."[66] In light of the two views, a worldview is used in this paper to signify thoughts and behaviors the Luo Muslims portray in regard to their former "ways" of conducting funerals.

The term *tradition* or *traditional* as used by both Beheraand Gilliland is synonymous with terms, "tribal," "indigenous," and "local."[67] It is also similar to the term "animism," which is derived from term *Anima*, a Latin word

---

65. Clifford Geertz, *The Interpretation of Cultures* (New york: Basic books, 1973), 126–127.

66. Nigel Rapport and Joanna Overing, *Social and Cultural Anthropology: The Key Concepts*, 2nd ed. (New York, NY: Routledge, 2007), 431.

67. M. C. Behera, *Tribal Religion: Change and Continuity* (New Delhi: Commonwealth, 2000), 93; Gilliland, *African Religion Meets Islam*, 1.

meaning soul. It conceives of human being as passing through a life surrounded by the ghostly company of powers and elements mostly impersonal in character.[68] Therefore, *traditional view* speaks of the invisible world of the spirits (the living dead and the ancestors) that the Luo Muslims are still attached. The term *Luo traditions* as used in this study also include material objects and practices that are embedded in kinship relations and the sociality of everyday life that guide important events such as dealing with death.[69] The way Luo traditions have found their way into the belief and practices of Luo Muslims is referred here as *Continuity*. Behera refers to continuity as "holding on to the legacy of cultural heritage handed down through generations."[70] Behera also writes of *Change* or *Discontinuity* as referring to "adaptation by which a society faced with evolving paradigm 'adapts' to the changing expectations."[71] In relation to the Luo Muslims, the term discontinuity denotes the fact that Luo traditional beliefs and practices are no longer adhered to by the Luo Muslims in their understanding death. In other words, they have completely been discarded and are therefore no longer followed or practiced in their day-to-day living.

The term *conceptualization* refers to the mental and emotional or psychological processes by which Luo Muslims have gained the understanding and explain their experiences on death and its related rituals. The term *Contemporary* as used in this study refers to the Luo Muslims living in Kendu Bay between 1930 and 2015. *Syncretism* is another term that has been used in this study. In line with Braukamper's thinking, it is used in this paper to mean the coalescence of cultural traits in its broadest sense, but is normally employed with reference to the realm of religion. It is used to denote not only the phenomena and processes taking place within a single religion but also occurring between two or more religions.[72] The two religions or cultures that are being referred to in this context are Islam and Luo traditions. The

---

68. Behera, *Tribal Religion*, 93.

69. Ruth Prince, "Christian Salvation and Luo Tradition: Arguments of Faith in a Time of Death in Western Kenya," in *Aids and Religions Practice in Africa*, eds. Felicitas Beeker and P. Wenzel Geissler (Netherlands: IDC, 2009), 66.

70. Behera, *Tribal Religion*, 95.

71. Behera, 95.

72. Ulrich Braukämper, "Aspects of Religious Syncretism in Southern Ethiopia," *Journal of religion in Africa* 22, no. 3 (1992): 194.

Luo traditions have been divided into two. The first one is referred to the *former or old Luo traditions* while the second is referred to the *current or latter Luo traditions*. The former or old Luo traditions are those Luo funeral beliefs and practices that the contemporary Luo Muslims have adopted from their forefathers. The current or latter Luo traditions are the Luo beliefs and practices that Luo Muslims follow. They have modified those funeral beliefs and practices from the traditions of their forefathers.

Besides Christianity, Islam has also had a great influence in many parts of Africa. It has penetrated and affected the traditional customs of the African people. A good case lies in funeral practices among the Luos. The story of the death and the burial of S. M. Otieno attests to the fact that the majority of the Luos are rooted in their traditional customs. But with the majority of Luo-Muslim population in Kendu Bay signifies that there is an extent to which Islam has influenced them. This influence may, however, not be very comprehensive due to the fact that elements of Luo traditions are still being followed.

CHAPTER 2

Literature Review

Introduction

Rather than being viewed as static, Islam is a religion on the move. Islam has been described by Faloloa, Braswell and Ayoub as a religion that has spread quickly to different parts of the world.[1] Of particular interest especially in Faloloa's writing is the mention of Africa as a place where the spread of Islam has affected the socio-economic and political systems in different communities.[2] The systems that Faloloa refers to are cultural. If that is so, then the situations surrounding death should be taken as one of those areas where such systems have been affected. The subject of death is of great significance in many of the African communities. This is because it is an area where many traditions that have been passed on by the forefathers still prevail. Such traditions include practices such as mourning of the deceased, widow inheritance, the food eaten by mourners, funeral speeches and dirges.

Various sources point to the Luo as a community that follows elaborate traditional rituals of death. These rituals are mostly socio-economic and political in nature. Van Doren, for instance, views S. M. Otieno's death as "a social event that is believed to be vital in keeping touch with the spirits of ancestors of the ethnic group."[3] Apart from pointing to death as a social

---

1. Toyin Faloloa, "The Spread of Islam and Christianity and Their Impact on Religious Pluralism in Africa," *Dialogue & Alliance* 2, no. 4 (1988): 5; George W. Braswell, *Islam: Its Prophet, Peoples, Politics, and Power* (Nashville, TN: Broadman & Holman, 1996), 207; Mahmoud Ayoub, *Islam: Faith And History* (New York: Oneworld, 2004), 70.

2. Faloloa, "Spread of Islam and Christianity," 6.

3. van Doren, "Death African Style," 337.

event, van Doren also indicates that it contains some ties with the spirit world. Her perspective makes it clear that it is not merely on social grounds that the burial and other activities are undertaken but also on account of the deceased's spirit. In other words, the deceased is believed to be capable of inflicting harm on the living. This explains why keeping in touch with the spirits through rituals is a necessary overture. In line with her thinking, Kisiara also observes: "a [Luo] kin is willing to contribute an ox to be slaughtered to feed mourners, but is most likely not to agree to contribute the same towards the treatment of an ill relative, or to pay school fees or to bail a relative out of jail."[4] The fact that the dead are treated differently from the living is testimony of the view that the Luo people hold concerning their dead ones. However, it is not clear from van Doren and Kisiara whether such treatment to the deceased is out of fear or respect for the deceased.

A recent story that appeared in one of Kenya's daily newspapers about the demise of Senator Otieno Kajwang of Homa Bay gives a clear revelation about how death affects the socio-economic and political systems of a Luo funeral.[5] In these systems, both the essence of fear and respect to the deceased are always evident. The essence of fear comes out of a belief that unless proper rituals are carried out, the deceased's spirit might turn against their immediate relatives and the community at large. Proper rituals include burying the deceased in his ancestral land. If the deceased has a home that he has built himself, like the late Kajwang, he must be buried in his home. Respect or honor to the deceased is demonstrated by the large number of mourners who turn up for burial. It is also characterized by slaughtering many cows, goats and chickens during the funeral. Just as it was in the case of the late Kajwang, the presence of many politicians and several cars at the deceased's funeral also attest to the fact that the deceased has been honored. It also tells of what kind a person the deceased was.

---

4. Kisiara, "Some Sociopolitical Aspects," 130.

5. According to the *Daily Nation*:
   Otieno Kajwang died on 19 November, 2014 from a heart attack. He has been the senator for Homa Bay county where Kendu Bay, the place of research lies. He is being accorded a heroic send off by the slaughtering of 60 bulls, 50 goats and 500 chickens. Besides this, 20 buses have been hired to carry people to his burial home. Many political big weights are expected to attend his burial. (*Daily Nation*, 26–27 Nov, 2014).

But apart from the slaughtering of many animals, other scholars while citing the case of S. M. Otieno have also revealed that the body of the deceased has to be transported and buried in his Luo ancestral home.[6] There is no doubt that the task of transporting the body is economically involving. This is in addition to the huge expenses that are incurred during the period of time that the body is put in the mortuary. However, the body may also be kept in the mortuary due to other reasons. In the case of the late Otieno, his body was kept in the mortuary for one year before it was finally laid to rest. It took this long due to a legal tussle in court between his clan and his wife over who should bury him. But the fact that the body can stay in the mortuary for such a long time and even if buried is still accompanied by many rituals, reveals the level of commitment that the Luos hold towards their traditional beliefs and practices. Considering this level of commitment, the question as to whether the Luo Muslims have fully embraced Islamic teachings in their funeral beliefs and practices cannot go without being asked.

The insistence that a Luo can only be buried in his ancestral land as has been noted in S. M. Otieno's case brings the feeling that there are some social ties that Luos still attach to their dead ones. But apart from such social ties, Egen also gives a different understanding that the Luos may be holding concerning their ancestral land. This he does by quoting a Luo lawyer, Richard Kwach who was representing S. M. Otieno's clan in his burial saga: "Among the Luo, men never leave their homes, they always return, dead or alive."[7] The statement gives a contrast between a "home" and a "house." As it has been pointed out in the previous chapter, a home refers to one's ancestral land while a house is a place where one dwells outside his ancestral land. The fact that one's remains must still be transported back to the ancestral land provides evidence that the Luo are still following the traditions of their forefathers.

---

6. Nancy L. Schwartz, "Active Dead or Alive: Some Kenyan Views about the Agency of Luo and Luyia Women Pre- and Post-Mortem," *Journal of Religion in Africa* 30, no. 4 (2000): 435; Kisiara, "Some Sociopolitical Aspects," 134; Daniel Branch, "The Search for the Remains of D'iddahn Kimathi: The Politics of Death and Memorialization in Post-Colonial Kenya," *Past and Present* 206, no. 5 (n.d): 304.

7. Sean Egan, ed., "SM Otieno: Kenya's Unique Burial Saga," *Daily Nation Newspaper* (Nairobi, 1987), 12.

If it is true that Luos still follow their old customs especially the ones about funerals, then the view that Islam has affected such areas as Faloloa argues becomes interesting to study.[8] This is particularly so among the Luos who have embraced and follow Islamic faith in Kendu Bay. Are the current Luo Muslims still honoring their dead ones as their forefathers used to do? To what extent has the teachings of Islam affected their Luo traditional view of death and its related practices? How do the Luo Muslims view and carry out their ceremonies of death? As important as these questions are, it is through field research that the answers were appropriately provided.

The Influence of Islam on Luo Traditional View of Death

Sharkey uses the term "Arabization"[9] to describe the impact that the Arab culture has had on the Sudanese Nubians. She places an emphasis on inter-marriages as having caused the impact. Sharkey however, gives little indication of a possible exchange of culture that might have occurred between the Arab Muslims and the Nubians. The concept of Arabization denotes that the Nubian culture simply conformed to that of the Arab Muslims. If that conjecture holds, then it implies that the Nubians' approach to death and its related practices must have been borrowed from those of the Arab Muslims. While this argument may sound logical, it is almost impossible to avoid thinking of what might have happened to the Nubians' culture that they have followed for many years before making contact with the Arab Muslims. Though the possibility of assimilation may not be ruled out, it is, however, not clear to what extent it has taken place. In spite of the hard questions that the concept of Arabization pose, Sharkey has nevertheless helped the understanding that Islam is a religion that has culturally impacted the Nubian people.

By pointing also to the Nubian context, Sharkey has given a hint to the possibility of a common ancestry with Luo Muslims in Kendu Bay. This possibility of sharing a common ancestry is due to the belief that the Luo

---

8. Faloloa, "Spread of Islam and Christianity," 6.

9. Heather J. Sharkey, "Sudan," in *Muslim Cultures: A Reference Guide. Coughin*, ed. Kathryn M. Coughin (London: Greenwood, 2006), 177.

originated from Bahr-el-Ghazal province of the Republic of Sudan where Nubians also come.[10] Since the Nubians' contact with Islam came much earlier[11] before the Luo migration into Kenya,[12] it is likely that the descendants of the present Luo people must have had contact with Islam in Sudan just like their Nubian counterparts. However, this information about the origin of the Luo does not necessarily imply that the Islamic influence on the current Luo Muslims in Kendu Bay is related to their original homeland in Sudan.

The inquiry by Mazrui whether one can be a Muslim and still follow the African traditional religion gives an impression that both Islamic and traditional cultures can co-exist.[13] His question comes out of his study on the Yoruba of Nigeria. He notes that despite the influence of Christianity and Islam, traditional customs are still thriving among the Yoruba.[14] The Yoruba context can be compared to Kendu Bay where those three religions are also found to exist.[15] However, such comparison may not necessarily mean that the Luo Muslims in Kendu Bay have reverted to their Luo traditions in same way as the Yoruba people. But if they have reverted, then the same question may be asked of them concerning their identity as Muslims. In other words, can they be considered as true Muslims on the basis that they don't mix their practices with their Luo traditional beliefs and practices? If the answer to

---

10. William R. Ochieng', *People around the Lake* (London: Evans Brothers, 1985), 45; John W. Ndisi, *A Study in the Economic and Social Life of the Luo of Kenya* (Uppsala, Sweden, 1974), 7; Okot p'Bitek, *Religion of the Central Luo* (Nairobi: East African Literature Bureau, 1971), 8; D.W. Cohen, "The River-Lake Nilotes from the Fifteenth to the Nineteenth Century," in *Zamani: A Survey of East African History*, ed. B. A. Ogot (Nairobi, Kenya: Longman Kenya, 1974), 135.

11. "Islam had its first encounter with Sudan around mid of seventh century when Muslim Arab armies reached the fringes of Nubia and signed a peace treaty with its rulers" (Sharkey, "Sudan," 177).

12. The Luo migration to Kenya is estimated to have been around 1500–1800 CE (M. G. Whisson and J. M. Lonsdale, "The Case of Jason Gor and Fourteen Others: A Luo Succession Dispute in Historical Perspective," *Journal of the International African Institute* 45, no. 1 [1975]: 52; Samson O. Gunga, "The Politics of Widowhood and Re-Marriage among the Luo of Kenya," *Thought and Practice: A Journal of the Philosophical Association of Kenya* 1, no. 1 [2009]: 166).

13. Mazrui, "African Islam and Competitive Religion," 504.

14. Mazuri, 504–505.

15. Gideon S. Were, Ben E. Kipkorir, and Elias O. Ayiemba, *South Nyanza District: Socio-Cultural Profile* (Nairobi: Institute of African Studies, 1986), 24.

the question is positive, then the idea of Arabization or Islamization that both Sharkey and Mazrui have acknowledged may not fully be said to have replaced the African traditions.[16]

Both Lewis and Pouwels also describe the Islamization process in East African coast.[17] They observe that Islam became the religion of the majority of the Coastal people in early centuries because of its spread. By adopting the religion, the coastal people could have followed Islamic practices such as in the case of death. While this may have been the case, it is not easy to say with full certainty that the Muslim practices were carried out alongside the traditional ones. Sperling mentions that it was the *Mijikenda* (in Swahili, meaning, nine tribes) who were the ones occupying the Kenyan coast.[18] Going by his sentiment, the *Mijikenda* tribes were the first people to have had contact with Islam during its early period of the spread along the coast. But while Sperling's focus on the nine tribes is general, the study by Sesi is specific. It centers on Digo as one of the *Mijikenda* tribes. His study also reveals that the majority of the Digo population (99 percent) is Muslim.[19]

---

16. Sharkey, "Sudan"; Mazrui, "African Islam and Competitive Religion."

17. I. M. Lewis, "Sufism in Somaliland a Study in Tribal Islam," *BSOAS* 17, no. 3 (1955): 584; Randall L. Pouwels, "The East African Coast, C. 790 to 1900 C.E.," in *The History of Islam in Africa*, eds. Nehemia Levtzion, and Randall L. Pouwels (London: James Currey, 2000), 251. The idea of Islamization has in mind the way in which Islam penetrated to various societies with focus on Africa. Loimeier writes that the process of Islamization has to be characterized thus, on the one side, as a process of gradual and selective adoption and in-culturation of the greater framework of Islam by communities of Muslims. The process was accompanied by processes of contestation and reconfiguration of an established consensus and consequently never came to an end (Loimeier, *Muslim Societies in Africa: A Historical Anthropology* [Bloomington, IN: Indiana University Press, 2013], 17–18). He presents Islamization as an ongoing process. This implies that even among Luo Muslims in Kendu Bay, they are still incorporating new cultural forms of Islam. Nehemia Levtzion notes that Islamization has its emphasis on what was common to Islam and to local religions (Nehemia Levtzion, Michel Abitbol, and Amos Nadan, *Isalm in Africa and the Middle East: Studies on Conversion and Renewal* [Aldershot; Burlington, VT: Ashgate/Variorum, 2007], 5). This "commonness" is what el-Aswad refers to the interaction between Islamic doctrines and local traditional beliefs (el-Sayed el-Aswad, *Muslim Worldviews and Everyday Lives* [Lanham, MD: AltaMira, 2012], 18).

18. David Sperling, "The Coastal Hinterland and Interior of East Africa," in *The History of Islam in Africa*, eds. Nehemia Levtzion, and Randall L. Pouwels (London: James Currey, 2000), 276.

19. Stephen Mutuku Sesi, "Prayer among the Digo Muslims of Kenya and Its Implications for Christian Witness," (PhD thesis, Fuller Theological Seminary, Pasadena, CA, 2003), 13.

Although it is not clear from Sesi's study whether Digo has the highest population among the *Mijikenda* tribes, the percentage he has highlighted is quite informative. It shows the extent to which Islam has affected the Digo's perception of life. With this influence, there could be no doubt that the Digo people follow Islamic customs in matters to do with deaths and their related practices. But while Sesi's study makes it clear that Digo tribe is predominantly Islamic, the little or no mention of how other *Mijikenda* tribes have interacted with Islam at the coast raises some questions. Could it be that other *Mijikenda* tribes were resistant to Islam at the time it made its way to the Kenya coast? Or could it be that they made some contact with Islam but still carried on with their traditional way of life? If the latter is true, then it is possible that these other *Mijikenda* tribes are practicing both Islam and their traditional culture. Regardless of the answer, it is clear that Islam must have influenced the *Mijikenda* tribes differently. This difference may be possible if it is taken that other *Mijikenda* tribes had very little participation in trade and commerce as compared to the Digos.

Since trade and commerce between the Arab Muslims and the African natives were very common at the coast as Trimingham suggests, they must have been the mode of contact with Islam.[20] This contact at the coast is significant since it is through it that Islam found its way into the interior parts of Kenya as Said affirms: "The penetration of Islam to Mumias and Kendu Bay in late nineteenth and early part of the twentieth century is traced from its early contact with the coastal people."[21] Said is very specific about areas where Islam reached in Kenya. By highlighting these two areas, Mumias and Kendu Bay, he has thus shown that they are related to each other (see appendix C). The understanding of this relationship is vital since it makes it clear how Islam moved to Kendu Bay. It negates the thinking that Islam as practiced in Kendu Bay came directly from the Kenyan coast. By pointing to Mumias as the place where Islam moved from to Kendu Bay, Said further provides an idea of where some of the Luo-Muslim practices such as those

20. J. S. Trimingham, *The Influence of Islam upon Africa*, 2nd ed. (London: Edinburgh House Press, 1986), 38.

21. Ahmed Salim Said, "An Outline History of Islam in Nyanza Province," in *Islam in Kenya: Proceedings of the National Seminar on Contemporary Islam in Kenya*, eds. Mohammad Bakari and Saad S. Yahya, (Nairobi: Mewa, 1995), 20.

on funeral could have originated.[22] Since it is these funeral practices among Kendu Bay Luo Muslims that are being investigated, a cultural study of Mumias with regard to how it encountered Islam and its eventual spread to Kendu Bay becomes paramount.

Mumias is part of the Abaluhya community in western Kenya while Kendu Bay is part of Nyanza. While linking the two, Ochieng argues: "Any inquiry to the origin, migration and evolution of the Nyanza people must be done in relation to the history of the Abaluhya."[23] Ochieng examines both contexts from a historical and cultural perspective. These two perspectives are evidenced by the fact that both Nyanza and Abaluhya have lived and interacted together from their early periods of history.[24] Culturally, the Luhya-Luo relationship can be traced through marriage. Osogo confirms this: "Some of the Shiundu's (the father of king Mumia of Wanga) wives were from South Nyanza. They bore him children including his eldest son, Mumia."[25] Shiundu must have married his South Nyanza wives according to the Luhya customs. The same Luhya customs should also be seen to have been followed in matters of death. Shiundi's intermarriage thus suggests that the Luos of South Nyanza are related by blood to the Luhyas of Mumias. It is on this basis of relationship that their customs including those they follow when somebody dies can be said to be similar.

But while marrying from a different ethnic group has a cultural implication in the sense that a woman who has been married adopts same values as those of her husband, the spread of Islam from Mumias to Kendu Bay must have had also some bearing on Luo customs. It meant that as a cultural religion, the Luos who converted to Islam had to follow its teachings in every aspect of life. However, this may not be the case going by Osogo's sentiment that Luos in South Nyanza have a blood relationship with Luhyas.[26] As

22. Said, "Outline History of Islam."

23. William Robert Ochieng', *An Outline History of Nyanza up to 1914* (Kampula: East African Literature Bureau, 1974), x.

24. William Robert Ochieng', *A History of the Kadimo Chiefdom of Yimbo in Western Kenya* (Nairobi: East African Literature Bureau, 1975), 27; Ogot, *History of the Luo-Speaking Peoples*, 485.

25. John Osogo, *Nabongo Mumia of the Baluyia* (Nairobi: East African Literature Bureau, 1969), 6.

26. Osogo, *Nabongo Mumia*, 6.

neighboring communities in the western part of Kenya, the Luo and Luhya share some common traditional values. This includes the way they handle their dead ones. The writing of Munday makes it clear that the Luhya community that has converted to Islam still follow traditional funeral customs.[27] This implies that as neighbors and as a people who are related by blood, those Luos who have converted to Islam in Kendu Bay may still be following their Luo traditional ways of doing funeral rituals. The writings by many scholars such as Ongong'a Stamp, Ochieng, Odaga and Prince, portray Luo as a people who still follow their old customs of burying the dead.[28] They particularly cite cases like widow inheritance, burial in the ancestral land and loud wailing as practices that have prevailed among the Luo people. Although their writings cover Luo community in general, what they are saying is not exclusive to the Luo Muslims who reside in Kendu Bay. This is most likely due to the fact that Kendu Bay is part of the Luo Nyanza. It is located in the South of Luo Nyanza. What is true with other Luos in other places is also true to them. What those scholars have pointed out also reflect what the Luo Muslims in Kendu Bay may currently be experiencing. This is due to the fact that their writings are more recent compared to when Islam was first established in Kendu Bay. They are therefore aware of the presence of Islam in such places in Luo land.

While the work of other scholars provides little information as to whether the Luo Muslims in Kendu Bay follow Islamic teachings in every aspect of their lives, Said's writing on Mumia's change of name to Muhammad is in itself a point of reference towards the understanding of how Islam has impacted Kendu Bay.[29] Using Mumias' case to understand the situation in Kendu Bay is partly necessitated by the fact that the two communities have many cultural practices in common. The suggestion by some scholars,

---

27. E. J. Munday, "The Luyia Response to Death: A Case Study from Wanga, Western Kenya," (PhD diss., University of Oxford, 1983), 249.

28. Jude Ongong'a, "The River-Lake Luo Phenomenon of Death," in *Rites of Passage in Contemporary Africa: Interpretation between Christian and African Traditional Religions*, ed. James L. Cox (Cardiff: Cardiff Academic Press, 1998), 231–232; Stamp, "Burying Otieno," 825. Ochieng', *People around the Lake*, 130; Asenath Odaga, *The Luo Oral Literature and Educational Values of its Narratives* (Kisumu, Kenya: Lake, 2011), 50; Prince, "Christian Salvation and Luo Tradition," 52.

29. Said, "Outline History of Islam."

including Said,[30] concerning the spread of Islam from Mumias to Kendu Bay also makes it possible to believe that the Luo Muslims encounter a similar experience of change of names. But while Said points to the change of name as an indication of being a true Muslim,[31] Osogo looks at it differently. He in fact, impugns this claim: "Mumia was neither a Christian nor a Muslim."[32] Osogo's claim suggests that Mumia was either somebody who was between Christianity and Islam or simply a traditionalist. If it is understood that he was in between the two religions, then both Said and Osogo's arguments are valid. Said's point is valid in the sense that Mumia could have easily embraced his new Muslim name without any serious commitment to Islam. On the other hand, Osogo's assertion implies that Mumia had no serious allegiance to any of those two religions. He could change them at will.

Osogo's dispute obviously raises a very fundamental question as to why Mumia had to change his name. Was it for economic and political reasons? While the answer to this question remains unclear, Kasozi's input on the life of Kabaka Mutesa of Baganda kingdom in Uganda provides a hint as to why Mumia may have changed his name. Kasozi puts it that besides better communication that Muslims offered him, Kabaka toyed with Islam for political motives.[33] Since the two are rulers with similar experiences on how they encountered, it is not difficult to believe that Mumia's acceptance of Islam was politically motivated just like Kabaka's. Apart from Kasozi's observation about Kabaka, Nanji, who has also written widely about his (Kabaka's) leadership, adds: "Kabaka's new faith in Islam made him reject certain traditional practices such as hunting with dogs."[34] Nanji's remarks imply that although Kabaka accepted Islam, he did not abandon or reject all of his traditional practices. Even though he does not point to it, death is one of the areas in Africa where the demand to follow traditional customs

30. Said, 21.

31. Said, 21.

32. Osogo, *Nabongo Mumia*, 4.

33. A. B. K. Kasozi, *The Spread of Islam in Uganda* (Nairobi: Oxford University Press, 1986), 20.

34. Azim Nanji, "Beginnings & Encounters: Islam in East African Contexts," in *Religion in Africa: Experience*, eds. Thomas D. Blackely, Walter E. A. Van Beek and Dennis L. Thomson (London: James Currey, 1994), 49.

is usually very high. It is therefore most likely that Kabaka did not abandon the traditional death customs of the Baganda.

A study on the character and leadership styles of both Mumia and Kabaka is very significant. In the first place, their account confirms that the spread of Islam was significant. This significance lies in the fact that the message of Islam was first to kings and rulers of the African societies. Once the rulers had accepted Islam, it almost became obvious that the people they led would follow without any question. Making contact with the rulers first was a strategy that the Arab Muslims employed in many places in Africa. The Luo Muslims in Kendu Bay therefore, could not have been exceptional. However, this reasoning may not be regarded as conclusive without first considering the kind of leadership structure that the Luo community followed. Just as it is in the case of Mumia and Kabaka, there is need to investigate whether conversion to Islam by the Luo people in Kendu Bay has anything to do with the influence of an opinion leader. However, such an opinion leader does not necessarily need to be a king as were true to both Mumia and Kabaka. Since the role of opinion leaders is always expansive and covers almost every area of life, there is little doubt that the kind of funeral beliefs and practices that people follow are as a result of their influence. This thinking makes it helpful to identity the kind of opinion leaders that Luo Muslims follow and how what they believe and practice concerning funerals are related to the kind of teachings that are given to them by their opinion leaders. How these teachings have affected their lives is something that cannot also be ignored.

While their role as agents of the spread of Islam to their respective kingdoms is something that could be viewed as positive, the change of name and accepting Islam for political reasons that were linked to Mumia and Kabaka in their respective areas of jurisdiction, may not necessarily suggest that they were fully committed to their Muslim faith. It actually casts doubt as to whether their conversion to Islam was one that was not without other motives attached to it. Their actions show that Islam is a religion that subscribes to multiple meanings. In other words, they have simply indicated that conversion to Islam means different things to different people. Although holding such a perspective gives the impression that Islam has no single common identity, it nevertheless creates the need to examine Islam in its context rather than generalizing it. It points to the fact that one single context may altogether give a different meaning from the other. Finally, since both Mumia and Kabaka are seen to have been friendly to European missionaries and their colonial counterparts,[35] it shows that they had interest in Christianity as well. But going by Kasoza's, Nanji's and Osogo's writings, it is almost impossible to ascertain whether their level of interest was greater in Islam or in Christianity.[36] This remains a matter for speculation.

The Influencing Nature of Islam

Various factors have popularized Islam in Africa. While focusing on Kendu Bay, both Ayubi and Mohyuddin attribute the spread of Islam in the region to intermarriages.[37] The fact that Islam is cultural and is patrilineal makes it clear that the customs of the head of the family are being followed in such intermarriages. This means that it is the customs of a male Arab Muslim that should be practiced in such matters as death. Besides intermarriages, Arab Muslims are also viewed to have accessed the local people through trade, recruitment of the natives to serve as porters and through other missionary initiatives that promote people's welfare in areas such as socio-economic development, and peace building.[38] The discussions pointing to the way Islam has gained considerable following are revealed in the qualities and the level of impact it embodies. It is through such qualities and impact that Islam may be defined in terms of what it stands for. In other words, the identity of Islam as a cultural religion is displayed by its character. Exploring this subject about its character, therefore, becomes very necessary. It is a means

---

35. Both Kabaka and Mumia encountered European missionaries. Missionaries were closely associated with European colonialists. In the case of Kabaka Mutesa, he had become happy and pleased with the Europeans and also their religion. When the missionaries did arrive, Mutesa was full of expectations. Islam had to be brushed aside for the moment (Kasozi, *Spread of Islam*, 37). The same applies to Nabongo Mumia of Wanga who interacted and became friendly to Europeans such as Karl Peters and Fredrick Lugard, and Thomas and Martin (Ogot, *History of the Luo-Speaking Peoples*, 613; Osogo, *Nabongo Mumia*, 9).

36. Kasozi, *Spread of Islam*, 20; Nanji, "Beginnings & Encounters," 49; Osogo, *Nabongo Mumia*, 4.

37. Shabeen Ayubi and Mohyuddin Sakina, "Muslims in Kenya: An Overview," *Institute of Muslim Minority Affairs Journal* 15, no. 1–2 (1994): 146–147.

38. Elizabeth Richards, *Fifty Years in Nyanza: 1906–1956: The History of the C.M.S. and the Anglican Church in Nyanza Province, Kenya* (Maseno, Kenya: Nyanza Jubilee Committee, 1956), 6; Said, "Outline History of Islam"; John Spencer Trimingham, *A History of Islam in West Africa* (London: Edinburgh House Press, 1962), 27–28; Susan Kilonzo, "The Ahmadiyya Muslim Community and Peace Building in Kisumu District, Kenya," *Journal of Peace Building and Development* 6, no. 1 (2011): 82.

of understanding the teachings that Islam conveys to its people concerning death.

Universalizing quality of Islam

The idea of universalism brings into mind, a quality of Islam. Although it is a theological term and mostly related to Christianity, universalism is used here to represent the wide acceptance of Islam by the majority of the people. It basically bears the idea of adoption as Munday illustrates: "The shrouding of the body, which was introduced by the Muslims on the coast, has now been adopted by Christians of Wanga in Western Kenya."[39] The fact that Christians have followed the Muslim way of preparing the body for burial is an indication that the universal quality of Islam is one that surpasses religious boundaries. Munday's mention of Wanga is also significant due to the relationship it shares with Luo Muslims of Kendu Bay in South Nyanza.[40] If this relationship is true, then it is most certain that the Christians in Kendu Bay have also adopted into their practice, the Muslim way of covering the body. However, this may not be the case due to the cultural and doctrinal differences that the Christians and Muslims have in their respective religions.

By describing Islam as a catholic and tolerant towards the African traditional religion, Lewis has simply presented another face of Muslim universalism.[41] In this case, he sees Islam as accommodative and as a religion that does not necessarily require one to abandon their old customs such as the ones practiced during the burial of the dead. Both Lewis and Munday give similar perspectives concerning Muslim universalism. The only difference is that Lewis discusses universalism in respect to conversion whereas Munday presents Islam as involving practices such as burying the dead and animal slaughter in funerals.[42] They are adopted by other religions without necessarily changing one's religion to Islam.

Even though Christians have adopted certain Muslim practices, it should not be construed to mean that Christianity is not universalizing. It

---

39. Munday, "Luyia Response to Death," 244.

40. Ochieng argues that the Luo of South Nyanza are part of the splinter group from Abawanga from where Nabongo Mumia was the paramount chief (Ochieng, *Outlline History*, 33).

41. Lewis, *Islam in Tropical Africa*, 60.

42. Munday, *Luyia Response to Death*, 244–245.

is universalizing except that it has been perceived to be indifferent to the indigenous culture as Madid explains: "Christianity's universalizing ethos was seen as a threat to the indigenous culture whereas Islam, while itself universalizing, was viewed as strengthening the traditional and indigenous culture."[43] Madid's remarks helps to explain why in many places where both Christianity and Islam co-exist, the majority of the indigenous people prefer Islam than Christianity. The strength that Islam is believed to be carrying can partly be derived from Sanneh's sentiment: "It [Islam] demands no major radical adjustments and that it is easily incorporated into the rhythm of African life."[44] In this case, Islam serves as a reservoir of African cultures. This implies that whenever there is death, traditional customs take full precedence. This position however, presents Islam as a single unified religion which is inclusive of the indigenous customs.

The idea of uniformity of Islam is something that Loimeier believes does not exist in Africa or in any other Muslim world.[45] Although his view appears to be general in the sense that it points to the whole of Africa, Loimeier has nevertheless provided the need to examine each context of Islam differently. This therefore implies that while examining a case such as the Luo Muslims, the possibility that Islam may have rejected, adopted, partially or fully synthesized with the Luo old funerary rituals should not be ignored. The view that any option is possible is further underscored by Conn. In his classification, he considers rituals of marriage to be predominate in traditional African practices while death rituals are predominate in Islam.[46] Conn's classification first points to the fact that there is incompatibility of certain cultures that the African Muslims follow. But, by providing such categories, it becomes easy to predict the customs Muslims would follow at a given time. This distinction, however, could lead to a different form of generalization. It also limits the input by other scholars such as Lewis, who argues that the elements in Islam are variously combined with the

---

43. Abdur Rahman Madidi, *The Spread of Islam in Southern Africa and Its Impact on Society: A Geographical Perspective*, 3rd ed. (South Africa: University of Stellenbosch, 2003), 46.

44. Sanneh, *Crown and the Turban*, 7.

45. Roman Loimeier, *Muslim Societies in Africa*, 11.

46. Conn, "Islam in East Africa," 85.

indigenous burial rituals.[47] Lewis points to the possibility of mixing Islam and traditional cultures. However, it is not easy to establish the ratio of the mix of these two cultures.

Eliminating and filtering the nature of Islam

Quinn describes the turning of Mandingo funeral culture by Islam from elaborate into just a wrapping of the body in white cloth, hence a simple burial.[48] Quinn shares the idea that Islam changed the Mandingo's perspective on burial. This change, however, may not have been so sudden considering that Islam assimilates gradually. It is in this course of assimilation that Islam is believed to filter and carefully ignore whatever it does not want. However, Kennedy's remarks that the orthodox Muslims had eliminated and prohibited funeral dancing and continuous wailing among the Nubian Muslims, presents a radical process.[49] By this, it is easy to understand that while in some parts the African traditional customs have been gradually assimilated into Islam while in other places it has been total elimination. The former is what some scholars such as Kim and Musk, believe to characterize popular Islam while the later is official or formal Islam.[50] The discovery of these two forms of Islam is significant. It provides the need to examine each context with the understanding that it can be either formal or popular Islam, or both.

The Luo-Muslim Teachings of Islam on Death

As a religion and as a culture, Islam has a body of teachings that its adherents are expected to follow.[51] From various sources of Ḥadīth, it is clear that Islam has many teachings in areas of its beliefs and practices.[52] But while all

---

47. Lewis, *Islam in Tropical Africa*, 70.

48. Charlotte Quinn, *Mandingo Kingdoms of the Senegambia Traditionalism, Islam, and European Expansion* (London: Longman, 1972), 72.

49. John G. Kennedy, *Nubian Ceremonial Life: Studies in Islamic Syncretism and Cultural Change* (Cairo, Egypt: American University in Cairo Press; Berkley, CA: University of California Press, 1978), 226.

50. Kim, *Islam among the Swahili*.

51. P. M. Holt, Ann K. S. Lambton, and Bernard Lewis, *The Cambridge History of Islam. Vol. 2B: Islamic Society and Civilization* (Cambridge: Cambridge University Press, 1970), 569.

52. Karim Ginena and Azhar Hamid, *Foundations of Shari'ah Governance of Islamic Banks* (West Sussex: Wiley, 2015); Muhammad Abdalla Riday, *Masahaba kumi waliobashiriwa pepo* (Mombasa, Kenya: Adam Traders, 1993).

the areas are important, it is the teachings on matters related to death that are most relevant to this study. The fact that it is the subject of death that has widely been explored by the above scholars points to its significance in Islamic doctrines. Karim for instance, deals with the uncertainty of death.[53] He points to the death of Jesus and Muhammad. The essence of resurrection, trial and judgment and the aspects of heaven and hell are all covered in relation to death.[54] The same is true of Siddiqi. He devotes a consideration amount of space in both of his books; one relating to the subject of death to humanity and the other one is on rituals of death.[55]

Rippin and Jan and Ayoub's claim that Islam has incorporated both the Jewish and Christian cultural elements in its practices implies that the teachings which Muslims offer contain some elements from those two cultures.[56] But in comparison, AbuSulayman suggests, the contrary: "Muslim's way of thinking, their concepts and associated values have emerged from their Qur'anic worldview."[57] He gives little indication that other cultures such as Judaism and Christianity may have also informed the beliefs and practices in Islam. His idea also gives little consideration that practices such as those of death have been informed by the Qur'an. But since the Qur'an is reputed as having emerged from a context which was predominately Jewish and Christian, AbuSulayman should be considered as complementing rather than contradicting what Rippin and Jan and Ayoub have said.[58]

AbuSulayman's "Qur'anic worldview"[59] signifies that the Qur'an provides teachings that inform the way a Muslim views life. Teachings such as these on death are numerous in the Qur'an. For instance, the Qur'an points to the relationship between God and death. In this relationship, Allah is

---

53. Ginena and Hamid, *Foundations of Shari'ah*, 78–88.

54. Ginena and Hamid, 178–88; 449–463; 93–118; 52–179.

55. Abdul Hamid Sidiqi, *Sahih Muslim: Arabic-English*, vol. 1 (New Delhi: Idara Isha'at-e-Diniya, 1983); Abdul Hamid Siddiqi, *Sahih Muslim: Arabic-English*, vol. 3 (New Delhi: Idara Isha'at-e-Diniya, 2007).

56. Andrew Rippin and Jan Knappert, *Textual Sources for the Study of Islam* (Chicago: University of Chicago Press, 1990), 5; Ayoub, *Islam*, 13, 16.

57. 'AbdulḤamīd Abū Sulaymān, *The Qur'anic Worldview: A Springboard for Cultural Reform* (Hernsin, VA: International Institute of Islamic Thought, 2013), 3.

58. Rippin and Knappert, *Textual Sources*, 5; Ayoub, *Islam*, 13, 16.

59. Abū Sulaymān, *Qur'anic Worldview*, 3.

believed to be the source of death (67:2; 44:8),[60] he wills and determines it (4:78, 3:185).[61] This is contrary to the belief in African traditional society, which views death as caused by magic, sorcery and witchcraft.[62] Those three agents of death are always believed to be from a human source. They are also believed to be intentionally caused.[63] The teaching that death is divinely caused as in Islam, and humanly caused as in African Traditional Society (ATS) must be very confusing to some Muslims who are still attached to their traditional customs. God is also believed to determine the existence of humanity (6:2; 16:70; 26: 80–81; 53:44; 56:60). This means that the fate of every individual rests entirely on God.

The Qur'an describes death differently. It depicts it as a return to God (2:256). Scholars have contradicting opinions concerning whether it is the soul or the body that returns to God. According to Mardini, it is the soul while according to Jonker, it is the body.[64] But the elaborate rituals of death that Muslims are known to offer[65] and its accompanying beliefs about the future existence in the invisible world[66] present both the soul and the body as significant. In other words, the soul and the body may not be separated from the other. This invisible world[67] is also described as a new and eternal existence.[68] The Qur'an clearly specifies that the eternal existence is either in heaven, a place for the righteous (2:82), or hell, a place for the wicked

60. Thomas J. O'Shaughnessy, *Muhammad's Thoughts on Death: A Thematic Study of the Qur'anic Data* (Leiden: Brill, 1969), 53.

61. Kamyar Hedayat, "When the Spirit Leaves: Childhood Death, Grieving, and Bereavement in Islam," *Journal of Palliative Medicine* 9, no. 6 (2006): 1285.

62. Mbiti, *African Religions and Philosophy*; *Introduction to African Religion*; Parrinder, *Religion in Africa* (New York: Praeger, 1969).

63. John Beattie, *Other Cultures* (London: Routledge and Kegan Paul, 1966), 75.

64. Souran Mardini, *Islam: Worldly Life and the Hereafter* (Istanbul: Murat Center, 2013), 80, 82–84; Gerdien Jonker, "The Many Facets of Islam: Death, Dying and Disposal between Orthodox Rule and Historical Convention," in *Death and Bereavement across Cultures* (London: Routledge, 2000), 152.

65. Claudia Venhorst, et al., "Islamic Ritual Experts in a Migration Context: Motivation and Authority in the Ritual Cleansing of the Deceased," *Mortality* 18, no. 3 (2013): 235.

66. el-Sayed el-Aswad, "Death Rituals In Rural Egyptian Society: A Symbolic Study," *Urban Anthropology and Studies of Cultural Systems and World Economic Development* 16, no. 2 (1987): 211.

67. el-Aswad, "Death Rituals," 211.

68. Jane Idleman Smith and Yvonne Yazbeck Haddad, *The Islamic Understanding of Death and Resurrection* (Oxford: Oxford University Press, 2002), 3.

(11:108; 47:15). The picture presented about the Boni community concerning heaven, is that it is a place where celebration with women abounds.[69] Such a description about heaven implies that Muslims treat death as a means to an end. The belief in the resurrection of the dead as Qur'an explains (6: 61–62, 98; 11:6) and the subsequent judgment of God (79:34–41; 81:7) where the believers will be separated from the believers (79:1–2), speak a lot about the kind of life a Muslim is expected to live.

Apart from doing righteous deeds which also includes continued "remembrance of death,"[70] the living, the dying and the dead are also confronted by other forms of rituals. For instance, when one is nearing death as Khan explains, "There is reading of the Qur'an and uttering prayers for the dying by family members and relatives."[71] The prayer being made is not meant to heal or restore the dying but that God may do his will. This may mean that the fate of an individual lies solely in God. Death in this sense is not necessarily viewed as evil but as something acceptable since it originates from God. This goodness lies not so much on death itself but on the fact that it is God who has purposed it to happen.

This goodness cuts across the board. In the case of the dying, they are expected to recite the creed.[72] Individual Muslims are always expected to

---

69. Faulkner exaplains:
Bargoni of Boni paints a picture of the Islamic perspective about life after death in heaven. First, the emphasis is not on seeking to restore a sense of harmony and wholeness among the living community in this world, but the focus switches to seeking the joys of heaven in the afterlife. A dualism is introduced in which this life is a penitential preparation for the rewards of heaven where, it was said, things far surpass what is at hand in this world: women are far more beautiful and available than in the here and now and thus one must not allow oneself to be attracted by earthly female beauty since this is but a dim reflection of what awaits the pure man in heaven. Likewise, one must refrain from a few bottles of beer sure in the hope that there will be rivers of beer in the after-life.
(Faulkner, *Overtly Muslom, Covertly Boni: Competing Calls of Religious Allegiance on the Kenyan Coast*, Studies of Relgion in Africa, vol. 29 [Leiden: Brill, 2006], 174).

70. Khawaja Muhammad Islam, *The Spectacle of Death: Including Glimpses of Life beyond the Grave* (New Delhi: Adam, 1992), 12.

71. A. S Khan, *Muslim Culture and Traditions: Information Pack* (Belfast: Al-Nisa Association NI, 2006), 16.

72. Abu Hamid Muhammad ibn Muhammad Ghazzālī and Timothy Winter, *The Remembrance of Death and the Afterlife: Book XL of the Revival of the Religious Sciences, Iḥyā' 'ulūm al-dīn = Kitāb Dhikr al-mawt wa-mā ba'dahu* (Cambridge: The Islamic Text Society, 1989), 48.

remember death. A case is cited about the prophet saying that one who reminds himself of death frequently becomes alive in heart and death is also easy for him.[73] But rather than taking this literary, death as an easy affair should be understood to mean that Muslims are taught to approach death with courage. This courage stems from the belief that death is from God, and therefore it must be held as good. It should be from this same courage that the relatives to the deceased of the same gender are allowed to purify their body in readiness for burial.[74] Without courage, some relatives could be terrified with the site of the body. But courage is a virtue which is build with time. It may not be realized immediately due to human emotions which always manifest during such times as death. Stensson's remarks that HIV/AIDS is believed to be a punishment from God by the Muslims,[75] reveals a different stance on death. It shows that whereas death in itself is viewed as something natural and inevitable in Islam, the circumstances leading to it may not necessarily be deemed in the same way. This explains why acts such as stealing and promiscuous living are punished by stoning.

Goldziher's writing indicates that the Shafi'ite's School of Law has spread in many parts including East Africa.[76] Since Luo Muslims in Kendu Bay are part of East Africa, is it highly speculated that they are following Shafi'ite's teachings. According to Musa, "It was Idris al-Shafi'i who laid the foundations which eventually established the Ḥadīth as the second revelatory source of law and guidance for the vast majority of Muslims."[77] Musa has given credit to Idris al-Shafi'i as having established Ḥadīth as a source of authority in Islam. In Musa's case, Idris al-shafi'i considers Ḥadīth as a second source

73. Islam, *The Spectacle of Death: Including Glimpses of Life beyond the Grave*, 13.

74. Nathalia Maria Dessing, *Rituals of Birth, Circumcision, Marriage, and Death among Muslims in the Netherlands* (Leuven: Peeters, 2001), 145.

75. Jonas Stensson, "Muslims Have Instructions: HIV/AIDS, Modernity and Islamic Religious Education in Kisumu, Kenya," in *Aids and Religious Practice in Africa*, eds. Felicitas Beeker and P. Wenzel Geissler (Netherlands: IDC, 2009), 209.

76. Ignaz Goldziher, "On the Veneration of the Dead in Paganism and Islam," in *Muslim Studies*, vol. 1, ed. S. M. Stern, trans. C. R. Barber and S. M. Stern (London: Allen & Urwin, 1967): 209.

77. Aisha Y. Musa, "Al-Shafi'i, the Hadith, and the Concept of the Duality of Revelation," *Islamic studies* 46, no. 2 (2007): 164.

of revelation while in Lowry's, Idris al-shafi'i puts it at par with the Qur'an.[78] But despite their apparent differences, both scholars have revealed the importance of those two scriptures as sources of Shafi'ite's teachings. It thus implies that as members of Shafi'ite's School of Law, the Luo Muslims in Kendu Bay follow the teachings from the Qur'an, Ḥadīth, *Ijma*, and *Qiya*s.

Outcomes of Islamic Teachings on Luo-Muslim Death and Its Related Rituals

The argument by Vannaprasert and Jittpoosa that Muslims all over the world follow similar patterns of beliefs and values based on the Qur'an gives no indication of a possible change due to differences in cultures.[79] It also generalizes Islam as a culture that is totally conservative. Although this notion of conservatism may apply to orthodox Islam, there is also need to accept that Islam is diverse.[80] Diversity is a concept that acknowledges that other cultures are equally contributive. Relating this to the context of the Luo Muslims, it means that both Luo and Muslim cultures have impacted each other. This makes it almost impossible to delineate one culture from the other. Such a context has created what some scholars have referred to as popular or ordinary Islam.[81]

Both Qur'anic and diverse Islam is simply an outfit of official and popular Islam respectively. The Nubian Muslims' case in which the soul of the deceased is believed to return every year for a feast and to visit relatives illustrates that they are popular Muslims.[82] However, their use of Qur'anic scriptures as the basis of explaining their human existence points to fact that they have also some elements of official Islam.[83] The argument that the Nubians are generally more popular Muslims than official may still be

---

78. Joseph E. Lowry, *Early Islamic Legal Theory: The Risāla of Muḥammad Ibn Idrīs Al-Shāfiʿī*, Studies in Islamic Law and Society (Leiden: Brill, 2007), 8.

79. Chawīwan Vannaprasœt, Phīrayot Rāhimmūlā, and Mānop Čhitphūsā, *The Traditions Influencing the Social Integration between the Thai Buddhists and the Thai Muslimsi*, trans. Prachitr Mahahing and Kate Ratanajarana. (Pattani, Thailand: Faculty of Humanities and Social Sciences and Centre for Southern Thailand Studies, Prince of Songkhla University, 1986), 33.

80. Mellisa S. Carr, *Who Are the Muslims?: Where Muslims Live, and How They Are Governed* (Broomall, PA: Mason Crest Publishers, 2004), 11–12.

81. Kim, *Islam among the Swahili*; Musk, *Unseen Face of Islam*.

82. Kennedy, *Nubian Ceremonial Life*, 228.

83. Kennedy, 228.

valid since a majority of popular Muslims usually use Qur'anic writings in dealing with their life issues.

While describing the context of Luo traditions, Ogot writes: "The departed spirit (*juogi* in Luo) continues to relate with the living members of the society."[84] Ogot and Kennedy give similar approaches to the spirit-world of both Luo and Nubian Muslims. The only difference is that Ogot's focus is purely on the Luo traditional customs. His argument cannot be thus deduced to include completely the belief in *juogi* by the Luo Muslims. The belief that the spirit of the dead has some contact with the relatives of the deceased, symbolizes that death is not an end but a passage to the next world. It is, however, not explicitlt clear from Ogot whether the kind of influence *juogi* has depends on the nature of death, social status and the gender of the deceased.[85] Giving such indications could probably have been helpful in determining the kind of rituals that are carried out on the deceased.

Al-Bili describes a practice that is mostly common in official Islam: "The dead is washed, covered with a simple cloth, and buried with the head facing the *Kaaba*."[86] He has described Islam as if it were a single whole. However, such procedures of preparing the body before burial are not necessarily done by the official Muslims but also by ordinary Muslims. It can therefore be said that those procedures demonstrate that an Islamic influence has taken place. Whereas it is not quite conclusive that Al-Bili has discussed one particular group of Islam, Santen provides a clear cut between official and popular Islam. On one hand, he explains that the dead in Islam go to Allah to be judged, and from there they go either to paradise or to hell.[87] On the other hand, Santen remarks that the dead person usually comes to visit the mourners in dreams as a way of consoling them.[88] The Al-Bili's argument

84. Ogot, *History of the Luo-Speaking Peoples*, 494.

85. Ogot, 494.

86. ʿUṭmān Sayyid Aḥmad Ismāʿīl al-Bīlī, *Some Aspects of Islam in Africa* (Reading: Ithaca, 2008), 39.

87. Josepha C. M. van Santen, *They Leave Their Jars Behind: The Conversion of Mafa Women to Islam (North Cameroon)* (Leiden: VENA, 1993), 244.

88. van Santen, *They Leave Their Jars Behind*, 224.

is a position that is contained in official Islam while Santen illustrates a "popular or ordinary"[89] Muslim belief.

By asserting that death rituals are intended to facilitate the transition of the individual from life on earth to a state of heavenly bliss, Faulkner has in a way clarified the purpose of rituals among the Boni.[90] This, however, does not in any way indicate whether Boni are official or popular Muslims. His description that they are: "overtly Muslims and covertly Boni,"[91] signifies that part of their life is completely Islamic while the other part is traditional. It is, however, not easy to dissect which part of their lives is Islamic and which part is traditional. Despite this shortcoming, Faulkner has nevertheless highlighted the possible mix between Islamic and traditional customs. What comes out clearly from Faulkner, Al-Bili, Santen and many other scholars whose writings have been analyzed in terms of their practices is that the majority of Muslims in Africa are mainly popular Muslims.[92] It is on this account of the majority that the belief that the Luo Muslims of Kendu Bay can also be categorized as popular or ordinary Muslims is based. However, arriving at such a conclusion may be still premature. In order for such resolute to be undertaken, it first requires that the various funeral rituals are analyzed and put into different categories as Islamic, traditional or both. Practicing both customs could then be construed to mean that the said group consists of ordinary Muslims. There are so many areas in a funeral where the rituals involved may provide a clear outcome concerning the kind of Islam being practiced by a particular community. The two most common ones, which also relate to the context of Luo Muslims, are mourning and burial rituals.

---

89. In his article, "Considering 'Ordinariness' in studying Muslim Cultures and Discipleship," Kim has used the term ordinary in many places. The term refers to the life experiences that a Muslim has after mixing their Islamic and traditional customs (Kim, "Considering 'Ordinariness,'" 178–191). The term carries the same meaning to "popular Islam" (Kim, *Isalm among the Swahili*).

90. Faulkner, *Overtly Muslim*, 175–176.

91. Faulkner, 175–176.

92. Faulkner, *Overtly Muslim*; Bīlī, *Some Aspects of Islam*; Santen, *They Leave Their Jars behind*.

Outcomes of Islamic teachings on Luo-Muslim mourning rituals

There is a clear teaching in Islam that death is predetermined by God (Q 40:67, 69; 22:5; 35:11–12).[93] The idea of predestination portrays death as something which is bound to happen at anytime.[94] Fosarelli also describes death as something that can occur suddenly.[95] The teachings on remembrance of death (*dhikri* in Arabic) as in the case among Sufi Muslims, also abound.[96] All these teachings are meant to build a consciousness about death in every Muslim. The kind of responses Muslims give to death should therefore be used as a basis of determining the strength of the teachings they are provided. Wambui is categorical that the prolonged period of mourning in Luo helps them in shaping their identity.[97] Although she is not very precise on whether the same applies to the Luo Muslims, her view on mourning as shaping the Luo identity is both sociological and cultural. If mourning is viewed from a perspective that it also includes wailing, then Wambui's observation may only be limited to non-Luo Muslims. This is due to the fact that Islam prohibits wailing.[98] Halevi and Goldziher trace the history of why wailing is prohibited back to the days of Muhammad.[99] Goldziher in particular emphasizes this prohibition as applicable only to women: "Women were forbidden to wail since they could tear their clothes, recite funeral dirges, and incite blood revenge and civil unrest."[100] By concentrating on women alone, Goldziher has thus identified that Islam prohibits wailing in a particular gender.

---

93. O'Shaughnessy, *Muhammad's Thoughts on Death*, 58.

94. Huda Kassatly, "Local Traditions and Islamic Tradition The Dynamics of a Conflict Seen Through the Study of a Specific Case: Funeral Rites in a Shi'ite Village in South Lebanon," *Islam and Christian-Muslim Relations* 2, no. 1 (1991): 33.

95. Patricia D. Fosarelli, *Prayers & Rituals at a Time of Illness & Dying: The Practices of Five World Religions* (West Conshohocken, PA: Templeton, 2008), 59.

96. Ismail Raje, *Death and Beyond*, vol. 26 (Bradford: Jamea Publications, 1998), 3.

97. Kamau Wambui, "A Strategic Seclusion – Yet Again! The 1997 General Elections in Luo Nyanza," in *Out of the Count: The 1997 General Elections and Prospects for Democracy in Kenya*, eds. Marcel Rutten, Alamin Mazrui and Francois Grignon (Kampala: Fountain Publishers, 2001), 498.

98. Raje, *Death and Beyond*, 26:42.

99. L. Halevi, "Wailing for the Dead: The Role of Women in Early Islamic Funerals," *Past and Present* 183, no. 1 (2004): 5; Goldziher, "On the Veneration of the Dead," 241.

100. Goldziher, "On the Veneration of the Dead," 241.

Hussain and Bah are, however, in agreement that mourning is allowed since it expresses the grief of the heart.[101] Bah identifies weeping as part of mourning that Islam allows.[102] This is insightful since it reveals that mourning has various components and is understood differently depending on the group. For example, in some communities wailing is encouraged as part of mourning. The Luo community is a case in point. According to Prince, the Luo justify following such practices on the ground that they are ensuring the well-being and the continuity of people, animals and land.[103] Among the Muslims, wailing is prohibited while weeping is allowed. The question of whether the Luo Muslims follow their Luo traditional customs of wailing or weeping as Islam allows in mourning, becomes very interesting to establish.

Both Akrong and Azumah describe African Traditional Religion (ATR) as: "The substructure and as the software for both Islam and Christianity."[104] They imply that it is ATR that gives both Islam and Christianity their identity. In other words, the kind of Islam that is practiced by a people in a particular context is determined by their ATR. By treating ATR as central, it is not hard to predict which direction the mourning could tend to. The kind of approach that Akrong and Azumah have given to ATR makes both wailing and weeping to be possible practices among the Luo Muslims in Kendu Bay. The contributions of other scholars on the subject of wailing also identify other reasons why it is prohibited in Islam. For instance, according to Muḥammad and Khadija: "the dead person is tortured when his family wails for him."[105] Abu-Lughod on his part describes wailing as fighting the will of God.[106] Here "fighting" symbolizes resisting that which

---

101. Zamir Hussain, *A Gift for the Bereaved Parent: A Remedy for Grief from the Islamic Perspective Using Quotes from the Qur'an and Ahadith* (London: Ta-Ha, 2010), 6; Alpha Mahmoud Bah, *Glimpses of Life after Death: A Collection of Hadiths on the Transition from This Life to the Hereafter, the Entrance to Paradise or Hell* (London: Ta-Ha, 2001), 26.

102. Bah, *Glimpses of Life after Death*, 26.

103. Prince, "Christian Salvation and Luo Tradition," 66.

104. Abraham Akrong, "Hermeneutical and Theological Resources in African Traditional Religions for Christian Muslims in Africa," in *The African Christian and Islam*, eds. John Azumah and Lamin Sanneh (Carlisle: Langham Monographs, 2013), 75.

105. Muḥammad ibn Aḥmad Qurṭubī, Reda Bedeir, and Khadija Ford, *An Authentic Selection of Imam al-Qurṭubī's At-Tadhkirah fī aḥwālil-mawtá wal-ākhirah = in remembrance of the affairs of the dead and doomsday* (Egypt: Dar-Al Manarah, 2004), 29.

106. Lila Abu-Lughod, "Islam and Gendered Discourse on Death," *International Journal of Middle East Studies* 25, no. 2 (May 1993): 196.

God has already decreed to happen. Death, as it has been explained and as Lybarger writes, "is the divine act of God."[107] Therefore by wailing over the dead, one is believed to be defying the will of God. This is against the Shafi'ite's teachings, which emphasizes obedience to God and the Sunna of Muhammad.

Both Abu-Lughod and Lybarger explain the ideal situation, which identifies with a purely Muslim society. However, the story may be different in the Luo-Muslim situation. This is due to the fact that they have also been influenced by their Luo traditions. Critical tension or conflict between Islam and Luo traditions could therefore be apparent. Both Levine and Black discuss Jewish cultural perspective of mourning.[108] They are in agreement that in Jewish customs, weeping is allowed during the first three days after the funeral. Their discussions are relevant due to the fact that Jewish culture has had a great influence upon Islam. Besides, they are both Semitic cultures, as such, they have similar practices. However, since Islam has adopted and is evolving due to its contact with other cultures, the belief that it has retained the Jewish culture in the Luo-Muslim context is very minimal.

Outcomes of Islamic teachings on Luo-Muslim burial practices

Halevi observes that it was Al-Shafi'i who recommended quick burials in Islam in all cases, except in dubious deaths.[109] The possibility that the Luo Muslims are also engaged with quick burials is high. This is based on the understanding that they are following teachings in the Shafi'ite's School of Law. The exceptions pointed out to quick burials may thus suggest that Shafi'ite's School of Law classifies some deaths as good while others are bad. The good deaths are buried quickly while the bad ones may take longer period before burial. But unlike Halevi's reports on the teachings from Shafi'ite's School of Law, Ja'far Sharif makes no such distinction in burials. According to him, "A

---

107. Loren Lybarger, "The Demise of Adam in the Qisas al-Anbiyā: The Symbolic Politics of Death and Re-Burial in the Islamic 'Stories of the Prophets,'" *NU Numen* 55, no. 5 (2008): 521.

108. Ellen Levine, "Jewish Views and Customs on Death," in *Death and Bereavement across Cultures*, eds. Colin Murray Parks, Pittu Luangani and Bill Young (London; New York: Routledge, 2000), 114; John Black, "Death and Bereavement: The Customs of Hindus, Sikhs and Moslems," *Bereavement Care* 10, no. 1 (1991): 7.

109. Leor Halevi, *Muhammad's Grave: Death Rites and the Making of Islamic Society* (New York: Columbia University Press, 2007), 158–159.

good man [or woman] is quickly buried so as to reach paradise faster while a bad man [or woman] is speedily buried in order that his [or her] unhappy lot may not fall upon others."[110] Going by Halevi's assertion, her difference from Sharif as far as quick burial is concerned can only be said to be representing two different perspectives in the same Shafi'ite's School of Law. Since the kind of Islam that a particular community follows is determined by the local culture, the Luo Muslims may be doing and explaining their burials differently. Although Halevi and Sharif have given different reasons to explain why Muslims do quick burial, they are, however, in agreement that haste burials are practiced in Islam. Halevi on her part narrates that this hastiness was Muhammad's move as a way of bringing about a communal distinction of Islam from Jewish and Christian burials.[111] Sharif on the other hand, focuses on the need to hasten the burial for the sake of the deceased, who must go through judgment.[112]

Achieng's list of "bad deaths"[113] signifies that the Luos have also different categories of death. In their writing on Luo mythology, Onyango-Ogutu and Roscoe and Ochieng attribute bad death to have been caused due to the negligence of the chameleon who delayed in delivering a message from God to human beings on time.[114] Despite classifying some deaths as bad, none of those scholars has made any reference to "good deaths" among the Luos. By not referring to "good deaths," the Luos have thus been represented as simply

---

110. Ja'far Sharif, G. A. Herklots and William Crooke, *Islam in India or, the Qanun-i-Islam; the Customs of the Musalmans of India; Comprising a Full and Exact Account of Their Various Rites and Ceremonies from the Moment of Birth to the Hour of Death* (London: Curzon, 1972), 91.

111. Halevi, "Wailing for the Dead," 159.

112. Sharif, Herklots and Crooke, *Islam in India*, 90–91.

113. According to Achieng, bad deaths include:
death of a virgin woman, a widow dies whilst still wearing the funeral dress (*dhako otho gi kode* in Luo), a bride dies before she is confirmed (*orise* in Luo), a woman dies without giving birth (*dhako otho sunu* in Luo), death of a pregnant woman, the death of a person with abnormal swelling, the death of a hunchback, the death of a newly married man, a man died leaving a pregnant wife, a widow conceives whilst still wearing the funeral dress (*kode* in Luo), a married man dies in his father's homestead.
(Jane Achieng, *Paul Mboya's Luo Kitgi Gi Timbegi* [Nairobi: Atai Joint, 2001], 119–125).

114. Benedict Onyango-Ogutu and Adrian A. Roscoe, *Keep My Words: Luo Oral Literature* (Nairobi: East African Educational Publishers, 1974), 43; Ochieng', *People around the Lake*, 130.

having the single category of "bad deaths." It is in this line of bad deaths that Prince asserts: "*ter* (in Luo, meaning, widow inheritance) is meant to avert the spirit of bad death."[115] She has also partly explained why many rituals are called for in times when a loved one passes on among the Luo. Unlike in Islam, where speedy burial is seen to depend on the deeds of the deceased, Achieng and Prince present the Luo burials as entirely depending on the external circumstances that the deceased was faced with at the time of their demise.[116] In other words, while there is evidence of quick burials in both cultures, Islam's hasty burial is for the wellbeing of the deceased, while in Luo the overall goal is to protect the living. How such views correlate among the Luo Muslims is something that is of interest and should be studied.

Apart from Halevi and Sharif, Levine also adds another reason for quick burial: "[It] is preferred in order to allow the bereaved to start the mourning process without the pain of delay."[117] Levine's argument underscores the concerns to the bereaved. Based on the account of the Luo customs where some deaths such as S. M. Otieno's[118] have taken a long period of time before the burial takes place, the question of whether the Luo Muslims have resorted to quick burials could simply signify that they are following Islam. But since the Luo traditions also allow for hasty burials, there is need to establish why a burial has been conducted hastily. The reasons would help in categorizing such quick burial as tending towards Islam or Luo traditions.

Several rituals such as the washing of the body, shrouding, prayer[119] and the reading of the Qur'an to the dying[120] are believed to be important part of the burial processes in Islam. Prayer has been identified as an alternative

---

115. Prince, "Christian Salvation and Luo Tradition," 52–53.

116. Achieng, *Paul Mboya's Luo*, 119–125; Prince, "Christian Salvation and Luo Tradition," 52–53.

117. Levine, "Jewish Views and Customs," 106–107.

118. David William Cohen and E. S. Atieno Odhiambo, *Burying SM: The Politics of Knowledge and Sociology of Power in Africa*, Social History of Africa (Nairobi: East African Educational Publishers, 1992), 59.

119. Khan, *Muslim Culture and Traditions*, 16.

120. 'Abd Allāh ibn 'Alawī 'Aṭṭās and Badawî Mostafâ, *The Lives of Man: A Sufi Master Explains the Human States : Before Life, in the World, and after Death* (Louisville, KY: Fons Vitae, 1997), 45.

to wailing.[121] Marranci, also regards it as: "a freedom given to the human soul from hardship; it allows the soul to experience happiness and freedom in the afterlife."[122] Seedat, on his part, recognizes that different prayers are made for both male and female asking God to forgive them.[123] Since these prayers are made by the living, it is believed that the living should act on behalf of the dead. The dead in this case are regarded as helpless. This is contrary to the Luo traditional society in which many rituals surrounding the dead give the impression that they are more superior to the living. This is expressed through loud wailing by women,[124] insistence in burying the dead in the ancestral land,[125] and providing plenty of food to the mourners.[126] Failure to conduct those rituals is believed to make the spirits of the ancestors angry. They may as a result of anger, cause harm to the community.[127] The practice of widow inheritance has also the fear of the dead in mind.[128]

While prayer has been marked as one of the most important rituals, its significance is limited to the dead. This is captured by Fosarelli's, who reasons that many Muslims do not name an ill person in their prayers.[129] He also portrays Muslims as being very selective in their prayers. But is it not so obvious that in any religion the ill would be prayed for? Being different, as Islam is, may be because of its fatalistic view of God. Fatalism attributes God as the source of all forms of suffering including illnesses and death. In this sense, praying for the sick or the dead with a view to restore them back to good health is regarded as contradicting Allah's will. It is out of this fatalism that the call to surrender to God's will is emphasized in the teachings of Islam.

121. Islam, *The Spectacle of Death: The Scene of Death and What Happens after Death* (Delhi, India: Adam, 2001), 85.

122. Gabriele Marranci, *The Anthropology of Islam* (Oxford; New York: Berg, 2008), 25.

123. Noorjehan bint Faqir Seedat, *What to Do When a Muslim Dies* (London: Ta-Ha, 2004), 15.

124. Ndisi, *Study in the Economic*, 81–82; Odaga, *Luo Oral Literature*, 49–50.

125. Stamp, "Burying Otieno," 825; Parker MacDonald Shipton, "Debts and Trespasses: Land, Mortgages, and the Ancestors in Western Kenya," *Journal of the International African Institute* 62, no. 3 (1992): 362.

126. Odaga, *Luo Oral Literature*, 51.

127. van Doren, "Death African Style," 337; Ocholla-Ayayo, "Death and Burial," 90.

128. Prince, "Christian Salvation and Luo Tradition," 66.

129. Fosarelli, *Prayers & Rituals*, 58.

Whereas in Islam prayers are made *for* the dead,[130] in African traditional perspectives prayers are made *to* the dead.[131] In the ATR perspective, prayers are invoked; the dead are asked to keep a watchful eye over their children.[132] They are also asked for help.[133] The fact that the dead are prayed to should not be construed to imply that the African traditional religion (ATR) has no understanding of God. In fact, the opposite is true. This is according to Mbiti, who posits that the African traditional religions view God as supreme. They understand God through intermediaries such as the ancestors.[134] The idea of intermediaries is very central in analyzing and understanding the Luo-Muslim context. Their context can be the path through which Christ as the intermediary can be introduced, especially if they are still holding on to their Luo traditional customs. "Prayer to the dead" and "prayer for the dead" provide the basis for establishing whether the Luo Muslims still follow their Luo traditional customs or they are fully in Islam. If they are praying to the dead as well as for the dead then it demonstrate that they are popular rather than official Muslims.

Unlike in Luo customs where the dead are to be buried in their ancestral land, the place of burial has no significance in Islam.[135] Raje also presents Islam as discouraging the transportation of the dead body. This does not only mean that a Muslim can be buried anywhere but also the expenses involved are kept minimal. More importantly, the difference between Luo traditions and Islam concerning where the dead should be buried lies in their understanding of an afterlife. Being buried in ancestral land as it has been claimed about Luo customs is a means of keeping the relationship between the dead and the relatives intact. In this regard, burying outside the ancestral land is considered as inviting the wrath of the deceased's spirit against their

---

130. Khan, *Muslim Culture and Traditions*, 16; Seedat, *What to Do When a Muslim Dies*, 15; Islam, *The Spectacle of Death: The Scene of Death and What Happens After Death*, 85.

131. Taiwo O. Olaleye-Oruene, "The Yoruba's Cultural Perspective of Death with Special Reference to Twins," *Twin Research* 5, no. 3 (2002): 154; Francis-Xavier Sserufusa Kyewalyanga, *Traditional Religion, Custom and Christianity in Uganda: As Illustrated by the Ganda with Some References to Other African Cultures and Islam* (Freiburg: Krause, 1976), 204.

132. Olaleye-Oruene, "Yoruba's Cultural Perspective," 154.

133. Kyewalyanga, *Traditional Religion*, 204.

134. John S. Mbiti, *Concepts of God in Africa* (Nairobi, Kenya: Acton, 2012), 51.

135. Raje, *Death and Beyond*, 40–41.

family members and relatives. Burying anywhere, as is done in Islam, places the focus not on the relatives but on the destiny of the deceased. In other words, the discussion establishes that Luos carry out rituals on the dead for the sake of the living while in Islam the death rituals are mainly for the sake of the deceased. The apparent difference may imply that the Luo Muslims are uncertain about which customs they should follow. Following either way or both will define what kind of identity they hold as Luo Muslims.

In contrast to Luo burials where women play many roles, El-Aswad limits their role to the following funeral procession, but at a distance.[136] According to Granqvist and Peters, menstruating women in particular are prohibited from coming into contact with the deceased since they are regarded as impure.[137] It is not clear what kind of relationship exists between the impure woman and the deceased. But Sharif's discussion on *ghusl* (in Arabic) and *wudu* (in Arabic)[138] provides a basis for understanding their relationship. According to him, purifying the body ensures that the deceased is ready for burial.[139] This is a task that is carried out by people who are without any impurities, and of the same gender as the deceased. This therefore disqualifies menstruating women. But such impurity should also be considered as hindering the deceased from traveling to their final destination. The role of women also covers post-burial rituals. Dubisch relates this with the Greek women who in post-burial periods bring food and flowers to the graves and attend to the needs of the dead.[140] The belief that Muslim women are practicing a similar culture to that of Greek women is made possible out of Dubisch's remarks that Greek culture has had an impact on Islam.[141] But the influence of Islam on the Luo culture may not necessarily produce a similar effect as that of the Greeks on Muslims due to their difference in context and the changing of times.

---

136. el-Aswad, "Death Rituals," 218.

137. Hilma Granqvist, *Muslim Death and Burial: Arab Customs and Traditions Studied in a Village in Jordan* (Helsinki: Societas Scientiarum Fennica, 1965), 63; F. E. Peters, *Islam A Guide for Jews and Christians* (Princeton: Princeton University Press, 2003), 218.

138. See the table on transliteration.

139. Sharif, Herklots and Crooke, *Islam in India*, 92–93.

140. Jill Dubisch, "Death and Social Change in Greece," *Anthropological Quarterly* 62, no. 4 (1989): 190.

141. Dubisch, "Death and Social Change," 190.

Luo Traditional Elements in Luo-Muslim Perception of Death

By characterizing Islam as both catholic[142] and adaptive[143] in nature, makes it possible to believe that Luo-Muslim funerals still have some traces of their old customs. This possibility is also founded on Sanneh's claim: "the ATR is also adaptive and able to modify or reject that which was not in conformity or was in conflict with its values."[144] Both scholars, however, show very little concerning the possibility that ATR is equally impacting. Without providing such possibility, the ground upon which both Luo traditional and Islamic customs can be considered as influencing each other becomes very limited. But by reasoning that neither Christianity nor Islam has managed to expunge aspects of indigenous religion in East Africa,[145] Shipton, has thus recognized that ATR is also impacting. He cites sacrifices offered to the ancestors and other spirits as an area that has encountered very little change. This simply means that it is generally in death that both Christianity and Islam have achieved very little impact. But the obvious question especially in the context of the Luo Muslims is why this is so?

Kaniki also identifies another area of strength in ATR: "African Muslims in many societies have retained widow inheritance despite the Qur'anic explicit prohibition."[146] Even though he is not referring to Luo Muslims in particular, the issue Kaniki raises about widow inheritance and Qur'anic prohibition are certainly very familiar to them. Examining Luo Muslims from Kaniki's perspective gives a possibility that they are still practicing widow inheritance despite the Qur'anic prohibition. This would then mean that they are popular rather than official Muslims.

---

142. Lewis, *Islam in Tropical Africa*, 60.

143. Sanneh, *Crown and the Turban*, 7.

144. Sanneh, 22.

145. Parker Shipton, *Mortgaging the Ancestors Ideologies of Attachment in Africa* (London: Yale University Press, 2009), 69.

146. Martin Hoza Y. Kaniki, *The Impact of Islam on African Societies* (Dar es Salaam: University of Dar es Salaam, 1974), 9.

Luo-Muslim Perspectives on Luo Traditional Expressions of Death

Musk, in his book *The Unseen Face of Islam*,[147] provides a very substantial study on the life of ordinary Muslims. The book is therefore relevant since it covers details that are relevant in understanding the lifestyle of the Luo Muslims in Kendu Bay. Although Musk's comparison is between the Western and popular worldviews, his writings nevertheless highlights the underlying assumptions that characterize a life such as that of Luo Muslims. He provides various categories of concepts of "being" in popular Islam.[148] One such category that is relevant to this study is the "trans-empirical realm."[149] According to Musk, this realm contains many forms of "life." The souls of the recently dead are seen as present or near at hand.[150] This view should correspond to that of the Luo Muslims, especially if they have adopted a lot of cultural practices from their traditional background. Viewing the dead as alive though in a different state is a common belief that many African communities hold, including the Luos. Therefore, if such a view is what the Luo Muslims reflect, then it implies that they still hold some Luo traditional beliefs despite the fact that they are Muslims. Musk, further states that such a view of blended cultures is especially evident in cultures where the faith of Islam has rested largely as a veneer over more traditional views of the world.[151] To describe Islam as a veneer is to regard it as thinly distributed in such a context as the Luo-Muslim one. Taken from that perspective, the existence of the Luo traditional practices may simply be explained by Luo Muslims as a way of conserving their cultures.

Although his context is the Philipino Muslims, Parshall[152] outlines another aspect that characterizes practices of ordinary Muslims. He explains that much superstition centers round the graveyard, where candles are lit due to the belief that the spirits of the dead visit the living during this

---

147. Musk, *Unseen Face of Islam.*

148. Musk, 178–183.

149. Musk, 179.

150. Musk, 179–180.

151. Musk, 180.

152. Phil Parshall, *New Paths in Muslim Evangelism: Evangelical Approaches to Contextualization* (Grand Rapids, MI: Baker Books, 1980).

time.[153] Since Parshall writes about ordinary Muslims, his description of their practice on the cemetery fits well with the Luo Muslims whose worldview is still not alienated from the world of the spirits. This lighting of fire by the graveside, as Parshall observes, is a way of showing respect to the dead.[154] Sharing such a similar context could mean that the Luo Muslims are also lighting the fire. But in keeping with their Luo traditions, there is more to fire than just showing respect. The Luo light the fire (*magenga*) as a way of inviting the deceased to warm himself or herself. A male deceased warms himslef as he watches over his homestead. The fire is also meant to chase away evil spirits that might be hovering around the homestead.

Gilliland writes: "When the cult of the tribe has been retained, it is because there are features which are more absolute and vital for practice in the tribe than Islam can offer as options."[155] Even though Gilliland's account does not directly relate to matters of death, his writing generates a principle which can be used in evaluating the Luo-Muslim context. This is particularly so if it is confirmed that the Luo Muslims have retained old practices from their Luo traditional background. Retaining their traditional customs should then signify that there is a lack of an option in their new religion of Islam. Mtoro, whom Allen quotes, contributes to the discussion. He cites cases where the body of the deceased is treated following both Swahili and the Muslim customs: "The digging of the grave under the deceased's bed follows the traditions of the Swahili, while washing and wrapping is provided for in accordance to Islamic religion."[156] He represents Swahili Muslims as partly traditional and partly Muslim. Although the Swahili death and burial procedures may not directly relate to the Luo-Muslim context, the general approach to traditions is similar. This similarity is noted in Mtoro's claim that the dead is given the observances of his religion.[157] Mtoro's perspective gives the possibility of practicing burial rituals as both a public and a private affair. In the case of the Luo Muslims, this could mean that publicly

---

153. Parshall, *New Paths*, 73.

154. Parshall, 73.

155. Gilliland, *African Traditional Religion*, 150.

156. J. W. T. Allen, *The Customs of the Swahili People: The Desturi Za Waswahili of Mtoro Bin Mwinyi Bakari and Other Swahili Persons* (Berkeley, CA: University of California Press, 1981), 142.

157. Allen, *Customs of the Swahili*, 142.

the dead is laid to rest following the Muslim customs while privately other death rituals are performed in obedience to the wishes of their forefathers or ancestors. Mtoro's perspective also elicits the need to examine what guides and determines a public and a private funeral ritual.

Apart from Mtoro, Bunger also discusses the mixed practices that are evident among the Swahili people in the coast. He differentiates the rituals of prayers and Qur'anic reading from the ritual of the "ghost."[158] He claims that this ghost ritual is a practice which is connected with their former customs. By distinguishing the two contexts, Bunger has underlined the fact that the former customs are still evident among the contemporary Muslims. It is, however, not very clear what the ghost ritual is all about. The idea of a ghost signifies that there is a belief in life after death. But since Swahili people are Africans, their belief in the ghost is thus comparable to that of the Luos, who in their traditions, respect and offer sacrifices to the ancestors. If the Luo Muslims hold a similar perspective by the virtue of their traditional heritage, then there is no doubt that the kind of Islam they follow has both Luo traditional and Islamic elements. The mixed custom is, however, not easy to separate since there are no clear boundaries between the two customs.

Kassatly's writing on Lebanese Muslims demonstrates that both traditional views and official Islamic views of a funeral exist alongside each other. This is marked first by the washing and the shrouding of the body. At the burial time, women wail and express their emotions to the supreme power of God, while men pray and invoke God's mercy.[159] The procedures involving the treatment of the body, prayers and invoking the name of God, are part of the official Islam, while wailing and lamenting by women can be categorized as traditional. The Lebanese Muslim's context is a case in point where the local culture has influenced Islam. This is regardless of the geographical location that Islam interacts with. By the virtue of existing alongside each other, there is obviously tension between the official Islam and traditional customs. One side might be pulling towards the official Islam, while the other side reverts to its former customs. If such tension is apparent among the Luo Muslims, it implies that one side wants to fulfill the traditions by

---

158. Robert Louis Bunger, *Islamization among the Upper Pokomo* (Syracuse, NY: Eastern African Stuides Program, 1973), 151.

159. Kassatly, "Local Traditions and Islamic Tradition," 31.

demanding wailing over the dead, while the other side insists on following the Qur'anic teachings, which accept death as God's predetermined will. Inclining towards Luo traditions or Islam gives the impression that the Luo Muslims follow both Islam and their Luo customs as two separate traditions. This conclusion, however, may not be so practical since they identify themselves as Muslims.

Kennedy highlights the Nubia Muslim experience in which an animal was slaughtered and left for the spirits on top of the grave. This, together with the fact that some Qur'anic verses are repeatedly read during a funeral,[160] explains the co-existence of the old customs alongside Islam. But while Kennedy has provided the evidence upon which the Nubian Muslims may be regarded as practicing popular Islam, he has done very little in explaining why such co-existence is apparent. Since the Luo originated from Sudan, its experiences with Islam may have some correlation with that of the Nubian Muslims. This correlation is the basis upon which both Luo traditional and Islamic customs may be said to be similar to that of the Nubian Muslims in matters regarding death. Using Kennedy's view concerning the Luo-Muslim situation may, however, provide very little explanation as to why some Luo Muslims revert to their Luo traditional funeral beliefs and practices while others follow the Islamic teachings.

Although the studies by Kumar[161] and Geertz[162] are outside the scope of Africa, their remarks that, despite the influence of Islam the indigenous practice of funeral rituals has still remained in place, is relevant. Kumar, for instance, argues that the Yanadis Muslims of India attribute any sudden death to have been caused by the malevolence of a deity or to the wrath of deceased kinsman.[163] They explain death in terms of a soul (*jivan*) leaving the body to be with God (*swami*). The Yanadis' view in regard to the causality of death is certainly not Islamic per se. Their original Hindu culture has contributed to the way they comprehend those attributes of death. Geertz,

---

160. Kennedy, *Nubian Ceremonial Life*, 228.

161. G. Stanley Jaya Kumar, *Tribals from Tradition to Transition: A Study of Yanadi Tribe of Andhra Pradesh* (New Delhi: M. D. Publications, 1995).

162. Clifford Geertz, *Islam Observed: Religious Development in Morocco and Indonesia* (Chicago: University of Chicago Press, 1971).

163. Jaya Kumar, *Tribals from Tradition to Transition*, 65.

illustrates the significance of the indigenous culture by citing the case of Java in Indonesia. The idea behind their quick burial is so that the spirit of the dead that flies around like a bird can return to its natural home, otherwise it could cause harm to the survivors.[164] It is evident that Javanese haste burial is due to their fear of the deceased's spirit rather than on God's impeding judgment as Islam teaches. The Javanese practice of quick burial and their fear of the deceased's spirit indicate that they are following both Islamic and traditional teachings. Such a mix of cultures signifies that despite them being predominantly Muslims, and just like Yanadis, the Javanese have not abandoned their indigenous customs. This is quite surprising, since India and Indonesia, where Yanadis and Javanese respectively come from, are predominantly Islamic. The fact that they are still accustomed to the indigenous practice in funeral rituals signifies that both Yanadis and Javanese are popular Muslims. Their context has thus helped to reveal that in a strong Muslim presence such as Kendu Bay, Luo Muslims may still be reverting to their Luo traditional customs. But while this may be evidently so, both Kumar and Geertz have not adequately explained why following old traditions is still prevalent among the Yanadis and Javanese Muslims.[165]

Explaining Luo Traditionalism in Luo-Muslim Perspective of Death

Unlike Kumar and Geertz, Sicard and Munday offer some hints that are very helpful in explaining why indigenous culture is still being followed among some Muslim communities.[166] In his writing, Sicard observes that the Antankarana people of Madagascar were previously Muslims who have now reverted to their former traditional way of life. He attributes this change to have been caused by lack of proselytizing zeal among the Muslims, as well as the strength and coherence of Malagasy culture and society.[167] These two combinations give the understanding that the practices of Antankarana are mainly traditional. The aspect of falling back to the traditional customs may

164. Geertz, *Islam Observed*, 68.

165. Stanley Jaya Kumar, *Tribals from Tradition to Transition*; Geertz, *Islam Observed*.

166. S. von Sicard, "Malagasy Islam: Tracing the History and Cultural Influences of Islam in Madagascar," *Journal of Muslim Minority Affairs* 31, no. 1 (2011): 101–112; Munday, "The Luyia Response to Death."

167. von Sicard, "Malagasy Islam," 107.

justify the saying, "East or West, home is the best." Sicard describes a situation in which a people have taken pride in their traditional lifestyle. It, however, remains speculative whether this lifestyle is inclusive of funeral rituals.

Munday also underlines this sense of pride in her reference to Luhya community. She remarks that while Christians view death as an occasion for rejoicing, the Luhya are expected to wail. If one fails to wail then they risks being accused of "sorcery."[168] Rejoicing rather than mourning, as Munday alleges concerning Christians, lies in the belief that the deceased has gone to heaven. Due to sharing similar beliefs between Muslims and Christians with regard to the hereafter, it is almost certain that Luhya Muslims would view death in a similar way to that of their Christian counterparts. Although wailing has been presented as bearing some sense of pride in Luhya context, it has also been considered as a source of curse for those who fail to undertake it. The Luhya case also provides the understanding that mourning is viewed as traditional while the act of rejoicing over death is considered as being religious. If Luhya Muslims share the same view, then their traditions and their Islamic faith are pulling from both ends. The fact that Luhyas are neighboring Luos may also imply that the same tensions exist among them. However, this can only be speculated since the Luo-Muslim context is different from the Luhya Muslim one. Munday has mainly approached the subject surrounding mourning from both religious and traditional perspective. Her case has not dealt with how to deal with emotions. A growing body of literature has described the psychological and sociological aspects that surround the ritual of mourning. In their contribution, Klass, Silverman, and Nickman give the indication that it is natural for the bereaved to react with emotions due to the attachment they have had with the deceased.[169] Through this, they have thus acknowledged that expressing emotions, which in many cases comes through the shedding of tears, is a natural process. The aspect of naturalness signifies that the act of mourning should not only be considered from a cultural and religious perspective, but also from a psychological perspective.

---

168. Munday, "Luyia Response to Death," 249.

169. Dennis Klass, Phyllis R. Silverman, and Steven L. Nickman, *Continuing Bonds: New Understandings of Grief* (Washington, DC: Taylor and Francis, 1996), 58.

The psychological part in a mourning situation is, however, difficult to establish since culture also assumes the bonding that exists between the bereaved and the deceased. On his part, Durkheim provides a sociological dimension to mourning. He emphasizes the aspect of solidarity by the deceased's family and relatives due to their common sharing of a misfortune.[170] According to this view, the need for group assembling together is necessitated by the death of an individual. In this case, it is clear that a funeral ritual such as wailing is done by the group out of a sense of belonging. Durkheim also advances the belief that funeral rituals are used to unify the affected individuals. He has thus highlighted the significance of individual feelings in a mourning process by focusing on norms that the group shares. His perspective further underscores the need to examine the weeping or wailing of individual mourners in a funeral with a view to establishing any relationship with the wider mourning group.

But different from Durkheim, Hertz emphasizes the impact that the death of an individual brings to the society.[171] He sees death as significant both to the deceased and the bereaved.[172] To the deceased, elaboration of rituals is correlated with their social importance. This means that the children as well as the most elderly are little mourned due to their limited social participation in the society. Hertz's description of death highlights the fact that various rituals are carried out depending on the cultural or social significance of the deceased. But in the case of the bereaved, he implies that the more an individual is closer to the deceased, the more rituals they are required to do. It is, however, not very clear concerning the kind of restrictions Hertz is referring to. It can only be inferred that these restrictions center on the rigor of rituals that a family member or a close relative to the deceased is expected to carry out. In a more practical sense, Hertz has established that there is a relationship between rituals of death on one hand, and the deceased and the bereaving on the other hand. This understanding is helpful in categorizing the mourners in the Luo-Muslim context as close and distant

---

170. Emile Durkheim and Joseph Ward Swain, *The Elementary Forms of Religious Life.* (Stilwell: Neeland Media LLC, 1965), 445.

171. Robert Hertz, *Death and the Right Hand* (London: Free Press, 1960); Robert Hertz, *Death and the Right Hand,* 2nd ed. (London: Routledge, 2004).

172. Hertz, *Death and the Right Hand,* 51–52, 79–80, 84–86.

relatives of the deceased based on the kind and the frequency of rituals they are involved with. In order to adequately establish such a distinction, funeral rituals should be assessed right from the time of death up to the post-burial.

Effects of Luo Traditional Discourses of Death on Luo Muslims

The writings of Klass, Lalande and Bonanno, show that there is a continuing bond between the deceased and the living.[173] The idea of a bond highlights the critical role that funeral rituals play. They strengthen the relationship between the living and the dead. There is no doubt that the main beneficiaries in this relationship are the living ones. This is due to the fact that they are the ones who conduct funeral customs. The benefit derived should be that of safety to both the deceased's family and their relatives. The discussion centering on both the dead and the living signifies that traditional customs have not been abandoned. This suggestion implies that in a case where Islam has an influence, such as that of the Luo Muslims in Kendu Bay, rituals "to" the dead are carried out with a view to protect the living. But if this is the case, then how has the teachings in Shafi'ite's School of Law been influencing the lives of the Luo Muslims? Has it replaced their traditional understanding of death or does it simply co-exists alongside their old customs?

Whitehouse provides a different approach to the subject of bonding. He describes the cognitive process as having two divergent modes of religiosity: the imagistic, and the doctrinal.[174] In the imagistic mode, Whitehouse explains that rituals, which are often traumatic in their performance, have a lasting impact on people's minds through their memories, influencing in this way how people conceive religion. By contrast, in the doctrinal mode, he discusses that religious knowledge is spread through, mainly, intensive and repetitive teaching. For this reason, religious communities in the imagistic mode tend to be small, exclusive and de-centered, while in the doctrinal

---

173. Dennis Klass, "Continuing Bonds in the Resolution of Grief in Japan and North America," *American Behavioral Scientist* 33 (2001): 742–764; Kathleen M. Lalande and George A. Bonanno, "Culture and Continuing Bonds: A Prospective Comparison of Bereavement in the United States and the People's Republic of China," *Death Studies* 30, no. 4 (2006): 303–324.

174. Harvey Whitehouse, *Modes of Religiosity: A Cognitive Theory of Religious Transmission* (Oxford: AltaMira Press, 2004), 65.

mode, religious communities are large, inclusive and centralistic.[175] His discussion has provided two categories by which Luo-Muslim rituals of death may be classified. Imagistic perspective provides the understanding that their rituals associated with death affect the participants for a long time. This should be due to the memory ties or bonding that the living shares with the dead. There is, however, no indication of how long the effects of rituals can last.

The doctrinal mode points to bonding through teachings. This view relates to Shafi'ite's School of Law, where teachings on doctrinal issues are also emphasized. The doctrinal mode implies that the Luo Muslims are given teachings related to the issues of death. These teachings are in turn effectual concerning the way the Luo Muslims view death. But if both imagistic and doctrinal modes explain the bonding aspect among the Luo Muslims, then such bonding should be viewed as tending towards traditions (imagistic) as well as to the official Islam (doctrinal). Whitehouse's classification is therefore insightful in exposing where the Luo Muslims are leaning. But the presence of both modes may imply that there is a mix in their funeral rituals. This then qualifies them to be categorized as popular rather than official Muslims.

Marranci also alludes to the fact that rituals in Islam are based mainly on the doctrinal model.[176] However, Marranci's approach is more subjective since he portrays Islam as a universal entity. He does not recognize that Muslims are varied in their beliefs and practices due to the differences in the local context. Sanneh describes the Nupe Muslims in Nigeria as using Islam only as a boost in their ideas on death and funeral. He notes that where substitution is possible, they follow a parallel path.[177] Although Sanneh is not very direct on this, he notes that Islam is being followed only in matters where it does not contradict itself with the local customs. Funeral practices are such areas where conflict is bound to happen. In that case, the local rather than Islamic customs are followed. His reference to Islam as a boost can either mean that it is abandoned once it has fulfilled its mandate or is followed passively. Even though Sanneh points to a different case, his view of Islam in relation to the local context is relevant. He highlights the

---

175. Whitehouse, *Modes of Religiosity*, 66–74.
176. Marranci, *Anthropology of Islam*, 24.
177. Sanneh, *Crown and the Turban*, 16.

preference given to the local customs in the expense of Islam. His argument
indicates that the local customs are still being followed by the very people
who have converted to Islam.

But whereas Sanneh does not clarify on what might lead to substituting
a certain practice in Islam, Gilliland,[178] covers it. In his focus on the influence of Islam on the traditional practices of Northern Nigeria, Gilliland
presents Islam as a religion of influence. However, instead of being dogmatic,
Gilliland provides a fair judgment by underlining areas of conflict between
African traditions and Islam.[179] The two major areas of conflict that he writes
about are the ethnocentric African worldview versus supra-tribal Islam on
one hand, and the immediacy, or utilitarian aspect of traditional religion
versus fatalistic acceptance of life in Islam, on the other hand.[180] While
discussing why such worldview differences exist, Gilliland submits that the
traditional ethos in most cases is a non-negotiable aspect of indigenous
religion.[181] The fact that traditional ethos cannot be compromised means
that they are still being followed by the indigenous Muslims. The reason
why following traditions abound in a local Muslim setting may be because
of the need to bond with the spirits of their ancestors. Denying such a
relationship is viewed as detrimental both to the deceased's family and relatives. Both Sanneh's and Gilliland's theoretical framework, in which Islam
is viewed as a boost and traditional ethos as non-negotiable respectively, is
therefore relevant. It gives the understanding of a possible cultural conflict
among the Luo Muslims between following their old traditions and the
Islamic teachings to which they are now exposed. Both writers have also
provided the awareness that in the case of such conflicts, the choice to go
traditional is most likely.

Nyaundi views the peaceful co-existence of Islam with other religions
in Kenya to have been made possible by the fact that Islam has been
Africanized.[182] This idea that Islam has been Africanized implies that the

---

178. Gilliland, *African Traditional Religion*.
179. Gilliland, 82–96.
180. Gilliland, 85.
181. Gilliland.
182. Peter T. N. Nyaundi, *Religion and Social Change: A Sociological Study of Seventh-
Day Adventism in Kenya* (Lund, Sweden: Lund University Press, 1993), 89.

Kenyan Muslims are conducting their ceremonies such as funerals following the African customs rather than the "foreign" practices of Islam. This, by extension, means that the Luo Muslims act like "Africans" when it comes to performing death rituals rather than "Muslims." This, argument, however, minimizes the fact that Islam has also had some considerable influence on the African society and in Luo land in particular. Nyaundi's view contradicts the one advanced by Levtzion and Pouwels and Robinson, who point to the African societies as Islamized.[183] The contention between "Africanized-Islam" and "Islamized-Africa" underscores the need to acknowledge that both African and Muslim customs have mutually influenced each other. But the nature and the extent of this influence among the Luo Muslims could be established by examining the different funeral customs that they practice. The concepts of Africanized-Islam and Islamized-Africa may simply be reflected in a context such as that of the Luo Muslims. Such sharing is likely to give rise to an African-Islamized society in which both African and Islamic funeral elements are reflected. The question as to why such sharing should exist needs to be asked.

The case of Rendille Muslims, as Schlee and Shongolo write, also provides evidence of an African-Islamized existence.[184] They view a curse as a socially accepted speech in which a specific prayer is made to God to kill someone.[185] The concept of curses is a very familiar practice in most of the African traditional settings. It is mostly associated with the breaking of traditions that have been set by the forefathers. This means that the harm or the punishment to the individual who has broken the *taboo* (curse) comes from the ancestors. The Rendille Muslims' case is different since it provides both traditional and Islamic fatalistic perspectives. Death is here regarded to be caused by God, while humans play the role of transmitting that curse from God through their utterances. Such a mix as found among the Rendille context identifies them as popular rather than official Muslims. Their belief in curse related

183. Nehemia Levtzion, Michel Abitbol, and Amos Nadan, *Islam in Africa and the Middle East: Studies on Conversion and Renewal* (Aldershot; Burlington, VT: Ashgate/Variorum, 2007); David Robinson, *Muslim Societies in African History* (Cambridge: Cambridge University Press, 2004).

184. Günther Schlee and Abdullahi A. Shongolo, *Islam and Ethnicity in Northern Kenya and Southern Ethiopia* (Rochester, NY: Boydell & Brewer, 2012).

185. Schlee and Shongolo, *Isalm and Ethnicity*, 92.

deaths in which both God and human are involved, provide the need to identify and to categorize such deaths as divine-human. This could become the third category besides classifying death as a divine or human causality.

Factors Contributing to Continuity and Discontinuity

Rosander argues that the line between indigenous custom and Islam is often ambiguous. But the line of division is becoming increasingly important due to the Islamization process to the extent that the boundary between tradition and religion, which was once blurred, if at all recognized by people and particularly not by rural people is becoming more clear-cut than before.[186] Rosander's argument is useful in categorizing the indigenous customs and Islam into continuity and discontinuity. The aspect of continuity is represented by the nebulousness that exists between the two cultures while the discontinuity is marked by their apparent division. It sounds quite ironic to attribute the apparent division between the indigenous and Islamic customs to Islamization. The opposite should have been true, in which as a result of Islamization, the practice of indigenous customs becomes obsolete.

Rosander is also categorical that the boundary between the two cultures is increasingly becoming more evident among the people in the urban than the rural areas. This makes it almost impossible to differentiate indigenous customs from Islam among the rural Muslims. Their beliefs and practices are interwoven together. Her urban-rural category is useful in dividing the Luo Muslims in Kendu Bay into two categories: urban or town, and rural Muslims. Hypothetically, it is expected that the Muslims in the urban or the town setting of Kendu Bay are different from their Muslim counter parts in the nearby villages in the way they practice funeral rituals. In other words, the two contexts should provide a clear-cut between official and popular Muslims. Apart from geographical proximity, the urban-rural theoretical framework can also be used in a psycho-cultural sense. This is where the influence of urban life comes in. It is understood that the lifestyle of urban dwellers, even if they have moved and settled in the rural areas, is completely different from those who have lived in rural areas most of their lives. Since

---

186. Eva Evers Rosander, "The Islamization of 'Tradition' and 'Modernity,'" in *African Islam and Islam in Africa: Encounters between Sufis and Islamists*, eds. Eva Evers Rosanders and David Westerlund (London: Hurst & Company, 1997), 6.

these former urban dwellers could still be holding their urban view of life, the way they conduct their funeral rituals may be different from their rural counterparts. However, this difference could be minimal due to the influence from the rural setting.

Mazrui observes that both Christianity and Islam face intense competition in Africa more than anywhere else in the world. Africa is the arena and platform for the rivalry between them.[187] In so doing, he has thus demonstrated that Africa is very significant to both Christianity and Islam. Although Africa's significance can also be a political one, Mazrui's context is mainly cultural. This means that funeral rituals are included. If that is the case, then the competition may be viewed as an attempt by both Christianity and Islam to bring change to the African funerary practices. Mazrui's context has a lot in common with that of Kendu Bay, where both Christianity and Islam co-exist. His theory of competition between Christianity and Islam in Kendu Bay therefore becomes applicable. But knowing the nature of both Christianity and Islam, this competition is bound to pull from opposite sides. The need to revitalize Christianity could mean that the Luo funeral practices that are viewed as traditional are either ignored or prohibited. On the other hand, Islam could be accommodating and adopting the Luo traditional customs. Whereas the competition theory helps to establish which side of the divide between Christianity and Islam the Luo people have mostly converted, the critical question as to why a majority of them have converted to that particular religion and not the other remains unsolved.

But while Mazrui's content hints at conflict from without, Kassatly and Adogame and Harvey, are mainly focusing on the conflicts that abound within those in Africa who have already embraced Christian or Islamic faith.[188] Kassatly views the clash between the tribal life and the Islamic tradition as pulling towards the opposite direction, with each side being determined to

---

187. Ali A. Mazrui, "Islam between Ethnicity and Economics: The Dialectics of Africa's Experience," in *Africa, Islam and Development: Islam and Development in Africa-African Islam, African Development*, eds. Thomas Salter and Kenneth King (Edinburgh: Universtiy of Edinburgh, 2000), 43.

188. Kassatly, "Local Traditions and Islamic"; Adogame Afe, "Practitioners of Indigenous Religions of Africa and the African Diaspora," in *Religion in Focus: New Approaches to Tradition and Contemporary Practices*, ed. Graham Harvey (London: Equnox Publishing, 2009), 75–99.

substitute the other.[189] His remark begs the question as to why such a conflict should occur. The answer lies in the kind of Islamic teachings to which the indigenous people have been exposed. The conflict can also arise due to some cultural values that are non-negotiable. Touching on such areas can easily be protested by the indigenous people. But the apparent conflict also means that some aspects of traditional and Islamic life are continued among those who are Muslims. It can, however, be speculative where continuity and discontinuity are realized, since Kassatly gives no indication of such. Adogame centers on an area that could be causing conflict. He remarks that the indigenous African peoples preserved aspects of their belief and ritual cosmos but also adjusted to a new socio-cultural milieu.[190] This explains why indigenous practice is still a reality among the African Muslims. The adjustment means that they have adapted Islamic life but at the same time revert to their former beliefs and rituals from time to time. Since there is very little information concerning why some aspects of indigenous beliefs and practices have been preserved, it could be interesting to venture into this through a field research. But if the saying, *mkosa kabila ni mtumwa* (in Swahili, meaning, the one who forsakes traditions is a slave) is true, then the perception that preserving a culture is meant to give a sense of belonging, becomes convincing. It provides a sense of identity not only to one's community but also the ancestors.

While writing about Samuel Crowther's[191] reaction to traditional practices, McKenzie identifies burial as the point where traditional religion was faced with radically different Christian practices.[192] Samuel Crowther was reacting to Christian burial in Sierra Leone where he noted that the people were prepared to tolerate all their proceedings except on one thing, that they bury their dead in the bush instead of the house. There could be no

---

189. Kassatly, "Local Traditions and Islamic Tradition," 26.

190. Afe, "Practitioners of Indigenous Religions," 82–83.

191. He was a very famous Christian leader and the first African Anglican bishop. He was born in Nigeria and rose from being a slave boy to a national hero as far as the Christian missionary movement of the nineteenth century is concerned. In his work in several West African countries, Crowther's view point was that Christianity was revolutionizing to the indigenous traditions. He exposed areas in the indigenous culture such as burial customs as having conflict with Christianity.

192. Peter R. MacKenzie, *Inter-Religious Encounters in West Africa: Samuel Ajayi Crowther's Attitude to African Traditional Religion and Islam* (Leicester: Blackfriars, 1976), 24.

doubt that the same attitude by the indigenous people prevailed against the Muslims since they co-exist together with Christianity in most parts of West Africa. Even though burying in the bush may not be what is presently practiced by the indigenous people in Sierra Leone due to change of times, the kind of insistence that was there then may only had transformed to a different form but which is still, indigenous. Sharkey's account on Sudanese Muslim acknowledges that Arab fostered the expansion of Islamic and Arabic culture in the Sudan. But he also observes that the Arab Muslims and the local culture did not erase nor harmonize each other: "Their co-existence has led to a new, ever-changing, and overlapping cultural formations."[193] This means that the Sudanese Muslims being referred to are partly Muslim and partly indigenous in their practices of rituals such as that of burial. If that is so, then the argument confirms that their customs carry the aspects of both continuity and discontinuity. The common history of origin that the Sudan shares with the Luos makes this study relevant in examining the Luo-Muslim context. But very little is found from Sharkey that can be used in explaining why the Arab Muslim culture is incompatible with the Sudanese indigenous one. Adequate response would be necessary, since, it provides the basis upon which the Luo-Muslim context can be appropriated.

Continuity of Luo traditional customs in Luo-Muslim funerals
The whole idea of continuity raises certain questions that some writers are grappling with. In his analysis of the cultural and political definition among the Luo, Parkin asks questions that seek to indicate that the subject of continuity is a very complex one: "Is it the practice of the custom which has persisted through changing condition? Or has the practice itself altered with the emic meaning of the custom persisting? Or have the ideas as well as the practices been altered?"[194] The same questions would guide in establishing whether the Luo old customs on matters of death have persisted or have been altered by the virtue of being Muslims. If there is alteration, has it retained its meaning from a traditional perspective or has the meaning and the form altered? If the latter applies to the Luo-Muslim context,

---

193. Sharkey, "Sudan," xxi, 137.

194. David J. Parkin, *The Cultural Definition of Political Response: Lineal Density among the Luo*. (London: Academic Press, 1978), 21–22.

then it means that discontinuity is also represented in a very limited way. Overall, Parkin's questions point to the nature of continuity. Its nature is a complex one and has given rise to discontinuity. Parkin has thus established that there is a correlation between continuity and discontinuity. In applying this to the Luo Muslims, their current death practices should be examined in the light of their former ones. Carrying on the same practices shows that there is continuity. The elements which they are continuing from their Luo traditional culture should in turn be examined against those that they have discontinued. Such an evaluation helps in establishing the link between continuity and discontinuity. But on the other hand, Parkin's questions provide the need to examine the aspect of continuity on the basis of whether it is a deliberate or a non-deliberate experience. A deliberate experience is where the Luo Muslims are practicing their Luo traditional customs related to death but with full knowledge that these customs are against Islamic teachings. Non-deliberate is where they are following their customs without being aware of the divide between Luo and Islamic customs.

While continuity remains complex among some indigenous Muslims, Horton provides a parallel observation in Christianity: "Christianity has not alienated the Africans from their indigenous world-views but instead, has reworked and integrated some key concepts into their own framework."[195] Horton demonstrates that African Christians have simply re-framed their Christian practices in order to suit their own local context. Considering that ATR has had a similar approach to Islam, Horton's observation becomes relevant in examining the Luo-Muslim context. His perspective gives the belief that the Luo Muslims may not have rejected Islamic teachings and practices concerning death, but instead they have simply re-worked and integrated them into their system. He also gives the understanding that the Luo Muslims have ignored those Muslim funeral practices that are not consistent with the customs of their forefathers, to which, they are still attached. Gilliland provides a perspective which is different from that of Horton. While admitting that the ancestral mindset is still troubling the conscience of the Muslims, Gilliland explains that if Islam has a strong influence where there was once an active ancestor cult, the practices that center

---

195. Robin Horton, "Tradition and Modernity Revisited," in *Rationality and Relativism*, eds. Martin Hollis, and Steven Lukes (Oxford: Blackwell, 1982), 223.

on the dead will be modified to fit the Muslim pattern.[196] Whereas Horton's emphasis is on Africanized Islam, Gilliland emphasizes on Islamized Africa. Both, however, have not minimized the fact that there could be traditions or Islamic practices which are being followed in either way. Despite the contrast, the accounts by Horton and Gilliland concerning the experiences of Christians and Muslims in Africa in respect to their traditional customs, give a basis for continuity.

Studies by Mbiti, Lawson and Parrinder,[197] have describe the continued presence of African customs in their new found religion. In reviewing the relationship between African traditional religion and Abrahamic faiths (Christianity and Islam), they are in agreement that indigenous customs and values have remained so deep despite the influence that the current religion has brought. In a more specific way, Ogutu envisions no change to the Luo practices of their forefathers.[198] Such practices also include the way a dead person is disposed. Ogutu has thus implied that the Luo Muslims are still disposing their dead ones in accordance to their Luo traditional customs. This is possible considering also, Odaga's[199] remarks: "up to the present time, a large percentage of the Luo community, still believe that a widow must go through *ter* or *chodo okola* (in Luo, meaning, widow cleansing)". He underlines the seriousness of this custom: "If the widow fails to observe this rite, her male children would experience lots of difficulties in their life."[200] In both Ogutu and Odaga's writing, it has become clear that the traditions that have been passed on by the ancestors cannot be ignored. This is insightful because, apart from asking why the Luo Muslims believe in the ancestors, it also seeks to explain how their beliefs in the ancestors have affected their perspective on death.

---

196. Gilliland, *African Religion Meets Islam*, 106.

197. Mbiti, *African Religions and Philosophy*, 222, 253; E. Thomas Lawson, *Religions of Africa* (New York, NY: Harper & Row, 1984); Geoffrey Parrinder, *African Traditional Religion* (New York: Harper & Row, 1962), 140–145.

198. Gilbert E. M. Ogutu, "An African Perception," in *Mortality and Human Destiny: A Variety of Views* (New York, NY: Paragon, 1985), 104.

199. Odaga, *Luo Oral Literature*, 39.

200. Odaga, 40.

In her discussion, Prince also contributes to the debate that the Luo rules, along with concerns about *chira*,[201] dominates contemporary traditionalist discourse and are prominent in the everyday life of people in the village.[202] About the present deaths in Luo, she further exposes: "They [Luo traditionalists] argue that the death of today is a consequence of people leaving the traditions, which brings confusion to social relations and results in sickness and death, and that the only way to avoid personal, social and cultural crisis is by following the rules."[203] Looking at widow inheritance as a contemporary ritual begs the question as to whether the current Luo Muslims are observing it. If they are, do they do it out of fear that there could be mysterious illnesses and death or because of the need to identify with their forefathers? If the contrary is true, then both Odaga and Prince have provided a benchmark by which the Luo traditional and Islamic customs can be differentiated. In his other writing Ogutu in fact gives a loud call to tradition by alluding that it is something one must return to in order to identify and water one's roots.[204] He goes on to say that the Luo community is in a crisis of identity, of purpose, of legitimacy or trust, of direction and of survival. He poses a challenge to take a retrospective look at the roots in order to propel the community into tomorrow's inevitable cultural renaissance.[205]

A call to identify with traditions of the forefathers can sometimes be very strong, to the extent that those who are already Muslims could think of reverting. Reverting to the Luo traditional customs may not only happen because of such a call, but also whereby the religious faith may have failed to meet needs of the people. It is on this basis that Mbiti laments that unless Christianity and Islam occupy the whole person as much as, if not more than, traditional religions do, most converts to these faiths will continue to revert to their old beliefs and practices for perhaps six days a week, and certainly in times of emergency and crisis.[206] Mbiti's suggestion implies that

---

201. *Chira*, in Luo, is a taboo or an act that is believed to cause death if carried out.

202. Prince, "Christian Salvation and Luo Tradition," 68.

203. Prince, 68.

204. Gilbert E. M. Ogutu, *Ker Jaramogi is Dead: Who Shall Lead My People? : Reflections on Past, Present, and Future Luo Thought and Practice* (Kisumu, Kenya: Palwa Research Services, 1995), xi.

205. Ogutu, *Ker Jaramogi is Dead*, 19.

206. Mbiti, *African Religions and Philosophy*, 3.

both Christianity and Islam are not providing enough as they should. The people have been left with no option but to revert. While his argument may be valid, Mbiti has given no suggestion as to how Christianity or Islam can occupy the whole person such that there would be no reverting. But can it be true that Islam for the case of the Luo Muslims has not met their felt needs or is it just that inclination to their traditions has been too strong that the Islamic teachings cannot penetrate? Mbiti has nevertheless inspired the need to examine and to establish the relationship between practices of the Luo Muslims on death and Islamic teachings to which they are being exposed.

The aspect of continuity has also been identified by some scholars from various communities in Africa. In her study of Waso Borana Muslims of Kenya, Aguilar notes that they keep their Muslim public rituals but continue to stress their traditional practices.[207] Among the Boni Muslims, Faulkner, reiterates: "the Boni are nothing if not resilient and even in this sphere, where Islam exerts its most powerful influence, traditional ways are still respected and constitute a world in the background, an alternate memory to that of Islam but one that still exerts a powerful hold over the Boni imagination."[208] Among the Wanga community of Kenya that is related to the Luo, both geographically as well as culturally, Munday notes that there is an ambiguity or vagueness that still characterizes their religious practices. She observed from her informants that although they are Christians and Muslims, they would still carry out their very traditional customs which they had denied before.[209] Since Munday's context is on burial, her writing is relevant to the study of the Luo Muslims. Their change of mind to follow traditional ways of burial implies that traditionalism was never replaced by Christianity or Islam. But one can only speculate that these traditions are being followed secretly due to the conflict they may have with the Islamic teachings.

Ghana is one of the countries in Africa that has had Islamic presence in the region. While this is undisputable, some Islamic areas in Ghana have continued to follow their traditional customs. Kirby singles out this

---

207. Mario I. Aguilar, "African Conversion from a World Religion: Religious Diversification by the Waso Boorana in Kenya," *Africa: Journal of the International African Institute* 65, no. 4 (1995): 526.

208. Faulkner, *Overtly Muslim*, 187.

209. Munday, *Luyia Response to Death*, 245.

continuing trend of old customs among the Anufo of Northern Ghana. He observes that "the Islamic presence has affected some of their customs like dressing; it has not altered their tripartite problem-solving matrix, Islam has simply adjusted to the traditional mode."[210] Rather than the religion of the forefathers adjusting, it is Islam that is said to have conformed. This conformity means that there is co-existence between Anufo traditional and Islamic customs. In such a relationship, continued practice from either side is expected with the traditional customs taking precedence over Islamic ones.

But while the idea of continuing practices of traditional customs is a matter that has elicited several debates among the anthropologists, the need to explore the underlying factors that are contributing to it is necessary. Diene and Burrell, in explaining this phenomenon argue that it was African cultures, because of their age-old natural adaptability, that absorbed both Christianity and Islam.[211] Absorption in this sense does not do away with the traditions, rather, it incorporates new ones. Pobee and Emmanuel also view continuity in rites in such places as the father's death as a way of avoiding offending the ancestors.[212] Their explanation of this gives the understanding that a father's death has more rituals involved than other deaths. If this is related to the Luo Muslims, then it creates the need to categorize deaths and examine the rituals involved according to various ages, gender and social status. The purpose for carrying out such rituals should also be established. If those rituals are related to the way ancestors are viewed, then it simply means that the focus of the Luo Muslims is more inclined to their traditions than on Islam.

Continuity may also have been possible due to little or partial commitment to Islam. This is illustrated by the case of Kabaka Mutesa, who was one of the Ugandan kings. Kasozi describes him as an extremely intelligent man. He also describes Mutesa's enthusiasm for Islam as having arisen partly from academic and intellectual excitement and partly from the other causes that

---

210. Jon Kirby, "Cultural Change and Religion: Conversion in West Africa," in *Eperience and Expression*, eds. Thomas D. Blakely, Walter E. A. van Beek and Dennis L. Thomaon (London: James Currey, 1994), 63.

211. Diene and Burrell, "Dynamic Continuity," 17.

212. John S. Pobee and Emmanuel H. Mends, "Social Change and African Traditional Religion," *Sociological Analysis* 38, no. 1 (1977): 7.

may have nothing to do with religion.[213] Kasozi gives the impression that Mutesa was religiously Muslim but traditionally a Baganda. This uncertainty over his conversion makes it apparent that Mutesa could easily give priority to his traditions instead of Islam. But if one claims to be a Muslim and yet he is not, the issue of identity is questioned. The question of what makes one a Muslim or a non-Muslim also becomes valid.

Another factor is captured by Yannoulatos. He comments: "contrary to the over simple conviction of many, the old religious certainties do not yield so easily to modern technological civilization."[214] Yannoulatos has simply presented the difficulty that emerges with an attempt for any religion to replace the traditional one. The new religion in an existing one may be resisted all together or accommodated with some adjustments to suit the old traditions. In cases where the new religion is adopted into the old system, the traditional customs never die but pop up at the opportune times, like in the case of a funeral. Viewing the Luo Muslims in this light implies that they are faced with the challenge in which their old customs are still surfacing in their funeral ceremonies. Yannoulatos also provides the need to examine the approach that Islam has been used to bring about civilization. Failure of yielding by the indigenous people lies in this Islamic approach.

Discontinuity of Luo traditional customs in Luo-Muslim funerals

According to Olupona, Christianity and Islam have filtered and changed the people from traditional beliefs and practices.[215] Based on Olupona, the Luo Muslims should be understood to perceive death as purely Islamic with no traces of traditional worldview. Trimingham also shares the same thought in his three stages of the Africanization of Islam, which are (1) germination, (2) crisis, and (3) gradual reorientation. He sees the third stage as a place where reorientation and the old religious structures are consciously rejected.[216] This consciousness is a deliberate one, which might come about as a result

---

213. Kasozi, *Spread of Islam*, 26.

214. Anastasios Yannoulatos, "Christian Awareness of Primal World-Views," in *Mission Trends No. 5: Faith Meets Faith*, eds. Gerald H. Anderson and Thomas F. Stransky (Grand Rapids, MI: Eerdmans, 1981), 250.

215. Olupona, "Major Issues in the Study," 26.

216. Trimingham, *Islam in East Africa*, 43.

of comparing traditions with their Islamic faith. Rejecting traditions for the sake of the religion may be taken to mean that the people want to be associated with the new lifestyle rather than the traditional one. This life in the new religion rather than the traditions carries some aspects of discontinuity not only in local customs but also in Islam. This is Brodeur's perspective that whether real or imagined, Islam and Muslim identities are constantly being defined and redefined by Muslims, generation after generation, in order to provide an integrated self-understanding in the midst of an increasingly complex world.[217] The implication of this is that time should be considered as a very essential element in examining the Luo-Muslim death rituals.

The sense of wanting to identify with life in the new religion is indeed a factor that contributes to discontinuity. Striving for change is a concern that faces both Luo traditionals and Muslim practitioners. Ogbuagu has this in mind when she states: "Due to technological innovations, methods of burying the dead have undergone tremendous transformation."[218] This implies that rituals such as wailing in a funeral have taken a different turn. Economic affluence and new thinking have resulted in hiring professional mourners. This, however, puts the genuineness of such mourning into question. Booth also advances reasons for discontinuity by claiming that to think of African traditional religion and culture as unchanging is a dangerous trap.[219] Although Booth is not very specific about the agent that causes change, his idea nevertheless implies that what was practiced and believed by the Africans many generations ago, is not the same in today's world. Jindra and Noret join this debate on discontinuity in their observation that over the last few centuries, sub-Saharan Africa has witnessed a series of broad and linked changes that have inescapably altered its funeral rites. They cite colonialism and the large scale adoption of world religions as the

---

217. Patrice C. Brodeur, "From Postmodernism to 'Glocalism': Toward a Theoretical Understanding of Contemporary Arab Muslim Constructions of Religious Others," in *Globalization and the Muslim World: Culture, Religion, and Modernity*, eds. Birgit Schäbler and Leif Stenberg (Syracuse, NY: Syracuse University Press, 2004), 188.

218. Stella C. Ogbuagu, "The Changing Perception of Death and Burial: A Look at the Nigerian Obituaries," *Anthropologica* 31, no. 1 (1989): 91.

219. Newell S. Booth, "Time and Change in African Traditional Thought," *Journal of Religion in Africa* 7, no. 2 (1975): 89.

most contributive "forces" toward change.[220] With colonialism comes the idea of industrialization and urbanization while religiously, Islam is rated as influencing the African funeral practices. Although they have touched on the change, Jindra and Noret give very little clarity concerning whether this change has meant the old customs have been totally replaced. However, absolute replacement of past practices may not be the case bearing in mind that other scholars have also argued for continuity.

Synthesis of Luo Traditional and Luo-Muslim View of Death

The above literary studies have demonstrated that there are vestiges of traditional worldview in African-Muslim funerary practices. Such understanding is also based on various discoveries, which have been made by some writers such as Kim.[221] In his book, *Islam among the Swahili in East Africa*, Kim underscores the fact that Islamic studies especially from the Western Christian missionaries have unconsciously overlooked the vital aspect of Islamic phenomena in relation to the local context.[222] This oversight, although not deliberate, has only resulted in a situation in which Islam is viewed more as an orthodox religion without considering its cultural nature, which is popular Islam. The former focuses on the ideologies while the latter on the practices of Islam. Although both are important areas of study, ignoring the synthetic nature of Islam in relation to the local context could only lead to emphasizing the official without regard to its popular nature.

The idea of how discontinuity and continuity play out in a Muslim group such as the Luo Muslims can be understood through Bhatti's view on popular religion. According to him, popular religion is an invisible reality. It is operated largely at the subconscious level. Those who believe in it may not be entirely conscious of the fact, and for a rational modern educated person, it is simply a survival of primordial superstitions.[223] Bhatti draws

220. Michael Jindra, *Funerals in Africa: Explorations of a Social Phenomenon* (Oxford: Berghahn Books, 2011), 16–40.

221. Kim, *Islam among the Swahili*.

222. Kim, 1–3.

223. Harvinder Singh Bhatti, *Folk Religion Change and Continuity* (New Delhi: Rawat Publications, 2000), 10.

a parallel between belief and disbelief in popular Islam. By pointing to both aspects of belief and disbelief, Bhatti has made a clear distinction between popular and official Muslims. His notion of unconsciousness makes clear an inseparable contrast in popular religion, such as the one the Luo Muslims are viewed to be practicing. The mixing of old customs with Islam or Christianity has been described differently as syncretism,[224] hybridity, naturalization or synthesis. According to Stewart: "the implied trajectory of syncretism moves from conflict and discrepancy to consilience, harmony, synthesis, integration, cross-fertilization, and other concepts that imply the fusion of difference into a new whole."[225] It is this "new whole" that the researcher describes as inseparable.

While contributing also to the idea of syncretism in a religious context, Behera views syncretism as religious entities that were originally separate but have now come together. He explains that this may occur in three possible ways. In the first place, what is superimposed predominates, while what is older survives. The second way is that the sub-stratum, that is, what is older and traditional continues to exercise dominance. The third possibility, at least at an ideal level, is that a balance may be established between the various components.[226] These three phases would be used as a theoretical framework for studying the Luo-Muslim context. In applying the first phase, the Luo Muslims should be examined and establish whether the traditions of their forefathers are still surviving despite their acceptance of Islam. The second phase is where the Luo traditional customs of funerals are studied concerning whether they continue to exert dominance in Luo-Muslim practice. The various areas where this can be established are in wailing, and in rituals associated with widowhood. In the third part, both the Luo traditions and Islamic customs are established concerning their state of being. Are they in a state of balance or one is overriding the other? The outcome would

---

224. The term "syncretism" usually refers to connections of a special kind between languages, cultures, or religions. Religious syncretism can be described as "an attempt to bring together and combine as, harmoniously as possible diverse religious views" (Encyclopedia Britannica, vol. 9, 739). The Oxford English Dictionary also defines syncretism as "an attempted union or reconciliation of diverse or opposite tenets or practices."

225. Charles Stewart, "Syncretism and Its Synonyms: Reflections on Cultural Mixture," *Diacritics* 29, no. 3 (1999): 40–62.

226. Behera, *Tribal Religion*, 80.

indicate whether there is a compromise on both sides over their cultural practices or not.

Similar to Behera, Broom shares three possibilities to religious syncretism: "symbiosis, acculturation, or superposition."[227] Very close to syncretism is symbiosis, which Behera describes as a social presupposition for the rise of a syncretism following the co-existence of various groups.[228] The group in question is similar to the Luo Muslims since they have integrated their old traditions and Islamic teachings into their practices and belief system. Unlike Behera and Broom, Kwenda, emphasizes "the use of naturalization as a viable term for assessing the impact of African religious or the host environment on missionary religions."[229] One of the missionary religions that Kwenda refers to is Islam. He further elaborates that to naturalize in this sense is not to take away anything but to give something a new release on life, a new way of being.[230] Kwenda uses "naturalization" as opposed to Africanization or indigenization, which he describes as vogue.[231] In relating his "naturalization" theory to the Luo Muslims, it implies that the Islam that was introduced to the Luos has been made to "look" and to "feel" as if it is native. This theory views the Luo Muslims not as diminishing but as flourishing in their new identity as Muslims. Naturalization, as Kwenda describes, carries the notion of dualism, since it only introduces something new (Islam) to the already existing (Luo traditional customs). "Naturalization" makes the line separating those two cultures identifiable.

The idea of naturalization may not convey the same meaning as synthesis or hybridity since, according to Clarke, synthesis or blend is due to the interactions with African society and culture. It has been unnoticeable in many parts of Africa where Islam has established itself.[232] Clarke gives the idea of

---

227. Broom defines acculturation as "culture change that is initiated by the conjunction of two or more autonomous cultural systems." Leonard Broom, "Acculturation: An Exploratory Formulation," *American Anthropologist* 56, no. 6 (1954): 974.

228. Behera, *Tribal Religion*, 80.

229. C. V. Kwenda, "The Jekhanke of Senegambia: A Study in Religious Naturalization," *Encounter* 53, no. 3 (1994): 294.

230. Kwenda, "Jekhanke of Senegambia," 294.

231. Kwenda, 287.

232. Peter Clarke, "Religion in the Service of Politics and Service in the Politics of Religion," 4 (1993): 35–42. Accessed at the Bodleian Library, Oxford.

a fusion of cultures. This, unlike the "naturalization," makes separating Luo and Muslim cultures difficult. While synthesis carries the idea of fusion of cultures, it is not clear whether Mafa burial in Northern Cameroon fits the description that Santen provides. He mentions that Islamized sons may bury their Pagan father the same evening, according to Islamic customs, while the funeral rites are carried out according to Mafa customs.[233] It is also not very explicit as to when and how the Mafa community conducts this interchange in burial practices. It is out of such ambiguity that the experiences of the Luo Muslims may be understood.

Luo-Muslim Experiences of Luo Traditional Understanding of Death

The arguments that so far have been presented in this study provide a clue to the kind of a worldview the Luo Muslims may hold concerning their beliefs and practices surrounding death. The foregone discussion has demonstrated that both traditional beliefs and practices surrounding death have either changed or have remained the same among Luo Muslims. However, holding such a view can easily lead to the suggestion that the Luo Muslims are dualistic in their beliefs and practices about death. But describing Luo Muslims as dualists does not fully reflect their perception of death. Dualism carries the understanding that their worldview is divided into two distinctive compartments. On one side is the continuity while on the other side is the discontinuity. However, according to Kim, such boundaries do not exist. His study of Swahili Muslims shows that their Islam is still one but has dynamic aspects; these two Islamic features (orthodox and popular) are not two separate entities, but are two aspects inherent in one reality.[234] What Kim states is relevant to the Luo-Muslim context. In the absence of such a distinction, the Luo Muslims by implication could regard themselves as Muslims. In fact, Kim refers to this by stating that the Swahili Muslims believe that both Islamic (more ideological) and folk traditions are ordained (or at least allowed) by Allah. Therefore, they are not different "kinds" of Muslims.[235] A Muslim experience which suggests this oneness is reflected by Ghazali in

---

233. Santen, *They Leave Their Jars*, 241.
234. Kim, *Islam among the Swahili*, 57.
235. Kim, 57.

his account about remembrance of death in Islam.[236] This *dhikri* practice is a lifetime experience which cannot be divorced from other areas of living.

Since popular Muslims regard their practices as ordained by Allah, the kind of experiences they face concerning their view of death, are driven by two forces. On the one hand, there is the aspect of boldness in instituting in what is claimed to be from Allah in a death situation. This includes prohibiting women from wailing. But on the other hand, there is the fear of what could happen if God is disobeyed. This kind of fear is not only centered on Allah, but also from the spirits of the ancestors, which are supposed to be honored in a folk Muslim context. This in part is in line with what Musk suggests that an ordinary Muslim sees himself or [herself] as confronted by a plurality of "powers."[237] Such "powers", are in the realm of the spirits.

But with the belief in two realms of "power," one from Allah and the other from "powers," it is certainly evident that there is a conflict of allegiance in the life of an ordinary Muslim. Musk focuses this in one of his chapters on "World in Conflicts?"[238] He begins by pointing out that it is plain that the beliefs and practices of ordinary Muslims contradict many formal aspects of Islamic faith.[239] Throughout his discussions, Musk draws a parallel between the orthodox and popular Islam. The third element which Kim describes as the "domain of total synthesis"[240] is seemingly missing in Musk's description of the life of ordinary Muslims. But on the other hand, contrary to Musk, who distinguishes between orthodox and ordinary Muslim, Kim, largely emphasizes on complete blending of the two sides as one whole.[241] The conflicts that Musk writes about are only between the two sides of Islam. It is Gilliland, who provides the understanding of the conflict in worldviews between Islam and traditional religion.[242] He has, however, not attempted to define the type of Islam he is focusing on.

---

236. Ghazzālī and Winter, *Remembrance of Death*, xiii.

237. Musk, *Unseen Face of Islam*, 197. "Powers" is a term referring to the invisible world of the spirits which include magic, sorcery, divination, *Baraka, dhikr,* evil eye, omens, vows, curses etc. (Musk, *Unseen Face of Islam,* 185–192).

238. Musk, 223–238.

239. Musk, 223.

240. Kim, *Islam among the Swahili,* 67–68.

241. Kim, 57.

242. Gilliland, *African Traditional Religion,* 82–85.

Although they share some differences and similarities, the writings of Kim, Musk and Gilliland should be used to establish whether there is a conflict in the Luo-Muslim beliefs about practices concerning death. The conflict could be an indication that they are still distinct in their orthodox and popular perspectives on death. Secondly, the concept of "total synthesis" should also be established if it has worked in their case. This means that the various cultural elements of death from both Luo traditions and Islam are examined in the light of what the current Luo Muslims are practicing. Having a different way of explaining what Luo Muslims do during funeral ceremonies could provide meaning to their new cultural life.

Luo Muslims' Explanation of Death through their own Experiences

The writings of Gilliland, Kim and Musk are relevant since they provide the information on how through their experiences Muslims in general and Luo Muslims in particular could be explaining their understanding of death.[243] Gilliland, for instance, outlines the ethnocentric quality by which tribal religion was regarded as one of the areas of conflicts between Islam and African traditional religion. The point he emphasizes is that such quality is in terms of traditional ethos, which is non-negotiable.[244] In most of the African customs, death is such an area where traditional ethos is hard to compromise. It means therefore that if there are conflicts between Islam and traditions in matters of customs of death, it is the traditions that carry the day. The traditional ethos is non-negotiable because it is associated with the world of the ancestors. The view that death is humanly rather than divinely caused is part of the experience that has been unconsciously inherited from the ancestors. Using Gilliland's approach, funeral rituals of the Luo Muslims could be categorized into negotiable and non-negotiable. What determines what is negotiable and non-negotiable should also be established. This assessment would in turn help to explain what really informs the experiences of the Luo Muslims in their understanding of death.

---

243. Gilliland, *African Traditional Religion in Transition*; Kim, *Islam among the Swahili in East Africa*; Musk, *Unseen Face of Islam*.

244. Gilliland, *African Traditional Religion*, 85.

In Kim's "total synthesis,"[245] the Luo Muslims become a single whole. However, cases of death are explained from both Islamic and traditional perspectives. For instance, while death is believed to be caused by God, the living dead and the ancestors are still venerated through libation and other rituals as these spirits demand. The dead may either be buried facing Mecca or in accordance to traditional customs. Kim's "total synthesis" would mean that the Luo-Muslim practices of death are analyzed to see how both customs have been synthesized into a single whole. It is expected that what they now practice is distinct from the two cultures. This calls for observing their death customs and separating what are Luo traditions from Islam. A thin layer between those customs would indicate that the Luo Muslims are popular rather official Muslims.

Musk considers beliefs and practices of ordinary Muslims as contradicting many formal aspects of Islamic faith.[246] The conflict signifies very little compatibility between formal and popular Islam. But he also observes: "[These] beliefs and practices are, however common and permeate the everyday life of human beings."[247] What Musk implies is that the day-to-day experiences of ordinary Muslims are mostly informed by their popular Muslim beliefs. Going by his idea, it is very easy to believe that the Luo Muslims are also informed by the same popular Muslim beliefs. But whereas this might be the case among the Luo Muslims, the role that the official Islam has played would remain speculative.

Conclusion

This study therefore has mainly examined how Islam has penetrated the African communities and the effects that this perforation has had on the African traditional customs. Much interest has been placed on death and the customs surrounding it. Various scholars have used terms such as Islamization and Arabization in describing the influence that Islam has made on the African customs. The impact of Islam on the various traditions of African communities has been due to its nature, which is catholic,

---

245. Kim, *Islam among the Swahili*, 67.
246. Musk, *Unseen Face of Islam*, 223.
247. Musk, 223.

accommodative and adaptive. Its character allows it not to ignore but rather to make necessary adjustments to the African cultures wherever necessary. Islamic teaching on death is very fatalistic. It puts God at the center of all that happen to human beings including death. Human beings are believed to be powerless. They therefore simply surrender to God's will.

Just like in Islam, ATR has also been described as adaptive and assimilative in nature. This means that although Islam has had significant influence on ATR, it has not managed to expunge certain aspects of indigenous customs. Elements such as widow inheritance and wailing have been retained despite Islamic prohibition. Reverting to those practices have been explained from the African perspective as a way of conserving the culture, paying respect to the ancestors and as lack of an alternative. A lot of contrasts have been displayed between the indigenous and Islamic customs. For instance, in African customs, prayers are made to the dead while in Islam prayers are made for the deceased. The death rituals are for the wellbeing of the deceased in Islam while in ATR they are meant to protect the living. Another area which has emerged is where Islam treats death as divinely caused, while African customs treat it as caused by human agents. Such contrasts are contributing to the debate on continuity and discontinuity of African culture in Islam. These two aspects have been seen to affect rural and urban people differently.

Different literary sources in this study of Luo traditional and Islamic perspectives on death have revealed three main issues. First, there is an aspect of continuity in which the African old customs are still being practiced in Islam. Second, there is a sense in which some traditions have been discontinued. Last, both former customs and Islam have been synthesized into one single whole. The latter treats Islam not as a separate entity but as a unified unit. These three areas have given a clear understanding that the majority of the African Muslims are practicing popular rather official Islam.

CHAPTER 3

Methodology

Introduction

The overall goal of this research is to describe how the understanding of death among the Luo Muslims has been affected by the Luo traditional funeral beliefs and practices. In his book, *Introduction to Missiological Research Design*, Elliston describes the research methods as addressing two fundamental issues: "the collection and analysis of data."[1] Although he is specifically referring to a missiological study, data collection and analysis are very fundamental in any field of research. In looking at the study of Islam, a lot of researches have been done that mainly focus on its theological,[2] historical[3] and political[4] aspects. Those studies have greatly contributed toward the understanding of the ideological nature of Islam. Despite the effort, the research into how Muslim beliefs and practices have been affected by traditional customs still remains scanty. The lack of a study in this area has led to an imbalanced view of Islam. Many people understand it only as a political religion. It has also been understood as a religion whose beliefs and practices are unchanging despite the local context under which it operates. The trend, in which,

---

1. Edgar J. Elliston, *Introduction to Missiological Research Design* (Pasadena, CA: William Carey Library, 2011), 74.

2. Tilman Nagel, *The History of Islamic Theology: From Muhammad to the Present* (Princeton, NJ: Markus Wiener, 1999).

3. Abdulkader Tayob, *Islam: A Short Introduction: Signs, Symbols and Values* (Oxford: Oneworld, 1999).

4. William Montgomery Watt, *Islamic Fundamentalism and Modernity.* (New York, NY: Routledge, 1999).

some communities have embraced Islam while at the same time follow their traditional customs is increasingly becoming very perplexing.

Questions have been asked as to how Islam has influenced such communities, what has become of their old customs and how they explain their experiences in relation to the local beliefs and practices. A community where a field research was conducted with a view to respond to those queries was among the Luo Muslims in Kendu Bay. The study was limited to understanding how Luo traditional views have affected the Luo-Muslim beliefs and practices surrounding death. Since the study centers on their experiences[5] on funerary issues, a qualitative method was used. As Creswell, explains: "A qualitative study is an inquiry process of understanding social or human problem, based on building a complex, holistic picture, formed with words, reporting detailed views of informants, and conducted in a natural setting."[6] Creswell's definition distinguishes qualitative research from other research methods. He also implies that a qualitative method is a sequential process that revolves around four areas: the issue being studied, approaches used in dealing with the issue being studied, persons interviewed and the social situation in which the research was carried out. Those four areas were very helpful. They enabled the researcher to identify and to concentrate on the main issues that were relevant to his study during data collection. After collecting data, it was analyzed and classified into different categories and domains. The Luo-Muslims' experiences in relation to Luo traditional customs surrounding death were then explained using those categories and domains. Kendu Bay is a town with about ten thousand people (1999 Kenyan Census). The population mainly consists of people from Islamic and Christian backgrounds. Though its population is scattered throughout the town, the majority of the Luo Muslims live in the old town of Kendu Bay. It is here that the research was conducted. The population size was put at sixty-five. This number was arrived at by considering those who were contacted and volunteered to be interviewed. Due to the nature of the research questions (see chapter 1), their age and gender were also considered.

---

5. Michael Quinn Patton, *Qualitative Research & Evaluation Methods: Integrating Theory and Practice* (Thousand Oaks, CA: Sage, 2002), 33.

6. John W. Creswell, *Research Design Qualitative and Quantitative Approaches* (Thousand Oaks, CA: Sage, 1994), 1–2.

Data Collection

Ethnographic method is generally understood as part of qualitative research methods.[7] However, the ethnographic method has been described as very descriptive and one which involves face-to-face interaction.[8] By adopting it, it was not only possible to hear the informants speak about their experiences on death but also to see what goes on in a Luo-Muslim funeral. In his two books, Spradley underlines the significance of interviews and observation in research.[9] These two methods were employed together with others that are also discussed in this chapter. The data was collected between May and August, 2015 in Kendu Bay.

Ethnographic Interviews

Whereas there are various forms of interviews, it was the open-ended question method[10] that was used. According to Fontana and Frey, this method has the purpose of "understanding the complex behavior of members of a society without imposing any *a priori* categorization that may limit the field of inquiry."[11] The interview was also unstructured.[12] The positive thing about open-ended question and unstructured interview methods was that the informants were able to describe in detail their behaviors and beliefs as far as their funeral procedures and activities are concerned. Some of them gave their own personal experiences of how they have participated in funeral processes. Their responses were very useful in generating new questions that were never thought about before. The face-to-face talk also made it possible to determine through their facial expression whether the questions they were asked made sense. Their body language was an important gesture that helped to adjust or improve on the questions accordingly.

---

7. David Silverman, *Doing Qualitative Research* (London: Sage, 2005), 5.

8. Margaret Diane LeCompte and Jean J. Schensul, *Designing & Conducting Ethnographic Research: An Introduction*, 2nd ed. (Lanham: AltaMira Press, 2010), 4–5.

9. James P. Spradley, *The Ethnographic Interview* (Orlando, FL: Holt, Rinehart and Winston, 1979); James P. Spradley, *Participant Observation* (Orlando, FL: Holt, Rinehart and Winston, 1980).

10. Spradley, *Ethnographic Interview*, 88.

11. Andrea Fontana and James H. Frey, "The Interview: From Structured Questions to Negotiated Text," in *Handbook of Qualitative Research*, 2nd ed., eds. Norman K. Denzin and Yvonna S. Lincoln (Thousand Oaks, CA: Sage, 2000), 653.

12. Spradley, *Ethnographic Interview*, 60.

Interviews were conducted in many different settings of the informants such as in their homes, at their work places, in the *madrass* and *barazas*.[13] The appointments were made to individual informants before interviewing them. These requests to interview were made through the research assistant, a Christian friend (he is the one who formally introduced the researcher to the Luo Muslims since he works with them in table banking) and directly to the informants themselves. Accessing the Luo-Muslim community through those individuals followed some kind of a cyclic sequence (see Spradley[14]) as illustrated in the diagram below.

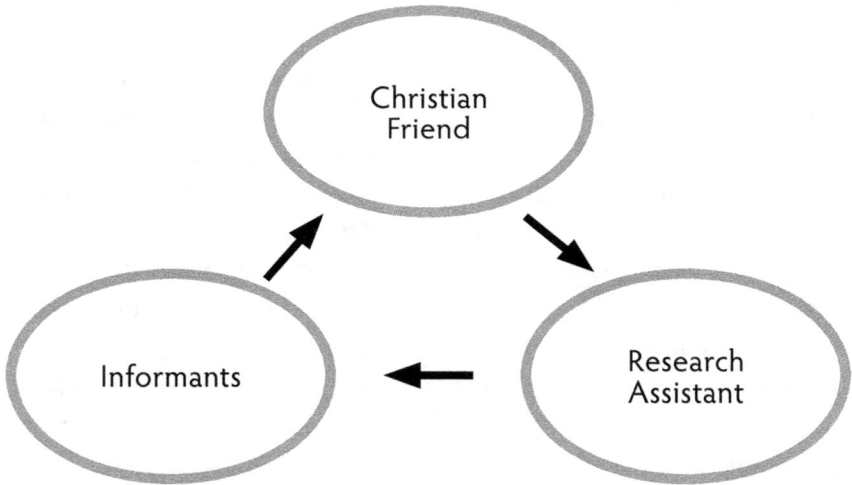

Diagram 1: Channels through Which Luo Muslims Were Accessed

Christian friend

As shown in the diagram, the way that the researcher got access to the Luo Muslims in Kendu Bay was through Christian friend. This happened in May, 2015 while he (the researcher) was on his way to meet another pastor whom he had contacted and was willing to introduce him to some Luo Muslims.

---

13. *Barazas* are village gatherings where the Luo-Muslim community would come together to be addressed on some issues that are affecting them. Except in a few cases, most of these gatherings consisted of men and women.

14. Spradley, *Participant Observation*, 26.

His friend Orega, works with the Luo Muslims in the business of table banking.[15] Because of his familiarity with those Luo Muslims, he became a very resourceful person for the researcher. It was through Orega that contacts with different groups of the Luo Muslims were made. Some of the people who were met on the way included the *imams* (spiritual leaders among the Luo Muslims) and certain officials in table banking initiative. They heartily extended their invitation to the researcher to visit them at their homes or in their *barazas*. The researcher was also introduced to the chief of the area. He was also very welcoming. In fact, as an administrative officer, he later became very resourceful in providing the information about the history of the different clans living in Kendu Bay Sub-County. These clans are a mix of people from different faiths and backgrounds.

The place where the chief's office is situated is very close to a tree which has been there for many years. It is under this tree as the researcher came to know later that many of the Luo-Muslim *barazas* take place. This was also the venue where some of his informants would direct him to meet with them there. Both the chief's office and the big tree are located in Kendu Bay old town. It is at this place where most of the Luo Muslims reside. Since the researcher's friend stays not far from Kendu Bay town (about fifty kilometers away), he just used to commute to and fro. Every time he comes to see how his groups were doing, he could also call on the researcher or take him to meet with other Luo Muslims. At times he would call some of his Luo-Muslim friends over the phone to come and chat with the researcher. The respect they accorded him made it possible to meet with many Luo Muslims of different ages and gender. They in turn became very friendly and were readily available to share information and their experiences about death.

---

15. This table banking is a type of a banking system in which various stakeholders come together to form a group. In some contexts it is known as *chama* (union). In the group, a committee consisting of a chairperson, a secretary and a treasurer is formed. They are in charge of the money contributed by their members. They also organize various forums to educate members on issues that are affecting them. The money is contributed monthly to the treasury. The difference between this banking and other banking systems is that in table banking, no interest (usury) is charged. The money is also not kept in the bank but rather kept by the treasurer of the group. Many Luo Muslims have joined it since it does not encourage usury. It is a registered organization and has many other branches in the other parts of Kenya. The group members are allowed borrow money in order to increase their businesses. The researcher's friend is its director.

Research assistant

Another resourceful channel as indicated in the diagram above was the research assistant. In the first few days after the introduction, the researcher used to visit the people he secured appointment with by himself. Occasionally his Christian friend would accompany him to their homes whenever he was around. As days went by, he got to know some of the people very closely. Since it was becoming problematic in translating and explaining some issues in Luo mother-tongue, the researcher decided to start using an informant whom he has already identified. His informant was a young Muslim *imam*. He was most suitable for the task due to his position and age. He knows all the Luo-Muslim communities in Kendu Bay by their names, their occupation, their ages and the places they stay. He was very much available in most of the *barazas* and other government or NGO (Non-Governmental Organization) meetings. He was very reliable and sometimes would organize meetings for the researcher to meet with different Luo-Muslim groups.

Once he accepted to be the research assistant, he was taken through the whole content of what the researcher was looking for. Being a Muslim *imam*, he was obviously knowledgeable in Arabic language and other Islamic issues. This worked positively since through him, the researcher got to know many terms in Arabic, which are related to death. But apart from being familiar with Arabic, he was also very fluent in both *dholuo* (Luo language) and Kiswahili. His ability to communicate well in *dholuo* was very encouraging. He would reframe or translate the questions in such a way as to make the informants understand. The researcher spent most of his time with him. This was not only during the interviews but also before and after the interviews. Spending time together was for the purpose of reviewing and clarifying certain questions or issues that were not clear during the interviews. It was also a moment to strategize on how to make contact with other Luo Muslims who could be available for the interview. Together with visiting some of them in their homes, *barazas* and *madras* (especially for children during their Saturday classes), others were interacted with as they came to visit the *imam*. So, through the research assistant, many other informants came on board.

Informants

The third source was the informants (see diagram 1). The whole pattern is described as cyclic in the sense that there is a connection between one source and the other. In other words, through the Christian friend, the researcher got to know the *imam* who later became his research assistant. The research assistant was not known in isolation. He was part of the Luo-Muslim group who was introduced to the researcher. He was therefore very familiar. Some people who became the researcher's informants were introduced to him by his Christian friend while others by his research assistant. These informants also introduced other people who also became researcher's informants. All these three categories (Christian friend, research assistant and informants) have a chain relationship. They know each other.

Once they had been contacted personally or through the friend and research assistant, the informants would tell each other about the *wendo* (in Luo, meaning, visitor) who is interested in knowing their funeral customs. Out of curiosity, they would come. Some informants would be seen beckoning their friends as they pass by to come and listen to *jaloka* (in Luo, literally means, a person from a different clan or dialect).[16] This is a very polite way of addressing their Luo tribes' mate. It is especially applicable if the people have accepted the person visiting in their hearts. As they come, they would be told by their colleagues how *jaloka* is a good man who is simply interested in knowing how customs of death are conducted in Islam. Such acclamation from their fellow Luo Muslims together with the fact that *jaloka* was introduced to them by the people they know very well, made them less suspicious about the whole matter of interview. Some questions were repeated to those who joined while the interviews were going on. The questions that were repeated to the newcomers were meant to find out if they could answer them is the same way their colleagues have done. Some would refer certain questions that they were not sure with to the research assistant. They also encouraged the researcher to contact their *imams* or other elderly people among them. They are believed to know a lot about the beliefs and practices of Islam.

---

16. The term *jaloka* literally means a male (*ja-*) person from abroad. It is interesting that this term is not used when referring to a European or anybody else who come from other parts of the world. For a white person, the term used is *msungu* (equivalent of *mzungu* in Kiswahili language). It has its root from the word English which means an English speaker. *Jaloka* means a person from the other side. Rivers and sometimes mountains are used as the marking points. In other times, the researcher was called by the name of the place he was born which is *jalego* (male person from Alego). They hardly call a Luo "visitor" by his name.

Categories of the informants who were interviewed

The informants who were interviewed were sixty-five in number. They were divided into three categories: Luo-Muslim adults, Luo-Muslim youths and Luo-Muslim children. The *imams* were part of the first category of the informants who were interacted with. Interviewing them was necessary in order to know what they teach their followers in matters related to death.

Under the category of Luo-Muslim adults, eighteen men and nine women were interviewed. They aged between thirty and eighty years. Luo-Muslim adults are old enough and therefore considered to be familiar with both Luo traditional customs and their present Islamic practices with regard to funeral rituals. The Luo-Muslim youths who were interviewed were fourteen in number and aged between eighteen and twenty nine while children were twenty four. They were between five and seventeen years old. Both Luo-Muslim youths and Luo-Muslim children were interviewed because they attend *madras* and other institutions of learning such as Islamic schools, colleges and universities, where Islamic teachings on the matters associated with death are taught. The researcher sought to elicit information from this group of informants regarding how much they know about funeral beliefs and practices in Islam and the extent to which such knowledge has affected their understanding of death. The same information was also sought from the mature Muslim adults. The diagram is summary of the different groups of the informants who were interviewed.

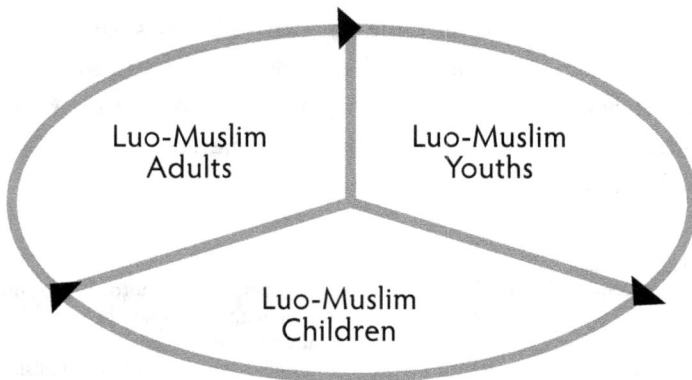

Diagram 2: Categories of the Informants

Different forms of interviews and places they were conducted

Apart from face-to-face interviews, some open-ended questions (see appendix A) were also used. These methods were applied during the *barazas*. The open-ended questions were administered to the Luo-Muslim adults and youths who due to their work and other commitments had very little time for the interviews. It was easy to administer the questions to them since they were already written. They would come early before the beginning of their *barazas* and then be taken through the questions. As for the Luo-Muslim children, focus group method was applied. After making an appointment with them through their *madras* teacher, Siraj, they were visited during their Saturday *madras* classes in one of their local Mosques situated in a Muslim primary school, in old town. Saturday was considered as the best day to meet with them since most of them go to school during the week days. Only a few of these children are in high school while the rest of them are in primary school. Everyone including the researcher and *madras* teacher sat on the mats that were spread on the floor. The girls sat with their legs stretched while the boys folded theirs. Unlike during prayers in the mosque, both boys and girls sat together, though on opposite ends. The fact that they sat separately from the opposite sex even though they were in the same room speaks of how some moral values are instilled in them right from their childhood.

During the first contact with the Muslim children, Siraj, the *madras* teacher wanted to excuse himself from the meeting. He felt that his presence would make the children feel very uncomfortable with answering the questions. Although his excuse was genuine, the researcher prevailed upon him to stay. It was necessary that he stay so that he could assist in any way that was needed. His input was so encouraging. He would repeat to the researcher some of the difficult names of the children as they pronounced them. He also assisted in writing and submitting the names and the ages of these Muslim children to the researcher at the end of every session.

Participant Observation and Steps of Data Collection

Spradley reveals five different types of participation.[17] He explains how they can be utilized as methods in a field research. He also identifies the various

---

17. Types of participation include: Nonparticipation, Passive Participation, Moderate Participation, Active Participation and Complete Participation (Spradley, *Participant*

contexts under which they can be used.[18] By discussing those participations in relation to their individual context, Spradley has made it clear of the need to select a method that is relevant to one's context. It thus follows his recommendation that both non participation and passive participation methods were adopted in the study of Luo Muslims. As he defines it, non-participation involves the collecting of data through observation only.[19] What Spradley implies is that one has to assess the sensitivity of the issue being researched on before deciding which participatory method to apply. Although those five participatory methods[20] have been illustrated[21] from a western perspective, the principles can be drawn that suit a local context such as Kendu Bay.

Methods of participant observation applied in the research

Death is one of the areas that has very memorable experiences. It does not only affect the lives of the people but also, depending on the community in question, is surrounded with many beliefs and practices. Due to emotions involved, death is an area that requires a lot of sensitivity. While this is very clear, going to the research also requires that one decides the extent to which they would like to involve themselves into the issues they are researching on. In this way, they would avoid making the mistake failing to identify the right participant observation as some secular anthropologists have done. As an outsider to the Luo-Muslim community, the researcher remained passive in his observation to the various activities that unfolded during the funeral. Spradley describes passive participation as being present where the activities are taking place but without playing any role. It also prohibits interacting with the people who are conducting the rituals.[22] Apart from being in a different religion, participating in a Luo-Muslim funeral either actively or moderately was also believed by the researcher to be quite distracting. Chances of losing focus on the major areas of interest to the research were believed to be very high. The people who were being researched on would

---

Observation, 58–59).

    18. Spradley, *Participant Observation*, 58–60.

    19. Spadley, 59.

    20. Spradley, 58–59.

    21. Spradley, 58–59.

    22. Spradley, 59.

also look at the researcher as someone who has very little or no respect for their customs.

But Spradley's description of non-participation observation as applicable to the scenes that do not allow for any participation,[23] should be understood as relative rather than absolute. It is relative in the sense that in the funeral, a person may be moved or called upon to assist in one way or the other. Even visitors who are not from the same religious faith may sometimes be called upon to offer prayers in one of the sessions of the funeral. This to some extent is a form of participation though in a limited sense. The researcher, however, did not encounter such experiences when he attended the two funerals that took place in Kendu Bay. He simply observed the proceedings as they unfolded from a distance. Occasionally, he would move close to where the body of the deceased was being attended to in order to get a glimpse of what exactly was taking place. But because Muslims are not very comfortable with male-female mixing, the researcher confined himself to observing only the male deceased as his body was being washed and shrouded. Concerning the details of how the body of the deceased female was being handled, he relied mostly on the information he gathered through the interviews and from other few procedures that were done in the public.

Steps that were applied for data collection

Creswell describes in detail a four-step strategy that may be utilized as a framework in data collection.[24] He has organized his steps in a way that follow a linear sequence (cf. Spradley[25]). Most of social science researches use linear sequence.[26] As is common with the linear sequence, there is no direct relationship between one step and the other in Creswell's strategy. A precaution was therefore exercised when applying his four-step strategy. This

---

23. Spradley, 59.

24. Creswell's four steps are: "(1) The first step is to identify the purposefully selected sites or individuals for the proposed study, (2) the type of data collected should be indicated, (3) highlight both the weaknesses and the strengths of the type of data collection used, and (4) inclusion of data collection types that go beyond observations and interviews" (Creswell, *Research Design: Qualitative, Quantitative, and Mixed Method Approaches* [Thousand Oaks, CA: Sage, 2003], 185–188).

25. Spradley, *Participant Observation*, 27.

26. "[I]nvestigators usually know what they are looking for" (Spradley, *Participant Observation*, 26)

was mainly because this research followed a cyclic rather than linear pattern (see Spradley[27]). Creswell's strategy was used selectively. His approach that is defined by the four steps, was believed to be very systematic. It underscores the need to be intentional and to purposefully lay down a procedure that would assist in collecting the data.

Following such a clear road map goes a long way in uncovering the right methods to use. This was in turn expected to meet the overall goal of the research. Chatting with a few Luo Muslims during the initial stages of the visit to Kendu Bay was very insightful. It was from this contact that a systematic structure that was in line with Creswell's strategy was developed on how best to go about collecting data. The things that were thought through in this structure included: the exact location of the research, the population size and tools or methods for data collection.

Combination of Both Interviews and Observation in Data Collection

Sometimes both interviews and participant observation were conducted together while at times separately. They were used in different stages: before the funeral, during the funeral and after the funeral. In the first stage, data was collected through interviews. These interviews were in three different forms: face-to-face interviews, open-ended questions and focus group method.[28] Interview methods were applied before any news of death was heard. Here, the informants were simply asked to explain and to describe their funeral beliefs and practices. It was in the course of conducting these interviews that news about the demise of two members of the Luo-Muslim community, a female and a male was heard. The first news to be heard was that of Salama. There was an interval of one month between her death and that of Muhammad. In the funeral period (second stage), both passive and nonparticipant observation methods were applied. These methods were very resourceful in confirming what had already been heard from the informants through the interviews. Some new information was also generated through them. The period after the burial (third stage) was where some observations

---

27. Spradley, *Participant Observation*, 26.

28. The written open-ended questions were the same questions that were used in focus group and among some Luo-Muslim youths and children.

and interviews were conducted. Those who were interviewed included some of the informants who were present and or participated in one way or the other in the funerals. The group included the *imams* and a few relatives of the deceased.

Both interviews and participant observation were conducted together and almost at the same time during the funerals. This, however, came much later, almost towards the end of the period that the researcher spent in Kendu Bay. Interviews helped to reveal how much the informants know about their funeral beliefs and practices. The knowledge that they shared concerning those beliefs and practices was, however, not necessarily from what they have observed or experienced. Some of that knowledge came from the teachings that they follow. But even though the information they gave was believed to be truthful, getting the opportunity to physically observe some activities and other funeral ceremonies as they unfolded, was very exciting. By observing, it became very easy to relate what had already been given in the interviews with the actual happenings as were observed. Another advantage with observation was that it made it possible to see other details that were lacking from the information the informants provided. Whereas in the interviews the informants' feelings or behavior may not be so open, observation made it easy to see clearly how people behave during the funerals.

In both Muhammad and Salama's burial ceremony, the opportunity to observe was granted. However, this permission was very restricted in Salama's case because of her gender.[29] Being aware of the possible distraction in a funeral, a deliberate effort was made to pay full attention to areas that were of paramount to research questions. Observation was therefore concentrated on: the stages of Luo-Muslim funeral rituals, the kind of people (in terms of their age and gender) involved in conducting those rituals, sites or venues where such rituals are carried out, the kind of tools and equipment that were used, the kind of attire and facial expressions of mourners, treatment of guests/visitors and other mourners, reactions of the bereaved family, and how time was managed. These observations covered the period between death and burial. However, the events that transpired between Muhammad's death and transporting his body home was not observed. It was because those events

---

29. Islam does not allow the opposite sex to mix or see one's private parts for whatever reason.

took place where he died in Kisumu. It was through interviews with some of his close relatives that other details surrounding his death were obtained. Likewise, some areas such as the washing of the body and shrouding were also not observed in Salama's case. This was, however, due to her gender as it has already been mentioned. The women who were taking care of her body were the ones who gave the information that was required.

Interchanging Between Interviews and Participant Observation

These interviews were conducted immediately following the burials. Part of the reason was that after burial, there were signs that it would rain. Some people were therefore in a hurry to leave. Others returned hastily to the deceased's houses where they joined the *imams* in making final prayers for the bereaved family. After praying and eating the food that was prepared for them, they dispersed hurriedly to their different places. Another reason why interviews were not conducted soon after the burial was due to the concern for the bereaved families. It was felt that it would be too early to start interviewing people who have just buried their loved one. They needed more time to settle down and to come to terms with the loss of their loved ones.

Being aware of this fact, it was the observation rather than the interviews that was started immediately following the burial. While doing the observation, much attention was given on the deceased's families and the activities that were happening around them. Since many people had dispersed by this time, moderate participation[30] was applied. Being a fellow tribesman and as a religious person, the researcher felt necessary to empathize and to console with the bereaved family more closely than before the burial took place. He commiserated with the bereaved families in the company of his research assistant. While consoling, he was able to take note of the way they were responding to the talks through their tone of language and facial expression. All these observations were done with a view to establish how the loss of their dear one has affected their lives in post-burial period. Interviews followed three days later after conducting the observations. The three-day window period was left in order to allow time to contact both the bereaved families and some informants who were present at the funeral

---

30. Spradley, *Participant Observation*, 60.

of the intention to interview them. Some of those informants were among those who participated in various funeral activities while others did not. They were the first ones to be interviewed then followed by the family members of the deceased.

Specific family members who were interviewed on Salama's side included her children, her husband, brothers and sisters in-law. On Muhammad's side, his three wives, children and his two parents were interviewed. The interviews to both the informants and the families of the deceased were focusing on their experiences toward death and its related practices. Besides narrating how they felt about the demise of their loved ones, the informants also mentioned the different roles they played at the funeral. They pointed out the significance of these roles in the light of what they believed as Muslims. Being familiar with Luo traditions, they were able not only to describe areas where their funerary customs are similar to the Luo traditional ones but also explained why those areas are similar.

Following and Recording Funeral Procedures and Events

The data was collected and recorded with a view to answer the three research questions (3RQs). The first research question (RQ1) deals with the understanding of how Islam has influenced the Luo-Muslim view of death. This influence was measured by looking at how the knowledge of Islam was applied by the Luo Muslims while conducting their different funeral activities and procedures. In order to achieve this, the whole funeral ceremony was first divided into four sections: (1) Death to body shrouding, (2) Body viewing to the grave, (3) Burial and (4) Post burial activities. In each section, and as was permitted, the procedures, conversations and the various activities were observed and recorded using digital decoder. But since there were a lot of activities taking place in the two homes of the deceased before they were taken to the grave for burial, the researcher and his assistant decided to divide themselves so as to cover different areas of the funeral.

The researcher covered the activities that were being performed on the deceased while his assistant covered other events such as the cooking, mourners and how they were behaving. He used his cell phone do to this recording. While observing and recording different activities and procedures of the funeral, it was also of particular interest to see what elements of the Luo traditions are still being followed by the Luo Muslims. This was done in order to respond to the second research question (RQ2). Apart from recording, both the researcher and his assistant had a note book where each of them recorded the events. They drew two columns on their note books. In one column was where the activities and procedures related to Islam was recorded while on the other column was where Luo traditional elements of death were recorded. They put asterisk on the activity/ practice that they believed bordered on both Islam and Luo traditions.

It was out of this exercise that similarities and differences of Luo traditions and Islamic practices were drawn. In the section of analysis, an area where both domains were found to be similar was classified in the category of continuity while an area where they were found different was put in the category of discontinuity. These two categories of continuity and discontinuity based on similarities and differences between the Luo old and Islamic funeral customs were in turn helpful in identifying the kind of Islam that the Luo Muslims in Kendu Bay follow. Questions that were posed to some of the family members and relatives of the deceased centered on their feelings about death and how it has affected their lives. Their view on Luo funeral customs of death was also sought. The answers that they gave helped to respond to the third research question (RQ3). It sought to describe how the mixing of both Luo and Muslim elements of death has affected the Luo-Muslim understanding of death and the rituals surrounding it.

A Work Plan for Keeping Data and Other Witnessed Funeral Activities

In order to ensure that no important information has been ignored or lost during the field research, a work plan was devised. Items that were posted in this work plan included the review of the data that was collected. Going through the information that was collected during the day was done every night. It was done with a view to identify areas that needed some clarifications from the informants. It was also conducted with a view to elicit more questions for the research. These questions were added to the list of other questions that was already being used. After establishing areas that needed clarification as well as obtaining a list of some new questions, more contacts with the informants were then planned for. The informants included both the previous ones who had already been interviewed (they were consulted again in order to clarify certain areas that were not quite clear) and the new ones (they responded to the new questions that emerged). Contacts to the informants were made by calling them directly using a phone call, personal visits to their homes or their work places and or through the research assistant. No interview was scheduled on a Friday. This was so in order as a show of honor and respect to the informants' prayer day.

The number of people who attended the two funeral ceremonies that were witnessed was simply approximated. This was because they were so many and scattered in different places of the funerals. They were also very mobile and kept on moving from one place to the other. This movement was largely so during the viewing of the body where most of them were seen pressing so hard in order to pay their last respects to the deceased. In the compound of the two deceased, some women were involved in cooking while others went to fetch water and fire food. The cemetery lay a few kilometers from the deceased's home. Here, a group of men were busy preparing the grave. Apart from taking note of the different activities as they were unfolding during the funeral services, the amount of time spent was also recorded. This recording of time in those events was considered necessary in order to establish the value that the Luo Muslims place on death. The different people groups who were present at the funeral on the basis of their age,[31] gender and different roles they were playing at the funeral were also noted. This was done with a view to establish how age, gender and roles affect the kind of responses that the Luo Muslims have given to the dead.

Strengths and Weaknesses of Interviews and Participation Methods

Both participant observation and interview methods that were applied in this research were not without weaknesses and strengths (see Creswell[32]). A strength gained in participant observation was that it provided the opportunity to see practically the different people groups who were engaged in different activities of the funeral. It also made available the opportunity to see the nature of the tools they were using at different stages of the funeral. But due to some events happening simultaneously such as preparing the

---

31. Age was assessed under the category of being Luo-Muslim adults, Luo-Muslim youths or children.

32. Creswell, *Research Design: Mixed Methods Approaches*, 188.

body and digging of the grave at the cemetery, it became almost impossible to watch all these events at the same time. There was also very limited access in observing the rituals that were being carried out on the female deceased. Occasionally, some mourners could simply switch off their conversations upon realizing that they were being listened to. Others, particularly those who were actively involved with the rituals on the deceased felt nervous once they sensed they were being watched by a stranger.

The strength of the interview method was that it enabled the researcher to meet face to face with the informants. This was useful in administering the questions prepared in advance as well as generating some other questions that were equally important and relevant to the study. Some challenges were encountered in the use of the interview method. It was discovered that some informants were uneasy discussing matters related to death. Areas they felt uncomfortable to answer included: their preparedness to face death and what they perceive to be the final destiny of the deceased. Their discomfort in answering the questions often propmted the researcher to keep on thinking and searching for the right way to present the questions. This, however, proved to be a time consuming task despite the helpful tips that his research assistant provided him on how well to present the questions. Some informants were completely unable to respond to the questions about death as were posed to them. This was particularly so among the informants who still held fresh memories about the demise of their loved ones. Asking them the questions which are related to death was like opening afresh the wounds that were already healing.

Data Analysis

The researcher sought to analyze the data after a successful collection of data. The first step was to examine some data analyses approaches, concepts and methods that have been used by other writers such as Kim's Domain of Total Synthesis and Synthetic Triangular Approach (STA),[33] Gilliland's concepts of "'Non-negotiable ethos', and 'Immediacy and Futuristic-View,'"[34]

---

33. Kim, "Considering 'Ordinariness,'" and Kim, *Islam among the Swahili.*
34. Gilliland, *African Traditional Religion.*

Conn's concept of Ultimate Synthesis,[35] Strauss and Corbin's Grounded Theory Methods (GTM)[36] and Spradley's Developmental Research Sequence (DRS).[37] It was through those approaches, concepts and methods that frameworks that analyze the researcher's own data were generated. Data analysis was conducted with a view to responding to the three research questions (see chapter 1). These research questions seek to describe the extent to which Luo traditional perspectives have influenced the way that the Luo Muslims view and practice their funeral customs.

Approaching Funeral Experiences of the Luo Muslims Using Kim's STA

Kim's Synthetic Triangular Approach (STA) has been utilized as a theoretical framework due to its focus on the ordinary life of the Muslims. It provides a systematic approach on which a study among the Luo Muslims in Kendu Bay was based. In his writing, "Considering 'Ordinariness' in Studying Muslim Cultures and Discipleship," Kim contrasts between conventional and non-conventional approaches. He explains that conventional approaches in Islamic studies mainly center on "ideological and other complex issues critical in political sphere between Muslims and non-Muslim worlds."[38] He also believes that conventional approaches don't deal adequately with religio-cultural issues that come from Muslims' experiences in daily life. On the other hand, he considers utilizing a non-conventional approach as the appropriate way of looking into Muslim's lived experiences.[39]

Since this study is to know how Luo old customs have affected the Luo-Muslim understanding of death, it is the non-conventional approach that has been applied. It explains the cultural experiences that ordinary Luo

---

35. Conn, "Islam in East Africa."

36. Juliet M. Corbin and Anselm Leonard Strauss, *Basics of Qualitative Research: Techniques and Procedures for Developing Grounded Theory* (Newbury Park, CA: Sage, 1990); Anselm Leonard Strauss and Juliet M. Corbin, "Grounded Theory Methodology," in *Handbook of Qualitative Research*, eds. N. K. Denzin and Y. S. Lincoln (Thousand Oaks, CA: Sage, 1994), 272–285; and Juliet M. Corbin and Anselm L. Strauss, *Basics of Qualitative Research: Techniques and Procedures for Developing Grounded Theory*, 4th ed. (Thousand Oaks, CA: Sage, 1998).

37. Spradley, *Ethnographic Interview*, and Spradley, *Participant Observation*.

38. Kim, "Considering 'Ordinariness,'" 178.

39. Kim, 178–179.

Muslims encounter as far as their Luo funeral traditions are concerned. Apart from describing it as quite integrative, Kim also points out that STA, which is non-conventional in its approach, has three important research components: "a (cognitive) philological study on the topic under investigation, an anthropological study with ethnographic fieldwork in the cultural area with which the topic is concerned, and an interdisciplinary analysis of the data drawn from the previous two researches."[40] In the diagram below, an illustration of those three research components has been given.

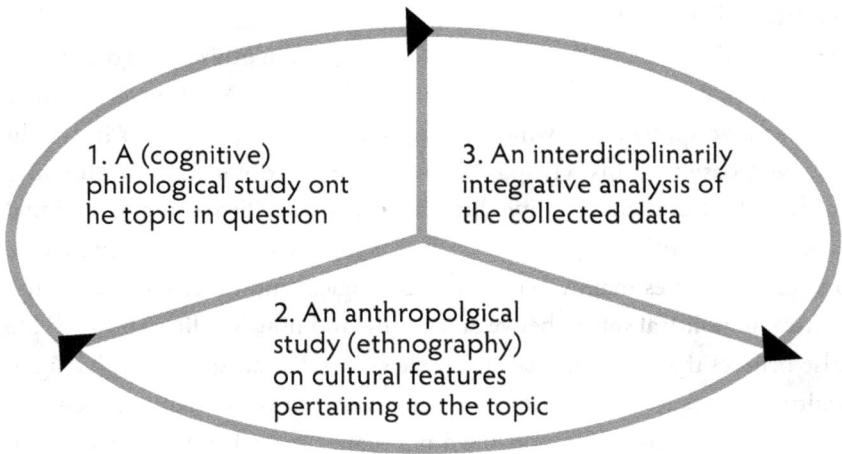

1. A (cognitive) philological study ont he topic in question

3. An interdiciplinarily integrative analysis of the collected data

2. An anthropolgical study (ethnography) on cultural features pertaining to the topic

Diagram 3: The Synthetic Triangular Approach in Studying Muslim Cultures[41]

A Theoretical framework one as developed from Kim's STA

From his line of thinking, a framework that holds Three Areas of Research Study, "TARS,"[42] was formulated (see diagram 4). It consists of: (1) Textual Study, (2) Interviews and Participants Observations and (3) 1 and 2 Integrated. Under Textual Study, both the Qur'anic and the Ḥadīth scriptures that touch on Muslims' understanding of death were examined. The study

---

40. Kim, 183.

41. Kim, 183.

42. "TARS" basically outlines a three-order plan that was systematically followed in the whole dissertation writing.

on those two scriptures was further narrowed down by focusing on what the Shafiʻite School of Law teaches. The rationale is that it is the dominant School in Kenya and other parts of East Africa.[43] This means that in terms of the way they deal with death, the Luo Muslims in Kendu Bay primarily subscribe to the Shafiʻite teachings. The Shafiʻite teaches that both the Qurʼan and the Ḥadīth are more important than *Qiyas* ("analogy"), and are followed in degree of importance by *Ijma* ("consensus") as the legitimizing basis of law[44] (cf. Watt[45]). Those three areas in Shafiʻte's School of Law have been classified as the Three Step Order of Law (TSOL).[46] It was presented in response to RQ1. It explores the kind of Islamic teachings that the Luo Muslims follow and how those teachings have affected their perspective on death. The study was based on the rituals that are undertaken right from the time somebody demises to the time of their burial and beyond.

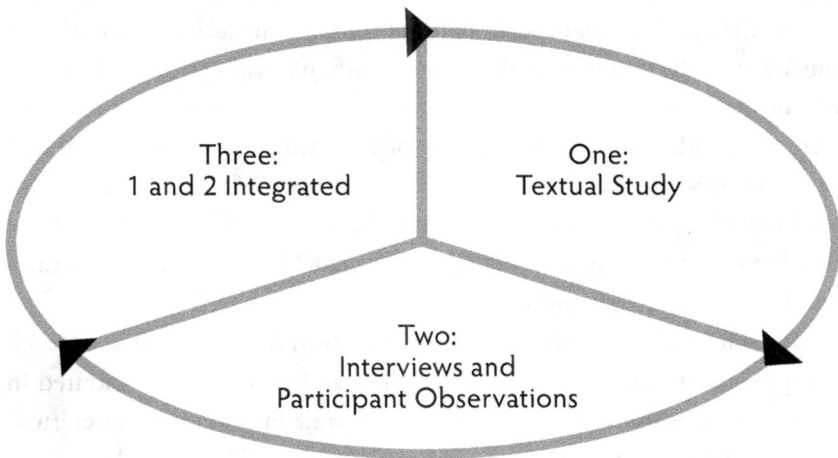

Diagram 4: Three Areas of Research Study (TARS)

---

43. Anwar Ahmad Qadri, *A Sunni Shafiʻi Law Code* (New Delhi: Islamic Book Service, 1997), v.

44. Cyril Glasse, *The New Encyclopedia of Islam. Revised Edition of the Concise Encyclopedia of Islam* (New York: Altamira, 2001), 416.

45. W. Montgomery Watt, *Islamic Philosophy and Theology* (Edinburgh: Edinburgh University Press, 1985), 56–57.

46. Three Step Order of Law (TSOL) is a term that has been coined by the researcher. It displays the various elements that are contained in the Shafiʻite's teachings in their varying degrees.

In order to determine the various degrees under which Shafiʿiteʾs TSOL
has influenced the way the Luo Muslims explain death and their subsequent
funerary practices, the informants were first asked questions related to the
meaning and causes of death in Islam. They were then asked to describe the
various funerary rituals that are usually conducted following the demise of
an individual up to the post-burial periods. As they described the events,
they were also required to mention what they believe are the meaning and
the causes of death, the kind of people who are required to participate at
the rituals and the different stages they are expected to get involved, the
significant of the rituals and how mourners and participants should behave
during the whole funeral ceremony. A diagram was drawn to demonstrate the
order by which TSOL affects the Luo-Muslims' view of death (see diagram 5
below). On this diagram, the elements of Shafiʿiteʾs TSOL (the Qurʾan and
the Ḥadīth, *Qiyas* and *Ijma*) were each placed on a circle respectively. An
arc was used to demonstrate how they are interconnected with each other
among the four important socio-cultural components relating to death and
funeral, namely, meanings and causes of death, mourning rituals, rituals to/
for the deceased, widow rituals and other family members of the deceased
were all classified under the category of Luo-Muslim Funeral Beliefs and
Practices. It was placed in one cycle at the center of TSOL. An arrow was
used pointing from each of the Shafiʿiteʾs TSOL to the Luo-Muslim funeral
beliefs and practices. It indicates the effects that TSOL has had on the Luo-
Muslim funeral beliefs and practices.

The effects that were discovered were in turn described based on each
component of Luo-Muslim funeral beliefs and practices as illustrated in
diagram 6. On the vertical side was placed four important socio-cultural
components that are contained in Luo-Muslim funeral beliefs and practices.
Each component has the Shafiʿiteʾs TSOL in which blue color represents
Qurʾan/ Ḥadīth, Red stands for *Qiyas* while Green symbolizes *Ijma*. The
horizontal side that is numbered one to five shows the level of impact that
Shafiʿiteʾs TSOL has on each component of Luo-Muslim funeral beliefs and
practices. However, this variation in the impact as shown on the chart has
simply been used to show Shafiʿiteʾs TSOL as provided in the textual study.
It does not therefore necessarily reflect the actual findings as were received
from the Luo Muslims in Kendu Bay.

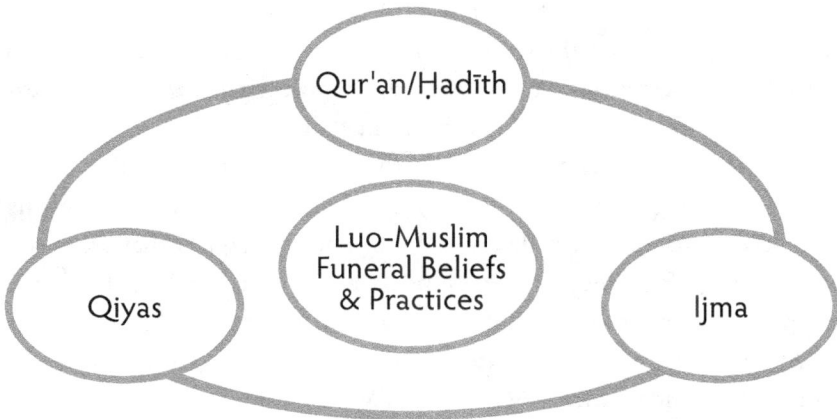

Diagram 5: Relationship between Shafi'ite's TSOL with Luo-Muslim Funeral Beliefs and Practices.

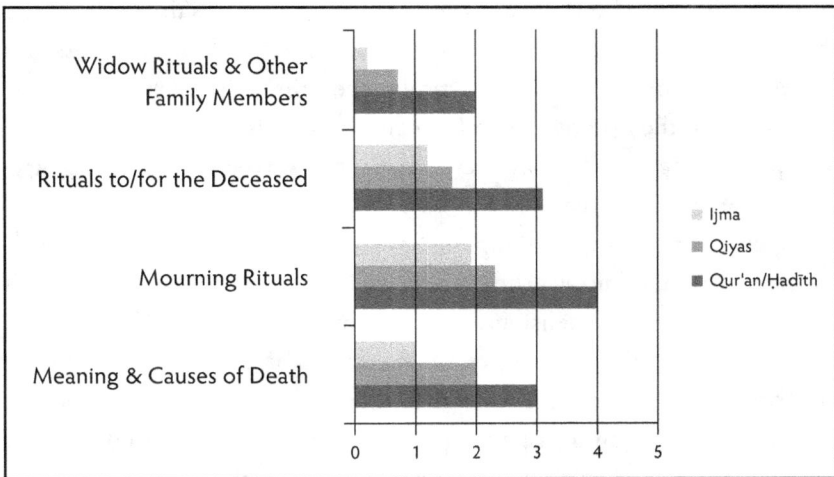

Diagram 6: TSOL's Impact on Luo-Muslim Funeral Beliefs and Practices

A Theoretical framework two as developed from Kim's STA

The second component of TARS (see diagram 4) consists of interviews and participant observations. They are methods that have been used to collect the data as shown under the section of data collection. The third category (diagram 4) integrates the textual study together with the interviews and participant observations. For example, the knowledge gained from the textual study of Shafi'ite's TSOL has been integrated with the experiences of Luo Muslims that have been acquired through interviews and participant observations regard to their funerary beliefs and practices. The resulting insights are what have been described in the finding chapter. They are meant to respond to RQ1. Such integrations have also been conducted in other areas as a response to the rest of the research questions (RQ2 and RQ3).

Apart from covering Shafi'ite's Three Step Order of Law, Strauss and Corbin's Grounded Theory Method (GTM) and Spradley's DRS were also found relevant in forming a theoretical framework. This framework seeks to establish concepts that have emerged from the Islamic teachings on death that Luo Muslims in Kendu Bay follow. The outcome of this process was meant to respond to the part one of RQ1 (see ch. 1). While describing its concept, Strauss and Corbin point out that the GTM has three phases: "Open coding, axial coding and selective coding."[47] It was the open coding that was found applicable to this area of study. According to Strauss and Corbin, open cording: "is the analytical process through which concepts are identified and their properties and dimensions are discovered in the data."[48] This phase of open coding, as Creswell puts it, "is basically meant to generate categories of information."[49]

Open coding was used alongside Spradley's DRS[50] in order to generate concepts from the Luo-Muslim funeral beliefs and practices together with their properties and dimensions. The concepts were then classified into different categories. These categories were identified based on the Luo-Muslim view on areas that are related to death and the rituals surrounding it such as: *Dhano* (in Luo, meaning a person), *Saa* (in Luo, meaning, time), *Kamoro* (in Luo, meaning, place) and *Kido/ranyisi* (in Luo, meaning, symbol). Under these four areas, descriptions were made concerning their relationship within each category (intra-relationship) as well as the relationship between one

---

47. Corbin and Strauss, *Basics of Qualitative Research*, 101.
48. Corbin and Strauss, 101.
49. Creswell, *Research Design*, 191.
50. Spradley, *Ethnographic Interview*, 107–120; Spradley, *Participant Observation*, 87–98.

category and the other (inter-relationship). The purpose of describing these relationships was to offer an explanation on how the understanding of death by the Luo Muslims affects their day-to-day life.

The second phase of GTM is described as "axial coding."[51] It was used as a framework in describing how Islamic teachings in Kendu Bay have affected the Luo-Muslim view of death. This is the phase in which one of the categories is selected and positioned within a theoretical model (cf. Creswell[52]). It is also where connections between a category and its sub-categories are made using a coding paradigm. According to Strauss and Corbin, the coding paradigm focuses on three aspects of the phenomenon: "the conditions or situations in which phenomenon occurs; the actions or interactions of the people in response to what is happening in the situations; and the consequences or results of the action taken or inaction."[53] Glaser also covers similar concept though he describes it differently as "theoretical coding."[54] Since the subject of death is the bedrock upon which the coding paradigm and theoretical coding were based, it was used as the main category, as illustrated on the diagram below:

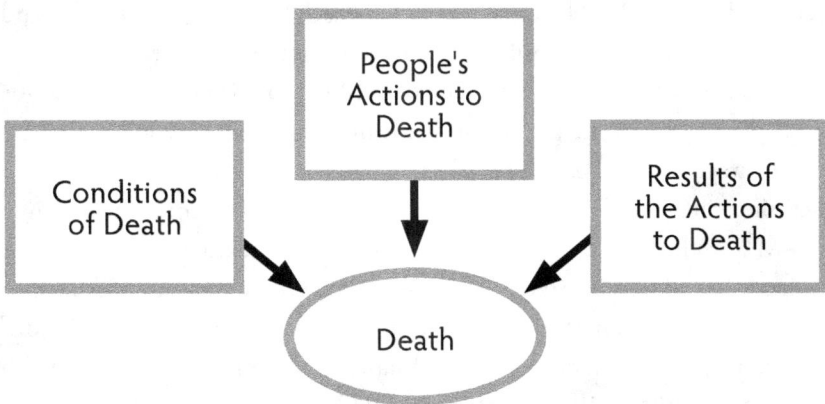

Diagram 7: Luo-Muslim Perspectives of Death in Relations to Its Rituals

---

51. Corbin and Strauss, *Basics of Qualitative Research*, 4th ed., 97.

52. Creswell, *Research Design*, 191.

53. Corbin and Strauss, *Basics of Qualitative Research*, 4th ed., 99, 123.

54. Barney G. Glaser, *Basics of Grounded Theory Analysis: Emergence vs Forcing* (Mill Valley, CA: Sociology Press, 1992), 74, 76.

Under this category of death, three other sub-categories (conditions of death, people's actions to death and results of the actions to death) were developed by using Strauss and Corbin's interrogative pronouns such as "who, what, why, where, how and when"[55] around death. All these interrogative pronouns were utilized in the main category of death and as part of the coding paradigm. In the main category of death, the pronouns that were applicable were "who, when and why." These interrogative pronouns speak of the person who has died (this is in reference to gender and age) and when they died (time). Under the sub-category of conditions of death, the circumstances leading to death were described using "what and why." In the category of people's actions to death, people attending and participating in different funeral functions were described by using "who and what" pronouns. Procedures for activities surrounding death, place for the burial of the deceased and for conducting other rituals of death, and the meaning/significance that the Luo Muslims attach to these rituals of death, were all described under the category of the results of the actions to death. The interrogative pronouns that were used in their case were "how, where, what and why." The diagram below is a summary of how interrogative pronouns were used to shoe the relationship between death (as the main category) and the ritual activities surrounding it (other sub-categories of death).

Selective coding is the third phase of GTM. Strauss and Corbin describe it as: "the process of integrating and refining the theory. The analyst selects a core category and then relates all other categories to the core as well as to the other categories."[56] Following this criterion another core category in a Luo-Muslim funeral was picked. Selection for this core category was done by determining what is central in the funeral processes of the Luo Muslims. In order to do this, taxonomic analysis as described by Spradley was utilized.[57] Through it, an understanding was obtained that helped to classify death processes into three different categories: (1) Initial stage – this is the period between the passing on of a loved one and preparing for burial; (2) Middle stage – this covers the time the body is removed from the mosque/homestead to burial at the graveyard (cemetery or homestead) and (3) Later stage – this

55. Corbin and Strauss, *Basics of Qualitative Research*, 123.
56. Corbin and Strauss, 116, 143.
57. Spradley, *Ethnographic Interview*, 132–154; Spradley, *Participant Observation*, 113–121.

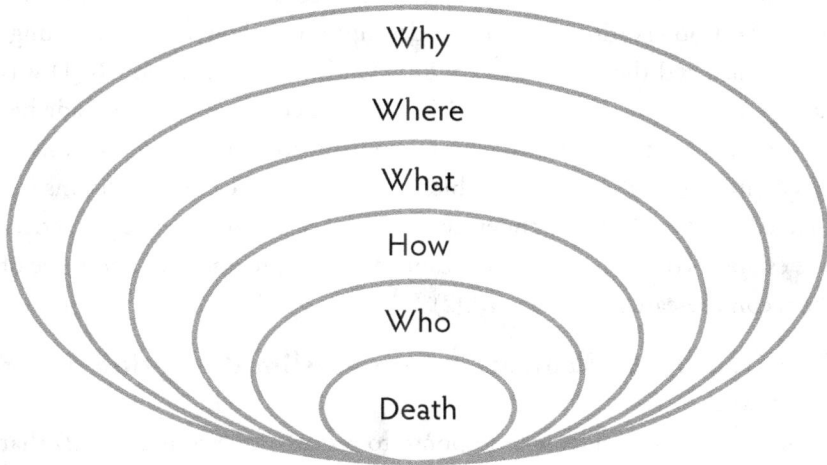

Diagram 8: Relating Death with Its Surrounding Rituals by Using Interrogative Pronouns

period spells what happens after burial. As the outline demonstrates, both stages 1 and 2 mainly center on the deceased while stage 3 centers on the bereaved. The kind of people who attended the funerals, and the ones who got involved with various rituals and activities, were classified and categorized into those three stages on the basis of their age, gender and relationship to the deceased. The objects/items that are used, dress code and other behavioral expressions at the funeral were also identified and placed in any of those three stages as was found relevant. In each stage of the funeral activity, different interrogative pronouns were applied. The one that was most frequently applicable in those three stages was used to determine the core category. The other interrogative pronouns were utilized in creating the sub-categories as found relating to the main category.

Componential analysis as advanced by Spradley[58] was also found useful. A paradigm worksheet as Spradley illustrates in his eight-step method for

---

58. Spradley, *Ethnographic Interview*, 173–184; Spradley, *Participant Observation*, 130–139.

making a componential analysis, was prepared.[59] It contained the various activities, elements and persons as were captured during the interviews and participant observations. From it, a description on how Islamic teachings have influenced the contemporary Luo-Muslim view of death (RQ1) was easily made. Through componential analysis, a contrast was also made between Luo traditional and Islamic funeral customs. It was on the basis of this contrast that the extent to which the perception of Luo traditions has affected the Luo-Muslim understanding of death and its related practices was established. This was partly meant to respond to part two and three of the second research question (RQ2).

Luo Traditional Elements in Luo-Muslim Perception of Death

In order to provide adequate response to research question 2 (RQ2) that seeks to describe the kind of Luo traditional elements that still exist in the contemporary Luo-Muslim perception of death, Gilliland's concepts of Non-negotiable ethos, Immediacy and Futuristic-Focus[60] were adopted as a framework. In his non-negotiable ethos, Gilliland highlights two basic factors that have led to conflict between Islam and African traditional religion (ATR) as pegged on the fact that ATR is both "ethnocentric and 'immediacy' or utilitarian."[61] He further identifies a type of tribal ethos consistently embedded in ATR.[62] From the explanation, it is clear that the concept of non-negotiable ethos carries an element of conflict. This conflict may be due to the fact that some traditional beliefs and practices that are ancestor-related have been retained. The idea of a conflict was so helpful in this research for several ways. First, it was through such knowledge that a discovery was made concerning what elements of Luo traditions still exist in the Luo-Muslim understanding of death. Those elements were identified

---

59. Spradley's eight steps in making a componential analysis are: "Select a domain for analysis; Inventory all contrasts previously discovered; Prepare a paradigm worksheet; Identify dimensions of contrast that have binary values; Combine closely related dimensions of contrast into ones that have multiple values; Prepare contrast questions for missing attributes; Conduct selective observations to discover missing information and prepare a complete paradigm" (Spradley, *Participant Observation*, 133–139).

60. Gilliland, *African Traditional Religion*.

61. Gilliland, 85–97.

62. Gilliland, 86.

on the basis of their link with the ancestor. They were thus classified under the domain of non-Islamic element. This domain shows that Luo Muslims still follow in the footsteps of their old Luo customs. They have not been, therefore, affected by Islamic teachings.

Second, with the discovery that there are areas of conflict also came the idea that there are areas in a Luo-Muslim funeral where Luo traditional customs may be similar to those of Islam. Such areas were classified as partial-Islamic-element. Classifying to the domain of partial-Islamic-element implies that there are certain elements in a Luo-Muslim funeral that border between Luo traditions and Islamic customs. The influence of Islam on them was regarded as minimal. Last, the fact that Luo Muslims follow Islamic teachings means that there are areas in their funeral beliefs and practices where those teachings have totally changed their perception from those of their Luo traditions. Such areas were therefore identified and classified in the domain of total-Islamic-element. The elements under this category have no relationship with the ancestral customs of the Luo. Thus by utilizing Gilliland's concept of non-negotiable ethos, a framework was developed that classified the responses from the informants and the observations that were categorized into three domains, that is, non-Islamic-element, partial-Islamic-element and total-Islamic-element as illustrated in the diagram below (see diagram 9). The bigger cycle under which those three categories have been placed represents the Luo-Muslim funeral beliefs and practices as a single whole.

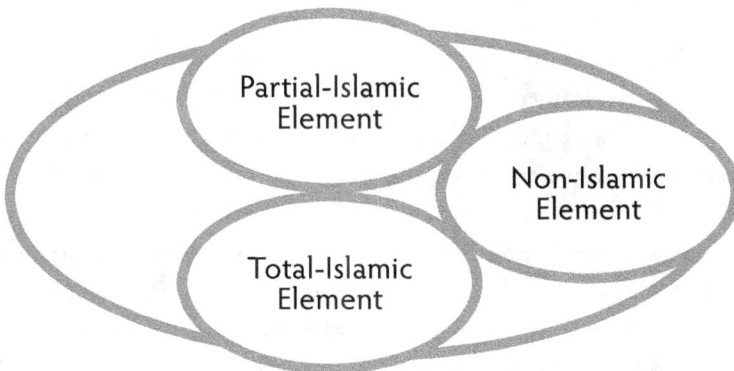

Diagram 9: The Domains of Luo Traditional and Islamic Elements in Luo-Muslim Funeral.

But apart from establishing the different levels of influence, such classification was also helpful in identifying areas where the Luo and Islamic cultures are compatible as well as areas where they are not compatible with each other. Compatibility and incompatibility of the elements were the basis upon which the existence of Luo traditional view in the Luo-Muslim perception of death was explained. This was done as a response to the first part of RQ2. Both partial-Islamic-element and non-Islamic-element were the two categories where the compatibility and incompatibility of both Islam and Luo funeral customs were drawn from. The three domains (non-Islamic-element, partial-Islamic-element, and total-Islamic-element) gave the basis for establishing the relationship between the Islamic funeral practices that the Luo Muslims in Kendu Bay follow and the Luo traditional ones. How the Luo traditional view affects the way Luo Muslims understand death and its related practices was also explained in the light of their shared relationship. This was done as a response to the second part of RQ2. It was also through the effects that those three domains have brought upon the Luo-Muslim beliefs and practices that the aspects of both continuity and discontinuity were described. This was in response to part three of RQ2.

Gilliland's concepts of Immediacy and Futuristic-View[63] were also found to be equally relevant. They were utilized as alternative frameworks toward the understanding of the existence of Luo traditional elements in the Luo-Muslim perception of death. Immediacy represents an African traditional perspective while the Futuristic-View is predominantly Islamic. As Gilliland explains, the immediacy or utilitarian paradigm seeks for "here-and-now" answers. In contrast to Islam's futuristic-view that centers on the divine and eternity, the immediacy focuses on individual persons and ancestral spirits.[64] Those two concepts were considered necessary due to the fact that they both point to the day-to-day life experiences of ordinary Muslims. The context under which they have been discussed relates very well to that of the Luo Muslims in Kendu Bay. Classifying funeral beliefs and practices of the Luo Muslims under the categories of immediacy or futuristic-view was done following the response from the informants. In their responses they described how they understand death in terms of what causes it and where

63. Gilliland, 92.
64. Gilliland, 92–93.

the souls of those who die go to. They also gave information regarding the procedures that are followed in disposing the body, the kind of rituals they carry out in every stage until the dead is buried and after, the kind of people involved in conducting these rituals and the purposes to which these procedures and rituals serve both to the deceased and also to their family members and relatives.

Following Gilliland's concepts of immediacy and futuristic-view, the categories of "here-and-now" and "there-and-then" were created. The concept of immediacy is centered on the Luo traditions that the Luo Muslims follow in the present time while the futuristic-view represents Islamic customs that are followed with future in mind. But in order to accommodate the elements that bordered on both the two concepts of immediacy and futuristic-view, a third category was created. It was termed as a "mix."[65] Information received from the informants that points to the different elements as found in their funeral rituals was then entered using a diagram as illustrated below.

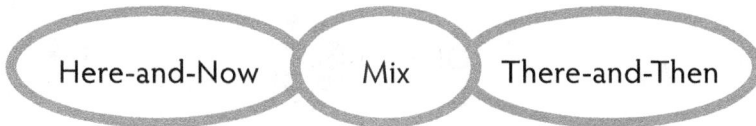

Diagram 10: The Concept of Time and Its Practical Values in Luo-Muslim Funeral Beliefs and Practices

The use of interrogative pronouns in different sub-categories of the Luo-Muslim as indicated in both diagrams six and seven were also utilized in response to part three of RQ2. This part of RQ2 seeks to determine the aspects of continuity or discontinuity of the Luo traditional view of death among Luo Muslims in Kendu Bay. The interrogative pronouns were used to highlight areas where the Luo-Muslim funeral beliefs and practices are similar or different from those of the Luo tradition. These similarities and differences were used to argue respectively, for both continuity and discontinuity of the Luo traditional view in Luo-Muslim funeral beliefs and practices.

---

65. The term "mix" refers to the funeral beliefs and practices that are followed by the Luo Muslims. They are Islamic but similar to the Luo traditional customs. The informants simply identified them as Islamic.

Developing a Theory of Synthesis on the Luo-Muslim View of Death

The need to explain the relationship between the official Islam (as derived from the researcher's textual study) and the actual experiences of the death of beloved ones that the Luo Muslims have (ethnographic study), requires a synthetic approach. It is for this reason that Kim's concept of the Domain of Total Synthesis (DTS),[66] and Conn's concept of Ultimate Synthesis[67] were used. These concepts helped to develop a framework that relevantly describes the synthetic nature of the Luo-Muslim's perception of death in Kendu Bay. In his DTS concept, Kim describes the relationships that exist between official, popular and *mila* aspects of Swahili Islam. He uses the "Swahili-Islamic Phenomena" as cover term for all his four domains, namely, "Domain A: Integration of *Dini* and *Mila*; Domain B: Integration of *Mila* and other popular Islamic practices; Domain C: Integration of *Dini* and other popular Islamic practices; Domain D: Domain of total synthesis."[68]

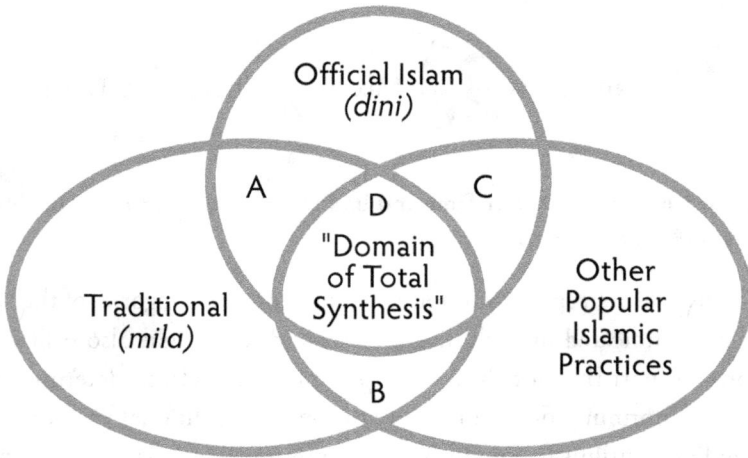

Diagram 11: Kim's Swahili-Islamic Phenomena[69]

---

66. Kim, *Islam among the Swahili.*
67. Conn, "Islam in East Africa."
68. Kim, *Islam among the Swahili*, 59–68.
69. Kim, 59.

It is evident from Kim's analysis that Domain D is the point on which other domains converge. This domain is also important for the present research in that it speaks of a synthetic nature of local Islam as also found among Luo Muslims. However, other domains are also useful since they contribute to the understanding of the day-to-day experiences of ordinary Muslims. Kim describes Domain D as representing "the integration of Islamic ideology and non-ideological elements, both African and non-African."[70] In that sense domain D was used as a framework by which the synthesis of Luo traditional and Islamic perspectives of death was demonstrated. This was done with a view to answering the third research question (RQ3). Kim's terms and diagram were used to present religio-cultural domins of Luo Islam in Kendu By. Domain D is the focal point upon upon which the Luo-Muslim elements were classified relating to death such as mourning styles, composition of funeral participants, tools and equipments, and burial procedures. The classification as shown on the diagram (diagram 12) below was done under three categories: *Timbe Luo* (in Luo, meaning, Luo traditions), official Islamic practices (*Kiarabu*),[71] and other ordinary Islamic practices. The last category lies between *timbe Luo* and *kiarabu*.

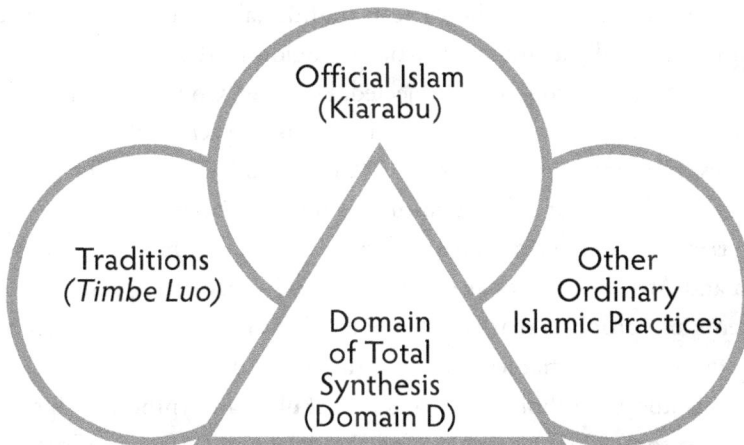

Diagram 12: Synthetic Nature of Luo-Muslim Funeral Customs

---

70. Kim, 67.

71. *Kiarabu* is a term that is used to refer to both pre-Islamic and Islamic funeral beliefs and practices that Luo Muslims follow.

Those three categories were then compared in order to establish the relationship that they have in common with each other and to Domain D. The discovery that was made about their relationship was in turn used to establish what kind of experiences that the Luo Muslims have in their understanding of death and its related practices. This was done with a view to responding to the first part of the third research question (RQ3). The question (see the second part of RQ3) of how the experiences of the Luo Muslims explain their conceptualization of death was done by looking at Kim's domain of total synthesis (Domain D). Their explanation of death was used as a main criterion, and so was the degree of both traditional and Islamic influences upon their understanding of death. The outcome helped to determine whether the domain of total synthesis (Domain D) has a complete synthesis of both *timbe* Luo and *Kiarabu* or there are some areas that have not been totally synthesized.

Conn's concept of Ultimate Synthesis[72] was also found relevant to this study. He has developed his concept by modifying Trimingham's idea of Africanization. In his idea, Trimingham sees the process of Africanization as a process marked by three stages: germination, crisis, and gradual reorientation.[73] Trimingham uses the analogy of a seed to explain the contact that Islam has made with the African traditional religion. In the process, Islam has gradually assimilated African religion to the extent that the old religious structure is consciously rejected. However, Conn sees Trimingham's concept as inadequately addressing Islamization in terms of time by which it moves from one stage to the other.[74] Conn also feels uncomfortable with Trimingham's view of African culture as merely "the passive factor" while Islam is viewed as "the vital cohesive factor." On the contrary, Conn sees both Islam and African cultures as manifesting both active and passive receptor elements and proposes that Islam interacted with African culture symbiotically, an interaction that leads to an ultimate synthesis.[75]

In this study, the choice of Conn's idea of ultimate synthesis is significant for two reasons. First, by recognizing that Islam and African cultures have

72. Conn, "Islam in East Africa."
73. Trimingham, *Islam in East Africa*, 60; Trimingham, *Influence of Islam*, 42–43.
74. Conn, "Islam in East Africa," 80.
75. Conn, 80.

influenced each other in the course of their interaction, provides a framework upon which the Luo-Muslim context should be examined in order to establish the nature of the relationship. This therefore called for the need to identify and classify the elements that the Luo Muslims practice during funerals in relation to their former Luo or Islamic customs. Furthermore, Conn's idea of ultimate synthesis in which both cultures are believed to have integrated into a single whole carries an element of time. In other words, both the African and Islamic cultures did not just integrate at once but rather it was a gradual process. This concept of time as used here is not so much of duration but rather of quality in terms of lived experiences by the Luo Muslims. This experience is based on the assumption that the Luo Muslims who have joined Islam in the later part of their lives have not lost their memories about Luo traditional funeral customs of the past. The fact that they are now Muslims makes it even more interesting to know how they are dealing with both their old and the new customs that they have found in Islam.

Both Conn's ultimate synthesis and Kim's domain of total synthesis present a similar idea on how African and Islamic cultures have interacted with each other. The merging of the two approaches was very useful in developing a theoretical framework. It was through this framework that the synthetic nature of Luo-Muslim perception of death was made clearer for description. By utilizing both Conn and Kim's concepts, a diagram was drawn (see diagram 13 below) that reflects the kind of experiences and relationships that a Luo-Muslim in Kendu Bay has had.

Additionally, it was also noted that there were different ways by which Luo people became Muslims, so the first task was to divide the informants according to the way they became Muslims. Although there could be several other ways to do it, the Luo Muslims were divided mainly into two categories. The first category consists of Luo Muslims who were converted to Islam at a later point in their lives while the second one consists of those who were born and raised as Muslims. The need to divide them into two groups was because their level of understanding, perspectives and experiences vary in their funeral beliefs and practices. Issues of engagement for the two groups included: their understanding of death, the integration of their traditional and Islamic customs, the results of such integration, their feelings towards integration of the two cultures, and the effects that have resulted from the integration of cultures. The two groups of the informants were considered differently.

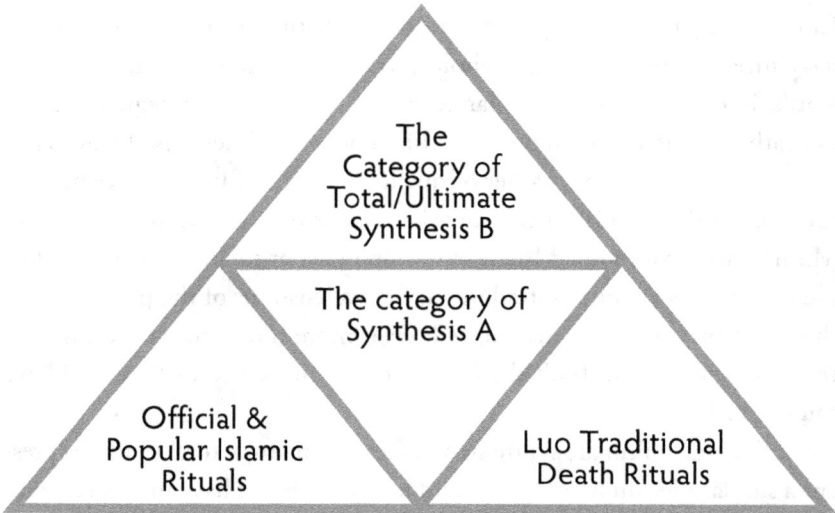

Diagram 13: Experiences and Relationships that a Luo-Muslim in Kendu Bay Has

In this diagram (see diagram 12), the area of Luo traditional rituals of death, represents the knowledge and experiences that the Luo person holds. On the extreme left signifies official and popular Islamic rituals. The rituals are Islamic in nature. This category represents experiences and knowledge that a Luo-Muslim person has. The Category of Synthesis A that is between the Luo traditional death rituals and the official and popular Islamic rituals represents an expected outcome from the process of integration between the two. This domain explains what Conn describes as symbiotic relationship.[76] Conn implies that African and Islamic cultures relate in such a way that they both benefit from each other. However, it is not clear what form of synthesis Luo Islam would acquire. It is for this reason that it was simply labeled as Synthesis A. It is the product of the two cultures interacting with

---

76. Conn, "Islam in East Africa," 80.

each other. The climax of Conn and Kim's concepts, that result into total and ultimate synthesis, was used to develop the category of Total/Ultimate Synthesis B (see diagram 13). This category was the product that emerged from the category of Synthesis A. The synthetic nature of Luo-Muslim view of death was described based on Synthesis A and Total/Ultimate Synthesis B.

Validity and Reliability

As Elliston puts it, "validity refers to asking the right questions, securing the right information and making the appropriate applications."[77] The researcher admits his personal biases in this qualitative research. But in order to obtain accurate information with minimal biases, the researcher utilized some aspects of Creswell's four-step method of validation.[78] In line with his suggestion, the researcher, after collecting the data, went through the questions once more with a few of his informants who were selected randomly. Their input was meant to verify the validity of the answers they provided during the interviews. Their input was also helpful in ascertaining whether the observations made during the funerals were truthful to the beliefs and practices as taught in Islam. The same procedure was followed after writing the whole research. A few key Luo-Muslim leaders from Kendu Bay were contacted. The whole content of the findings was presented to them. They were asked to verify whether the information that was written captured what they had mentioned in the interviews.

Elliston describes reliability as referring to "consistency or stability of the results."[79] According to Mugenda and Mugenda, this consistency of the data can be affected by "random error, inaccurate coding, vague instructions to the subject and the biased perspective of the researcher."[80] In order to minimize such factors that could have otherwise affected the reliability

---

77. Elliston, *Introduction to Missiological Research*, 55.

78. "Using different data sources, checking the data with the interviewees, in some cases, the interviewer could use the particular interview's script and describe it richly and thickly, so that readers can share the experience of the researcher. The self-reflection of the researcher in order to clarify the biases the researcher reflected in the study" (Creswell, *Research Design: Mixed Methods*, 196–197).

79. Elliston, *Introduction to Missiological Research*, 55.

80. Olive M. Mugenda and Abel G. Mugenda, *Research Methods: Quantitative and Qualitative Approaches* (Nariobi, Kenya: Acts Press, 1999), 95–96.

of the data, the researcher applied Elliston's "Equivalent Forms" method.[81] Under this method, the researcher called and asked some of his informants if they could remember providing information on death as was recorded in the findings. Their acceptance of the information was therefore an indication that the findings were reliable.

Ethical Issues in Research Field

In conducting an ethnographic research, the researcher has the mandate to "safeguard the rights, interests, and sensitivities of the informants."[82] Since the researcher was conducting his research in a Luo-Muslim context, he first clarified to his informants for what reason he was seeking to interview them and observe some of the funeral activities that they were involved with. The consent to participate in the interview and to have their voices recorded was then sought from each of the informants as well as the permission to observe their funeral participations and activities. The researcher also assured his informants that all the information that was obtained from both interviews and participant observations was confidential and would only be used for the purposes of study. The permission to use their names in the research findings was also sought and was granted.

Conclusion

Different research approaches have been utilized to compose theoretical frameworks in order to build a theory that was aimed at describing the impact of Luo traditional view on the contemporary Luo-Muslim understanding of death within the context of Kendu Bay. Kim's STA provided a systematic order through which the whole study was approached. In using the first part of Kim's approach, a textual study concerning aspects of death in Islam was reviewed. These aspects of death were traced from the perspective of Shafi'ite's school of law, which is followed by the Luo Muslims in Kendu Bay area. The Shafi'ite's School of Law emphasizes the application

---

81. According to Elliston, "The procedure of administering equivalent forms (sometimes referred to as alternate or parallel forms) is used when the group might recall their responses to a previous test" (Elliston, *Introduction to Missiological Research*, 63).

82. Spradley, *Ethnographic Interview*, 36.

of both the Qur'an and Ḥadīth into its various cultural practices. Therefore the researcher reviewed how both scriptures have informed the perspectives of Luo Muslims with regard to death and funeral practices. It was also out of the study of Shafiʿiteʾs School of Law that the Three Step Order of Law (TSOL) was appropriated. Besides the Qur'an Ḥadīth, the TSOL adds other components such as *Ijma* and *Qiyas* in order of their importance. They are part of what is emphasized in the Shafiʿiteʾs School of Law.

The second part of Kim's STA involves an ethnographic research. In this area, both books of Spradley and Creswell's methodologies were utilized. Interviews and observations were very helpful for data collection. The Kim's third stage of Kim's STA was useful in analyzing all the collected data. It was done in order to identify categories, domains and the meaning that the Luo Muslims in Kendu Bay give to death. It was at this stage that approaches from other scholars were also utilized toward building researcher's own theory. The collected data was analyzed using a theory that was formulated from Corbin and Strauss's Grounded Theory Methods (GTM), in *Basics of Qualitative Research*,[83] and Spradley's Developmental Research Sequence, (DRS).[84] Other approaches such as Gilliland's immediacy and futuristic view,[85] Conn's Ultimate Synthesis[86] and Kim's Domain of Total Synthesis[87] were also used as a means of analyzing the synthetic nature of Luo Muslims' funeral beliefs and practices.

A total of sixty-five informants participated in this research. They were divided into three different categories (Luo-Muslim adults, Luo-Muslim youth and Luo-Muslim children). Through the help of his research assistant, the researcher conducted interviews with each of these groups. In some cases, these interviews were carried out on the one-to-one basis while in other cases the researcher conducted focus group and written interviews. The researcher generated sub-questions out of his research questions and administered them to his informants as open-ended questions. Within a period of four months (May to August, 2015), the researcher managed to observe two funeral

---

83. See also, Strauss and Corbin, "Grounded Theory Methodology."
84. Spradley, *The Ethnographic Interview*, and Spradley, *Participant Observation*.
85. Gilliland, *African Traditional Religion in Transition*.
86. Conn, "Islam in East Africa: An Overview."
87. Kim, *Islam among the Swahili in East Africa*.

activities for one male person and one female. Muhammad was forty-three years old while Salama was in her fifties by the time they died. Both were married and had children. Muhammad died after suffering from pneumonia while Salama's death was abrupt. Although it was regrettable to hear about their deaths, it nevertheless gave the researcher an opportunity to observe how Luo Muslims conducted their funeral ceremony.

The deaths also provided the opportunity to hear practically what his informants have narrated to him with regard to funeral rituals. Regarding ethical issues, the researcher sought the consent of informants in order to interview and to observe their various funeral activities. He assured informants that he was not collecting the data for the purpose of soliciting funds but for the purpose of his study. The findings were then confirmed as valid and reliable by presenting it to some of the few and randomly selected informants in Kendu Bay. They authenticated it as representing the views as they have shared with the researcher.

CHAPTER 4

The Influence of Islam on Luo-Muslim Traditional View of Death

Introduction

After being given a letter of recommendation, the researcher carried out his research among the Luo Muslims living in Kendu Bay town. The research was conducted between May and August 2015. Kendu Bay town is located on the shore of Lake Victoria, in Rachuonyo North District, Homa Bay County in Nyanza Province of Kenya. According to the informants, Kendu Bay is the birthplace of the late Barack Obama Senior, the father of the former US President Barack Obama. According to the 2009 Census by the Kenya Bureau of Statistics, the population in was about 25,000 – a figure that has naturally gone up since. Since the researcher's main interest was on the Luo Muslims, he inquired from the *imams* and other informants about their current population. Most of them gave an estimate of about 10,000 Muslims. Imam Omar and Zachariah pointed out that this number could be higher since some of the Muslims who come from Kendu Bay, live in other parts of Kenya.[1] This estimate implies that the Luo Muslims who reside there are about half of the area's population. But in addition to Islam, other faith communities also exist in Kendu Bay. They include Christian denominations such as the Seventh Day Adventist (SDA), Pentecostals and African indigenous churches.

---

1. Oginga Omar, interview with author, Kendu Bay, 3 May 2015; Juma Zachariah, interview with author, Kendu Bay, 22 July 2015.

The way Islam penetrated and was established in Kendu Bay has been covered in the introduction chapter. However, a brief history about the old town of Kendu Bay was deemed necessary. It was the base through which Islam functioned and spread. According to Rashid, the old town of Kendu Bay was named so due to the many years it has been in existence. He confirmed that it was built by the Arab Muslims who visited the area in the beginning of the twentieth century.[2] This must have been in 1902 when an Arab Muslim man by the name Nasal Nyasoro visited and married a Luo woman in Kendu Bay.[3] But although the name "old town" is still being used, Rashid said that many people like referring to the place after Nasal Nyasoro's name as "Kanyasoro."[4] After Nasal there were also other Arab Muslims who came and settled in the old town of Kendu Bay. Some of them also married Luo women.[5]

Rebecca Osiro gives full report about Arab Muslims and Christianity in Kendu Bay. According to her, Islam seems to have come earlier than Christianity thus negating Adede's notion that Christianity was there first.[6]

This intermarriage was very significant in two ways. First, many children were born out of it. As a result, the population in the old town grew very fast. According to the informants, these children were identified as Luo by birth and Muslims by religion. Second, marriage with the local Luo women also gave the Arab Muslims an acceptance by the local Luo people. They became the relatives[7] of the Luos. Because of this relationship, the Arab Muslims and the local people would visit each other freely. It was through these visits that they got to learn each other's culture very closely. They

---

2. Alamin Rashid, interview with author, Kendu Bay, 2 August 2015.

3. Lawrence Oseje Odhiambo, *A Study of the Influence of Islam in the Traditional Death, and Burial Rites of the Luo Community in Kendu Bay: Implications for Christian Witness* (Nairobi: NEGEST, 2009), 85.

4. Rashid, Interview with author, Kendu Bay.

5. Omar Siraj, interview with author, Kendu Bay, August 2015.

6. Rebecca Osiro, "Women's Views on the Role of Khadi's Courts: A Case Study of Kendy Bay, Kenya," in *Sharia in Africa Today*, eds. J. A. Chesworth and F. Kogelman (Leiden: Brill, 2015), 197.

7. According to the informants, a relative (*watna*, in Luo) also includes a foreigner or an outsider to the community who has marriage a Luo person. He or she is no longer treated as a stranger but rather as "one of us." Such a person is different from *jadak* (non-resident). The latter lives among residents but has no marriage relationship with them. He or she may one day return to their home of birth.

realized that they have some things in common within their cultures. One such thing was polygamy. Just like it was in the Luo customs, the Arab Muslims were not opposed to the marriage of many wives. In fact, they were already married to other wives in their home country before they came and got married to the Luo women. These customs, which they had in common, further deepened their relationship.

Apart from the marriages with the local Luo women, the Arab Muslims also encouraged different Luo clans living outside Kendu Bay to come and stay with them in the vast land that they had occupied in the old town of Kendu Bay. This was quite pleasing to the Luo communities since the majority of them were already faced with the problem of land. Land had become scarce due to their high population. Interestingly, and as some informants put it, it was not lack of a place to do farming that was worrying to the Luos. Rather, lack for a place to be buried when one dies. Being settled in the old town of Kendu Bay was therefore a solution to their need. The Arab Muslims also designated a place within the old town where the dead could be buried. They were known as *makaburini* (in Swahili, meaning, graveyard). As one enters Kendu Bay from Kisumu, the old town lies on the right. The same road goes to Homa Bay and beyond. It has literally divided Kendu Bay into two regions. On the left side of the road is where many Christian churches are located, while Muslims live on the right hand-side. Where the Muslims live is also close to the shore of lake Victoria. They do some fishing in the lake. Some Luo Muslims live in the old houses that used to be occupied by the Arab Muslims. Others stay in houses that were built in *miji* (in Swahili, meaning, homesteads). These homesteads have over five hundred houses in total. The rest of them stay in their own homes (*mier* in Luo).

In order to provide leadership to the Luo community who were residing in the old town of Kendu Bay, the Arab Muslims worked very closely with the Luo elders (*jodo'ngo*, in Luo). Their main responsibility was to mobile the community for any function that was called for by the Arab Muslims. Some of these elders were women. They were in charge of the affairs of their fellow women. One such function that was regularly conducted by the Arab Muslims was teaching. These teachings included how to relate with each other in the community, the existence of a God called Allah, and the life in paradise or hell. Saleh, one of the elders, remarked that the last two teachings were the most interesting to the Luos. They had never heard it before.[8] It was through these teachings that most of the Luos became Muslims. Their perspective on life and death, which was centered on Luo tradition, began to change. At first, Muslim teachings were being offered under a big tree that was located at the center of the old town. With time, the mosques were built. At the time of the research, there were seven mosques spread across the whole area of Kendu Bay old town. Other institutions that were built in the old town and became centers where Islamic teachings were disseminated included *madras*, Islamic schools and colleges. These centers have been the means by which knowledge in Islam has been passed on from one generation to the other. This is to say that the majority of the Luo Muslims who reside in the old town of Kendu Bay are Muslims by birth. Out of the sixty-five informants who were interviewed, only a few were converted to Islam at a later stage of their lives. Those who were converted were mostly women. They got married to Luo-Muslim men.

The Islamic Teachings on Death That the Luo Muslims in Kendu Bay Follow

As has previously been noted, the practices that the Luo Muslims follow when somebody dies are mainly as a result of the teachings that they receive from the mosques, *madras*, and other Muslim learning institutions. According to Mariam, the teachings, especially those that are centered on the afterlife, have significantly influenced them to live virtuously on earth.[9] They are now concerned about what will happened to them when they die rather than just thinking about where they will be buried. This eschatological thinking implies that their perspective on death has somehow shifted from what they originally held in their Luo tradition. The way the informants described how they view death and the rituals accompanying it, and the subsequent observation that was made during the two funeral functions, confirmed that the Luo Muslims have some Islamic elements in their system.

In looking at the kind of Islamic teachings that the Luo Muslims in Kendu Bay follow, the researcher applied one-to-one and focus group

---

8. Okello Saleh, interview with author, Kendu Bay, 6 June 2015.

9. Abubakri Mariam, interview with author, Kendu Bay, 24 May 2015.

interviews with his informants. He divided them into three categories: Luo-Muslim adults, Luo-Muslim youths and Luo-Muslim children. Each group was interviewed and interacted with separately, and at different times. Before exploring the subject matter with them, they were first asked some preliminary questions. These questions had to do with their names, age, social and marital status, their former religion (if any), how long they have been Muslims, how they became Muslims, and their experiences in Islam. Some of these preliminary questions such as their former religion and the period of time they have been Muslims were mostly applicable to the Muslim adults who had converted to Islam at a later time of their life.

The sole purpose for looking at the kind of Islamic teachings that the Luo Muslims provide in matters related to death was to establish how the Shafi'ite's Three Step Order of Law (Qur'an and Ḥadīth, *Qiyas*, and *Ijma*)[10] has influenced their understanding of death. In order to accomplish this, the researcher first centered on the teachings that the Luo Muslims receive about death and what causes it. These Islamic teachings that they follow were based on two sources. First, it was based on their direct mentioning of those teachings as explained in any of the Shafi'ite's Three Step Order. It was also based on the descriptions they gave about their perception of death, and the rituals that they undertake after somebody has died. Their descriptions were important since they showed how practically they have applied the teachings. The details of their descriptions were then viewed in the light of the Shafi'ite's Three Step Order (Qur'an and Ḥadīth, *Qiyas*, and *Ijma*). The reason for doing this was two-fold. First, it was to determine which element of the Shafi'ite's Three Step Order of Law (TSOL) has affected the perception of the Luo Muslims on death and its surrounding rituals. It was also for the purpose of confirming or refuting the claim that the Luo Muslims in Kendu Bay follow Shafi'ite's School of Law. By confirming, it means that the funeral beliefs and practices that the Luo Muslims follow are linked to the Shafi'ite's Three Step Order. That is, the Qur'an and the Ḥadīth come first followed by the *Qiyas*, and then, *Ijma*. By refuting the claim, it means that

---

10. The Shafi'ite's Three Step Order (Qur'an and Ḥadīth, *Qiyas*, and *Ijma*) has been dealt with in the Literature Review chapter. It defines what the Shafi'ite's School of Law is all about. As it was noted in the Literature Review, most of the Muslims in East Africa follow Shafi'ite's School of Law. Since the Luo Muslims who are being studied are in East Africa, this section was aimed to confirm or refute the claim that they too follow Shafi'ite's School of Law.

such an order has not been realized and therefore the Luo Muslims cannot be said to follow the Shafi'ite's School of Law.

Islamic Teachings on Meanings and Causes of Death That Luo Muslims Follow

There is an *imam* in every mosque that is situated in the old town of Kendu Bay. His responsibilities include teaching and leading the other Muslims in prayers in the mosque (his other religious functions have been described in the chapters that follow). It was interesting to learn from almost every adult Muslim who was interviewed that the teachings they receive in the mosque are centered on death. The same was learnt from the Luo-Muslim youths and children. They gather every Saturday in their *madras* in order to hear teachings from *maalim* (a mixture of Luo and Swahili, meaning, Muslim teacher). It is clear from what has been shown that all the three categories of the informants (Muslim adults, youths, and children) that were interacted with and by extension all other Luo Muslims that they represented, have some understanding on what Islam teaches about death. Also, the fact that it is taught frequently gives the impression that it is a very important subject in Islamic beliefs.

Islamic teachings on the meanings of death that the Luo Muslims follow

Islamic teachings that the Luo Muslims follow have made them view death differently. Shaban, an imam in one of the mosques, used a phrase that highlighted the meaning that the Luo Muslims have attached to death: "*giko oloyo chakruok*" (in Luo, meaning the end is better than the beginning).[11] When taken literally, this phrase means that the day (the end) a person dies is better than the day they were born (the beginning). However, Shaban attached a different meaning. He meant that at birth, a person comes into this life (life on earth) but in death, they goe into another life – either paradise or hell. According to him, life here on earth is full of suffering and hard labor.[12] He therefore sees the end (the time of death), as a period when the dead rests from their suffering and hard labor. This perspective defines the

---

11. Otieno Shaban, interview with author, Kendu Bay, August 2015.
12. Shaban, interview with author.

meaning that the Luo Muslims put on death. They view it as an entry point into the life in the hereafter.[13]

The same phrase, *giko oloyo chakruok*, was also used by other informants to describe how they understand death. According to them, *chakruok* (the beginning), represents *ngi'ma* (in Luo, meaning life) that Allah has graciously given through the birth of a new born child. The parents are encouraged to celebrate the birth of their child with their relatives and friends. But this celebration is less compared to the one that is anticipated at the end of one's life. The idea here is that, while it is very much in order to celebrate and appreciate Allah for the giving of a gift of a child to their parents, and to the entire Luo-Muslim community, much celebration is required when Allah takes back that gift. This implies that a Luo Muslim considers what Allah has taken back (through death) to be more important than what Allah has given (through birth of a child). This framework of thinking is informed by what Luo Muslims are taught.

One significant teaching to the Luo Muslims is that Allah is at the center of everything that happens in the world. The death of a person is therefore understood to be in his control. In support of their claim that Allah is the source of life and death, the informants quoted several passages from the Qur'an (40:68, 10:56, 15:23, 23:80, 39:42, 44:8, and 55:29). They also explained based on those passages that Allah is the only one who can take away the soul of a person. Their emphasis on Allah as the creator of life and death, and as the only one who has the power to give and take away life, is very significant. It shows that the deceased has died at the time that Allah had planned for them. This knowledge that everyone has been designated a time to die is meant to discourage the Luo Muslims from harboring the feeling that the deceased has died prematurely. Such feelings are discouraged because they make people view God as being unjust. This is especially true in instances where a person has died before getting married or had just started

13. Both the Luo Muslims and non-Luo Muslims use the Luo term, *polo* to denote to hereafter or heaven. As it has been explained in a different chapter, *polo*, in the mind of a Luo Muslim refers to paradise (heaven) or hell. But according to Shaban, the immediate place a Muslim goes to after their death is *barzakh* (in Arabic). He associated it to a veil that places the deceased between this physical world and the next life as they wait for the Day of Judgment (Shaban, interview with author, 2015). The term *barzakh* was, however, not often referred to by the ordinary Luo Muslims. This implies that the degree by which Luo Muslims have grasped Islamic teachings vary.

their career in life. The unjust feeling towards Allah may also apply where death has occurred to a couple who has just gotten married.

In order to minimize the feeling that Allah has taken the life of an individual so prematurely, the bereaved is expected to say: *ina lilahi waina ileyi rajiun* (in Arabic, meaning, we are all from Allah and all of us must return to him). Those words should be the first response from a Luo Muslim who has been told or has witnessed the death of their fellow Luo Muslim. As the family members, friends, and relatives converge and make the necessary arrangements for the burial, they are still expected to speak the same words to each other. The words carry both the meaning and the belief of the Luo Muslims about the cause of death. The former is dealt with here while the later has been captured in the next section. The more they utter those words the more any negative feeling about Allah disappears. *Ina lilahi waina ileyi rajiun* are also meant to remind the people that life on earth is temporary. This explains why many Luo Muslims engage in doing good deeds such as helping the needy, attending prayers and teachings in the mosque and in *madras*, and building new mosques. They believe that the many good deeds they do in their lifetime, the more pleasing they become to Allah when they die. By pleasing Allah, it means that they have a higher chance of entering paradise.

Another meaning to death that was explained from the words, *ina lilahi waina ileyi rajiun* was that it is a transition that everyone would face. The terms that they often used to describe this transition are *nindo* (in Luo, meaning, sleep), and *wuoth* (in Luo, meaning, a journey). The two terms refer to death not as something that annihilates life but rather a means to a different form of existence. Just as there is waking up from the sleep or returning from a journey, the Luo Muslims use *nindo* and *wuoth* to signify that the deceased's spirit (*chuny* in Luo) lives on, but in a different state. The spirit of the deceased is also believed to be close to Allah. It has, however, very little or no contact with human beings. According to Abdallah, this is contrary to the view that the Luo tradition holds: "*echike mag joLuo* (Luo traditions), the spirit of the dead is always in contact with the living."[14]

---

14. Onyango Abdallah, interview with author, Kendu Bay, 23 May 2015.

It is clear from Abdallah's claim that in Luo tradition, death is seen as a transition that makes a person become close to the living while in Islam, death is viewed as sending a person away from the living. They become close to Allah but very far from the living human beings. Although they follow the teachings in Islam, Abdallah and other informants consented that contacting and relating with the spirits of the dead are practices that have not been completely abandoned among the Luo Muslims. This means that whereas Islam has influenced the way Luo Muslims view death, that influence has not completely erased their Luo traditional beliefs. The understanding of death as a transition in which the deceased's spirit moves close to Allah explains why many Luo Muslims attend the funeral. It also explains why loud wailing is discouraged. They come in big numbers in order to appreciate Allah for allowing the deceased to move on to the next level of life in the hereafter. It is by their presence and active involvement with the funeral activities that show their appreciation for what Allah has done.

Islamic teachings on causes of death that Luo Muslims follow

The Luo Muslims refer to death as *almaut* (in Arabic). They also use similar Arabic words to distinguish between male and female deceased. The male deceased is *almarhum* while the female is *almarham*. According to Saleh, the prefix *al*, as contained in *almout*, *almarhum* and *almaham* are all linked with the name, Allah.[15] This means that it is Allah who is believed to cause death.[16] Death is something that is predetermined by Allah while one is still in their mother's womb: "When a child is about four months in the womb, everything is written for him or her including what will kill him or her and when he or she will die. There is nothing to do to stop death. Allah plans for everybody and death is in his will."[17] Many informants also had the same view. The distinction that the Luo Muslims make between the deceased male (*almarhum*) and female (*almarham*) is also very important. It shows that it is the gender of the deceased that determines the kind of rituals to be conducted (more details on the kind of rituals offered to both *almarhum* and *almarham* has been given in the next section).

---

15. Saleh, interview with author, Kendu Bay.
16. Saleh, interview with author.
17. Nabil Hasan, interview with author, Kendu Bay, 16 May 2015.

The understanding of death by the Luo Muslims is that God is the one who determines the death of a person. It centers on the teachings that God is absolutely responsible for every human affair including sickness and death. Hoskins provides the understanding of what fatalism is all about: "Allah has no personal relationship with his creation. He is transcendent and everything he does should not be questioned."[18] In this case, the participation of human beings in making life's decisions is very minimal. This passivity implies that death and other misfortunes of life are accepted as originating from God. However, within this concept of predestination the question of God's sovereignty and human responsibility is raised. For example, how do we explain deaths caused by careless driving? How about deliberate abortion, murder or wrong prescription of drugs which lead to premature death? Who is responsible? If it's God, should the victims seek for justice concerning the death of their loved ones? These are just but a few questions that ring in the mind of a Luo Muslim whenever they lose their loved one. If one is not convinced that God is involved in the death of their loved, then other options may be pursued.

The idea that God has predestined death explains why the Luo Muslims believe that they should not suspect someone as having caused it. However, this is not to say that they don't experience pain over the loss of their loved ones in whichever way death has come. It does not also ignore the fact that they are aware of some human acts such as driving while drunk, over speeding, violence and other forms of inhuman treatment that may cause death. Whereas the majority of the Luo Muslims believe that death is solely a decree and an act of God, some of them do not share in this belief. These include Aisha and Ahmad.[19] They believe that God does not cause death but rather allows it to happen through the "channels" which he has designed. These "channels" as some of them point out include: sicknesses and diseases (Hakim, Rashid, Swedi, Hisham and Saidi),[20] accidents (Rashid and

---

18. Edward J. Hoskins, *A Muslim's Mind: What Every Christian Needs to Know about the Islamic Traditions* (Colorado Springs, CO: Dawson Media, 2012), 87.

19. Shamar Aisha, interview with author, Kendu Bay, 18 June 2015; Aware Ahmed, interview with author, Kendu Bay, 15 June 2015.

20. Abuor Hakim, interview with author, Kendu Bay, 3 July 2015; Rashid, interview with author; Karim Swedi, interview with author, Kendu Bay, 28 May 2015; Zakaria Hisham,

Zarika)[21] and murder (Ahmed).[22] Rashid also believes that death comes when its time is right.[23]

However, some informants held that the process or the channel of death does not matter. Omar is one such example. He stated: *ina lilahi waina ileyi rajiun* (we are all from Allah and all of us must return to him). By this he meant that death is the gate through which all people must pass.[24] His statement gives the understanding that the Luo Muslims are cognizant of the fact that the physical life is temporary. In other words, he meant that one's life here on earth would soon come to an end according to the decree (*Qadar*, in Arabic) of Allah. This view makes the question of the cause of death secondary. It also serves to explain why Muslims use the phrase *inshallah* (in Arabic, meaning Allah's will) in conversation. The term is used to signify that it is God who permits the death of an individual. The understanding that God is the one who causes death is meant to keep away the feeling that a fellow human being has caused the death of the other. This feeling is shown to have been minimized when a Luo Muslim mourns the deceased without uttering words like *ng'amonegi yawa?* (in Luo, meaning, who has killed you [the deceased]) Or *itimonigi ango?* (what have you [the deceased] done to them to deserve this death). Suspecting a fellow human being as the one who has caused death is a belief that was said to be imbedded in Luo tradition. It comes clear through the loud wailing. The person, who weeps silently without uttering words that are suspecting, is therefore considered to be a Muslim who understands what Islam through its holy books teaches.

The informants gave many references from the Qur'an (56:60, 3:185 and 63:11) to show that the death of an individual solely lies with Allah. In other words, it is Allah who has decreed death. This means that death is something that must tasted by everyone. The legitimate question is therefore not if but rather when death comes. This question of "when" points to the uncertainty of death. Being aware of the fact that death may strike

---

interview with author, Kendu Bay, 7 June 2015; Idi Simba Saidi, interview with author, Kendu Bay, 16 May 2015.

   21. Rashid, interview with author; Akinyi Zarika, interview with author, Kendu Bay, 11 June 2015.

   22. Ahmed, interview with author.

   23. Rashid, interview with author.

   24. Omar, interview with author.

any time is the reason why the majority of the Luo Muslims are very much involved in doing good deeds. The more good deeds one does during their lifetime, the more convinced they become that Allah would permit them to enter paradise when they die. This means that it is the good deeds that Allah uses at death and then decides where to place the deceased – either in paradise or hell. Omar quoted a section of the Ḥadīth to explain why the good deeds are important to a Luo Muslim. He said that the moment somebody dies their plans are cut off except three things: the works of charity that the individual did (for example, water drilling for the community, building mosques, schools and hospitals), education or knowledge which one acquired and is helping somebody else, and a good child who has been educated or trained by the deceased.[25] The child is believed to be praying for the deceased who had been helping them. Since those three things are what count after one's death, the life of a Luo Muslim should be seen to be centered on them.

Islamic Teachings on Funeral Rituals That the Luo Muslims Follow

A lot of Islamic teachings are also given concerning the various activities that take place following the death of a Luo Muslim. A combination of the Grounded Theory Methods, "GTM" (Strauss and Corbin)[26] and Developmental Research Sequence, "DRC" (Spradley),[27] was used to sort out and arrange into various categories the different funeral activities that the Luo Muslims practice. These activities also included the different names and the objects which they use during funeral functions. These funeral activities or rituals were then classified into four categories namely: mourning rituals, rituals to or for the deceased, widow rituals, and rituals for the family members and relatives of the deceased. To gain a better understanding, the researcher went through each category of funeral activity.

---

25. Omar, interview with author.

26. Corbin and Strauss, *Basics of Qualitative Research*; Strauss and Corbin, "Grounded Theory Methodology."

27. Spradley, *Participant Observation*; Spradley, *Ethnographic Interview*.

Islamic teachings on mourning and rituals surrounding it

Immediately after somebody has died, the news about their death is spread within the community and to the distant relatives and friends. As it has been noted, those who have witnessed or have been told that a fellow Muslim has died must respond by saying, *ina lilahi waina ileyi rajiun*. These words mark the beginning of the mourning period. Mourning is supposed to go on even after the burial has taken place. It is therefore a single ritual that is followed in all other areas of the different funeral activities. The one who utters the words, *ina lilahi waina ileyi rajiun*, acknowledges that Allah has done what is best to him in taking away the life of their fellow Muslim. Omar suggested that as Muslims, they are encouraged to weep upon hearing or witnessing the death of their loved one. But this weeping should not be loudly.[28] There are several reasons to this.

First, frenzy weeping shows very little concern for the deceased. As one wails loudly, he or she (mostly it is women who wail loudly) also utters words such as, *mosna ngane* (in Luo, meaning, greet for me my relative [this relative is somebody who died some years back]. It is assumed that both the deceased and the one who died some years back are both together in the afterlife), *ngamo negi?* (who has killed you?), and *iweya gi nga?* (who have you left me with?).[29] As it is evident, these words center on the deceased. Uttering them go against the Islamic teachings that require that the mourner remains thankful to Allah. Centering on the deceased is therefore something that annoys Allah. When Allah is displeased, the deceased get punished so severely, their chances of entering paradise are reduced.

Second, loud wailing is very detrimental to the ones who practice it. It makes Allah annoyed for expressing *kufr* (in Arabic, meaning disbelief) towards him. Those words they utter also cast doubt in Allah as the provider and the source of life.[30] Another reason is that the Prophet Muhammad outlawed the loud wailing that used to be practiced by the Arabian women. These women would wail as they tore off their clothes, beat themselves and

---

28. Omar, interview with author.

29. These words express the loneliness that the wife of the deceased encounters. They may also be uttered by the mother to the deceased. They signify that the deceased was the bread winner and now that he is dead, life will be very unbearable.

30. Shaban, interview with author.

rolled on the ground.[31] Muhammad considered these actions as indecent and therefore forbid them. Luo Muslims defer to this position, despite coming from a culture where loud wailing in mourning is the norm.

Some informants said: "the dead should be left alone." This implies that wailing disturbs the dead. The idea of being left alone should be understood in relation to the Judgment which is believed to be awaiting the deceased. As one of the informants put it: "the worst place is after death because you are alone until the Day of Judgment when others will be brought."[32] This "loneliness" carries the notion that the deceased is in a state of thinking and self-reflection. They therefore require ample time to go through all the processes toward their Judgment without being disturbed (in the form of loud wailing).

Whereas wailing in which people tend to direct questions to the deceased is greatly discouraged in Islam, there are certain questions which may be asked. These questions include: inquiry to where the deceased was killed and what killed them? These questions according to Shaban are necessary in cases where one has received information that their parent has died and that they did not know where their parent was. In this case, one might ask: where did they die?[33] This question is meant to reveal where the person is so that an inquirer (family member or a relative) may begin the funeral arrangements. Another purpose of such inquiring is to enable the people who are making funeral arrangement to bury the deceased on time. The questions that are allowed are those that are meant to hasten the burial of the deceased. They are directed to the living (family members and relatives) rather than to the deceased. Still, respect for the deceased is widespread in Islamic funeral rituals. For example, a Muslim stands up when the *geneza* (Swahili, meaning, bier) is passing by. Respect for the deceased can involve the family complying with the wishes that the deceased had made concerning their burial. Such wishes may not necessarily be influenced by Islamic teachings and in some rare cases may slightly deviate from them.

The burial of the late Salama Suedi is a case in point. After her sudden death on 10 June 2015, it took two days to bury her. This was very unusual

---

31. Siraj, interview with author.
32. Jamar Rehema, interview with author, Kendu Bay, 5 August 2015.
33. Shaban, interview with author.

since Islam teaches that burial should take place almost immediately. Salama Suedi had – when alive – expressed the desire that her children be present in her burial. Her husband relayed this desire to the religious community. Out of respect for the dead, the burial was delayed to allow the children travel from Mombasa – more than 500 kilometers away.[34] Clearly, it is not always that Islam holds sway when there is a tension between Islamic teachings and the Luo or African culture. Luo culture places a high premium on a deceased being buried in their ancestral home. This is contrary to the claim by some informants that a Muslim can be buried anywhere so long as they have identified themselves with the Muslim community in that area.

Sometimes when a Luo Muslim of the group under review dies in a distant place, the relatives do request for a delay in the burial date to facilitate transportation of the body to the ancestral home.[35] Islam itself is less rigid about the burial period on some occasions. For example, if somebody dies on religiously significant days such as Friday or at the closure of the month of Ramadhan, the burial is postponed.[36] Respect to the deceased is also measured in terms of the number of people who attend and participate in the burial, a big number indicates that the deceased person was virtuous and therefore liked by other people (Razia and Zainab).[37]

Islamic teachings on rituals to or for the deceased

There are four rituals which Luo Muslims are supposed to do after somebody has died: the washing of the body (*ghusl*), shrouding (*kaafi*), prayer (*salah*) and burial (*dafiq*). These steps follow a cyclical pattern[38] as illustrated below:

---

34. Suedi Swaleh, interview with author, Kendu Bay, 15 July 2015.

35. Rashid, interview with author.

36. Saidi Jimila, interview with author, Kendu Bay, 13 June 2015.

37. Apiyo Razia, interview with author, Kendu Bay, 3 August 2015; Hamed Zainab, interview with author, Kendu Bay, 26 June 2015.

38. This cyclic pattern is what ethnographer tends to follow (Spradley, *Participant Observation*, 27).

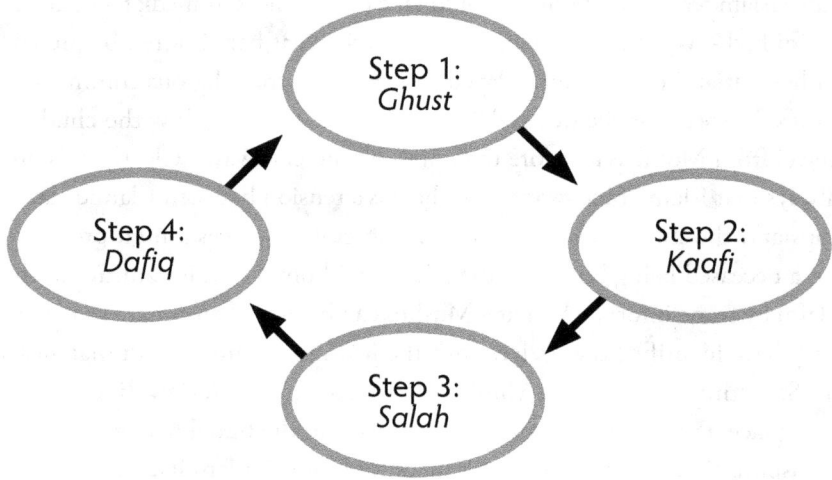

Diagram 14: Steps in the Luo-Muslim Funeral Rituals

Step 1: *Ghusl* (body washing)

This first step, which is the washing of the body, comes almost immediately after death. According to the wishes of the family, the *ghusl* can be conducted in either of the two places – the cemetery or at the deceased's house. For Salama, it was in the house. The people who wash the body should be of the same gender as the deceased. The issue of gender is very significant not only in this washing ritual but also in other areas of life such as during prayer time in the Mosque and other public gathering. Both male and female are not allowed to mix in any of these forums since to do so is viewed as immoral. The same applies to funerals where the Luo Muslims regard it as immoral for a man or a woman to see the private parts of the deceased who is of the opposite sex. This further explains why Muslim women are required to wear clothes that cover their entire body particularly in funerals, other public functions or when they are entertaining guests in their homes. The researcher's visit to their houses in *mijini* (homesteads) is an example of such occasion where he witnessed some women who dashed to their houses when they saw him and after a while came out with their heads covered in order to meet him. The reason why these women rushed back into their houses and coming out with their hair covered by a piece of cloth before meeting the visitor was because they considered themselves not to have been properly dressed. It was as if they were in a public meeting without covering their heads as their religion demands.

1. Instances where gender requirement is exceptional

While it is required that the deceased are washed by the persons of the same sex, there are some cases where this rule may not apply. For instance, Rashid and Siraj pointed out that if a Muslim couple has been living in a place where there are very few Muslims and one of them dies, the remaining one can wash their spouse.[39] The washing of the deceased by their own spouse is generally allowed even in places where there are many Muslims. The reason why it is not commonly practiced is because the person bereaved should be helped since they are in pain over the loss of their dear one. This is also the best time to show that the Luo Muslims are indeed *umma* (Arabic, meaning community). Helping each other or carrying the burden of the bereaved is also believed to be part of the *sadaka* (Swahili, meaning offering) that Allah is pleased with. It increases the rewards for those individuals who carry them out. Other informants also mentioned that washing of the opposite sex is allowed in a situation where a child has died. In this case either of the parent or somebody else of the opposite sex can wash the deceased. The order of priority in the washing of the deceased body is as follows: first to the close family members, relatives, volunteers and paid workers. According to Shaban, most people who do the washing even if they are not part of the family members or relatives simply do it voluntarily without expecting to be paid.[40] They do it voluntarily as a way of paying honor or respect to the deceased and as also part of their offering to Allah as it has been pointed out.

2. Importance of the number of people washing the body

Apart from the issue of gender, the number of people who conduct the washing ritual is also important. The informants pointed out that the number required for this exercise should be an odd number such as: three, five or seven depending on the weight of the deceased. The reason why this odd number is called for is to keep the "secrets" from the deceased body intact.

---

39. Rashid, interview with author.
40. Shaban, interview with author.

These "secrets" are the physical things that those who wash the body are able to see on the deceased. The informants believed that if people who are washing the body are in even numbers they can easily talk about those "secrets" with each other. The presence of the third or the fifth person is therefore believed to make it difficult for such conversation to go on. This requirement for an odd number of the people in washing the body, which ensures that the "secrets" of the deceased are kept, has certain implications. First, it implies that talking about the dead is something which is viewed as shameful. As it has been pointed out earlier on, Luo Muslims have a great respect for the dead. This is particularly understood from the way they carry out rituals pertaining to death. Talking about the dead particularly in a negative manner is like revealing their secrets. This is disrespectful and injurious to the deceased. It is an obstacle that hinders a smooth transition of the deceased to their destiny. If that happens, then the deceased is viewed to have been treated unjustly by the people who talked negatively about them. Such a talk brings shame to the living and disrespect to the dead.

It is not only the negative talk that is considered as unfair to the deceased but even the positive ones. In other words, the informants were of the view that once somebody has died there is no need to talk about them, whether positively or negatively. The deceased's fate and destiny, in terms of the life they have lived are well known by Allah. Speaking about the dead is like taking the place of God who alone is the Judge of all humankind. This also explains why the giving of eulogies or testimonies about the dead at the funeral are very minimal among the Muslims. The way to demonstrate one's love for the deceased is not found in talking about them but rather in attending and actively participating in their funeral. Second, talking about the dead minimizes concentration and delays the burial program. According to Shaban,[41] those who are carrying out this washing ritual should fully concentrate on what they are doing. Talking about the dead is to be destracted from the duty that the washers came together to do. Lack of concentration delays the burial. This delay, it is feared, may make the deceased fail to meet with the two angels who are believed to have been waiting by the grave side. Missing such an opportunity for questioning by the two angels is regarded as adding sorrow to the deceased.

41. Shaban, interview with author.

Talking about the dead is also discouraged on the ground that one's death offers a prophetic lesson that everyone will face death. This means that instead of talking about the one who has died, the washers should in silence be reflecting about their own deaths. This self-reflection is on the basis of one's deeds in relation to God. The demand that the number of people washing the body should be an odd number is therefore meant to minimize the temptation of revealing the "secrets" of the deceased. The idea of an odd number is said to be from Hadith.[42] Besides ensuring that those who are involved with *ghusl* are an odd number, they are first and foremost required to be people who can keep secrets. This is why the first priority for the washing is given to the close family members. They are believed to be the least likely to reveal the secrets of the deceased. It is just like in a household where it is almost impossible for a spouse to reveal the secrets of their partner.

3. Items used in the washing of the body and their significance

The washing of the body is done using clean water. This requirement for clean water is in the sense that it has no *najis* (in Arabic, meaning impurities) such as urine, feces, blood stain or alcohol. The use of clean water is symbolic. First, it signifies that the place where the deceased is going is clean. The view here is that the deceased is heading towards *Jannah*.[43] However, there is no certainty that the deceased has gone to heaven. This is due to the Luo-Muslim belief that one's destiny is determined by God. The washing of the body using clean water also symbolizes that the deceased was a true Muslim. As some informants indicated, Islam is about cleanliness from birth to death. The use of clean water is therefore part of the Islamic requirement in ritual practices such as prayers in the Mosque. The Muslims use clean water to wash their legs, arms and other openings of the body (*wudu*) in preparation for prayers. The same applies to the washing of the deceased body (*ghusl*). Clean water is an act that symbolizes one's readiness to stand before a holy God during the Judgment day.

---

42. Rashid, interview with author.

43. According to Shaban, *Jannah* is a beautiful garden whose description cannot completely be comprehended by any human mind (Shaban, interview with author). The Luo term which is equivalent to *Jannah* is *polo*. This term literally means the sky or heaven. It is however rarely used by the Luo Muslims. The reason is that it refers to what is seen physically. The word which is often used in the place of *Jannah* is paradise. It describes the invisible state where those who have pleased Allah enter.

Besides clean water, other items that are used in the washing of the deceased body are soap and gloves. Shaban pointed out that the soap which is used should not have any content of alcohol.[44] Since alcohol is associated with drunkenness which Muslims prohibit, soap which is non-alcoholic signifies that the one whose body is being washed was a faithful follower of Islam. The use of gloves according to Siraj is simply for the sake of protective measures against the health of those who are charged with washing the body.[45] This safeguarding of one's health is said to be necessary in order to avoid contracting the disease which may have killed the deceased. The washing of the body follows a very systematic order. As it was witnessed during the washing of the body of the late Muhammad, three men positioned themselves accordingly. These men were the cousins of the deceased. They started washing from the right to the left of the deceased. The same formula applies when washing the female. It symbolizes equality by which every Muslim is treated at death. The washers wash in silence although there are times in between in which they could talk to one another especially when asking for an item to wash with. The whole body remained covered while the washing was going on. This according to Ramsam, one of the deceased cousins who was washing the body, the covering is to ensure that his nakedness is protected.[46]

While commenting on the same, Shaban who is one of the *imams* in Kendu Bay clarified that in Islam one's nakedness is something that is protected from the time one begins their adolescent stage to the time of death.[47] This is quite interesting bearing in mind that in the first place the mandate to wash the body is always given to close family members. The reason as to why they are given the first priority to perform this *ghusl* ritual is because they are able to keep the "secrets" (nakedness) of the deceased. If this is true, then one would expect that the deceased would be washed completely naked since they are being handled by a people who would not go around revealing what they have seen on the body of the deceased. Besides, one of the requirements for an individual to participate in the washing is that they

---

44. Shaban, interview with author.
45. Siraj, interview with author.
46. Shaban Ramsam, interview with author, Kendu Bay, 20 July 2015.
47. Shaban, interview with author.

must be somebody who can keep what they have seen from the deceased body to themselves without disclosing it to somebody else. This is not to mention that the washing team should be an odd number. Since the covering of the deceased while washing their body is an obligation which is strictly observed despite having all these other rules in place, it shows that confidentiality of the deceased is something that is highly valued among the Luo Muslims. Moreover, the idea that nakedness is something which is protected since childhood until the person demises adds to the understanding of the various aspects of morality and its quest to guard it. The call to cover the head, hands and the legs by both young and elderly women in the mosques, *madras* and other public gatherings signifies that the Luo Muslims consider morality to involve the outward appearance of an individual.

4. Procedures followed in the washing of the body

While washing, the stomach of the deceased is squeezed. This squeezing takes place after the body has been made to sit up right on a metallic bed with a hole in it. It is done in order to remove the "dirt" in the body. This dirt passes through the hole in the metallic bed in a container which has been placed down below the bed. The washer applies oil on their hands and gently squeezes the stomach. The waste is then taken and is disposed in a pit latrine or in a hole dug some distant away from where the washing is taking place. During the washing of Muhammad's body, it was observed that the waste from his body that came out through his anus was disposed of. The squeezing as Omar explained it is very symbolic. Since it removes the feces, it ensures that the dead is light and not burdened with anything that can hinder his "journey."[48] The understanding here is that the deceased is on a journey to their destiny. As a good support to them, the washers must make every effort to remove any obstacle that could make this journey cumbersome. The removal of human waste is also believed to be part of the cleaning practice which Islam requires. In some cases warm water may be used. This is however not necessary according to some informants. It may just be used as the washers so wish in order to boost the "comfort" to the deceased while traveling to their destiny.

---

48. Omar, interview with author.

5. The cases of the second washing

The deceased is sometimes washed twice. This second washing according to Zacharia and Saidi may be carried out mainly for two reasons.[49] First, it applies in case family members request to be given more time in order to prepare for the burial of their loved one. In this case the first washing is done immediately the person passes on and the second one is done a few hours before the burial. Such a request is made to an imam but it should not exceed three days. This was the case with the death of Salama. She passed on while being taken to Kendu Bay district hospital. Her husband requested for more time so that their children who were living in Mombasa could come and attend their mother's burial. The *imam* who was approached with this request consulted with his colleagues, and by *Ijma*[50] (in Arabic, meaning consensus), they granted the permission.

The second washing, as was also the case for the late Muhammad, applies in a situation where the deceased has died in a far distant place. Muhammad died in Kisumu on 2 August, 2015 while undergoing treatment in a hospital. Immediately after his death, the first washing was performed on his body in the nearby mosque. This washing is the one that is required for every Muslim who has passed on. It is done regardless of where the deceased would be buried. Since the deceased family requested that the body be transported to his ancestral home, it meant that it could not be buried immediately. It was preserved in his house in Kisumu and brought to his home in Kendu Bay after two days. The second purification ritual was then conducted on Muhammad's body the very day it was brought to his home. It was important that the body be washed for the second time in order to remove the dirt that may have accumulated on it in the course of traveling. This practice is part of

---

49. Zachariah, interview with author; Saidi, interview with author.

50. *Ijma* is one of the components in the Shafi'ite's Three Step Order. It is related to the Swahili word, *Ijumma*, which means, a Friday. It also refers to a gathering. *Ijma* as a gathering of *imams* is convened to discuss matters of death where the Qur'an and the Ḥadīth give no clear direction. Because they use the same principle, *Qiyas* was used interchangeably with *Ijma*. *Ijma* is called for in order to allow Christians to bury a Muslim. This happens when a Muslim dies in a Christian dominated area. Second, it applies in a situation where a Muslim parent insists that they want to bury their child in a coffin made of nails. This is prohibited in Islam. Finally, *Ijma* applies where the family members of the deceased request for more time before burying their loved one. This may be necessary in order to allow other family members and relatives who are abroad to attend the burial. *Qiyas* was explained as not different from *Ijma*. See appendix D for relationships in *Ijma, Jumia* and *Ijumma*).

the belief among the Luo Muslims which indicates that Allah requires them to be clean at all times. This belief is about worship in which the worshiper must appear before a holy God in absolute purity.

The fact that the deceased is believed to be in a journey towards their creator makes it all clear why thorough cleaning must be conducted on their body just a few hours before the burial. Apart from removing the dirt from the body, the second washing is also conducted due to the changes that the deceased body has encountered.[51] According to Saidi, the washing is meant to restore the body to the state it was before the deceased died.[52] In other words, the body should be flexible with little or no swelling. Warm water and perfume may be used if necessary in order to reverse these conditions from the body of the deceased.

The need to treat the body in this manner is associated with the belief that though dead physically, the deceased is still regarded as alive wherever they are. Their body should therefore reflect the state of their life in the hereafter. In other words, the body is treated in such a way as to make somebody think that the deceased is just but sleeping. This notion of the deceased being asleep implies that the Luo Muslims believe in life after death. But the question of whether the deceased has gone to paradise or is in hell (*Jahannam*) is something that Luo Muslims cannot be certain about. They consider it to depend on one's own deeds in the sight of God.

The ritual of *ghusl* is significant in a number of ways. First, it is part of the purification ritual which Islam teaches right from the time on of birth to the time of death. Second, Islam teaches that everybody including the dead should present themselves to God when clean. In death, the deceased is believed to appear before God's judgment. This cannot happen in an unclean state. Finally, Luo Muslims practice *ghusl* due to their belief that no unclean person can enter paradise. It is from this fact that animals such as pigs are treated as unclean. Someone who eats or domesticates anything unclean is also viewed as unclean and therefore cannot enter heaven. But as it has been pointed out, the choice for heaven or hell is a matter which God alone can decide. It goes beyond good deeds as well as one's cleanliness.

---

51. This change on the deceased body is what Saidi calls in Luo language, *loko kido*. In Islam, it refers to *gaira* (Saidi, interview with author).

52. Saidi, interview with author.

Step 2: *Kaafi* (shrouding)

Once the washing has been done and the sweet smelling oil[53] is applied on the body, the washers move on to the next step where the body of the deceased is shrouded. In this stage, *sanda* (white sheet of cloth) is used to cover the body. According to Omar, Saidi and Shaban, white *sanda* is preferred but is not necessarily a must.[54] Being wrapped with white *sanda* signifies that the deceased was clean and therefore they were a true Muslim. It also signifies peace as well as a kind of a reminder to both the deceased and the living that *Kiama* (judgment day) awaits them. To the dead white *sanda* becomes a reminder that the journey to their final destiny has begun. To those who are still alive, it reminds them that they too will one day travel the same path of judgment. This reminder motivates the living to keep up doing good deeds. The color white is a symbol that is also commonly used in other religious traditions. In some Christian denominations for instance, white stands for holiness or purity. It is associated with heaven – which only the pure will enter.[55]

It may not be necessary to use a new *sanda* in the shrouding. This is in fact according to Shaban. He was very categorical that the old *sanda* is what is supposed to be used for the dead.[56] He said this while referring to the Ḥadīth in which one of the companions of the prophet, Ali bin Abutalib, is believed to have said that the new is better for the living while the old is good for the dead. This statement has both economic and religious implications. Economically, it means that some money has been saved that could have otherwise been used to buy a new piece of cloth. This money is instead channeled in support of the bereaved family. In a religious sense, it

---

53. Saidi reported that sweet smelling oil is smeared on the deceased body. It is a sweet smelling aroma that when applied it pleases even the angels of Allah (Saidi, interview with author).

54. Omar, interview with author; Saidi, interview with author; Shaban, interview with author.

55. In Islam it is only the dead that are shrouded with white *sanda*. Other Christian denominations however encourage their adherents to wear white clothes. It is a sign to them that they belong to heaven and not of this world. Besides some Christians putting on white garments, the Legio Maria sect in Kenya also uses white candles and rosaries while conducting prayers. The candles and rosaries are of different colors. The white color speaks of their nearness to God.

56. Shaban, interview with author.

implies that the ultimate focus in a Muslim's death is centered on hereafter rather than on the outward attires. Since in the prophet's death *sanda* was used, the Luo Muslims use it as a way of demonstrating their identity with him as well as in following after his footsteps. This is in line with Rashid's comment that white is the practice of the prophet.[57] Although white *sanda* is preferred, any other piece of cloth with a different color may be used. According to Saidi, the most important thing is that the deceased is covered by a piece of cloth that is plain.[58] What Saidi meant was that the cloth must only have one color which is either white or black.

Shrouding is done differently to both men and women. Males are covered with three sheets while females are covered with two sheets. While covering the body of the male these three sheets are placed on top of each other. For the deceased female one sheet is made into a skirt-like piece and a head covering. This skirt-like cloth is meant to cover her legs while the head covering is for the face. The remaining sheet is spread in such a way as to cover her entire body. The people who conduct the shrouding also use cotton wool to cover every opening on the deceased body. The use of cotton wool is very symbolic in that it represents the pure state of the deceased before God. The covering of the mouth and other open parts of the body of the deceased is also meant to prevent any impurity that may have remained from coming out. If that happens then the deceased is again rendered unclean. This calls for another purification in which the body is again pressed gently using warm water.

While shrouding is being done behind a closed door, one of the *imams* conducts teachings to the crowd who have attended the funeral. These teachings are centered on how people should come to God in worship and what death means to a Muslim. The fact that the subject of death is explored during this time of the funeral and in other Muslim gatherings signifies that it is important. It instills knowledge to the Luo Muslims about death and significant rituals involved. The extent to which this knowledge has impacted their lives was evident during the researcher's interactions with them. The responses from different informant groups concerning this subject of death

---

57. Shaban, interview with author.
58. Saidi, interview with author.

and the way some of them were actively involved in various funeral activities clearly demonstrated that they were acquainted with matters related to death and the rituals accompanying it.

Step 3: *Salah* (prayer)

Prayer is very vital in the life of every Muslim. It is one of the pillars of Islam. Muslims make prayers in mosques and other Muslim functions and gatherings. One such ceremony where prayer must be made is during a funeral service. According to some informants and through the observation that was made during the two funeral services witnessed in Kendu Bay, praying to God for the deceased is the best gift that one can give. It is more valued than offering plenty of food in order to feed mourners.[59] This high regard for prayer instead of the slaughter of animals points to the fact that the Luo Muslims conduct some rituals differently from their Luo traditional heritage. The reason why they put more value on prayer is because unlike food, intercession is purely directed towards the support of the deceased.

The big catering and great celebrations which are occasioned with eating and drinking are deemed not to be helping the deceased in any way.[60] This therefore means that the Luo Muslims conduct funeral rituals with the purpose of benefiting the deceased. However, these celebrations are not all considered unnecessary. They provide a platform on which mourners from both far and near are able to socialize with one another and to accord the deceased a nice send-off.

1. *The person who offers* salah *and procedures involved*

As it was evident during the funeral service for both Muhammad and Salama, it is the imam who conducts prayers. This comes immediately after the body has been shrouded but before the public is allowed to view and to pay their last respect to their loved one. The body can either be prayed for in the mosque or it is placed in the open field or around the deceased's home. Although this prayer is just like any other prayer such as the one which is offered in the mosques, it is conducted differently. It has also different components. While conducting these prayers, the imam stands in different places

---

59. Saleh, interview with author.
60. Shaban, interview with author.

depending on the gender of the deceased. For a female such as Salama's case, he conducts prayers while standing in front of the *geneza* (bier), somewhere in the middle. For Muhammad, the imam stood in front of the bier but near the chest of the deceased. The reason that the informants gave for standing in these different positions by an imam is that they follow in the footsteps of Prophet Muhammad who, according to the Ḥadīth, is said to have prayed for both male and female in those two different positions.

This prayer for the deceased is uniform in nature (*swalatul janaiza/mait*, in Arabic). In other words, the imam leads it and the rest of the Muslims follow in reciting some areas of it. *Swalatul janaiza/mait* carries four components: Sura al-Fatihah, *Swalatu ala nabi* (in Arabic, meaning a prayer to the prophet), *Somo Dua* (reading prayer) for the deceased, and for the rest of the Muslim community. These four components signify that although the deceased is the reason why *salah* is offered, other individuals, both the dead and the living, are also remembered. Prayers that are made to the deceased and the rest of the people are centered on the greatness (*takbirat*, in Arabic) of Allah. *Takbirat* comes from the same root as *Allah Akbar* (in Arabic, meaning, God is great).

2. Reciting al-Fatihah and Swalatu ala Nabi

Sura al-Fatihah (the first chapter of the Qur'an) is recited by the Muslims after the *imam* has uttered the words, *Allah Akbar* (God is Great). People recite Sura al-Fatihah while standing. It is then followed with the words, *Allah Akbar* from the *imam*. This utterance by the *imam* marks the end of the first component of *swalatul janaiza/mait*, and ushers in another. In *swalatu ala nabi*, Prophet Muhammad and Ibrahim together with their families are prayed for. The prayer is for God's blessings to be with them. The fact that these prophets are prayed for even though they have been long dead implies that the Luo Muslims believe in life after death. It also implies that they respect and honor their Prophets. An attempt by the researcher to understand from the informants why *swalatu ala nabi* is only limited to the two prophets and their families whereas there were several prophets who Muslims believe in did not bear any fruit. Some of them simply indicated that they are taught that way. Others said that those two prophets are the most famous ones while others did not have any idea why that is so.

3. A prayer of forgiveness to the deceased

The third component of *swalatul janaiza/mait* is the *dua* (prayer) which is made for the deceased. This prayer is offered to any deceased, irrespective of their gender, social status and age. In this prayer, God is requested to keep the deceased soul in eternal peace. God's forgiveness to the deceased is also sought. Asking for forgiveness for the deceased is based on two reasons. First, it is out of the belief that no human being is perfect. Incidences such as looking at someone with an ill motive, backbiting, killing and prostitution were cited as some of the human weaknesses that require that the deceased is interceded for. Second, seeking for forgiveness to the deceased by their fellow Muslims signifies comradeship. It is a sign of goodwill to the deceased. It shows that the deceased is loved by their fellow Muslims despite being physically absent. According to some of the informants, saying a prayer of forgiveness for someone else will guarantee them to be prayed for in the same way when they die.

This *dua* for the deceased also entails some practical actions. For instance, the imam asks the crowd if there could be somebody whom the deceased owed anything. Imam also asks if there is someone in the gathering or elsewhere who owed the deceased anything. This may be in form of money or any other property that was borrowed. It might also be a grudge that one has had with the deceased. Although the researcher imagines that nobody can respond to such a question as raised by the imam for fear that one may be haunted by the spirit of the dead, Luo Muslims think differently. According to some of the informants, if one does not truly and openly admit that there was a debt or a grudge between them, then the deceased is affected. This failure to admit is believed to bind and immobilize the deceased in such a way as to hinder their "journey." Since every Muslim wants the best for their beloved ones who have demised, the attitude of not wanting to reveal anything which has happened between the individual and the deceased is not very desirable.

The practice of declaring publicly that one had an issue with the deceased is something which is not common in many of the African societies. This difficulty lies in the fact that the dead are in most cases feared rather than respected. The fear is due to the perception that they are now in a changed status where they can see and hear everything that goes on in the face of the earth. Since this "seeing and hearing" has some negative repercussion of being tormented by the spirit of the dead, it becomes safe for the individual whom the dead owed money not to speak openly. In fact, forgiveness here is something of the heart. However, in some funeral settings, something similar to what Luo Muslims are practicing as far as this area of forgiveness is concerned has been noted. In a recent burial of his Christian cousin, the researcher heard the wife of the deceased announcing in her eulogy that anybody who owed her husband any money to come forth and see her after the burial. She likewise said that if her husband owed money or property to anybody, the family would be willing to pay back. The difference between this announcement and that of the Luo Muslims is that in the case of the cousin's wife, she was the one who took upon herself the burden to say that. In the Luo Muslim one, it is the duty of an imam to make such pronouncement. Another difference is that in the cousin's case, those who may respond and give the widow what they owe to her late husband can only do so secretly whereas among the Luo Muslims, such payment of debts are expected to be done publicly and before the body is buried.

Unlike in other non-Muslim Luo societies where people fear to admit that the deceased owed them something, the Luo Muslims in Kendu Bay consider it dreadful if one fails to acknowledge that the deceased owed them something. Forgiveness as practiced by the Luo Muslims also comes about when one simply declares openly that they have forgiven the deceased for any debt or any wrong that they might have caused them. In cases where repayment is required, the deceased family and relatives must quickly settle this debt before the body is buried.

As it was understood, the reason the debts must be sorted out before the burial is that the way of the deceased's path to paradise is made clear of any obstacle. Second, it is part of affirming that the deceased was a true Muslim who believed in God. Third, speaking out about debts and grudges that someone may have had with the deceased is a sign that his fellow Muslims wish him well in his "journey." The call to speak out publicly also minimizes talking ill about the deceased. Just as it is the requirement for those who are involved with the washing of the body to keep everything they have seen on the body of the deceased secret, so it is for the individual who has come up and has spoken openly about what was between him and the deceased.

It is shameful to talk again of such in secret. As it has been described, it is evident that this act of forgiveness is part of a deliberate effort by the Luo Muslims to ensure that their loved one is not stumbled in any way. This implies that the only debt which they cannot handle is that which involves the inner secrets of the deceased life. Since this is beyond them, they cannot but leave it to God who will deal with it during the Judgment Day. It is him who makes the ultimate decision as to whether the deceased will spend their eternity in heaven or hell.

4. Prayers for other Muslims

In the fourth *swalatul janaiza/mait, dua* is made for the rest of the Muslim community. The subject of this prayer, according to Omar, is to entreat Allah to give peace to the Muslims throughout the world and to stop any division that may occur among them.[61] Although these prayers to God for peace and unity among the Muslims are also made in the mosques, uttering them in the funeral has a different purpose. This prayer is essentially made out of a concern that some people especially family members and relatives of the deceased may react unresponsively toward the death of their loved one. As it has been pointed out earlier on, the belief among the Luo Muslims is that every death originates from God. This belief, however, does not necessarily stop people from suspecting that someone has killed their beloved one. This is especially so in a context where the Muslim who has died comes from a non-Muslim dominated background. The thinking and the utterances that someone is behind the death of their loved one may not come from a Muslim but from other mourners as they wail the deceased. In an *umma* community, what affects an individual is believed to affect the whole Muslim community.

The *dua* also goes a long way in remembering those Muslims who are living as minorities in other countries of the world. The prayer is for them to have peace amidst being persecuted in those countries. Acts of terrorism that are now widespread and political instability in some Muslim countries are becoming a challenge to the unity of the Muslim community. The *dua* is therefore meant to avert such happenings which may threaten to tear apart the oneness of the Muslim communities around the world. This *salah* is

---

61. Omar, interview with author.

significant to the Luo Muslims in many ways. First, it shows that they care for each other even after death. As it has been highlighted before, the ways by which the Luo Muslims express their love and support for each other are quite numerous. It is something which begins at birth or at the time one becomes a Muslim and moves on until one is buried. But even after burial, the support for each other is still practiced. The only difference is that it is now done not only to the deceased as such but also to their family. In most cases, this support is expressed by meeting the physical and educational needs of the deceased family.

It should be pointed out that this remembrance of the deceased by the Luo Muslims is different from the one held in Luo tradition. The former conducts the remembrance through prayer for the deceased while the latter through libation. Whenever prayers are performed among traditional Luos, this always means to appease the deceased. The second reason why *salah* is taken seriously is because it seeks forgiveness from God for both the dead and the living. As it has been discussed before, this prayer of forgiveness is meant to cater for the sins that have been committed unknowingly. Lastly, prayer is a way by which Luo Muslims acknowledge that God is the creator and that as human beings they find no problem with him taking back his own.

Step 4: *Dafiq* (burial)

Immediately after prayers and the viewing of the body have been made, men, especially young ones who have all along been waiting, carry the *geneza* to the burial site. According to Gudi, a Luo Muslim, the person who is mandated to conduct the burial ceremony is a sheikh or imam. In their absence, any other male person who has experience can conduct the burial. Shaban, an imam in the area said that a Muslim can be buried anywhere.[62] His point is that there is no specific place designated for the burial of a Muslim as it is practiced in Luo customs. This implies that if a Muslim dies far away from his ancestral land, there is no need to transport the body home for burial. Instead, he can be buried where he lives so long as it is done by a Muslim in accordance with the teachings in Islam. However, the decision as to where to bury the deceased lies squarely with the family or follows the wishes that

---

62. Shaban, interview with author.

the person has made before he dies.[63] This therefore means that there can still be a burial to the Muslim in the ancestral land.

1. The roles of Luo-Muslim men in burials and the burial processes

The burial processes are always a prerogative of men. This implies that it is the work of men to bury the dead, whether male or female. During the burial arrangement of Salama, her fellow women who were three in number washed and shrouded her. Their duty stopped after placing her body in a bier. They are not even allowed to go to the cemetery or be part of the burial procession since in so doing they would be mixing with men, a thing which Islam abhors. If the burial is in the cemetery as was the case with Salama, the *geneza* is carried by a group of young people who have volunteered to do so. Their availability in a large number coupled with their willingness and readiness to carry the *geneza* up to the burial site is informed by the belief that they would be rewarded by God for showing such commitment to the deceased. The level of how people loved the deceased is measured in terms of the number of people who have attended the funeral, the number of young men who have voluntarily offered to carry the *geneza* and the digging of the grave and the speed of their movement towards the grave.

Those who were seated would stand as the *geneza* passed near them on its way to the cemetery. Apart from showing respect and love, another reason for standing while the deceased is being transported to the cemetery is because they are still viewed as a human being.[64] In fact, this makes sense considering that the Luo Muslims still call the deceased by their name instead of referring to it as the body of so-and-so. The implication here is that the deceased has ceased to live physically but is alive spiritually. There is also a sense of egalitarianism in the burial of old, young, rich and poor, which stems from the belief that all people are equal before God. Once the body reaches the cemetery, the principle of odd number applies as in the case of the *ghusl*. The grave in which the deceased is laid to rest should be dug the very day of the burial. This is so because the grave is believed to be a house where the deceased begins their next life. Digging it the very day or some

---

63. Shaban Aboo, interview with author, Kendu Bay, 25 August 2015.
64. Siraj, interview with author.

hours to the burial ensures that it is clean with no impurities that can affect the transition of the deceased to God. This is also part of the reason why women are not allowed to come by the grave side. They may be in their menses period and thus making them ceremonially unclean. In addition, women are emotional and may burst in loud wailing which is to the detriment of the deceased person.

Preparing the grave the same day also means that the soil that is used as a pillow for the deceased is still soft and fresh. The grave is dug in two compartments. The first layer is broader and it is where some pieces of timber are placed close to each other once the body has been put inside. The informants referred to this compartment as a "sitting room." The inner layer, which is referred as a "bedroom" or *lahd* (in Arabic) is where the body of the deceased is laid. It is narrow and is usually made in such a way as to fit the body of the deceased. The two layers are identified so because of the perception which the Luo Muslims have about the dead. They believe that the deceased is alive and therefore requires some amount of comfort in the grave. To them, the deceased has simply been re-located to a new habitation. This new habitation (grave) is what they also believe another life (*barzakh* in Arabic) in the next world begins from. Their belief in the life after death is both spiritual and physical. The former is implied through their description which seems to suggest that the deceased has travelled (*odhi wuoth* in Luo). The fact this journey cannot be seen with the naked eyes makes it understood in the spiritual sense. The latter is understood through their reference to the deceased by their name. For instance, instead of referring to the body as the body of the deceased, they simply refer to it by their name. The name signifies that the deceased is a human being and thus physical.

The belief in life of grave was also confirmed by the way the men who were participating in the burial carefully handled the body. This was observed during Salama's burial. Three people entered and positioned themselves in the outer chamber of the grave. Two of them stood toward the end of both corners while the other one stood at the middle on one of the sides. A group of men then removed the body from the bier and handed it over to those three men. They lowered it very carefully into *lahd* while ensuring that the head faces North (*Qibla* in Arabic). The direction of North is very significant in Islam. First, north is where Mecca, the city where Muhammad was born, is situated. It is the greatest religious centre and the place where Muslims face while praying. To be laid facing it therefore means that the deceased is in a state of prayer while in the grave. But facing this direction is also believed to signify that the deceased is on his way to paradise.[65] This belief may seem contradictory since Muslims believe that it is Allah who alone determines whether the deceased goes to paradise or hell.

After they had committed the body into the inner layer, the three men then took several pieces of timber that were already on the site and arranged them very closely to each other on the outer chamber. This arrangement, according to Saidi, was done in order to prevent the soil from entering where the body was laid since it was believed that the body would be contaminated.[66] It is also believed that when the soil is poured directly on the deceased it could *deyo* (suffocate them). The only useful soil which is made into a pillow is that from inside. The two angels, Munkir and Nakir, who appear once the deceased is in the grave, are said to whisper certain questions in the ear of the deceased through this "pillow" of soft and wet soil. The soil must be soft so that the deceased may hear properly the questions that are asked by the two angels. The wetness of the soil means that the deceased would be alert during the interrogation period. It also symbolizes that the deceased is in their last and permanent residence.[67] But given the beliefs in Islam that those who have died either go to heaven or hell as determined by God, the description of the grave as an indelible place where the deceased dwells shows that the burial of the body is an important ritual to the Luo Muslims. The grave is the first place where the deceased begins their journey. This explains why unlike other communities, the Luo Muslims ensure that they bury their dead under the ground. The belief is that if the body thrown into the forest or left unburied, the deceased would miss the chance to be interrogated by the angels. Interrogation is a very necessary procedure since it is through it that the decease may move to the next stage of their journey.

---

65. Omar, interview with author.
66. Saidi, interview with author.
67. Shaban, interview with author.

2. Issues on gender and other Luo-Muslim regulations in burial
While the burial of a male (*almarhum*) and a female (*almarham*) deceased
are similar in many ways, there is a remarkable difference. Besides both being buried with their heads facing *Qibla*, a male is buried lying on his right
hand while a female lies on her left hand. Lying on the right hand, as some
informants claimed, is a symbol of authority or superiority. By this they
imply that a male deceased is still regarded as superior as compared to the
deceased female. This idea of superiority is also what lies in the Luo-Muslim
belief that there will be more men in heaven than in hell.[68] Through the
knowledge concerning the position where one is laid, together with knowing
where the direction of Mecca, it is possible to tell whether the grave where
the deceased was buried contains the remains of a male or a female.

It was interesting to learn that some Luo Muslims do not use coffins
that are made of nails to bury their loved ones. The reason is that a coffin is made of nails that are metallic. They believe through the Qur'anic
teachings (23:12–14; 40:67) that a human being was created from the soil.
Therefore, burying the person in the soil without using any metallic thing is
like returning the person to the original place that they were created from.
Other metalls such as rings and artificial teeth are also removed and sold.
The money received is used to support the bereaved family or other needy
people in the family. Coffins made without nails were used in the past in
burying people as Omar explains: "Originally in Arabia, Muslims could be
buried anywhere since there were vast pieces of land. Camels were used as
means of transportation because of the hot climate. Since the body could not
be placed properly on top of a camel to the burial site, *sanduku* (in Swahili,
meaning coffin) was used for that purpose only."[69] He also explained that
the dry climate in Saudi Arabia meant that the ground could not easily be
dug deep enough to keep the body. It therefore required a coffin that could
hold the body in a shallow grave for a long time.[70] The latter however, does
not apply to Kendu Bay since the soil is generally soft and can be dug to
the level that is required.

---

68. Rashid, interview with author.
69. Omar, interview with author.
70. Omar, interview with author.

Although the Saudi Arabian case may be different from Kendu Bay, it nevertheless highlights why the Luo Muslims use coffins that are not made of nails in disposing the dead people. By acknowledging and identifying with the Luo old traditions in which coffins were never used at all, the Luo Muslims have thus demonstrated that their burial customs are not purely Islamic. Unlike in the past, most of the burials that are conducted without a coffin at the cemetery in Kendu Bay are due to the limited land resource. In a dry place the body decomposes very fast. It then changes into soil. This makes it possible for someone else to be buried in the same place after a very short while. But when a coffin made with metal is used, it may take much longer for the body to decompose. This obviously adds to the already existing problem of land used. Unlike in the past, today's burial in many areas of Luo land is conducted using caskets that are made of nails. The fact that some Luo Muslims practice the same is a sure indication that they have adopted the current Luo way of burying the dead.

3. The activities in the grave where the deceased is laid

Before Munkir and Nakir start interrogating the deceased, it is the grave that squeezes them first.[71] This squeezing is for the purpose of removing urine that may have been left. The action of squeezing is believed to be part of the purification ritual that gets started right from the time of *ghusl*. Apart from cleansing ritual, the squeezing in the grave is also taken to be the beginning point of *chier mar rin'g dhano* (in Luo, meaning, resurrection of the deceased body). *Chier* (resurrection) was described as the moment in which the soul comes back to the grave and not to the body of the deceased. It is temporal and distinguished from the one that takes place in the afterlife. *Chier* in the grave is for the purpose of helping the deceased to respond to the questions that they will be asked by the two angels. The squeezing in the grave takes place last after everything else has been done including prayers. Since it happens in the invisible world, it is treated as part of what the deceased has to account for. Once the grave has done the squeezing, two angels, one on the right and the other one on the left begin to question the deceased about their faith. These questions and the answers which the deceased must give

---

71. Shaban, interview with author.

are indicated in the table below.[72] They have been written both in Arabic transliteration and translated in English.

Table 1: Grave Side Questions and Answers

Questions by Munkir and Nakir	Answers by Deceased
Man Rabbuuka? (Who is your Lord?)	*Allahu Rabbi* (Allah is my Lord)
Wa maa nabbiyyuka? (And who is your prophet?)	*Muhammadu Nabiyy* (Muhammad is my prophet)
Wa maa diinuka? (And what is your religion?)	*Al Islamu diyni* (Islam is my religion)
Wa maa qibllatuka? (And where is your *qibla*?)	*Al Kaaba qiblatiy* (The Kaaba is my *qibla* [direction of prayer])
Wa maa ikhwanuka? (And who are your brothers?)	*Al Muslimuna ikhwaniy* (Muslims are my brothers)
Wa maa kitabuka? (And which is your book?)	*Al Qur'anu kitabiy* (Qur'an is my book)

According to the informants, the dead is made to sit up before they can be questioned by the angels. This of course should not be taken in a literal sense since if the sitting up by the deceased and the question and answer forum inside the grave were experiences that take place physically, one would expect to see some cracks on the grave. However, the cracking of the grave may happen due to other natural forces and not necessarily the result of the physical experiences between the deceased and the angels inside the grave. Some pieces of timber that have been used to seal the outer layer in addition to the soil piled on top of it also makes it difficult to witness the unfolding of such happenings.

The questions that the angels ask look simple and can easily be thought of as obvious. However, according to some informants, the extent to which the deceased would answer those questions depends on the way they have lived

---

72. Shaban, interview with author.

their life on earth. This is to say that even if one crams these questions and their appropriate answers as a way of getting ready for that time, it will be in futility. As Abdul candidly put it during the interview, giving the answers to the questions is something that comes naturally based on one's deeds on earth.[73] This step of questioning determines the eligibility of the deceased to continue with their journey to where Allah has destined for them.

4. Activities that take place after the burial and their significance

After the burial is done, as was the case with the two burials that were witnessed in Kendu Bay, people dispersed. The majority of them however went back to the deceased's home to join their relatives in celebrating their life. This was particularly the case in Salama's burial since she was buried in the cemetery that was away from her home. The women served food in plenty and people got the opportunity to catch up with their relatives and friends whom they have never met for a long time. They are not supposed to talk about the deceased either positively or negatively, for the simple reason that there is nothing to be gained from such talk. The serving of food to mourners after burial is common among the Luo Muslims. This is a departure from the past tradition in which the mourners would bring food to the bereaved.[74] Several reasons were proposed for this change of practice. Some mourners come from too far and it is impractical for them to carry food with them. The new practice may have come from a Luo tradition where mourners are served food by the bereaved family. The current Luo Muslims in Kendu Bay are only from the second to fourth Muslim generation. They may have followed the footsteps of their progenitors who served food according to Luo tradition. If so, then the Luo Muslims of Kendu Bay have not totally abandoned some of the funeral tradition of their forefathers.

The idea of raising funds by friends and relatives of the deceased has become very common today. This mostly happens in towns and cities where the deceased was once residing. An example is in the case of Muhammad who died in Kisumu city. The need to have this fundraising was part of the reason why his family requested for the burial to be extended. It was in order

---

73. Rehman Abdul, interview with author, Kendu Bay, 15 June 2015.
74. Abdallah, interview with author.

to give his relatives and friends some ample time to raise funds that would cover funeral expenses. Expenses included: paying hospital bills, transporting his body from Kisumu to Kendu Bay, food and drinks for mourners at the funeral. Since the Luo Muslims claim that their religion is transparent, it meant that the money that was raised could only be used for the very purpose that was meant. Catering for mourners as it has been pointed out was part of that purpose. But together with meeting these expenses, it was also discovered that some money is put aside and is given to the bereaved family after the burial.

Providing plenty of food and other entertainment for mourners is part of what some informants described as giving the deceased *yiko malongo* (in Luo, meaning a decent burial) or *yiko mowinjorego* (in Luo, meaning a proper or a befitting send-off). Other features which are included in defining a decent burial are: high turn up of mourners, hasty or quick burial, and respecting the wishes of the deceased family in terms of when and where to bury their loved one. But, since those who die in Islam are treated with dignity and without partiality, the Luo Muslims make every burial look decent. This decent treatment, as Zuhura explained, may not necessarily be plenty of food and drinks that mourners were provided with.[75] In other words, for a Luo Muslim, what is described as a decent burial is more than just providing food to the mourners. A belief that the deceased is a person whom God created with a dignity makes the Luo Muslims conduct every ritual including burial very decently. Part of the reason why the Luo Muslims supply plenty of food in their funeral comes out of their understanding that a mourner is *wendo modhial* (in Luo, meaning special guest or visitor) to the deceased.

According to Siraj, *wendo modhial* in a funeral context could be simply a relative to the deceased but has been away from home for a long time.[76] What Siraj implies is that one is considered *wendo modhial* by the virtue of time and distance and not necessarily by non-blood relations. But since it is almost impossible to ascertain who is a visitor and who is not in a funeral, food is provided for everybody who is present. Providing food to every person in attendance is also part of the generosity that all Muslims are called to

---

75. Juma Zuhura, interview with author, Kendu Bay, 29 May 2015.
76. Siraj, interview with author.

practice. The sense of being a "special guest or a visitor" is also understood in terms of his relation to the deceased. Siraj showed this by pointing out that everyone who comes for the burial is said to be a "visitor" to the deceased.[77] Another aspect by which the concept of a visitor was examined was in relation to death. Here, the understanding of the Luo Muslims is that human beings are sojourners in this world. Their stay here on earth is temporary, and as such they are visitors. Death terminates this temporary visit and transits them to their permanent abode. This can either be heaven or hell depending on what God has determined for the individual.

Another reason why the practice of providing food by the deceased family is common in many of the Luo-Muslim funerals today is the religious heterogeneity by which some of them have found themselves. Some of the Luo Muslims in live in the same home with their non-Muslim family members and relatives. When a Muslim dies, the plans by their family members to provide food during the funeral are usually respected. Sometimes it happens that even non-Luo Muslims attend Luo-Muslim burial ceremony. This may be due to blood relations or just friendship with the deceased. Their presence makes it reasonable to prepare and to serve food not to them alone but also to the rest of those who have attended the function. According to some informants, the death is not a loss but rather a transition to the next life. This understanding means that death is something that is meant to be celebrated. The giving of food by the deceased family is therefore a form of celebration. It signifies that they are happy with God's verdict to take away their loved one.

Lastly, providing food to the mourners is a form of charity. It is considered as an opportunity for the Muslims to put into practice teachings in Islam, which encourage them to do good deeds. Part of the good deeds is to provide for the needy in the society. Those who attend the funeral include the needy people. Giving them food to eat, and by extension to everyone, is a good gesture showing that one is hospitable and therefore they are a true Muslim. Food also plays a cultural role. When the deceased family gives food to others, they are demonstrating that they are one as a Muslim community and that they harbor no enmity with anyone. The food that is offered in any

---

77. Siraj, interview with author.

funeral, whether it is for a Muslim or non-Muslim, involves the slaughter of
an animal. The slaughter is, however, done by a Muslim and in line with the
Islamic teachings. Although this is the case in many Muslim funerals, Rashid
gave an area where this may not apply. He said: "when a Muslim attends
a non-Muslim funeral where they are the only Muslim in that place, then
they are allowed to eat what non-Muslims have prepared."[78] This exception
is an illustration of how *Qiyas* is applied in the day-to-day life of a Muslim.
However, such an incidence is said to be very minimal due to the fact that
Muslims are found everywhere. It is therefore almost impossible for a single
Muslim to live by themselves in a particular place.

While the idea of feeding mourners by the deceased family has many
positive reasons behind it, Abdallah dismisses it as a mere show off.[79] He
cited some funeral cases where catering services were hired for the simple
reason that they wanted to outdo other previous funerals. But Abdallah
was not the only who disapproved the idea of spending a lot money in a
funeral. Other informants who were in agreement with Abdallah were almost a quarter of the sum total of the number of the informants that were
interviewed. The three quarters of the informants were part of the people
who gave positive reasons why they believe in spending a lot of money in
the funeral. The sentiment by Abdallah and that of the other informants
who were in agreement with him strongly suggests that incuring so much
expense in feeding mourners may be due to a wrong motive. But going by
the fraction between those who were for and against, it was clear that the
majority of the people find almost no problem with providing costly services
in the funeral. In this case their practice is similar to other non-Luo Muslims.
The minority of the informants who were against the practice mentioned
that it is because of their Muslim faith that makes them do things differently from the non-Luo Muslims. They in fact, doubted whether those who
hire expensive services in the funeral are genuinely Muslims as they claim.
The difference in the opinion between those two camps is a clear indication
that it is almost impossible to assume that the beliefs or practices of the Luo
Muslims are the same.

---

78. Rashid, interview with author.
79. Abdallah, interview with author.

5. Significance of grave burial to the Luo Muslims

The informants gave several reasons why burial is important to them. First, because a Muslim has an inherent dignity, putting the body beneath the earth and covering it with soil is a way of preserving that dignity. The idea of burying the body of their beloved ones is in sharp contrast to some African traditional practices where the dead body was simply thrown in the forest for wild animals to eat. Second, while referring to the relationship between life and death, some informants, using the Qur'an (such as 40:68, 15:23, 10:56, 23:80 and 23:12–14, 40:67, 36:77, 18:34–36, 80:19, 53:45–46), pointed out that, since a human being is created by God from soil, at death the person must be returned to the same soil. This understanding implies that at burial the person is simply returned to where they came from.

Third, the presence of a cemetery or any other grave where a Muslim has been buried is a reminder to the Muslim about death and God. This, according to Shaban, is something that Ḥadīth records.[80] Every Muslim therefore is encouraged to visit the grave often as a way of increasing the individual's faith. The researcher finds this practice of visiting the grave or the cemetery similar to what Luos used to encourage traditionally. The difference, however, lies on the purpose of the visit. Shaban[81] used the principle of *shibr*[82] that is recorded in the Ḥadīth to explain why it is dangerous to forcefully take another person's land. Such a misdeed would result in the offender being punished by being forced to carry the whole earth. The place where one is buried is so small (*shibr* in Arabic). It is for this reason that the Luo Muslims don't like to engage in quarrelling or fighting over a piece of land.

Luo Muslims believe that there are certain people and things that are used to *kowo*[83] (in Luo, meaning to escort) the deceased up to the grave, namely, family members and relatives, vehicles (if the body of the deceased

---

80. Shaban, interview with author.

81. Shaban, interview with author.

82. This is a saying among Muslims to describe something that is very small, yet important enough, that if ignored it could result in death.

83. *Kowo* is a term that is used to refer to the persons or items or one's character that accompany the deceased to their grave. They are mainly perceived as providing comfort or help the deceased gain acceptance from Allah. They are a witness to the fact that the deceased was indeed loved or well taken care of. They also give a testimony of the kind of life the deceased lived.

has been transported from elsewhere as it was the case with Muhammad's body), and the deeds of the deceased. Out of the three, only the last one goes to the grave with the deceased. It is on the basis of these deeds that one is rewarded in hereafter. Since deeds are what one would be buried with, it makes sense to understand why many Muslims are very active in performing good deeds. This reality makes every Muslim strive hard so that when he dies he would not be buried empty but rather with the good deeds he used to do while on earth.

Rituals associated with widows and other family members of the deceased

The rituals that the Luo-Muslim widowers follow are very few compared to the Luo-Muslim widows. It is for this reason that the rituals that have been described here are mainly linked to Luo-Muslim widows and their families. Just like in many African cultures, widows in Islam are expected to undergo more rituals than the other relatives of the deceased. Following the demise of her husband, a widow begins a period of *'iddah*. It usually takes four months and ten days. It is a period in which a widow goes through a moment of mourning for her husband. This period is characterized by a number of ritual activities. There is also a way in which a widow is expected to behave during this period of *'iddah*. The informants also used the terms *chola* or *okola* as they described *'iddah*. These terms are mostly used by the non-Luo Muslims. The way they have been used shows that the Luo Muslims are not completely ignorant of their Luo traditional roots. Their relationship with *'iddah* also remains very significant. They are however discussed in detail in the next chapter. The main focus that is kept in this section is to describe what happens during the *'iddah* period and how it affects the life of a Luo-Muslim widow and other members of the deceased family

The ritual and regulations associated to a widow in *'iddah* period

In a more specific sense, a widow begins her period of *'iddah* at the time her husband is laid to rest. Both Omar and Tatu outlined what the Ḥadīth teaches about this period to widows.[84] First, she is prohibited from talking or engaging in love affair with a man. She is unclean and therefore would contaminate those she gets into contact with. Second, she is not allowed to attend any wedding or decorate herself in any way. But when she is in her periods, she is allowed to apply perfume (*marashi* in Swahili) on her body. It was interesting to discover that on one hand, the widow is prohibited from attending a wedding while on the other hand she is allowed to attend a funeral. The informants were, however, quick to explain this irony. They understand a funeral unlike a wedding as a place where the bereaved express their emotions over the loss of their loved ones. In this case, it is the right for a widow to be in that mood since she is still grieving over the demise of her husband. A wedding on the other hand, is a place for jubilation. A widow cannot therefore attend it since her heart is still in pain. In other words, there is nothing for her to be happy about in a wedding ceremony. Third, she is expected to wear clothes that are either white or black. Although a widow can wear either a white or a black cloth, Prophet Muhammad is said to have recommended a white one.[85]

It was, however, not clear why Muhammad preferred a white cloth. It was simply equated with the widow's state of purity. Many informants also pointed that *'iddah* is a period that is primarily meant to establish whether a widow was left with pregnancy at the time her husband passed on. In case she was left with a child in the womb, she must first deliver before getting re-married. The idea of waiting until a widow delivers before she can re-marry applies also in divorce (*talaq* in Arabic) in Islam (see appendix E). The widow's decision to get married to another husband is something that is treated as new. In other words, the husband who wants to marry the widow must pay the dowry to her. Just as in death, which marks the end of a marriage contract between a husband and a wife, payment of dowry is a sign that a new contract has been entered.

---

84. Omar, interview with author; Amina Tatu, interview with author, Kendu Bay, 5 May 2015.

85. Omar, interview with author.

The ritual of *nika* and its importance to a widow who desires to re-marry

The marriage between the widow and the man she desires to re-marry her is not considered complete with the payment of dowry alone. The new couple must do the Islamic wedding (*nika*, in Arabic). This is a ceremony that is presided over by imam. It is done in the public. Many people including non-Muslims come to witness as the two are ushered into new marriage. The significance of *nika* cannot be underestimated. First, it signifies that the two who have gotten married are Muslims who follow Muslim practices truthfully. It is what brings a major difference between the Luo-Muslim *'iddah* and the Luo traditional *chola* or *okola* (the details are in the next chapter). Second, *nika* is the basis by which a marriage is recognized as Islamic. Without it, a couple is simply considered as co-habiting or fornicating with each other. The danger of this, according to Tatu, is that the children born out of such a kind of relationship or the woman herself who is co-habiting cannot bury her second husband when he dies.[86] A widow, who just enters into marriage without the wedding, is also looked down upon as an immoral person in the Luo-Muslim society.

The demand for a wedding between the man and the woman who wish to stay together as a husband and a wife as pointed out by the informants was meant to minimize promiscuity among the Luo Muslims in Kendu Bay. If a widow gives birth to a child of the deceased during the four months and ten days period, then *'iddah* comes to an end. The widow is free to re-marry after the lactation period is over. The decision to re-marry is entirely left to the widow. She is the one who should decide for her suitor and not the decision of the deceased husband's relatives as is common in the Luo traditional setting. Upon agreeing to re-marry, a wedding is planned. Apart from reducing immorality, a wedding in the Luo-Muslim context signifies a new life. In fact, the wedding involving a widow and her new husband is treated by the Luo Muslims not as a re-marriage as such but rather as a new marriage. This wedding nullifies the previous one. It is therefore considered and treated as something new that has never been before. It comes with new

---

86. Tatu, interview with author.

terms and conditions. First, a new couple is encouraged to agree on where they want to settle.

Some of these new couples have settled in the *miji* (homesteads) in old town of Kendu Bay. Their move to settle in *miji* is attributed by the fact that land is generally scarce in Kendu Bay. Houses in *miji* are meant to accommodate people who might find it hard to settle in their new marriage either at the widow's late husband's home or the new husband's home. Settling at *miji* is also viewed as a way of "running" away from the Luo traditions. This could be imposed on the Muslim widow who at the time of her husband's demise was living in a non-Muslim home. Sometimes this newly wedded couple may choose to stay at the widow's late husband's home, the home of the new husband, or anywhere they decide. The below diagram summarizes the various components that *'iddah* entails.

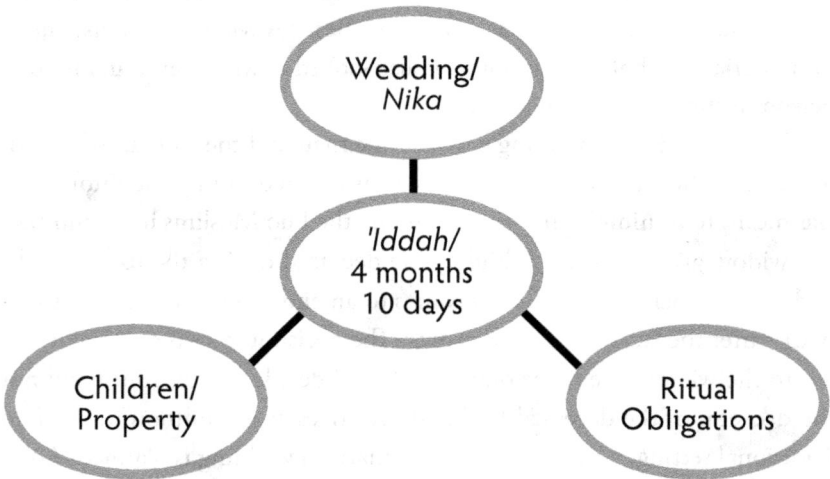

Diagram 15: *'Iddah* and Its Variant Components

Duties and obligations during and after *nika.*

As indicated in the above diagram, all the requirements that a Muslim widow is expected to follow are categorized as the ritual obligations. These rituals are required depending on the age of a widow. Younger widows are more restricted compared to the older ones. They are not supposed to leave their houses for whatever reason during their *'iddah* period. The older widows are allowed to go about doing their businesses like selling in the market. They are however not allowed to sleep outside in their *'iddah* cloth. The younger widows are more restricted out of a belief that they are young and can easily get tempted to have sex with men during their *'iddah* period. The wedding or *nika* component can be what marks the end of *'iddah*. But apart from being a platform by which the new couple decides where to stay, the wedding is also characterized by the giving of gifts. According to the Ḥadīth, it is the man who gives gifts (*mahr*, in Arabic) to the woman. A widow has a choice to contract another marriage with the husband of her choice. Some widows, however, may decide to carry on with their lives due to their advanced age or for some other reasons that have to do with their relationship with the in-laws or simply personal.

The component under "children/property" is very important. The children who were born before their mother was widowed and have followed their mother a new marriage after *'ddah*, are still identified as the children of the deceased. They are therefore called by the name of their late father. On the other hand, the children who are born through the union with the new husband are identified as his children. The property under the category of "Children/Property" includes what the widow owned with her late husband. Rather than transferring them to a new marriage, they are divided amongst the deceased's children. Dividing property follows Islamic teachings in the Ḥadīth where a son gets twice as much as a daughter. If in this marriage there was no son, then the male cousins of the deceased may divide their late cousin's property as equivalent to what his own son would have received.[87] The "property" also represents places where the new couple decides to stay. The new husband may want his bride to stay in the same home where his other wife or wives are staying. But due to scarcity of land many couples have decided to stay in *miji*. Settling at a particular place of residence usually comes after the *nika*.

---

87. Nabil Ikbar, interview with author, Kendu Bay, 18 June 2015.

Shafi'ite's Three-Step Order for the Luo-Muslim Beliefs and Practices

The above section has dealt with how the Luo Muslims follow Islamic teachings as far as their belief in death and its related practices are concerned. These Islamic teachings have been found to emerge from three distinct sources of Islamic Law: Qur'an/ Hadīth, *Qiyas* ("analogy") and *Ijma* ("consensus"). The researcher examined this Shafi'ite's Three Step Order of Law in relation to various categories of the Luo-Muslim funeral beliefs and practices. He has done this for two reasons. First, it has been done in order to establish what part of the Shafi'ite's Three Step Order of Law informs the various categories of the Luo-Muslims' funeral beliefs and practices. It has also been done in order to determine the extent to which Shafi'ite's Three Step Order of Law has affected the meaning and causes that Luo Muslims attach to death, mourning rituals, rituals to/for the deceased, and rituals to the widow and other family members of the deceased. The diagram below is a summary showing the relationship between the Shafi'ite's Three Step Order of Law and the Luo-Muslim funeral beliefs and practices.

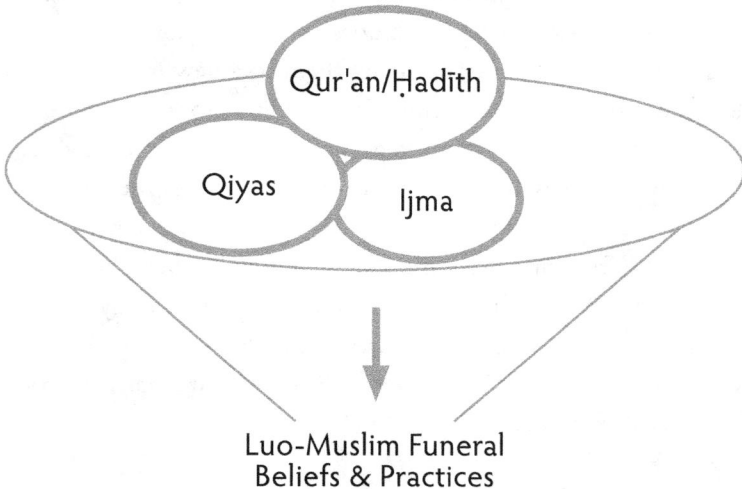

Diagram 16: Effects of Shafi'ite's Three Step Order on Luo-Muslim Funeral Beliefs and Practices

The shape for the diagram, which is like a funnel, has been chosen very deliberately. The wider open part of the funnel represents an entry point to the Islamic teachings about death that the Luo Muslims receive in their day to day life. They receive those teachings from different sources, namely, in the mosques, *madras*, funeral services, schools and other institutions of higher learning. On top of the funnel are the components that make up the Shafi'ite's Three Step Order. They are in different proportions but attached to each other. The arrow indicates the direction they move. As they move down, the components continue fusing with each other into one whole. The movement is rather gradual. It varies from one individual Luo Muslim to another. This movement represents the way a Luo Muslim grasps the teachings in Islam. Some are very quick to learn while others are slow. The way that was used to determine how much the Luo Muslims have grasped was through listening and observing them as they described and participated in different funeral activities. As represented in the diagram, the different sizes of the Shafi'ite's Three Step Order signify the level of influence that each component has had on the funeral beliefs and practices of the Luo Muslims. The diagram thus demonstrates that a lot of influences have come from the Qur'an/ Ḥadīth. It follows in that order by *Qiyas* and finally *Ijma*.

In their descriptions of what exactly takes place when somebody dies and the various rituals that they conduct during the funeral, the majority of the Luo Muslims kept referring to what the Qur'an/ Ḥadīth says. Under very minimal cases did they refer to *Qiyas* and *Ijma*. But in other times they could simply refer to Islam in general. For instance, when some informants were asked why loud wailing is discouraged, they simply responded that *Islamu wacho kamano* (in Luo, meaning that is what Islam says). This statement refers to the teachings that Islam gives. The same statement was quoted as an answer in their other funeral beliefs and practices. Speaking of Islam in general suggests three things. First, it may mean that some Luo Muslims are not aware of the various distinctions that exist in the Islamic Schools of Law. This was the case with the majority of the Luo-Muslim adults. They may have forgotten due to their advanced age or are just simply not interested. Second, their reference to Islam in general implies that they take it as a single whole. In other words, they don't see Islam as compartmental. To them, the voice of Islam is a single voice. Finally, due to mixing with Luo traditional elements, some Luo Muslims may find it difficult to distinguish what is Islam and what is Luo traditional. Since they are Muslims, it is safe and easy for them to consider their beliefs and practices as simply Islamic. If this last suggestion is anything to go by, then the Shafi'ite's Three Step Order should not be seen as operating in isolation but rather in a cultural setting that is equally influential. In that case and as was evident in the speech and the deeds of the Luo Muslims, its influence to the funeral beliefs and practices of the Luo Muslims is not purely Islamic. It contains some elements from the Luo tradition.

The Outcomes of Islamic Teachings on the Luo-Muslim View of Death

In the previous section, the kind of Islamic teachings that Luo Muslims in Kendu Bay follow during funerals have been displayed. These teachings apply from the time a Muslim dies up to the time they are buried. They also cover the period after the burial of the deceased has taken place. This is more particularly so in a situation where the person who has passed on was a married man. The widow would be required to follow and apply the Islamic teachings pertaining to the situation that she has found herself in. In this section, the researcher examines how those death-related teachings have affected the lives of the Luo Muslims. As it has been pointed out before, the Luo Muslims understand death as something that is determined by God. This does not in any way accuse him of any wrong doing, but rather it simply allows the Luo Muslims to know that death is a mystery, and as such it is beyond any human comprehension. Islamic teachings that the Luo Muslims follow have generated several outcomes in the way they view death.

The Outcome of Fear and Worry on the Luo-Muslim View of Death

The discovery that some Luo Muslims are afraid or are worried of death was made following the interviews. Out of the three categories of the informants that were interacted with, it was the category of Luo-Muslim adults that was found to have some of its members who felt very uncomfortable responding to the questions posed to them about death. Some could take long to respond while others termed the questions as hard to describe. Rukia, for instance, explained that talking about death is like inviting it.[88] Some people, as Shaban explained, do not want to hear about death even though they knew it is inevitable. He further narrated that when a sermon based on death is preached in the mosque the same people feel uncomfortable about it.[89] Their minds drift away. Lack of interest in the subject of death among some members of the adult category along with their fear of death is quite revealing about the role that age plays towards the understanding of death among the Luo Muslims. In other words, it simply demonstrates that as one gets older, the more cautious they are to discuss subjects related to death.

The reason why they are not comfortable talking about death is that as one gets older, they becomes less active in carrying out the good deeds. This is a source of worry because the less the good deeds, the less the chances of getting into paradise. The situation of the Luo-Muslim adults is contrary to the other two categories of youths and children. They were so open to talk about death. Their small age allows them to be very active in doing the good deeds. They have high hopes that when death strikes, their many deeds would increase their chances to enter paradise. The subject of death is a matter that many African communities including the Luos rarely discuss. It is simply left in the hands of fate.

While writing about beliefs and activities involved in rites of death among the folk-Muslims[90] in his book, *The Unseen Face of Islam*, Musk also observes that the subject of death is hardly discussed due to its consequences: "Death is not mentioned lest that invite its premature occurrence. Rather, focus is made upon positive words, even if the sick person is actually dying."[91] This belief is common especially in Africa among different cultures. Any careless words before a dying person is generally prohibited. In fact, even though the human causality of death like witchcraft is not very much pronounced among the Luo Muslims in Kendu Bay, Sarah who is a woman Muslim by birth admits that some Muslims use *majinni* (in Swahili, meaning spirits)

---

88. Adhiambo Rukia, interview with author, Kendu Bay, 14 May 2015.

89. Shaban, interview with author.

90. Although Musk uses the term "Folk Muslims," many anthropologists today including Kim (see Kim, "Considering 'ordinariness,'" and *Islam among the Swahili*) use the term "popular or ordinary Muslims" to refer to the same people.

91. Musk, *Unseen Face of Islam*, 101.

for their selfish motivates.[92] Some Luo Muslims even believe *jinn* as a cause of death. However, Saidi considers such people who use *majinni* as not true Muslims. He further reiterated that when the person who uses *majinni* dies, they are met with the severe judgment of Allah. There is also no place for such an individual in paradise.[93]

The belief that witchcraft, or *majinni*, can also cause death implies that there are mixed feelings about what or who causes someone's death among some Luo Muslims. Whereas some may genuinely surrender to God upon receiving news that their loved ones have passed on, others may have questions or associate their deaths with some human agencies rather than God. While some Luo Muslims believe in witchcraft as a possible cause of one's death, there are also some who believe that the power of witchcraft cannot kill the person whose time to die has not yet come. This is usually the case with those who might have fallen sick for quite a long time or have been involved in a road accident. Their recovery from sickness or being unhurt from an accident is explained as an example that their time of death has not yet been permitted by Allah. This means that even though some deaths may still be attributed to human causality, God is still believed to be the one who ultimately determines the fate of an individual.

Increased Awareness of the Value of One's Deeds

Apart from fear and worry, another outcome that the Islamic teachings on death have brought to the Luo Muslims is the increased awareness of the significance of their deeds. It is the eschatological teachings in Islam about heaven and hell that have brought about this awareness that one's deeds are important. The Luo Muslims have been taught that death is not the end of human existence. There is heaven and hell. The entry into heaven or hell is depended on what Allah has decided for the deceased. Although many Luo Muslims are not fully certain, Allah's decision as to whether the deceased should be allowed to enter paradise or hell is usually perceived to rely on their deeds.

These deeds that are talked about do not only consist of what one does to the other people and the community around them but also the behavior

---

92. Abdallah Sarah, interview with author, Kendu Bay, 9 May 2015.
93. Saidi, interview with author.

of the person. In other words, the deeds and the behaviors simply define the kind of a lifestyle that a Luo Muslim has. The awareness that deeds have consequences in the afterlife has made some Luo Muslims change their habits from bad to good. Some, particularly the older ones, spend most of their time in the mosques praying, meditating, and reciting/reading the Qur'an, repenting or doing *dhikr* (in Arabic, meaning remembrance of Allah). Others have gotten involved in helping the less fortunate people in the society. These are all good deeds. Their awareness that evil doers will be punished by Allah has also helped the Luo Muslims to keep on doing the good deeds. There is a lot of respect for one another. The dead are also respected. This is demonstrated in the way they are handle right from the time of demise to the time of burial. But together with such charitable deeds and good behaviors toward the living and the dead, a Luo Muslim is still not very certain about their future destiny. As Rukia remarked, "it is all for Allah to decide where to place us when we die."[94]

Mixed Feelings and Responses to Life and Death

The teachings in Islam about death have met with mixed feelings and re-sponses from the different Luo-Muslim groups (adults, youths and chil-dren). An example is in the teachings about a person's deeds. As it has been explained in the previous section, Islam teaches that once somebody has died, it is their deeds that Allah uses to determine where to place them in the afterlife. While it is clear in the mind of a Luo Muslim that it is the good deeds that Allah requires, it is the nature of what these good deeds entailed that they struggles to comprehend. Some Luo Muslims especially from the category of the youths have understood the good deeds to be entirely involving the things they do toward others and the community. They find fulfillment in life through what they do rather than through their conduct before Allah.

The emphasis on what one does rather than how one lives is indeed a dichotomy. It gives an understanding on how some Luo-Muslim youths view life. The feeling that they should exploit their youthful period to the maximum in worldly affairs is a reality to them. This reality is also is also driven by their feeling that they have many more years to live. They think

---

94. Rukia, interview with author.

that they would return to Allah (in repentance) during their old age. As Shaban puts it, this approach to life is discouraged in Islam.[95] Some Luo Muslims occupy a middle state. In other words, the message on the existence of death and life in the hereafter neither excites nor scares them. Most of the Luo-Muslim youths and children fall under this category. They feel that they should let things happen the way they are. Quite a number of Luo Muslims especially in the adult category are confused in relation to funeral rituals. Some would want to stick strictly to Islamic funeral practices while others would want to mix Islamic with Luo traditional rituals. In fact, some don't see the difference in some of their funeral practices. This includes burial procedures. For example, they argue that the way they bury without a coffin is the same way Luo people used to bury traditionally. A person was never buried in coffin as it is today but rather on a mat. If one is a prominent person in the society they could be buried in an animal skin.

Teachings on Islam that center on the funeral rituals give the Luo Muslims the ground to compare the Luo traditional and Islamic customs. An example was found in the area of providing food to the bereaved. In the Luo-Muslim funerals, friends and relatives to the deceased are encouraged to bring food to the bereaved. The food is supposed to be brought from outside rather than being prepared by those who have been bereaved. As some informants confessed, the same practice was also followed by the Luos of the past. This trend has, however, changed. In most of the Luo-Muslim funerals today, food is offered by the bereaved family rather than the outsiders who have come to mourn. It is the same practice even in non-Luo-Muslim contexts in Kendu Bay. This has thrown the Luo Muslims into mixed feelings. Some of the Luo Muslims are not able to say for certain whether such funeral practices have been borrowed from the Luo tradition or not. All that they said was that Prophet Muhammad passed to them practices that seemed similar to the Luo customs. They are, however, distinctively Islamic. This means that they view them as originating from Islam rather than from the Luo tradition. Other informants were of the opinion that the similarity in terms of the funeral practices is due to the fact that Islam is part of the Luo customs. Some Luo Muslims appreciate the simplicity of Islamic funeral rituals. They

---

95. Shaban, interview with author.

say that Islam does not burden them with many programs as witnessed in non-Luo-Muslim homes. An example that was pointed to was with regard to the rituals surrounding the widow. They felt that Islam is flexible and does not subject widows to undergo rigorous rituals as is practiced in the Luo traditional context. It is based on this simplicity that many widows have turned to Islam at the point they were bereaved by their spouses.

The Significance of the Place of Burial to the Luo Muslims

The impact of Islamic teachings on the Luo-Muslim view of death has also been felt in other areas of their life. Such include the aspect of burying their loved ones in cemeteries. As the researcher has highlighted before, Luo Muslims bury their dead in either cemetery or in the homestead. The choice for the place to bury always depends on the decision of the deceased family. The Luo Muslims have a designated place in the old town of Kendu Bay where they bury their members. The idea of a cemetery as the burial ground has brought a completely different perspective to the way Luo Muslims view land as well as life in general. There is little worry among them about where they would be buried when they die since they have a cemetery.

The concern for where to be buried is a very major issue in Kendu Bay due to the scarcity of land. It is also an area of concern to the wider Luo society where the insistence to be buried in one's ancestral land is very strong. For some Luo Muslims, this is not a problem anymore because of the teachings that a Muslim can live anywhere. This becomes important considering that many of those Luo Muslims residing in Kendu Bay such as Kaum, Wagwe, Kanyaluo, Karabondi and Koguta are outsiders. They have therefore no right to own land in Kendu Bay were it not for the fact that they are Muslims. The religion of Islam has united them together. They are therfore given the same treatment including the right to be buried at the cemetery just like any other Muslim. Those people who now reside in Kendu Bay and have become Muslims, simply burry their dead ones where they live. The question of transporting the body back to the birth place or the ancestral land of one's origin is almost impractical to them. It is impractical to them because they consider Kendu Bay to be part of their ancestral land.

The Importance of Cleaning the Body of the Deceased

In the interviews and the observations that were made, the Luo Muslims took seriously the practice of cleaning the body of the deceased. According to the informants, cleaning the body of the deceased is not optional. The cleaning of the body may take one or two days depending on the number of days the deceased takes before their burial. This washing of the body, which is referred to as, *ghusl* (in Arabic) is different from the washing of other parts of the body that a Luo Muslim does before entering the mosque for prayers. The latter is referred to as *wudu* (in Arabic). Cleaning of the body is not limited to washing only. It also includes spraying perfume on the body of the deceased (more details on cleanliness have been discussed in the next chapter). Once the washing of the body has been done, it is then covered with a white sheet of cloth known as *sanda* (in Arabic).

The cleaning of the body is considered a very vital ritual. It is done with the full view that the deceased would stand before Allah in judgment as they give an account of the deeds they have done on earth. The informants explained that Allah being holy, means everybody who comes before him must first and foremost be clean. Cleaning the body was also viewed as a way of affirming that the deceased was a true Muslim. Looking at the way Luo Muslims carry out cleaning in their homes and houses, perform *wudu* ritual before prayers in the Mosques, gives no doubt that they have great value attached to cleanliness. It has religious rather than physical values. This is because every form of cleanliness or purification is made in respect to paradise. To enter where God dwells, every attempt is made in this life to keep up with cleanliness or to reflect it.

A New Islamic Understanding of Widowhood and Death among Luo Muslims

Besides the effect that this concept of cleanliness has brought, there is also a new understanding of widowhood. This is most relevantly in the sense that a Luo-Muslim widow is expected to wed (*nika*) her new husband. The effect of this is that promiscuity and ridicule have been minimized. A widow who fails to wed and instead elopes with a man is treated as a prostitute, such that she loses the benefit of enjoying her identity as a Muslim. She is also viewed as an outcast. Facing such treatment and ridicule is usually too shameful not only to the individual but also to the Luo-Muslim society as a whole. The fear of being isolated makes the widow and other persons in the Luo-Muslim community follow Islamic teachings about good morals.

The view that death comes from God and that it is a secret that he alone knows brings on a new meaning. Apart from some that showed reservation about the subject of death, most of the informants expressed their readiness for death. This readiness is also founded on the fact that teachings about death are given at the Mosques, *madras* and other forums such as funerals, Muslim colleges and universities. Hearing the messages on death repeatedly makes them less scared about it. But on the other hand, the fact that no one knows when death would occur has caused some to be very anxious. The thinking of what would kill an individual is something that cannot be minimized.

New Concepts of Time and Death among the Luo Muslims

Islamic teachings on death have also brought about new meaning to the way Luo Muslims understand the concept of time. From the diagram below, it is clear that the essence of time touches on four areas. The first area is represented by burial before or after Mosque prayer. If somebody dies, they must be buried before or after prayers have been made in the Mosque. This order highlights the significance of prayer in a Muslim's life. It is something that cannot be postponed or pushed to another date just because somebody has died. This attitude however, does not in any way suggest that the Luo Muslims are less caring about those who have died. In fact, whether burial is conducted before or after, prayers are still made at the Mosques for those who have died including the prophet.

Another essence of time is represented by "many hands." Here, what the researcher means is that, once news of demise has reached people, they come in a large number to support the bereaved and give a befitting send-off to the deceased. All these including funeral rituals that are conducted are done with time in mind. The saying from the Luos that "many hands make light work," applies here. This saying originally comes from the words *lwedo achiel ok neg onywogo* (in Luo, meaning, one finger cannot kill lice). It is a statement that discourages people from doing things by themselves. It calls for group participation and solidarity. This concept explains why many Luo Muslims turn up and participate in different activities during the funeral.

Their overwhelming support at the time of the funeral is meant to save time especially for the deceased. As they combine their efforts together, the work that could have taken more time is finished within a very short time.

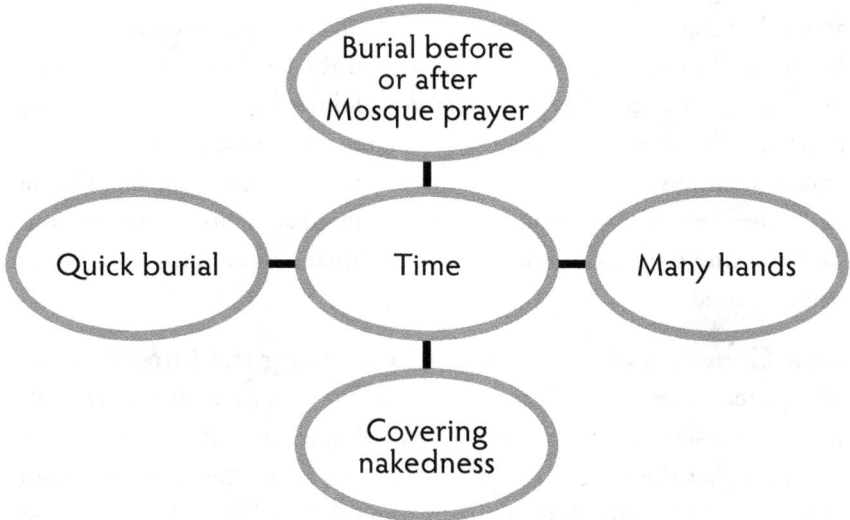

Diagram 17: The Concept of Time in a Luo-Muslim Funeral

The concept of time as represented by "Quick Burial," is also significant. As it has been pointed out in the previous section, Luo Muslims are known to conduct burial in less than twenty four hours. More time may be given only when the family of the deceased requests an extension. But this is rare. Conducting quick burial is essentially important for two reasons. First, it is meant to catch up with the two angels, Munkar and Nakir on the grave. They are the angels who interrogate the deceased about his life and deeds on earth. But also, quick burial is meant to give the deceased ample time to travel[96] to their destiny. The journey to the next life is so long such that the

---

96. *Odhi wuoth* is the concept behind the English word, "travel." The term refers to a visit that someone makes to a distant place. The one who visits is expected to come back at some point. When used in the context of death, it carries the meaning that the deceased is alive and that they would come back to life. According to some Luo Muslims, it is in the afterlife that coming back to life would be realized. However, some believe that coming back to life is an ongoing experience for those who have died. The latter's belief has been influenced by

earlier the deceased starts the better. The last area representing the essence of time is the "covering of nakedness." It was pointed out by some informants that a Muslim's nakedness is something that is guarded right from the adolescent stage to the time of death. It therefore comes as no surprise that at death the deceased is shrouded in such a way that their nakedness is not exposed. This covering of nakedness is exercised through modest dressing by all Muslims during their lifetime. When one dies the same is being conducted on their behalf by ensuring that there is no part of the deceased body that is exposed. Even the people who take care of the deceased in terms of washing and shrouding should not see their nakedness.

Conclusion

In this section, the researcher has looked how Islam has influenced the Luo traditional view of death in Kendu Bay. This influence was based on some of the Islamic teachings on the death that the Luo Muslims in Kendu Bay follow. A description was then given concerning how those teachings inform the contemporary Luo-Muslim view of death. The increasing number of Mosques and Muslims in the area is an indication that Islam is rapidly spreading. Among the many teachings that they receive, the informants were very categorical, that it is the subject of death that has widely been taught to them in the mosques and *madras*, different Muslim forums, and other Islamic institutions of higher learning. These teachings cover the beliefs and the practices that a Luo Muslim is expected to follow right from the time they get the news or witness the demise of a fellow Muslim to the period after the burial.

The beliefs and practices that the Luo Muslims follow during their funerals had many references from the Qur'an and the Ḥadīth. They also explained some few instances where *Ijma* may apply. They gave very little difference between *Ijma* and *Qiyas* (in Arabic, referring to the principle of analogy). According to them *Qiyas* was also used in situations where there was no clear ruling from both the Qura'n and the Ḥadīth. Their mention on those areas

---

the Luo tradition. It claims that the dead are dead physically but their souls are alive. They sometimes talk of seeing their loved ones who died sometimes back in a dream. It is for this reason that libation is offered to the dead in memory of them.

was a clear indication that the Luo Muslims follow the Shafi'ite's School of Law. It is based on the three Shafi'ite's Three Step Order, namely, Qur'an/ Ḥadīth, *Qiyas* and *Ijma*. The areas of Luo-Muslim funerals that were looked at in relation to the Shafi'ite's Three Step Order were: the meanings and causes of death, mourning rituals, rituals to/for the deceased, and rituals associated to widows and other family members.

As a result of the Islamic influence, the Luo Muslims describe death as simply a transfer into another life in an invisible world. Most of them especially youths and children talked openly about death as if it held no danger. The Luo-Muslim adults were, however, skeptical about the subject of death. They talked cautiously about it. This fact that the youths and children talk openly about death while the mature adults are a bit reserved about it is quite insightful. It is out of their own interpretation of what death means to them. For instance, despite the teachings that Allah is the one who causes someone to die, some Luo-Muslim adults still think otherwise. They claim that Allah is merciful and therefore cannot cause someone to die. They also don't see death as a mere accident but rather as something that has been caused by someone. They therefore look at other people with suspicion. The way they view death shows that they have combined their Islamic beliefs with the Luo traditional ones. On the other hand, most of the Luo-Muslim youths and children are convinced that death comes from Allah. This shows that they have remained true to the teachings that they have received about death. Their belief that everything that comes from Allah is good makes them view death positively. Their turning up in large numbers to assist in the burial arrangement is a fact that proves that they have accepted Allah's decision.

How the Luo Muslims respond to the news about death and the rituals which they carry out throughout the funeral have the indications that they have been influenced by Islamic teachings. The first sign is found in the way Luo Muslims mourn their dead. Most people wail and shed tears but not very loudly. Due to high emotions, some find it difficult to restrain themselves. They simply burst into loud wailing. Second, the preparation of the body through washing and shrouding is done by three people of the same gender as the deceased. This ensures confidentially to the deceased about their body parts. Third, in most cases, the burying of the body takes less than twenty-four hours. The consent about where to bury and what time to burry comes from the immediate family of the deceased. Permission is granted to the family members who would wish to defer the burial of their loved one until a later day (but not more than three days). By granting their wish, it shows that the Luo Muslims are flexible and easily adjust to the Luo traditional customs. Finally, the requirement that a Luo-Muslim widow who wishes to re-marry must do the Islamic wedding (*nika*) is also a sign that the Islamic teachings have an influence. In an instance where a widow stays with a man without the wedding is simply viewed as cohabiting. From the evidence mentioned, it is true that Islamic teachings have had influence on the Luo-Muslim view of death. However, this influence is not 100 percent. Some elements from the Luo cultural setting can still be identified.

CHAPTER 5

Elements of Luo Tradition in Luo-Muslim Perception of Death

Introduction

There is little doubt that Islam has affected the way Luo people bury their dead ones. As it has been discribed in the previous chapter, many of the funeral rituals that the Luo Muslims do right from the time one dies up to the burial period are mostly done in line with the Islamic teachings. However, a thorough scrutiny of these beliefs and practices has revealed that there are some areas where Luo traditional elements still surface. Apart from looking into those elements in this chapter, the researcher has also described how contemporary Luo Muslims explain the existence of Luo traditional views in their cultural perception of death. Further to this, he has explained how Luo traditional views have affected the understanding of the Luo Muslims about death and its related practices. Points of similarities and differences between Luo traditional and Islamic customs have been used in this chapter to describe the aspects of continuity and discontinuity of the Luo traditional understanding of death within the Luo-Muslim context of Kendu Bay.

Explaining the Existence of Luo Traditions in the Luo-Muslim Perception of Death

In order to provide a clear understanding of how Luo Muslims explain the existence of Luo traditional view in their cultural perception of death, the first task that was undertaken as indicated in the methodology chapter was to divide the Luo-Muslim funeral into three stages: (1) Initial Stage – death to body preparation, (2) Middle Stage – deceased body taken from the mosque/homestead to the grave and (3) Later Stage – activities and the events after burial. This was done using Spradley's taxonomic and componential analyses.[1] From these analyses, a paradigm worksheet was prepared. It contained descriptions of funeral activities, elements and the persons who were involved in each of those three stages of a Luo-Muslim funeral. Gilliland's concepts of non-negotiable ethos, immediacy and futuristic-focus[2] were used as a framework. A theory was developed. This theory classified the Luo-Muslim funeral activities, elements and persons who were involved into three different categories: non-Islamic element, partial-Islamic element and total-Islamic element. The criterion for developing this theory was undertaken by looking at both similarities and differences between Luo traditional and Islamic beliefs and practices as were found at every stage of the Luo-Muslim funeral.

Similarities and Differences in the Initial Stage

As pointed out in the previous section, the Initial Stage of a Luo-Muslim funeral covers the period between one's death and preparation of the body for burial. In this section, a step-by-step analysis of the various components in the Initial Stage has been conducted. Those components consist of the terminologies that were used by the informants to refer to death and the person who has died. They also include descriptions of how Luo Muslims react or respond to the news about the demise of their loved one and the areas of rituals such as washing and shrouding of the body. The findings were then made based on how similar or different the components are with the Luo tradition. A description that explains the similarities and the differences was also offered.

The Luo-Muslim beliefs in death and their responses to it

As covered in the previous chapter, death (*almaut*) is seen by the Luo Muslims as something that Allah has decreed. The circumstance that may have caused it is therefore taken to be part of Allah's plan. This explains why on hearing the news about death a Luo Muslim is expected to respond with the words:

---

1. Spradley, *Ethnographic Interview*, 132–154, 173–184; Spradley, *Participant Observation*, 113–121, 130–139.
2. Gilliland, *African Traditional Religion*.

ina lilahi waina ileyi rajiun (we have come from God and we will go back to him). But as some informants admitted, this utterance is not always what comes out of every mouth of the people who have witnessed or have heard news about the demise of their loved ones. Sometimes, as Shaban pointed out, people remember to utter those words after complaining or pondering in their hearts as to who or for what reason their loved one was killed.[3] Other informants also admitted that, although they are expected to utter those words which acknowledge that God is the source of life and death, it is not always possible to know whether they are confessed genuinely.

Those varied perspectives concerning how Luo Muslims respond to death have several implications. First, it implies that some Luo Muslims are not consistently following the teachings of Islam that require them to affirm that death has a divine causality. In bad times such as death, it is not difficult to understand why Luo Muslims may respond indifferently to Allah for what has happened. It has to do with the perception they have towards him. They view him as the source of both good and bad. Such a perception may be contrary to the idea behind the words, *ina lilahi waina ileyi rajiun.* These words are meant to praise and acknowledge that Allah is sovereign despite the death that has occurred. The concept exudes no division between good and bad in the attitude towards Allah.

The belief by some Luo Muslims that death is not an accident gives a hint as to where they direct the cause. It points to human agent. The claim that a certain person has caused the death of their fellow human beings is very common in many communities in Africa. Several authors have written about it.[4] It was even there before Islam was introduced to the African people. It was not therefore a surprise to hear some Luo Muslims making those assertions. It shows that they still follow *timbe* (Luo traditions) of their forefathers. They seek answers to their questions of who has killed their loved ones and for what reason from *ajuoga* (in Luo, meaning witchdoctor). This was proven by the presence of many *od bilo* (in Luo, meaning shrines) that are located in different places of Kendu Bay. In some shrines, the practitioners are Luo Muslims while in others, they are non-Luo Muslims. Some

3. Shaban, interview with author.

4. See Mbiti, *African Religions and Philosophy*; Mbiti, *Introduction to African Religion*; Parrinder, *African Traditional Religion*; Gunga, "Politics of Widowhood."

informants reported that the Luo Muslims who wish to get answers to their questions about who has killed their loved one and for what reason visit those shrines secretly. Unlike the Luo Muslims, non-Luo Muslims may visit those shrines any time. They go to those shrines secretly and sometimes at night in order to avoid being ridiculed by their fellow Luo Muslims. They also do so clandestinely in order to avoid being scoffed by non-Luo Muslims. They are afraid that non-Luo Muslims may accuse them of not being true Muslims as they claim.

Based on this encounter in which some Luo Muslims still follow the traditional customs, the uttering of words, *ina lilahi waina ileyi rajiun*, send some mixed signals. These mixed gestures provide several options that are helpful in classifying Luo Muslims. As it will be demonstrated shortly by a diagram after considering other beliefs and practices at the initial stage of the Luo-Muslim funeral, the options that can rightly be classified are: non-Islamic element, partial-Islamic element, and total-Islamic element. This classification is based on the extent to which Islam has influenced the cultural perception of death among the Luo Muslims.

Ways Luo Muslims express their emotions on death

While the words, *ina lilahi waina ileyi rajiun*, are expected to be verbal as some informants pointed out, some people may choose to ponder them in their hearts. The reasons are twofold. First, because of the closeness that one had with the deceased, emotional pain may be too much to think about anything else other than the vacuum that has been left in the relationship. In that case, what may be seen are tears rolling down the cheek. The shedding of tears is common among Luo-Muslim women. On the other hand, Luo-Muslim men express that they mourn by simply becoming quiet. This was the case with the late Salama's husband. Although ordinarily he is known to be a quiet person, he became quieter than before when the death of his wife occurred. His quietness was interpreted to mean that he truly loved his wife. While in today's society many Luo men mourn the death of their loved ones by shedding tears publicly, it was not the case in the traditional society.

The shedding of tears in public by men was viewed as a weakness. Such a person would always be referred to as *dhako* (in Luo, meaning a woman). The sense of *dhako* in this case points to a weakness that should not be tolerated in a male person. The habit of keeping quiet or talking less by men as a way of showing remorse over the loss of their loved ones is something that cuts across both Islam and Luo traditional customs. The difference is only apparent in the way this silence is interpreted. The Luo Muslims believe that the silence by the husband implies that he loved his deceased wife so dearly. He can only reflect quietly over the loss he has encountered. On the other hand, some Luo Muslims described such quietness from a Luo traditional perspective to signify that the bereaved husband is aggrieved by the death of his wife. His quietness makes it less suspecting that he could have killed his wife or wished her to die. Given the two perspectives, it becomes practically difficult to tell whether the quietness among the bereaved Luo-Muslim men is centered on Islamic or Luo traditional beliefs. Most of the individuals who were interviewed insisted that since they are Muslims, they follow the ways of Islam. However, with time it is possible to draw the line. This line can be drawn by looking at the behavioral pattern of the bereaved husband in the next couple of days following the burial of his wife. If he stays aloof and is still quiet most of the time, it is an indication that the man loved his wife. He should therefore be regarded as a Muslim who totally follows the Islamic ways of life.

Another area that was used as a benchmark in testing how Luo Muslims express emotions was in the issue of re-marriage. Although a Luo-Muslim man has fewer restrictions concerning when to re-marry after his spouse has died, he is viewed as lacking emotions if he just chooses to re-marry immediately after his spouse had died. The term often used to express lack of emotions is, *ne ok ohero jaode* (in Luo, meaning he did not love his wife). Such quick marriage is believed to be informed by the Luo tradition. Such a person despite being a Muslim is still viewed as one who is not fully committed to following Muslim ways. The above criterion of ascertaining whether the attitude of a Luo Muslim whose wife has passed on represents Islamic or Luo tradition was followed in testing Salama's husband, Saleh. It was done one month after the burial. His meeting with the researcher was not planned for. It was very deliberate. Arranging the meeting with Salama's husband in advance would have made him put on a face that may not have brought a true reflection of him as was expected.

Even without planning for the meeting, he was still found to be calm and quiet. He took his time to think through the questions that he was being asked before answering them. One specific area of interest was to find out if he had a future plan to re-marry. His answer was, *Nyasaye ema chano gik moko duto*, meaning, "God is the one who plans for everything."[5] Although this was an indirect answer, the fact that he mentioned God as the one who plans for people was enough proof that he was in no way planning to re-marry soon. This shows that he loved his late wife. Islam, however, encourages a widower to re-marry as soon as possible. Re-marriage is encouraged in order not to plunge the widower into much thinking about his late wife. It is also encouraged as a way of preventing the widower from being tempted to indulge in immorality. Saleh's decision not to re-marry soon has therefore been informed by his Luo traditional belief rather than Islam.

Abdallah, who was in his eighties, made a very interesting suggestion. He said, "Some Luo Muslims find it difficult to utter the words, *ina lilahi waina ileyi rajiun,* immediately after hearing or seeing a loved one die."[6] This difficulty as he explained lies in the fact that, when those words are pronounced immediately following the demise of a loved one, other people begin to think that the individual who has uttered those words participated in the death of the deceased. The pronouncer may also be seen as someone who has been harboring bad thoughts or had wished the deceased to die. Such thoughts are considered to be true especially if the person dies shortly after having a quarrel or bitter exchange of words with the other individual. They are therefore held as lacking emotions. A Luo Muslim who is hesitant to utter the words, *ina lilahi waina ileyi rajiun* do so due to the influence that they have received from their Luo traditional background. But since not all Luo Muslims are hesitant to utter those words, it is sufficed to say that the beliefs and practices of the Luo-Muslim's perception of death have partly been influenced by Islam and partly Luo traditional.

Terminologies used to describe the deceased and their implications

Another area in the initial stage of a Luo-Muslim funeral where a comparison can be made is terminologies that are used to refer to the deceased. As it has been made clear in the previous chapter, a Luo Muslim uses different

---

5. Saleh, interview with author.
6. Abdallah, interview with author.

terminologies to refer to the dead. This difference is based on the gender of the deceased. The male deceased is referred to as *almarhun* while the female one is referred to as *almarham*. Such differences are not common in the old custom of the Luo people. It simply refers to the dead as *ringre ng'ane* (the body of the deceased). This reference is made especially in cases where the body of the deceased is being transported or has been transported back to the ancestral land in order to be buried.

Besides differentiating the deceased in terms of gender, the Luo Muslims refer to the dead as simply *ng'ane* (in Luo, meaning the deceased himself or herself). *Ng'ane* carries the essence of a person who is still alive. In other words, they refer to the deceased by their name to indicate that life has not been lost. This life is not counted in terms of physical existence but rather in terms of the impact and the legacy that the deceased has left behind. This explains why Luo Muslims are encouraged to do good deeds. These righteous deeds, as have been mentioned previously, can be in the form of building mosques or educating some orphan children. The understanding here is that it is the good deeds that the deceased has done on earth that qualify them to be called by their personal name at death.

This truth implies that the Luo Muslim who dies is believed to have been engaged in doing good deeds. During the interviews and in the two occasions (the funerals of Salama and Muhammad), the words frequently used to refer to the dead were *ng'ane onindo* (in Luo, meaning the deceased has slept). Although Islam and Luo traditions use different terminologies when referring to the dead, the concept behind *nindo* is the same. It implies that, though the deceased is physically dead, he is alive spiritually. The way this life is demonstrated is however different. In Islam the treatment of the deceased as though he was alive is shown by the way the grave is dug into two compartments. Washing the body by an odd number of people as a way of preventing any secret of the deceased from being revealed just, as it has been described in the previous chapter, is another way. But in Luo tradition, as informants explained, the belief is that the deceased *nindo* (in Luo, meaning sleeping) is demonstrated by putting besides them items such as fishing net or a piece of cloth. Those items were buried with the deceased with the understanding that they would use them in the next world. Since *nindo* as Luo Muslims refer to have a common meaning in both Islam and Luo tradition, it shows a point of continuity. The reason why the Luo Muslims still follow Luo tradition is so that they may feel a sense of belonging to the wider Luo community despite being in Islam.

Comparison between Luo tradition and Islam on ghusl (washing)

The way the Luo Muslims conduct *ghusl* is also another area where comparison is made with reference to Luo old traditions. The claim that was made by some informants that a Luo person is naturally clean and should remain clean even in the grave is quite informing. First, the caring of the body of the deceased is a ritual that has been in practice for many decades by the Luo community. This implies that the washing and the other purification rituals that Luo Muslims do to the body of the deceased are just a continuation of what they have inherited from their past Luo tradition. However, the view by other Luo Muslims that these practices were introduced to them by the Arab Muslims when they first came to Kendu Bay is contradicting. It shows that Luo Muslims are divided in thoughts in some areas of their beliefs and practices. But while the views of the Luo Muslims about the source of *ghusl* may be different, they are in agreement of what it means to them. The meaning that can be derived from their practice of *ghusl* is basically eschatological. The body is purified as a symbol that the soul of the deceased is on its way to *Jannah* or *paradiso* (paradise). However, the decision the destiny of the deceased soul is entirely left on Allah.

The similarity in both Islam and Luo tradition is found on their view of *paradiso* and *polo malo*[7] respectively. In both contexts, heaven (*paradiso* or *polo malo*) is viewed as a holy (*takatifu* in Swahili) and clean (*ler* in Luo) place. The practice of purifying the body is therefore done with this understanding in mind. Last, the Luo Muslims purify the body of the deceased as part of showing their respect to them. But as Odaga claims, this respect is something that is not new to the Luos. They have practiced it in the past

---

7. *Polo malo* literally means heaven above. It is used to distinguish it from *Polo* (sky). Sometimes *Polo malo* and *polo* are used interchangeably by both Luo Muslims and non-Luo Muslims to refer to heaven or abode of the dead. Due to what they believe, some Luo Muslims like to make distinction between paradise and hell. They do this by using Arabic words, *Jannah* and *Jahanam* respectively.

up to the present.[8] Other Luo Muslims also expressed the same. This implies that it is the form by which the deceased body is purified that has changed, and not the meaning. The alteration of the form and not the meaning is very practical in many ways. First, in both Islam and Luo tradition, the washing of the body usually takes place. However, the specific and elaborate procedures attached to the Luo-Muslim *ghusl* with the requirement of an odd number of the washing people in the same gender are Islamic in nature. They represent the domain of total-Islamic element.

Similarities in the shrouding between Islam and Luo tradition

The meaning that the Luo Muslims attach to shrouding is similar to that of the Luo traditions. Just as in Islam, Luo people use a white garment to cover their dead ones in readiness for burial. The white garment or dress is mostly used for the female while a new suit and shoes are used for the male deceased. It should however be understood that the practice of dressing up a corpse is a recent development among the Luo people. In the very words of Abdallah, Luo traditionally used to simply wrap up their dead ones using an animal skin (this done mostly for *ruodhi* [in Luo, meaning chiefs and kings]) or a mat made of papyrus or banana leaves.[9] It was done with the purpose to cover the nakedness of the deceased. If Abdallah's statement is anything to go by, then there are two aspects under which Luo traditions can be viewed. The first one involves those beliefs and practices that are followed by the Luos of today just as they were followed in the past. Another aspect is where some customs have been modified with a view to remaining relevant to the present way of living. But whether the Luo culture has been adjusted or not, the intended meaning has always remained unchanged. The details that Abdallah provided can be considered reliable. This is because of his age (he is in his eighties) and his birth in a Muslim family. Both the former and the latter signify that he has a lot of experience in both Islam and Luo traditional customs. His experience also attests to the fact that the Luos who were born and raised in Muslim families have also some knowledge about the traditional funeral customs of the Luos. It is therefore not entirely true

---

8. Odaga, *Luo Oral Literature*, 49.
9. Abdallah, interview with author.

that those who got converted to Islam at some point in their lives are the only ones who comprehend what Luo traditional customs entail.

The issue of covering the deceased's nakedness as Abdallah mentioned[10] is another area where continuity is drawn. In Islam and according to what Luo Muslims follow, this is a behavior that is instilled to people right from the time they were children. Exposing one's private parts of the body is viewed by both Islam and Luo tradition as shameful. It is also believed to encourage promiscuous behavior in the society. But as for the dead, the covering of the body signifies that the deceased has secrets that are confidential and are only known to God. It is also a way of demonstrating respect and honor to the deceased. The Luo Muslims do shrouding to both male and female differently. This is a true indication that the issue of gender is important to them. As it has been explained in the previous chapter, they cover the deceased male with three sheets while the female is covered with two sheets of white cloth. The use of a white piece of cloth to cover the body of the deceased is a practice that is followed also in Luo tradition. The Luo Muslims therefore follow what is in both Islam and Luo tradition. This similarity is because of continuity. An area where the difference between Islam and Luo tradition lies is on the number of the white sheets of cloth that are used to cover the dead and the fact that this shrouding is done based on the gender of the deceased. According to Saidi, the difference in shrouding where a male deceased uses three pieces of white cloth while the female is covered with two is believed to mean that a man is superior to a woman.[11]

The opinion of the majority of the Luo Muslims was quiet contrary to that of Saidi. They explained that they do to every Luo Muslim who has died the same rituals regardless of their gender, age or social status. They claimed that their show of no partiality is informed by the teachings in Islam. They use *sanda* to cover the body of the deceased – an illustration that all Muslims are equal in the eyes of Allah. Since they were the majority, their view was as reflecting what many Muslims practice. On this note, it suffices to say that the three and two white sheets that are used to cover the bodies of the deceased male and female respectively have very little to

---

10. Abdallah, interview with author.
11. Saidi, interview with author.

do with who is superior or eminent over the other. But even if the claim that the Luo-Muslim men are superior to women was true, the majority of the informants still believed that it is important to look at the context. The general truth that was discovered in the Initial Stage was that the rituals are carried out for the wellbeing of the deceased. This is with regard to their destiny. The same truth applies to the other stages of the Luo-Muslim funeral beliefs and practices.

The nature of sanda and its relations to God and good deeds

As many informants pointed out, *sanda* does not necessarily need to be new. In fact, as noted in the previous chapter, the old is preferred. This is very different from the Luo traditional practices where almost everything used is new including the underwear for the deceased. This difference should be understood by looking at the meaning that both Islam and Luo tradition have attached to death. By preferring to use old *sanda*, the Luo Muslims are simply following what Ḥadīth teaches. They quoted one of the caliphs of Muhammad; Ali bin Abutalib said that the new is better for the living while the old is good for the dead. His statement was in no way despising the dead but rather it meant that it is while still living that one can do the best or provide good things to others. The implication is that it is the good deeds that are done to those who are still alive that pleases Allah. It is on this account that one may be allowed to enter paradise. It was also alleged that good deeds that the Luo Muslims conduct on the dead are not meant to benefit themselves but rather to help the deceased secure a place in paradise. But whether the righteous deeds are performed with a view to bringing benefit to an individual or to the deceased, it is all left for Allah to decide the destiny of the person. The diagram below illustrates the two aspects of good deeds in relationship to the destiny of the living and the dead.

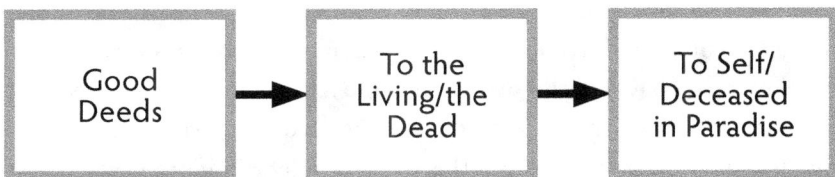

Diagram 18: Good Deed Concepts in Relation to the Dead and the Living

The idea behind the new and the old *sanda* should therefore be understood in the context of a relationship between the good deeds that a Luo
Muslim is encouraged to practice and its ultimate purpose to self or to the
deceased in the hereafter. What the good deeds imply should also be understood differently. The good actions that one does to his fellow humans
while both are alive that may merit him to enter paradise if Allah so wishes
includes: building a mosque, helping the needy, and educating the orphans.
On the other hand, the good deeds that the living are supposed to do to
the dead include: conducting *ghusl* as a group of an odd number, covering
the deceased with *sanda* as a way of keeping their secrets, praying for the
deceased, speaking publicly whether you owed anything to the deceased
or whether the deceased owed to you, and burying quickly. These events
are conducted with the hope that they would enhance the journey of the
deceased to his final destiny. They are also viewed as contributing to Allah's
fair judgment.

**Comparing the Luo tradition and Islam in relation to good
deeds and *sanda***

The idea of good deeds is also similar in Luo tradition. Whereas Islam emphasizes that the good deeds should be done to the living and the dead, the
emphasis from the Luo tradition is only on the dead. However, the fact that
it is the dead who attract considerable attention should not be construed
to imply that the Luo people do not encourage good actions and deeds
among themselves. Moral values and proper behaviors are issues that have
been passed on from one generation to the other. They are greatly cherished
by the community. But the way they perceive death and their belief in the
hereafter is what makes the difference in terms of their actions and the behaviors toward the dead. In the Luo traditional understanding the dead are
always regarded as more powerful than the living. They derive their powers
from the ancestors whom they are now very close to. They are directly and
actively involved with regulating human affairs in the community. But the
belief that they have control over human life means that they are depended
upon in every area of life. Such dependency requires that the people do
things that would please them. This explains why using old *sanda* or old
clothes for that matter does not apply in Luo thinking. It would make the
spirits unhappy. This state of being unhappy is considered very detrimental

to the community. Efforts are therefore made in order to ensure that the dead are happy. Such efforts are what are considered as good deeds. They are assigned different meanings according to different stages of the funeral. The diagram below points to the meanings that are attached to the good deeds at various stages of the funeral as viewed from a Luo traditional perspective.

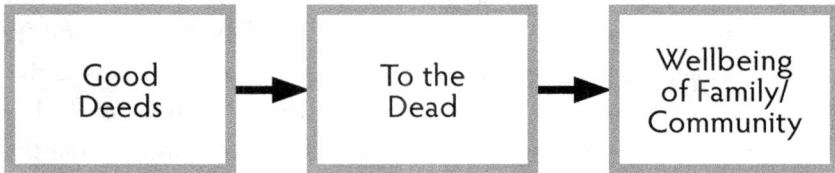

```
┌──────────┐      ┌──────────┐      ┌──────────────┐
│          │      │          │      │ Wellbeing    │
│  Good    │ ───▶ │  To the  │ ───▶ │ of Family/   │
│  Deeds   │      │  Dead    │      │ Community    │
│          │      │          │      │              │
└──────────┘      └──────────┘      └──────────────┘
```

Diagram 19: How Luo Traditions View Good Deeds in Relation to the Dead

Besides the new clothes and shoes that the deceased is made to wear, other areas that are considered as good deeds in the Luo traditional thinking include offering plenty of food and music entertainment to mourners. Libation and periodic visits to the grave of the deceased are also part of the rituals that contribute to the good deeds. In today's Luo society, *harambee*[12] is very common. Although it is conducted with a view to helping the bereaved keep on with life, the spirit behind it is to affirm to the deceased that they were dearly loved. Dignitaries who conduct this exercise and the amount of money realized attest to respect and love that the people have for the deceased. But far from pleasing the deceased, the good *deeds* are carried out with an aim of making the ancestors pronounce *gweth* (in Luo, meaning blessings) to the people, the animals, and the produce of the land. Overall, the understanding that the Luo Muslims have about *sanda* has been found to be similar in form but different in meaning to that of the Luo tradition. The similarity is historical in perspective and it relates with how the Luo used to bury their dead ones in the past. According to the informants, the Luo people never used to bury their dead ones using coffins as it is done

---

12. *Harambee* is a Swahili word that literally means pulling together. It was coined by the late Jomo Kenyatta who was the first president of Kenya. It is a call to the society to join and to put together their resources and strength in assisting each other or in order to accomplish a certain task. In today's Luo funeral, *harambee* spirit is demonstrated through fundraising. It has become part of the ritual that is done before the body is laid to rest.

today. They used to dispose the body using simple items like banana leaves except for the chiefs and kings who were buried using an animal skin (this has been pointed out in the previous section). The skin symbolizes authority. This authority was believed to continue in the next life.

Some informants believed that the *sanda* they use today in burying their loved ones actually originated from the Luo tradition. They therefore disregard the present Luo funeral practices such as putting the body in a coffin and clothing the deceased with expensive attire and shoes. They consider them as something that is nowhere near Luo tradition. Their perspective over what is traditional in Luo in relation to what they practice during funerals gives a clear indication that the Luo tradition has evolved over the years. By identifying with the old form of Luo tradition and disregarding the present one, the Luo Muslims have thus shown where their choice lies. The similarity with the old or former Luo tradition is explained in connection to how Islam first entered Kendu Bay. The Arab Muslims found many practices in Luo including the way bodies of the deceased are wrapped very similar to theirs. It was on the basis of this similarity that, as Abdul puts it, "the Arab Muslims readily identified themselves with the Luo community. They were even given Luo names."[13] Abdul's sentiment about the readiness by which Arab Muslims adapted to Luo traditions fits into the description that Lewis gives to Islam as a religion that is catholic in nature and tolerant to the African traditional religion.[14] This idea of tolerance implies that there are some Luo traditional funeral practices that the Luo Muslims still follow. They are not compatible with the Islamic practices. True to Lewis' argument, it is in the shrouding that the difference in terms of the meaning it holds has been realized. Such difference signifies that the meaning that the Luo Muslims have attached to their use of *sanda* has very little relationship with the meaning as understood from the Luo traditional perspective. It is this incompatibility of the meaning that has been classified under the domain of non-Islamic element.

But accepting and adapting to the Luo way of life by the Arab Muslims may have been intentional. This follows Omar's remarks that after settling

---

13. Abdul, interview with author.

14. Lewis, *Islam in Tropical Africa*, 60.

down and gaining some considerable converts, the Arab Muslims gradually began to change some areas of Luo practices. This included the way the dead were handled and clothed before being buried.[15] They introduced *sanda* for shrouding the body. This change is strategically religious. It supports Sanneh's view about Islam as a religion that modifies the fabric and introduces new strands and colors and patterns in the existing traditional practices.[16] *Sanda* fits very well the description pertaining to the changes that Arab Muslims have injected into the Luo funeral practices. Its use has also a lot of bearing on how Muslims view the dead people. Contrary to the Luo funeral where gender, age and social status count, *sanda* is used uniformly. In other words, those who die are covered with the same *sanda* regardless of whether male or female, old or young, rich or poor. This understanding gives very little doubt over the fact that a people who live in a society where such distinctions are common easily identify themselves with a system that accommodates them the way they are. *Sanda* is therefore used in this sense to signify the equality that all humanity have before God. This claim to equality was associated the teachings that the Qur'an provides.[17] But apart from bringing the sense of equality, *sanda* was also perceived by some informants to carry an element of hope in life after death. This hope is what its white color represents.

As it has been noted, the religious forms that the Luo Muslims hold about *sanda* are similar to the Luo tradition. There could be some similarities even in terms of its meaning between the two, but they are very minimal. The greater percentage of its meaning is completely Islamic. In other words, the meanings attached to *sanda* were much Islamic as they were passed on to the Luos by the Arab Muslims. They have been adopted into the system and are now understood and explained from an Islamic perspective. The Arabs are also believed to have replaced the way *sanda* used to be understood in the Luo traditional context. Such meanings that bear no relationship with the past practices of Luo community have been classified under the domain of total-Islamic element. But because of similarity in form and to a little extent in meaning over the way *sanda* is viewed, a third domain of partial-Islamic element was created. This domain is also associated with the middle and the

---

15. Omar, interview with author.
16. Sanneh, *Crown and the Turban*, 7.
17. Omar, interview with author.

later stages of the Luo-Muslim funeral. It is where both Islamic and Luo old customs are believed and practiced concurrently. However, some informants denied that this was the case. According to them, the similarity that is found in both Islam and Luo customs is coincidental. Some informants who were born and raised in Muslim homes denied that there is resemblance with the Luo traditions over what they believe and practice in funeral ceremonies. This denial is, however, expected since they have never known anything outside what they have been taught as Muslims. The majority of the people who fall under this category are the Muslim youths and children.

The reason why they are not exposed and can therefore not be able to tell any similarity or difference is because most of the burials for non-Luo Muslims take place on Saturdays. Those days find them in *madras*. But they also lack exposure due to the fact that what is inculcated in them at school or at home are the teachings that they are expected to follow as Muslims. This makes it difficult for them to begin thinking about what happens in other customs. Some informants even admit that there are people among them who still follow Luo traditions. They are, however, very categorical that such people are not true Muslims. Their claim provides the basis upon which one is judged. A true Muslim in this sense is defined by whether or not one is involved with Luo past customs.

The outcome of mixing Islam and Luo tradition in funeral

Keeping one foot in the old traditions and the other in Islam, as Sanneh describes,[18] is perceived by some Luo Muslims as turning against faith (backsliding). Others see it differently. They consider Islam as a religion that has evolved from the Luo tradition. In fact, Saidi describes it as a second Luo religion.[19] He meant that in terms of relationship, Islam is treated as a "son" or a "daughter" to the Luo tradition. This analogy of the father-son or father-daughter relationship implies that both Luo traditions and Islam influence each other. But while this is possible, the level at which one has influenced the other may not be equal. Saidi's description also makes it apparent what they believe and practice in the funerals are partly Islamic and partly Luo traditional. This perspective in which the Luo Muslims are believed to have

---

18. Sanneh, *Crown and the Turban*, 7.
19. Saidi, interview with author.

similar forms and meanings from both Islam and Luo tradition is in line
with what Lewis writes about:

> the ritual washing of the corpse to the accompaniment of
> prayer; the incensing of the body; the use of bier to carry the
> corpse to the grave; the standard type and orientation of the
> grave towards Mecca; the ritual funeral service conducted by
> clerics; the sprinkling of earth over the grave; the ritual mourn-
> ing of the bereaved (washing, seclusion, and purification); and
> observance of the subsequent ceremonies for the dead on the
> first, third, seventh, and fortieth days. All these elements or
> the majority of them are variously combined with indigenous
> burial ritual.[20]

However, Lewis' statement provides very little clue concerning what
kind of indigenous burial rituals are combined with Islam. It is also not very
clear whether this combination is something that happens naturally. But in
contrast, Saidi's description shows clearly that the union between the two
funeral customs is one that comes naturally.[21] However, this position may
not be taken as conclusive considering the claim by the majority of the Luo
Muslims that what they follow is purely Islamic. Due to their divergent
perspectives on what they believe and practice in the Initial Stage of their
funeral, the lifestyle of the Luo Muslim can thus be described as one that
is characterized by total, partial and non-Islamic element. However, the
degree of these influences varies greatly as illustrated in the diagram below.

---

20. Lewis, *Islam in Tropical Africa*, 70.
21. Saidi, interview with author.

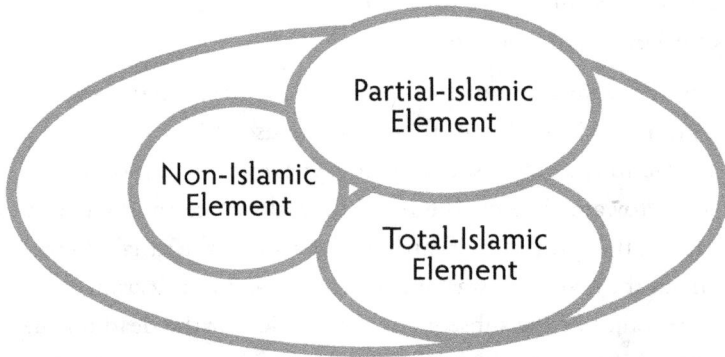

Diagram 20: Various Elements in the Initial Stage of Luo-Muslim Funeral

The total, partial and non-Islamic domains

This variation was realized based on three criteria: the ancestor-relatedness, areas of similarity, and changed perception of life. Elements in a funeral that are ancestor-related have been classified as non-Islamic element. They are represented by the small circle since they were found to be the fewest. It was followed by the domain of total-Islamic element. This is an area that shows how Islam has changed the perspectives of Luo Muslims. It is represented by the medium circle. The domain of partial-Islamic element covers the largest portion. It is therefore represented by the big circle. It shows that Islamic and Luo traditional funeral customs share many similarities and are even compatible with each other in a number of cultural areas. These three circles are quite close and not easily separable, so they are put bordering each other with the bigger circle surrounding them.

The findings as presented in diagram 19 shows that Islam has a lot of influences at the initial stage of the Luo-Muslim funeral compared to the Luo tradition. The reason that explains this is that unlike the Luo tradition, there are numerous rituals that Islam demands to be done on the body. The critical issues in Luo traditions are who has died and what or who killed the deceased. These questions were not asked out-right in the funerals that were observed. They simply came up from the informants during the interviews. They explained what would take place in a Luo traditional setting rather than what they were involved with as Muslims. It was in the shrouding, as it has been explained, that some similarities were found. The similarities are very common in form but few in meaning. This is a major characteristic of the Initial Stage of the funeral considering most of the various elements, activities, and the people involved.

Similarities and Differences in the Middle Stage

This stage covers the period between shrouding and committing the body to the grave. A common ground between Islam and Luo traditions was discovered. It is that once the body has been washed and clothed, it is displayed for public viewing. The difference was also realized. It was in relation to the duration given for the viewing of the body. According to some informants, the viewing of the body in the Luo tradition takes a longer time. This may go on as long as the body remains unburied. They however pointed out that in Islam, the time is usually shorter. But while it is true that there are differences in the approach to the viewing of the body, there are also some similarities. The similarities are due to the fact that the viewing of the body is a public affair. This means that both Luo Muslims and non-Luo Muslims attend. This was witnessed in the burial of Salama and Muhammad.

Islamic and Luo traditional perspectives of viewing of the body

The public viewing of the body was found to be similar for two reasons. First, it is a way of paying honor (*luoro* in Luo)[22] to the deceased. According to some informants, the dead must be "escorted" (*kowo* in Luo) regardless of their gender, social status, or the circumstances under which they have died. Rashid explains this process of *kowo* is very significant. It shows that the mourner is friendly and that he harbors no personal grudge with the deceased. In a broader sense *kowo* refers to attending the whole funeral of the deceased. However, the climax of it comes at the time of viewing the body and the burial.

---

22. According to the Luo Muslims, the word *luoro* denotes three things. First, it means respect. This respect is bestowed on a person on the basis of their age. But it is also bestowed on the deceased. This is regardless of their age, gender and social status. It is basically due to the new status that one has acquired after death. The second category of *luoro* is that of fear. This is mostly in the negative sense. For instance, the witchdoctors are feared because they can terminate one's life. The third category of *luoro* is to go round. Death in a way is believed to be in a form of *luoro*. The belief that the dead is alive is explained by this concept of *luoro*. *Luoro* as has been used in this context conveys the meaning of respect to the deceased.

The concept of *kowo* is also significant in other ways. It brings a sense of solidarity between the mourner and the deceased. It is a very important opportunity in the mourner's life that reminds them that they too will one day die and will be escorted in a similar way. It also carries the idea of a journey. As the Luo Muslims explained, the belief here is that the moment one dies, their soul begins to travel (*wuoth*). Ideally, they don't speak of their soul but the person themself. This is because there is no dichotomy between the body and the soul in their understanding. This journey (*wuoth*) may be very long and has very unpredictable outcomes. The presence of mourners and their individual participation in honor of the deceased are therefore believed to encourage them to travel smoothly and safely to their destiny. Rashid explained that both *kopo* (in Luo, meaning, to escort) and *wuoth* (in Luo, meaning, a journey) have their origin in Luo culture.[23] Although he was not very clear how the two terms relate to the Luo culture, a discussion by Ongong'a[24] over the term *luwo* (in Luo, meaning to follow) from which the term Luo originates from explains it (see the introduction chapter). Apart from using it to describe how the Luo people followed each other as they left South Sudan in search of pastures in other parts of Kenya, *luwo* also gives the sense of being together. This togetherness is one that speaks of offering support to each other in good and bad times. But since the deceased is not physically present, the support is offered indirectly through the mourner's own presence and by actively participating in the funeral functions.

Some senior informants like Abdallah and Bruck who were born and raised up in Muslim families and are now in their eighties and sixties respectively provided another perspective as to why Islam allows for the public viewing of the body.[25] They explained that it is a solemn moment where the mourner should take upon himself an opportunity to introspect his own life. But, whereas public viewing of the deceased is allowed, it is never forced on anyone. As a matter of fact, the time allowed is usually very limited. This is due to the fact that the deceased is required to be buried early in order to meet the two angels who upon interrogation would set them on to the next

---

23. Rashid, interview with author.

24. Ongong'a, *Life and Death*, 7.

25. Abdallah, interview with author, Kendu Bay; Said Bruck, interview with author, Kendu Bay, 17 May 2015.

stage of their journey. The interesting thing is that even with the limited time allowed, the group that are more interested in the view of the body are young Muslims. Part of the reason for this is that they still consider themselves to live youthful and active lives. The viewing thus makes them realize that they need to spend their years wisely and in full worship of Allah. Another reason why they are the ones more interested is that unlike the mature adult Muslims who are advanced in years, the Luo-Muslim youths talk freely about death. It is because they believe that they still have many years to live. More importantly is the thinking that, since they are young and have been faithfully attending teachings in *madras*, they carry very little wrongdoings compared to the older generation. The conviction that one would receive Allah's forgiveness and entrance to paradise is almost certain for them.

Kowo or *kopo* is also tied to a hero's send-off. Some Luo Muslims describe the dead as a hero (*thuon* in Luo). *Thuon* is a war-like term. It is used to show that the deceased has conquered the battles of this life and now has rested. The battle that the deceased is said to have conquered include sickness. Death in this case is not a battle but rather a passage by which the deceased has returned to his maker, Allah. Death is therefore never perceived in a bad light. Allah is also not blamed for causing death. Instead of harboring blame they praise and thank Allah for calling back to himself his own creation. Although there are some little variations to the way the concept of *kowo* or *kopo* and *wuoth* are described by the Luo Muslims, a bigger portion identifies with the traditional Luo. It is for this reason that they have been classified in the domain of non-Islamic-element.

The perceptions and the dynamics of prayer in Islam and Luo tradition

Apart from public display and the viewing of the body, prayer is another element where comparison and contrast are made. In both Luo and Islamic customs prayer is viewed as very vital. Among the Luo Muslims, however, prayer is made by an *imam* to Allah for the deceased. Others who have died, including Prophet Muhammad and Abraham, and their families are also interceded for. God is asked to forgive and bless them. In the Luo traditional society, the village elder is the one who prays. His prayers are however a plea to the ancestors to not send calamity or famine upon the living and their animals. Prayer in today's Luo society has greatly changed.

Even if the deceased or his family members are not Christians, a religious leader is always sought to come and conduct the burial. Depending on his religious background, he may pray to God to place the deceased in *mahali pema peponi* (in everlasting rest). Such prayers are similar to the prayers that a Muslim cleric makes for the deceased.

The way prayers are made carries both similarities and differences. The difference is apparent between Islam and the old tradition while similarity is evident between Islam and the current Luo practices. Based on these differences and similarities, suffice it to say that the initial stage of the Luo-Muslim funeral has a lot in common with the Luo old tradition while this middle stage identifies a lot with the current Luo funeral practices. The reason for this lies in the fact that the people who are mostly involved with the rituals in the washing and shrouding of the body in the initial stage are mostly adult Muslims. Due to their age, they tend to relate so much with the old tradition of the Luo. In contrast, the middle stage is mostly for the young Muslim adults. They are the ones with the most interest viewing the body. Since they have a lot of energy, they take upon themselves the responsibility to carry the bier to the cemetery. Their age bracket makes it easy for them to identify with the current perspective of Luo funerals that has also changed in many different ways from that of the old traditions.

The similarities and the differences in prayers to or for the deceased are explained in many different ways. First, some informants were of the view that such prayers (*dua* in Arabic) are not new. The Luo people have been offering them since the days of their forefathers. This perspective gives the assumption that the Luo person is religious. Mbiti holds to the same view when he writes that the African people are notoriously religious.[26] This sentiment almost makes it impossible to believe the argument that the *dua* were introduced by the Arab Muslims when they first came to Kendu Bay. The prayers that the Luo Muslims offer today for their loved ones who have died should be therefore viewed as having relationship with the prayers that are made from a Luo traditional perspective. The difference however lies on the meaning that is given to prayers. Luo Muslims pray for the deceased while Luo traditional prayers are made to the deceased. The former pray

---

26. Mbiti, *Introduction to African Religion*, 1.

with a view to benefiting the deceased while the latter pray with a view to benefiting the bereaved. The difference in meaning of prayer is believed to be due to where prayers are focused. Prayers in the Luo tradition are centered on the deceased. This, in the view of some informants, was done as a means of keeping in touch with the ancestors. But in Islam the offering of *dua* to Allah for the deceased is what is required. Praying to the deceased, as Siraj puts it, is a sign of lack of faith in God.[27] It also signifies that one has no *dini* (in Swahili, meaning religion). The attitude in which on one hand the Luo Muslims applaud the religion of their forefathers while at the same time denounce some aspects of it sends mixed signals. It shows that they have no single outlook with regard to the impact that the Luo traditions have made on their funeral customs. Their mixed reactions are also a gesture that they are living in a denial of the fact that they have been impacted by both Islam and Luo traditions.

Prayers beseeching God to keep the deceased's soul in eternal peace are done with the understanding that the deceased is alive though in the invisible world. The goal of such prayers is that Allah may allow the deceased to enter paradise. Although they also believe in the existence of hell, the wish and the prayer of every Muslim to their departed ones is for Allah to decide in favor of the deceased. However, the truth as to where the deceased has gone after death is something that Luo Muslims find it hard to explain. Giving direct answers would mean that they are passing judgment on the dead. This is something that only Allah himself has the prerogative to do. But not only do they struggle to explain it, they also feel uncomfortable discussing the issues of the deceased especially if they are negative. The reason for avoiding this subject is explained differently by the informants. Some simply described it as something that faith (*imani* in Swahili) discourages. By this they mean that once a person becomes a Muslim his lifestyle including the way he views the dead should conform to that of Islam. But while this is true, conforming is something that may take a long time. Even if it happens, it does not mean that one stops thinking about certain traditions that were once very fundamental to his forefathers.

---

27. Siraj, interview with author.

But the requirement to conform immediately also causes some Luo Muslims to view their religion as *polis* (in Luo, meaning a policeman or woman)[28] and themselves as victims. It further makes them portray God as someone who is always ready to pounce on the individual who speaks badly (*jaurima* in Luo) about the dead. In this case, being reluctant to talk about the dead is perceived as something that comes out of fear rather than out of the love for the deceased. This attitude of fear, though not directly to the deceased, is not different from the Luo traditional understanding. The influence from the Luo tradition on the behavior that the Luo Muslims have towards the dead cannot therefore be minimized. The difficulty to talk about the deceased was also described from a Luo traditional perspective. The informants claimed that the Luo people have been handling the dead with a lot of care right from the past. This care includes burying the dead in the grave instead of throwing it in the bush in order to be eaten by wild animals, as was the custom of other communities (they mentioned Kikuyu tribe as an example). This care also includes guarding against ill-talking (*wuoyo marach* in Luo) or bad wishes (*gombo march* in Luo) to the dead.

The concept of pwoyo/dendo/pako *in Luo-Muslim understanding of death*

The Luo Muslims attach different meanings to good deeds that are related to death. There are good deeds that a Luo Muslim does for others. These were said to be self-rewarding. In other words, they are the deeds that are pleasing to Allah. It is these good deeds that, if Allah permits, may secure a place in paradise for the person when they die. There are also some deeds that are conducted particularly in the funeral. These deeds are done in support of the deceased. In other words, the deeds are meant to be added to the good deeds that were done by the deceased when they were alive. Through these good deeds added by others, the dead person's chance to go to paradise can be more secured. All these good deeds that a Luo Muslim does whether for one's own sake or for someone else who died are described as non-verbal actions (*timbe ma wuoyo kendgi* in Luo). They are secrets that Allah alone knows. There should therefore be no bragging about the good deeds one

---

28. This term denotes to the aspects of Islam that some Luo Muslims are not comfortable with.

has done. The majority of the informants were in agreement that it is quite in order to acknowledge the good deeds that a person has done. For some, this is expressed to the person while they are still alive; for others it is done to deceased at their burial ceremony. The terms that the Luo Muslims use to refer to this recognition or praises are *pwoyo*, *dendo* or *pako*. They are usually used interchangeably (more details on these terms are in the sections that follow). But whereas there was a consensus about *pwoyo*, the way to do it was not made clear. Some Luo Muslims felt that it should be offered verbally while others were of the opinion that it should be offered non-verbally.

The Luo-Muslim concept of *pwoyo* (praises) in verbal and non-verbal Actions

In a verbal sense, *pwoyo* denotes the nice and friendly words that are uttered about someone who is still living or about the one who has died. As it has been pointed out before, in the case of the deceased, *pwoyo* is done after they have been buried. The informants described *pwoyo* as more related to the Luo tradition than Islam. According to Omar, *pwoyo* is a practice that is most commonly said for the deceased than to the living.[29] The reason given by Omar and other informants was that pouring praises to someone who is still alive would make them stumble. Stumbling here is due to the pride that may enter them. It is impossible for pride to affect the deceased. *Pwoyo*, especially when uttered about someone who is still living, was considered as a form of *sihoho* (evil tongue). Those who utter them are perceived to be doing out of ill motives. Their words are like poison that quickly brings someone's life to an end. Most of the people who are praised have made significant contributions in the community. They are labeled as "good people." According to some informants, it is these "good people" who die fast. The reason is that they receive a lot of praises from others. Since praises are like poison, receiving many of them is like receiving a lot of poison in the body. It does not take a long time before such a person dies. Abstinence from praising others is encouraged, so that they can live longer and also that people may not be accused of having killed others by evil tongue. Interestingly, some people may read mischief from someone if they fail to declare publicly in a funeral how the deceased was important to them. The good relationship the

---

29. Omar, interview with author.

deceased had with people and their positive contributions in the community are all expected to be brought in the hearing of mourners.

Praising the deceased in public exonerates the one doing it. It confirms that there was no bad blood between them and the deceased. But in the situation where one is suspected to have killed the deceased by their evil tongue, especially following a quarrel over a piece of land for example, their presence in the funeral proves their innocence. It is believed that, if they killed the deceased, it would be very difficult for them to appear at the funeral of the deceased. The reason is that the spirit of the deceased may revenge and cause them to die on the spot. If indeed there was a bad relationship between them, the suspect would come or send someone to the grave where the deceased was buried. The visit is mostly at night or any other time when nobody is watching. The intention for coming is to seek protection of oneself and their family from the spirit of the dead. They seek this protection by licking (*nango* in Luo) the soil that was used to bury the deceased. If someone is sent, they take back the soil to the suspect to lick it. Unfortunately, the person has to do this ritual of licking the soil even if their conscious is clear that they did not kill the deceased. They do this because they are aware that people might allege that they killed the dead. The context under which the person acts it is the same context under which praises of the living are perceived to be *sihoho* (in Luo, meaning, evil tongue or evil eye). In this context, being suspected is believed to poison the mind of the deceased. Once the mind of the deceased has been poisoned, they pounce on the suspect and their family with unbearable consequences such as mental illness or sudden death.

In the above discussion, it has come out clear that the Luo-Muslim concept of *pwoyo/dendo/pako* has both Islamic and Luo traditional elements. They are both similar and different in some ways. However, these similarities and differences do not lie in their meanings but in their forms. The living and the dead are praised differently by Luo Muslims. The words that are used interchangeably to signify praise in Luo-Muslim context are: *pwoyo, dendo* and *pako*. They all point to some significant contributions that somebody has made (this has been mentioned before). The same words are used in worship to Allah or the spirits of the dead as in the case of Luo traditions.

1. The significance of pwoyo *in verbal and non-verbal to the living*

During one's lifestyle, *pwoyo/dendo/pako* was said by the informants to be non-verbal. In other words, the good deeds and the positive actions that an individual has done are acknowledged, but not through words. The non-verbal aspect is due to two reasons. First, from a Muslim perspective, praises should be made verbal only to Allah. According to Rashid, praising (*pwoyo*) a human being with words (verbal) is like putting Allah on the same level as the human being. He further pointed out that praises offered to Allah are regardless of whether what has happened is good or bad.[30] Another reason why a person should not be praised is because whatever good deeds they do should be a secret between them and Allah. Verbal praises to the person are therefore viewed to be very displeasing to Allah. The person may be denied the reward or entry to paradise when they die. The people in the community are always aware of the good deeds that people do. They however keep them in their hearts. If they have to disclose them to other people, they do it by just whispering. The reason why they whisper is that the person who is being talked about may not know. During the research, the researcher encountered such an experience from his research assistant. He whispered to him about some young Luo Muslims who have built mosques and brought piped water to Luo Muslim *miji* single-handedly.[31] In order not to be construed as an evil tongue (*sihoho*), a Luo Muslim may praise another person by finishing with the word, *Mashallah* (in Arabic, meaning praise to God). This word is meant to nullify any evil effect or any bad intention that person may have had over the individual to whom they have offered praises. This simply implies that praise to Allah should be the ultimate goal of a Luo Muslim in whatever they do or say.

Some Luo Muslims offer praises to the living due to their cultural roots which they have inherited from the Luo tradition. As it has been pointed out previously, direct praise to someone is culturally unacceptable. Although there are other reasons for that, the most common one that was cited by the informants was that a person who is praised for the good he has done

---

30. Rashid, interview with author.
31. Shaban, interview with author.

is likely to die prematurely (this has been discussed before). The death of such a person is usually very mysterious. Examples include death in a road accident, a sudden illness, and disappearance to an unknown destination only to be found dead. Due to emotional, psychological and material effects that such mysterious deaths have on the family, relatives, and friends of the deceased, restraint from *pwoyo* is demanded. In some Luo traditional contexts, *pwoyo* goes beyond a person's good acts. It also applies to a situation where one person admires another or what they have. The person being admired may be handsome or beautiful. One may have a lot of wealth or beautiful and well-educated children. The words used for *pwoyo* in this context include *nganecha ber yawa* (somebody is handsome or beautiful) and *ngane nigi mwandu mangeny miwuoro* (somebody has a lot of wealth). Depending on the context by which someone speaks these words, they are never taken lightly. But the person may decide to whisper them to someone they are very close.

Somebody may also be praised non-verbally because of the good things they are doing to other people or institutions that they may not have any relationship with. Under such a context, any of these terms, *pwoyo*, *dendo* or *pako*, apply. They are non-verbally conveyed[32] by other people rather than the individual themself. On the other hand, if a person acquires wealth, education or any other achievement in life by their own effort and they use it for themself and a few people whom they are related to, the term that mostly applies is *pako*. *Pako* here becomes non-verbal. For examples, such a person may have most of their relatives staying with them. They feed them every day. *Pako* which is non-verbal can be conveyed by either an outsider or the person themself. If one uses it personally, then *pakruok* (in Luo, meaning self-praise or self-abasement) is noticed through one's expensive lifestyle and hosting many relatives in their house. The person has very little concern for the other people that they have no close relationship. Some Luo Muslims dismiss such a way of living. They term it as *gwondo* (in Luo, meaning

---

32. The non-verbal way of praise involves two things – the attendance in big numbers at the deceased and the body gestures. In the latter, mourners communicate their praises to the deceased by being very fast in the activity that they do for the deceased. For example, nobody wait to be told to go and fetch water or carry the bier to the grave. Instead of waiting to be told, the people look round to see what they can. Once they discover what to do, they do it quickly.

selfishness). Some also termed it as *sunga* (in Luo, meaning pride). They said both of them are condemned by *dini* (religion). The way that Luo Muslims practice *pwoyo* both verbally and non-verbally evidences that there are partial elements from both Islamic ethos and Luo traditions.

2. *The significance of* pwoyo *in verbal and non-verbal to the deceased*

There is a whole difference between Islam and Luo tradition concerning praises that are offered to the deceased (see the summary in table 2 below). Here the Luo Muslims have mostly been influenced by the Islamic beliefs and practices. They apply non-verbal praises. The reason why they do this is somewhat similar to the practice they carry out to the living. At the time of death, it is believed that the good or bad deeds that the deceased has been doing now speak for themselves. There is therefore no need to talk about them. Another reason is that to praise (*pwoyo*) the deceased verbally at this time is like saying that one is sure of where the soul of the deceased has gone. To use the words of Saleh, it assumes that the deceased has gone to paradise.[33] But since no human being knows the destiny of the deceased, the Luo Muslims prefer to keep quiet rather than speculating. After death, the non-verbal praises that are shown to the dead include one's presence and active participation in funeral activities. The great turnout of mourners at the funeral also communicates that the deceased was somebody who made a great impact upon the community. This large attendance and people's busy activities at the funeral are also informative. Other people who may not have known the deceased in a personal way see them and appreciate the kind of a person the deceased was.

Another form of non-verbal praise that Luo Muslims practice is by continuing to do the good things that the deceased used to do. For instance, if the deceased in their lifetime used to educate orphans and help other less fortunate people in the society such as widows, other Luo Muslims would practice the same. This means that, besides supporting the family of the deceased whose footstep they follow, those people that the deceased used to help would still continue to be assisted. But also, other Luo Muslims may decide to start similar projects elsewhere as a way of continuing in the

---

33. Saleh, interview with author.

footsteps of the deceased. Walking in the footsteps of the deceased in helping others is believed by the Luo Muslims to be a practice that has been passed on to them by their forefathers. This implies that it was a practice that was not originated by the Arab Muslims. Interestingly, following in the footsteps of their predecessors embraces a similar meaning with *luwo* (to follow). As it has already been noted, *luwo* is the root word from which the term Luo comes from.[34] In its application, it signifies that the Luo Muslims follow (*luwo*) what their forefathers used to practice. The basis of this practice lies on the understanding that the Luo people have about community. It is an institution where people share and help each other. Children are brought up with the full knowledge that any older people in the community, other than their biological parents, can also discipline and guide them in life.

This trend that is characterized by helping the less fortunate is something that as some informants attested has been very common in the Luo community. The late Tom Mboya, who was the minister of labor in the Kenyan government at the time, championed this course.[35] He used to do what famously became known as airlift to USA for his people from Suba Island. This was in the 1950s and 1960s. The airlift was an educational program where people were taken to the USA for studies. The beneficiaries of this program included people like the late Barack Obama Senior, who was the father of the former president, Barack Obama, of the United States of America. It was a program that was widespread in Luo-land. Those who have been helped were also meant to help others in the community. By so doing, they offered their appreciation indirectly or non-verbally to those who had helped them. This practice of appreciating what others have done in one's life is something that is very cyclic among Luo people. In other words, it has been followed by one generation after the other. It is for this reason that the Luo Muslims identify with it as a practice that is traditionally founded rather than Islamic. This fact makes it very obvious that it is a practice that Islam has very little influence over. It is therefore classified in the category of non-Islamic-element.

The Luo people also verbalize their praises to the deceased (see the summary in table 2 below). They also carry out positive actions and other good

---

34. Ongong'a, *Life and Death*, 7.

35. Sarah, interview with author.

deeds to the deceased. These include buying and dressing the deceased with new clothes, and *harambee* (fundraising) to meet funeral expenses such as buying food to feed the mourners. Turning out in large numbers at the funeral and other activities like digging the grave and cooking are also considered as part of the good deeds or positive actions. However, the latter are mostly done by the community members who live close. The verbal praises (eulogies) are given shortly before the burial takes places. The duration of the eulogy may be long or short depending on the social status of the people who have attended the funeral. Their social status is evident by the mode of transport they came by to the funeral. This in turn tells what kind of a person the deceased was in the society. According to the informants, the nature of the gathering of mourners that proceeds with the burial is generally the same in both Luo-Muslim and non-Luo-Muslim burials.

However, the difference is in giving of eulogies. According to some Luo Muslims, Islam does not encourage eulogies. Their argument is that the doing of good deeds is a religious obligation that every Muslim should carry out. There is therefore no need to talk about it. Second, they claim that the good deeds of a Muslim are his secret with Allah. The more secretive they are the greater acceptance is gained from him. This means that talking about them either by the individual when they are still alive or by others while that particular individual is dead simply reduces the chances of the person to receive rewards from God. Third, the good deeds that one does on earth or are done for them, when they die are not an end in themselves but a means to the end. The implication of this is that while good deeds may be rewarded, the ultimate reward that every Muslim looks forward to is entry into paradise. But since nobody is certain about this, it can only be hoped that keeping silence about one's good deeds would please Allah, thus granting entry into paradise.

While it is true that eulogy is not allowed in Islam, the Luo Muslims permit it under limited cases. It is accepted in a situation where the deceased comes from a non-Muslim background. In this case, their family members and relatives would ask the Muslim leadership that is charge of the burial to allow them to give a brief speech concerning the deceased. Even though the request is never direct, it always turns out to be the giving of eulogies. The time is, however, controlled so that the burial can take place as scheduled.

According to Azis, family members and relatives of the deceased are allowed to give their speeches as a way of showing that both the Luo Muslims and non-Muslims belong to each other.[36] What this signifies is that, despite being Muslims, their identity with their ethnic group as Luo remains strong.

Pouring verbal praises to the deceased has also been described by some informants as a practice that many past generations in the Luo community have followed. By allowing it to happen in the burial of a Luo Muslim is therefore viewed as following a tradition that has been passed on by the forefathers of the Luo community. In this sense, Ongong'a's[37] concept of *luwo* (to follow) applies. One of the concepts in a Muslim worldview that Parshall discusses is time. In looking at the value attached to it, Parshall states that Muslims have high respect for the past and tradition.[38] This implies that anything that is of the past or traditional is respected by Muslims. This truth applies to Luo Muslims in Kendu Bay. Based on this truth, allowing of time by the Luo Muslims for eulogies should be seen as part of giving respect to something which is valued by the Luo tradition. Remembering and putting into practice such traditional values signify that the old is not lost completely. It shows that the Luo tradition still thrives in some areas of Luo-Muslim funeral practices. Verbal praise that comes in eulogies has therefore been treated as representing the domains of partial and non-Islamic-element. The table below is a summary of what has been discussed in this section.

Table 2: Luo-Muslim Concepts of Praises to the Living and the Deceased in Kendu Bay

		The Living	The Deceased
Luo-Muslim Concepts of Praises: *Pwoyo/Dendo/Pako*	Islamic Perspectives	Praises are non-verbal. Mostly for positive actions or good deeds.	Praises are verbal. For positive actions or good deeds
	Luo Traditional Perspectives		Praises are verbal. For positive actions or good deeds

---

36. Odero Azis, interview with author, 15 August 2015.
37. Ongong'a, *Life and Death*, 7.
38. Parshall, *New Paths*, 66–67.

The reason for *gowi* (debts) before the burial

Although the Luo Muslims explain it differently, asking the crowd if they owed anything to the deceased or if the deceased owed them anything before the burial takes place is a similar practice in Luo tradition. The similarity is in the meaning. The reason why it is done is so that the deceased may be cleared of any obstacle as he travels to his place of eternity. It is a form of purifying the deceased from any blame that may hinder them or cause Allah not to permit them to enter paradise. The informants saw this practice as something not new in Luo customs. Many incidences were cited by the informants; a relative of the deceased, preferably a very close family member, asks the mourners before the burial is conducted if anyone owed the deceased anything or if the deceased owed anybody anything.

This asking by the spouse or any other close relative of the deceased is accepted in all Luo-Muslim funerals if requested. Otherwise it is the imam who usually does the asking. He does it out of the simple reason that the relatives of the deceased are still in pain and therefore may not have the strength to speak. But it is still taken positively when a relative or a close family member of the deceased announces it. In fact, it is considered much better as Ahmad puts it: "The [close family member or relative] knows the deceased better than anybody else."[39] So in this case, the important thing that matters is not who has done it, but rather whether it has been done. The question as to whether it has been done implies that it is the wellbeing of the deceased that is of great concern. This practice among the Luo Muslims shows a similar bearing between Luo tradition and Islam. The concern for the deceased in the case of the Luo tradition is however meant to benefit the living. The deceased is believed to be less troubled and therefore their spirit would not torment the living. But in the case of Islam, it is conducted with a view to benefiting the deceased. His soul would travel faster to its final destination. The fact that there is concern for the deceased gives a clear indication that both Islam and Luo tradition have influenced each other. With this view in mind, it is logical to talk of partial-influence in this part of the middle stage of the Luo-Muslim funeral.

---

39. Omar Ahmad, interview with author, Kendu Bay, 22 May 2015.

Transporting the body to the graveside

Once prayers which come after the viewing of the body have been made, the next step is to carry the body to the burial ground. This is usually done by men. The reason is partly because men are strong and partly because they are emotionally stable. As it has been noted in the previous chapter, the body can be buried either at the deceased's home or in the cemetery. The place where the body is to be laid always rests with the family of the deceased to decide. This is irrespective of whether they are Muslim or not. The burial of Muhammad that took place in his home is a typical example of how his family's choice was honored. When it is done at home, the rule that prohibits women not to come near the burial site may not be applied in its entirety. The reason for this is that the home has so many people who have come to condole with the bereaved. But while women are allowed to watch the proceedings, they do so at a distance.

Even though they are expected to be far away from where the burial is being conducted, the presence of women in the funeral points to the similarity with the Luo tradition. Their presence is however completely prohibited when the burial is at the cemetery. The dividing of the grave into two layers (inner and outer layers) and the laying of the body facing Mecca are all practices that are Islamic. The former signifies that the deceased is alive and is on a transition into the next life while the latter symbolizes that the deceased was a true Muslim who followed in the footsteps of Prophet Muhammad. Although other areas of funeral rituals are all important, it is the way someone is finally laid to rest in the grave that tells whether they were a true Muslim or not.[40] It therefore means that the direction that the head of the deceased faces is non-negotiable in the Luo-Muslim funeral. Since it is the last ritual that is believed to usher in the two angels who come to interrogate the deceased, it is considered fair for the deceased to be laid with their head facing Mecca. This is therefore totally an Islamic influence.

The apparent difference with the Luo tradition is also meant to minimize the perception that the Luo Muslims conduct funeral practices that are identical with non-Luo-Muslim practices. But the essence of facing a particular direction, even if not the same direction, is a common custom in

40. Omar, interview with author.

both Luo tradition and Islam. Unlike in Islam where both male and female are buried with their heads facing Mecca, in Luo tradition the direction that the deceased faces depends on the gender. It is also determined by their age. As other informants argued, facing only one direction is not only done out of the religious mandate but also viewed as simple a practice to follow Islam, not Luo tradition. The Luo tradition, they said, is very complicated since, besides gender and age, other factors such as the nature of death and the marital status of the deceased at the time of death are also considered. Burial in an Islamic way is also considered as not discriminating since both genders are accorded the same treatment. One of the reasons why the Luo Muslims prefer to bury their dead ones in the cemetery is due to the said complications in the Luo tradition. It is the very reason that has led some people to convert to Islam. Persons born in Muslim families also cite the difficulty as a reason why they have held on to their Islamic faith. For instance, Jimila who is in her fifties puts it: "*Yik mar joluo nigi chike mathoth.*"[41] What this literally means is that burial in Luo has so many traditions. The many traditions pointed out include the feeding of mourners and wife inheritance. They are discussed in the next section. In summary, Luo traditions have affected the Luo-Muslim funeral practices in different ways as illustrated in the diagram below.

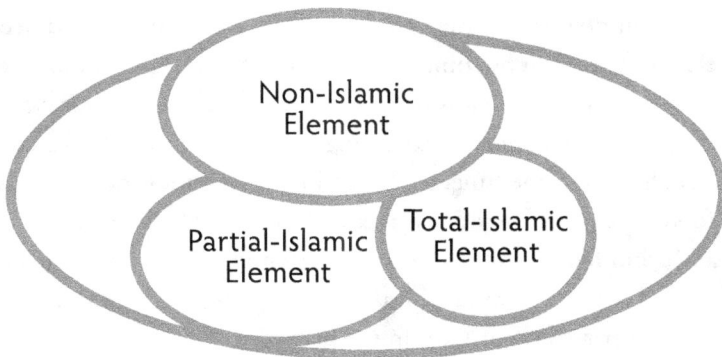

Diagram 21: Luo Old Customs in the Middle Stage of Luo-Muslim Funeral

---

41. Jimila, interview with author.

The total, partial and non-Islamic domains

As shown in the diagram, the area of non-Islamic element is the most dominant in the middle stage of the Luo-Muslim funeral followed by the domain of partial-Islamic element. The portion of total-Islamic element is the least category. The interpretation of this is that many of the Luo-Muslim funeral practices in the middle stage are basically Luo traditional in nature. This is represented by both the domains of non-Islamic and partial-Islamic elements. The domain of partial-Islamic element shows that the funeral practices being conducted are similar to both Luo tradition and Islam. They are therefore said to influence each other. Although some practices in this middle stage are purely Islamic, they are not as many as compared to those that are purely from Luo tradition or the ones that border between Luo tradition and Islam. The domains of non-Islamic element and partial-Islamic element are areas that show incompatibility and compatibility of both Islam and Luo funeral customs respectively.

Similarities and Differences in the Later Stage

As the name suggests, the later stage includes the activities that are conducted following the burying of the deceased. The two main activities are the feeding of mourners and the rituals pertaining to the widow in case the deceased was a married man. The former can also take place in the middle stage. This mostly depends on the population of mourners who have attended the funeral. If the number is very big and the burial is not to be delayed, feeding is done early. The claim by some Luo Muslims that feeding of mourners at the funeral is something that is never practiced in Islam makes it clear that they do it for a different reason. According to Saidi, in the beginning cooking was never allowed in the funerals. Instead it was the mourners who would bring food especially for the bereaved.[42] Saidi, who was born and raised up in a Muslim family and is now in his seventies, speaks out of his many experiences. He is acquainted with the teachings and the practices that the Arab Muslims passed on to Luos in the past.

---

42. Saidi, interview with author.

The Luo-Muslim concept of food in funeral

Food was brought to the bereaved because they were believed to be the ones experiencing sorrow and pain due to the loss of their loved one. It was a way of consoling and showing solidarity with the bereaved. But Saidi claims that with time this practice was easily assimilated into the Luo tradition.[43] It points to an area in Luo-Muslim funeral practices where Luo tradition has dominated. This is very much so considering that in the current Luo-Muslim funeral, cooking and feeding of mourners are very common. The change, which is basically Luo traditional, is followed for two reasons. First, the funeral is a social gathering that brings people from both near and distant places. According to Shaban, the Luo celebrates such a gathering with food.[44] It should be understood, however, that the context under which such social gatherings were climaxed with plenty of eating was ideally in the distant past. This was a period where there was plenty of food. The practice of offering plenty of food as it were in the distant past has been maintained in this present era by both Luo Muslims and non-Luo Muslims as well. This implies that Luo hospitality is a virtue that does not change with the changing of time. It therefore means that eating at the funeral would always continue in any season of the year and as long as there is a funeral within the community.

The Luo Muslims also practice cooking and supply food to mourners who have come from a distance. Most of the informants were in agreement that it is a shameful thing for someone to travel that far and go back again without eating. That the bereaved family is the one responsible for hosting the guests at the funeral is regarded as normal. It is abnormal, as some informants also put it, to carry food from a distance so as to come and eat at the funeral. It is viewed as shameful to the bereaved. However, the bringing of food to the funeral as Islam requires is still practiced in very rare occasions. Providing food to mourners in the funeral is part of the concept that defines what *yiko/kopo malongo* (in Luo, meaning decent burial) and *wendo* (in Luo, meaning visitor) are in a Luo-Muslim funeral. Diagram 22 shows the concept of decent burial and its components, and diagram 23 presents the meaning of *wendo* and its components that relate to it.

---

43. Saidi, interview with author.
44. Shaban, interview with author.

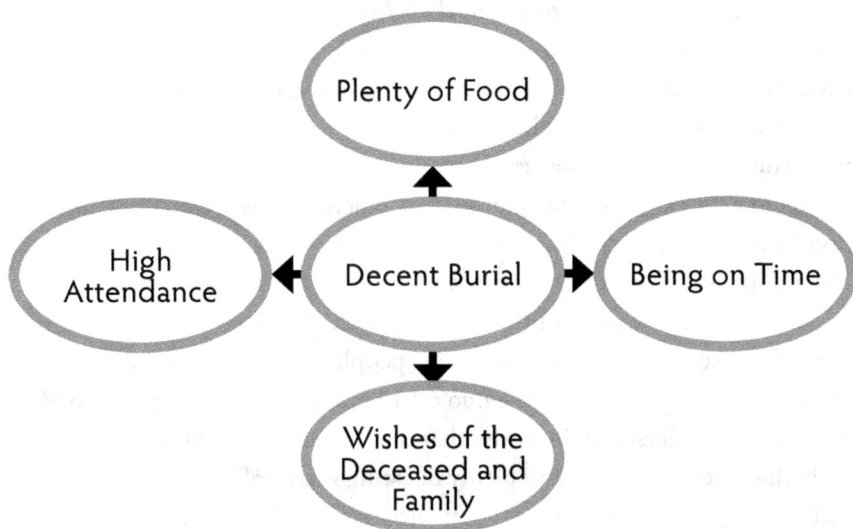

Diagram 22: The Concept of a Decent Burial in Luo Islam

The Luo-Muslim view of decent burial

The understanding that the Luo Muslims have about a decent burial (*yik mamungwana*/*yik mar ngama oyiedhi* in Luo) is not very different from the Luo traditional understanding of it. Out of the four components of a decent burial, it is the idea of burying on time that shows the difference. As diagram 22 shows, a decent burial is one that has plenty of food. A measure to determine the plenty of food is whether all the people present at the funeral eat and much food is still left. So, a Luo Muslim describes a well planned and successful burial as one that is characterized by plenty of food. The difference, however, lies in the slaughter of animal. The Muslims would always carry out the exercise of slaughtering an animal in line with Islamic teachings.

A decent burial includes being attended by many people. The presence of many cars and plenty of tents where the guests sit tell that the burial is a very special or unique one. The wishes of the deceased and their family point to another area that defines a decent burial. In other words, the decency is the sense that the burial has been conducted in the way the deceased had wanted it to be. The way they wanted it to be may have been communicated to their family members and relatives sometime before they died. It is mostly those who die out of sickness that would wish to explain to their family members what they would want to happen in their funeral. Sometimes family members may request to delay the burial in order to wait for other family members who live far away. The delay may also be due to waiting for what the deceased had wanted to be done in their funeral. If it involves incurring some expenditure, then at the opportune time when the funds to buy what he has requested are available, other procedures may be undertaken to complete the burial processes.

As it has been pointed out before, it is in the concept of time that Islam is different from the Luo tradition. The idea of burying on time (within twenty-four hours) is completely Islamic. However, the meanings that the Luo Muslims have attached to what they refer to as a decent burial share more in common with the Luo tradition than with Islam. Areas in decent burial of the Luo Muslims where Islamic and Luo traditional elements are compatible is because of continuity. Those compatible areas show a partial influence by Islam. Areas in the decent burial of the Luo Muslims where Islamic and Luo traditional elements are incompatibility show discontinuity. The difference represents a non-Islamic-element. In other words, the difference signifies that there are areas in Luo-Muslim funerals that some Luo traditional values are still attached to.

The Luo-Muslim understanding of wendo (visitor)

Diagram 23 shows the Luo-Muslim understanding of "visitor" in relation to the deceased. This concept and the "decent burial" are related to each other. They are the basis upon which Luo Muslims have developed the idea of preparing and distributing food to the mourners by the bereaved family and relatives. As it has already been pointed out, this is contrary to the practice that the Luo Muslims used to have during the early periods of Islam in Kendu Bay. There are four sub-concepts that are related to the Luo-Muslim concept of wendo: hereafter, deceased, time, and distance. The concept of visitor has been described in relation to each of its sub-category.

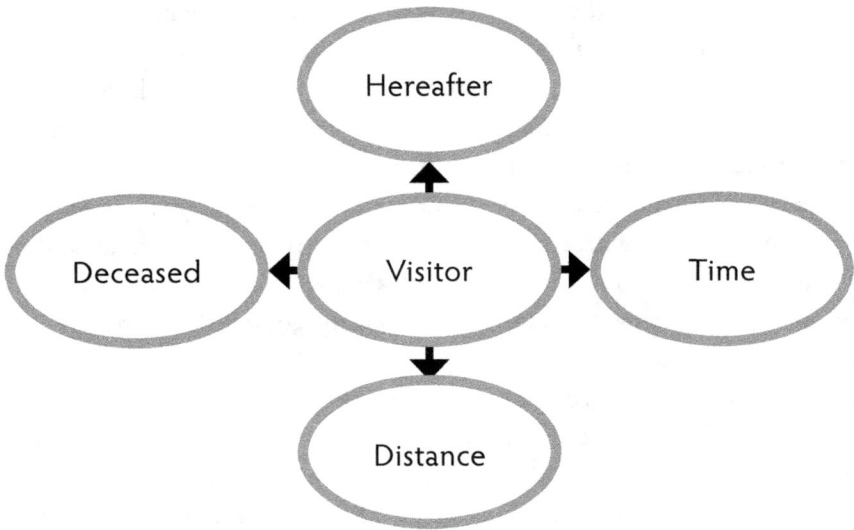

Diagram 23: The Concept of a Visitor in Luo-Muslim Funeral

The concept of visitor (*wendo*) in relation to time.
As indicated in the diagram, the concept of visitor is explained in four different ways. First, it is in relation to *ndalo* (time in Luo). The people who are in
this category are those who have not met with the deceased *ndalo mangeny*
(for a long time in Luo). Most of them are people whose homes are in the
neighborhood but currently live in the city or somewhere distant. They may
not be related to the deceased by blood but by the virtue that their original
homes are close by; they come home to mourn their departed community
member. Such a person under this category may not necessarily be a Muslim
like the deceased. In fact, at the time of death, one's religion matters very
little. What is greatly important is that a fellow tribesman or tribeswoman
has died. The Luos tend to ignore the religion to which they belong and
simply commit their time and energy to offer a deserving send-off to the
deceased purely on the grounds that they belong to the same community.
It raises a question as to whether Luo Muslims are first Luo then Muslim or
whether they are Muslim first then Luo? Mazrui also poses a similar question

with regard to Yoruba Christians and Muslims in Nigeria.[45] That question brings into doubt the possibility of being a Muslim or a Christian without having any relationship with the past tradition.

The past tradition here signifies the things that happened long time ago. It carries the value of time. Although distantly placed by time, the fact that Luo Muslims still do the rituals that are done within the context of Luo tradition is a sure indication that they still value those past traditions. They see no need to abandon the practice of providing a proper send-off[46] to the deceased. Time here plays a very significant role. It shows that the past is as good as the present. In fact, in some cases as have been explained in a different section, the past is viewed by some to be more important than the present. The past refers to the Luo traditions while the present refers to the religion of Islam that the Luo Muslims follow. These remarks, by some informants, that the past is as good as the present or more important than the present, imply that being in Islam does not completely alienate a Luo Muslim from their past tradition. Holding on to the Luo customs that have existed for many years makes it clear that the Luo traditions occupy a special place in the life of a Luo Muslim. The value that a Luo Muslim has placed on Luo traditions implies that their perspective on death is not purely Islamic but rather a mix of both Islamic and Luo traditions.

The concept of visitor (*wendo*) in relation to distance.
In relation to distance, a visitor is understood as someone who lives very far (*jaloka* in Luo). The person may have some blood relations with the deceased such as marriage. People in this category therefore include the in-laws or other relatives who once lived very close but moved to other places due to land issues or in search of better living standards. They cannot attend the funeral and go back without eating. Since they could be relatives by blood, going without eating is regarded as shameful. If, for example, they have married a woman from the deceased side and they have come to the burial

---

45. Mazrui, "African Islam and Competitive Religion," 504.

46. As it is in the Luo tradition, a proper send-off for a Luo Muslim involves the slaughtering of many cows and chickens and making sure that everyone who attends the funeral has eaten. It also involved burying the deceased in an expensive casket. The presence of many vehicles and dignitaries in the compound of the deceased is part of a proper send-off package (*kopo moyiedh* in Luo).

and gone back without eating, the woman will always be reminded after the funeral of how bad and disrespectful her people were. In fact, these distant relatives may go away protesting. This experience never fades from their minds easily. They would keep on referring and comparing it with other funerals that may come afterwards. In this sense, food becomes not only a social platform where people interact; it is also a cultural instrument to soothe the hearts of people toward each other. It also builds and enhances relationship between distant relatives and the host family.

The concept of *wendo* in relation to the distance also includes a person who lives far and yet is not directly related to the deceased. They may be a friend or a neighbor to the relative of the deceased. This friendship may be due to the business that they do together, a colleague in the workplace or a learning institution. It may also be due to the fact that the person who has lost their relative and their friend belong to the same religion. The friend or the neighbor of the person whose relative has died would attend the funeral of the deceased as well. This is a way of showing that even though they were not related or may not have known the deceased, on the account of their friendship or acquaintance with the relative of the deceased; they are now related. They would be served with food just like their friend that they have accompanied to attend the funeral of the deceased.

The concept of a visitor (*wendo*) in relation to the deceased

In relation to the deceased, every person who attends the burial is regarded as a visitor (*wendo*) to the deceased. This means that, whether one knows the deceased or not, the fact that they have come makes them considered as a visitor or guest for the deceased. It is for this reason that all sorts of people who attend the burial will, in turn, eat when the time comes. Giving food to everyone who has showed up for the burial signifies that the deceased was a very generous person. It is hard to deny someone food not only on religious grounds but also on the account of the deceased. If one is denied food or for any reason fails to eat, it is believed that this would turn to be a curse to the deceased.

Taking care of *wendo* (visitors) to the deceased is one of the greatest duties that people enjoy doing. They enjoy it because of the feeling that they are doing it for the deceased. It is as if the deceased was serving the people personally. The deceased is believed to be happy when they "see" the big number of people at their funeral. They also are thought to "feel" happy that they are being served with food. This, however, is a Luo traditional mindset. There are two reasons why the Luo Muslims enjoy serving food to the visitors on behalf of the deceased. First, it shows that the deceased was a generous person. Their generosity is believed to be part of the good deeds. It increases their chances to enter paradise. Serving food to mourners on behalf of the deceased also shows that the deceased was liked. This liking is a concept that is familiar in the Luo traditions. According to some informants, when a stranger comes to somebody's house and finds the owner is not around, neighbors or relatives of the host would take care of them. Upon the return of the owner of the house, they would feel pleased that their guest has been taken care of. It would prove that their neighbors and relatives who have taken care of their guest like them.

The concept of visitor (*wendo*) in relation to the hereafter

The last category is in relation to the hereafter. This is a religious perspective which takes into account that everybody, that is the deceased and those who have attended the funeral, view themselves as visitors in this world. The term *wendo* still applies here. It is during the post-burial period that, as people gather in small groups to eat, they begin to talk about how life is short. As it has been said elsewhere, they do not talk directly about the deceased but rather how Allah is good and that it has pleased him to take to himself the deceased. By directing their thoughts to Allah in relation to death, they are simply acknowledging that it is Allah who is the giver of life. But while this is going on, other small groups elsewhere also talk in low tones about the untimely death of the deceased. Their understanding of the untimely death is not only based on the age in which the deceased has died but also on the nature of death. The low tone in which they talk is because Islam does not allow such a talk. These mixed reactions and talk about the demise of an individual make it clear enough that the Luo Muslims hold both Islamic and Luo traditional understandings of death.

The belief that there is life in the hereafter makes every Luo Muslim consider themselves as *wendo* (visitor) on this earth. It is for this reason that the Luo Muslims use the term *onindo* (in Luo, meaning the deceased has slept) or *oyweyo* (in Luo, meaning the deceased has rested) when referring to the deceased. These terms have very little reference to hell or to someone who is believed to have gone there. In their Islamic teachings, hell is described as a place of *sand* (torment). There is no rest there. The same terms (*onindo* and oyweyo) are used in Luo tradition. In addition, they refer to where the deceased has gone, which is the same as *polo* (heaven or paradise). The concept of hell is very scanty in the Luo cosmology. How Luo Muslims describe the dead and the place to which they have gone is very similar to the Luo traditional understanding. This similarity makes it possible to believe that there could be sharing in both Islamic and Luo traditional beliefs. The fact that Luo Muslims hardly mention hell despite being part of the teachings that they follow makes it certain that they have inherited the mindset of Luo tradition. But this may not be taken as conclusive due to the uncertainty that they have about what Allah decides for those who have died.

The Luo-Muslim view of widow and her state

Besides supplying food to mourners, rituals pertaining to the widow are also conducted in the later part of the Luo-Muslim funeral. Interestingly, a husband whose wife passes on has very few rituals to perform. This means that it is largely women who get subjected to many rituals when their husbands die. The Luo people use the term *chi liel* to refer to a widow. It is a common word that even Luo Muslims use. There is therefore no difference in terminologies when describing a widow. However, the actual events and activities which are carried out or followed by a Luo-Muslim widow are where similarities and differences between Luo tradition and Islam can be made, as shown in the table below. The Luo-Muslim *'iddah* (in Arabic referring to a widow's waiting period), is related to *chola* or *okola* in Luo tradition.

Table 3: The Widowhood in Islamic and Luo Traditional Customs

'Iddah	*Chola* or *Okola*
If a widow was pregnant at the time of her husband's death, the child belongs to the deceased.	If a widow was pregnant at the time of her husband's death, the child belongs to the deceased.
Children born after in the marriage with the new husband belong to him.	Children born with the man who has inherited the widow belong to the deceased husband.
'Iddah period lasts for four months and ten days	No specified period in *Chola* or *Okola*
A widow can be re-married to the husband of her choice.	A widow is inherited; *ter* (cohabits with a man not usually of her choice). In former days *ter* was not allowed. A kin would take care of the widow and her children by providing materially. *Ter* applies today because of youthful age of many widows.
A widow is restricted to her house (younger widows are more restricted than the older ones).	A widow is restricted to her house (younger widows are more restricted than the older ones).
'Iddah begins from the time the husband is buried.	*Chola* begins from the time the husband dies.
Transition to a new life through a wedding (*nika*)	No wedding; Transition to a new life through sexual intercourse
The new couple chooses where to stay: (i) The deceased home (ii) The new husband's home (iii) The mijiji (Muslim homestead in Kindu Bay) (iv) Completely new place	Limited options for where to stay; A widow may not leave her deceased husband's home. The new husband does not also leave his home. He pays visit to the widow mostly for sexual purposes then goes back to his home.
The widow accepts gifts (*mahr* in Arabic) from her new husband as dowry. He may give some gifts (*kafa* in Arabic) to the widow's parents.	The wife takes a goat to her parents' home the following morning after sexual intercourse with the new husband.

Similarities and differences between *'Iddah* and *Chola* or *Okola*

There are similarities and differences between *'iddah* and *chola* or *okola*. The Luo Muslims apply the term *'iddah* as a way of avoiding what they claim to be the mixing of practices between Islam and the Luo traditions. The way they described *'iddah* period was found to be similar to the way *chola* or *okola* has been described in the Luo traditions. For example, Luo Muslims claimed that in the *chola* of the old Luo tradition, *ter* or wife inheritance was never meant to have any sexual relationship but rather, to provide material support to the widow and her children. The male relatives of the deceased took it as their responsibility to cater for these needs. The reason why this involvement was common was because of the belief that a wife is not only married to her husband but also to the entire community. Everyone therefore felt obliged to offer assistance to the family of the deceased. Providing for the needs of the widow and her children was also done as a sign of good will to the deceased. If a widow was still young enough to bear children, she was free to choose one of her brother-in-laws or a cousin of the deceased to take her as his wife. This was meant to preserve the deceased lineage since the children born were considered to belong to her late husband. According to some informants, sleeping with the widow and not providing for her needs and that of her family as are practiced by the non-Luo Muslims today are not true Luo traditions. The view that the informants hold implies that Luo traditions have two parts; the old or former and the new or latter traditions.[47] It is the old Luo traditions of *chola* or *okola* that the informants believed have a relationship with *'iddah*.

The freedom for a widow to choose whom she wants to re-marry makes it clear that there is continuity between *chola* and *'iddah*. This continuity, which is based on the similarity of the freedom that a widow has, is, however, linked with the former or old Luo traditions. Another example of continuity that also provides some form of similarity is on the restrictions that are imposed on the widow. In both *'iddah* and *chola*, it is mostly the younger widows who are more restricted. The restriction is out of fear that they may turn to

---

47. The old/former Luo traditions are believed to be the beliefs and practices that the forefathers of the Luos used to follow. The new/latter Luo traditions are the beliefs and practices of the current Luos. They are the new version of the old Luo traditions. The current Luos have modified them and therefore they consider them relevant. Some Luo Muslims relate to the old or former Luo traditions while others identify with the new or latter Luo traditions.

immoral living since they are still sexually active. The provision for *nika* (a wedding) has been made in order to minimize this immoral behavior. But this *nika*, as some informants admitted, is very recent. It has actually been modified from *ter* in Luo tradition. The reason for modification is because *ter* in which sexual intercourse is involved is considered very unfair to the widow. It is also considered as binding to the widow to have no choice over where she would want to stay. She is limited to stay at her late husband's home (all these limitations that a widow encounters are mostly associated with the new or latter Luo traditions).

By differentiating between the former and the latter Luo tradition, the Luo Muslims have thus underscored that the Luo tradition has gone through transitions. In other words, what is being perceived and understood today has very little relationship with what used to happen in the distant past. It is the similarity between *'iddah* and *chola* together with the modification that Luo Muslims have done, which have attracted many Luo widows to Islam. As it has been pointed out in the previous chapter, the point at which many Luo people get converted to Islam, especially women, is during the demise of their husbands. Women who are affected most are those who reside in Kendu Bay. The majority who live far away in the city and come home because they must bury their husbands end up going back to the city a few days after, if not immediately after the burial. They do this in order to escape *ter*. Wife inheritance is a concern that faces other religions as well. For instance, some informants reported how their Christian friends have been blaming each other for encouraging their daughters or daughter-in-laws to accept *ter*. Those who insist on *ter* argue that failure to do it would bring *chira* (in Luo, meaning curse) to their children.

Similarities and differences on the visit to the deceased's grave

Long after the deceased is buried, Luo Muslims are encouraged to be visiting the grave. It was explained that they do it in order to remind themselves of death, Islam and God. This is actually what is practiced in Luo tradition even though the reason for the visit is said to be different. It is not easy to make the distinction since besides being reminded about death, Islam and God, recalling the good memories and addressing the dead as if he was still alive cannot be avoided. Together with this is the temptation to pour libation. Those are deeds that are founded in Luo tradition. Acting or thinking about them simply implies that one has reverted to the old customs. In summary, there are similarities and differences of Islamic and Luo traditional customs as practiced in the later stage of a Luo-Muslim funeral as shown on the diagram below.

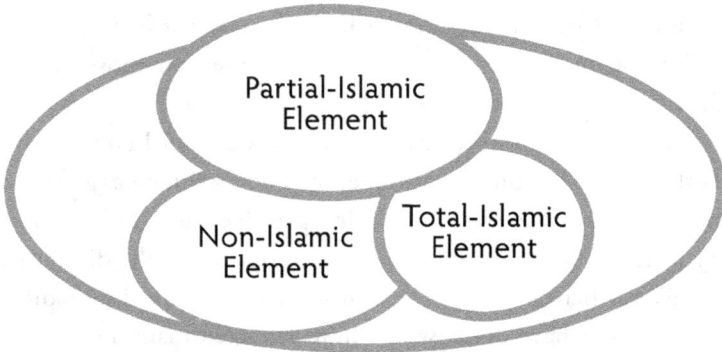

Diagram 24: Luo Old Customs in the Later Stage of Luo-Muslim Funeral

The total, partial and non-Islamic domains

As illustrated in the diagram, the domain categorized as the largest is partial-Islamic element. Both Islamic and Luo traditional practices were found to be compatible with each other in many ways. This implies that the majority of the practices that Luo Muslims conduct after the burial border between Islam and Luo tradition. The distinction is very minimal in those practices. The domain of partial-Islamic element is followed closely by the domain of non-Islamic element. A lot of the practices under this domain are basically Luo-traditional in nature. The last category is the domain of total-Islamic element. It is the smallest category and signifies that the Islamic elements that the Luo Muslims carry out in their later stage of a funeral are very few. Overall, the diagram shows that it is the Luo traditional customs that are mainly followed by the Luo Muslims in the later stage of their funeral. However, the bordering of each other makes it almost impossible to talk of one and not the other. The information about how the different stages of the Luo-Muslim funeral have been affected is presented in the following tables, which have used the taxonomic analysis by Spradley.[48]

Table 4: Type of Luo Traditions Impacting in Stages of Luo-Muslim Funeral

Stages	Type of Luo Traditions that are Impacting
Initial	Old/Former Luo traditions
Middle	Current/Latter Luo traditions
Later	Old/Former Luo traditions

Table 5: Participation by Age in Stages of Luo-Muslim Funeral

Stages	Participation by Age
Initial	Luo-Muslim Adults Muslims
Middle	Luo-Muslim Youths and children
Later	Luo-Muslim Adults Muslims

Table 6: Participation by Gender in Stages of Luo-Muslim Funeral

Stages	Participation by Gender
Initial	Both male and female
Middle	Male
Later	Female

Table 7: Impact of Luo Traditions in Stages of Luo-Muslim Funeral

Stages	Impact of Luo Traditions
Initial	Little
Middle	Moderate
Later	Great

---

48. Spradley, *Ethnographic Interview*, 132–154; Spradley, *Participant Observation*, 113–121.

The Influence of Islam and Luo Tradition in the Three Stages of Luo-Muslim Funerals

Table 4 shows the type of Luo tradition that has affected the different stages of a Luo-Muslim funeral. In the initial stage, it is the former Luo traditions that have affected it most. These are traditions that are said to have been the ones practiced by the forefathers of the Luo people. They are cherished mostly by adult Muslims (see table 5). The reason why adult Muslims value them is because most of them, by the virtue of being advanced in years, have good memories of the kind of Luo values that were passed on to them by their forefathers. They received those values way back, even before Islam entered Kendu Bay. Both genders participated in the initial stage (table 6). This participation is determined by the deceased. If the deceased is a female, it is the women who wash and shroud her body. But if the deceased is a male, it is men who clean and prepare his body for burial. The level of impact of old or former Luo traditions old or former is, however, little in the initial stage (see table 7). The reason for this is that it is at the initial stages following the demise of a loved one that the Luo Muslims come out in large numbers as a show of solidarity to the deceased. They therefore make sure that their actions and the deeds that they practice on the dead are Islamic. It is also believed that the way they respond and act after a fellow Muslim has died is the one that gives the first impression about Islam. The practices must therefore be predominantly Islamic.

In the middle stage the most dominant Luo traditional practices emerge from the current or latter Luo traditions (see table 4). The reason behind this is that the majority of the participants are Luo-Muslim youths and children (see table 5). It is easy to understand why that is so by looking at the activities involved. What is very crucial is the carrying of *geneza* (bier) to the burial ground. Young people in general are strong enough to carry it. They also include children attending to other needs in the funeral such as fetching water and firewood. But another reason is that the current or latter Luo traditions have a lot in common with contemporary lifestyle. The youths and children easily flow with that kind of a lifestyle. But while the group that is most involved in the middle stage consists of youths and children, the majority of the activities such as carrying and burying the deceased are limited to men (see table 6). Since they are in an age of influence and would want to do things according to the current fashion and in steps with their peers, the impact of the Luo traditions (new or latter) is moderate at this stage (see table 7).

The later stage of the Luo-Muslim funeral is characterized by the old or former Luo tradition (see table 4). The activities here are mainly feeding mourners and conducting rituals associated with widowhood. The former or old Luo traditions were viewed as offering a fair treatment to women as compared to the new or latter Luo traditions (see the section, "Similarities and Differences between 'Iddah and Chola or Okola"). Since the rituals mostly affect widows, the involvements by age are adult Muslims (see table 5). They are the ones who have good memories about their past heritage from their forefathers about the rituals that follow after death. In respect to gender, it is the female who mostly participate (see table 6). This is particularly so when they have lost their husbands. The participation of male adults, youths and children are very minimal at this stage even if they have lost somebody close to them. The Luo traditional impact (old or former) is great (see table 7). Luo-Muslim practices have a lot in common with the Luo traditions at this later stage of the funeral. It is also at this stage that adult Muslims are very active in sharing the good memories of the deceased. Since youths and children are less interested in such stories, their involvements become limited. A summary of how Luo traditions in relation to Islam have affected the different stages of a Luo-Muslim funeral is thus displayed in diagram 25.

The diagram shows how Luo Muslims have interacted with Islam and Luo tradition at different stages of their funeral. The figures on the vertical side of the diagram have been used to represent the level that each domain has reached in every stage of the Luo-Muslim funeral. Going by the figures,[49] partial-Islamic element has a total of 12.1 (4.3+3.5+4.3). Total-Islamic element has 8.5 (3.5+2.5+2.5) while non-Islamic element scored 10.4 (2.5+4.3+3.5). The scores place partial-Islamic element at the top followed by non-Islamic element. The least is the domain of total-Islamic element. An interpretation of this is that both Islam and Luo traditions have influenced the cultural elements, people involved, and the various activities and

---

49. The numerical figures as shown in the diagram are the researcher's own initiative. The numbers help him to understand the extent to which Islam and Luo traditions have influenced the Luo-Muslim view of death. The scores were arrived at by first getting the sum total of the partial-Islamic element, total-Islamic element and non-Islamic element in each stage of the Luo-Muslim funeral. The sum total was then dividing by those three domains.

events that occupy Luo-Muslim funerals. However, since the non-Islamic element comes second, the extent of influence is not equal, although there is sharing between Islamic and Luo traditional elements. Luo traditions exceed the Islamic in perceiving death and its related rituals. The diagram thus reveals that a Luo-Muslim is more Luo traditional than Islamic. The dominance of Luo tradition means that the past is still real and may affect more generations to come. The extent to which it has affected Luo-Muslim understanding of death is dealt with in the next section.

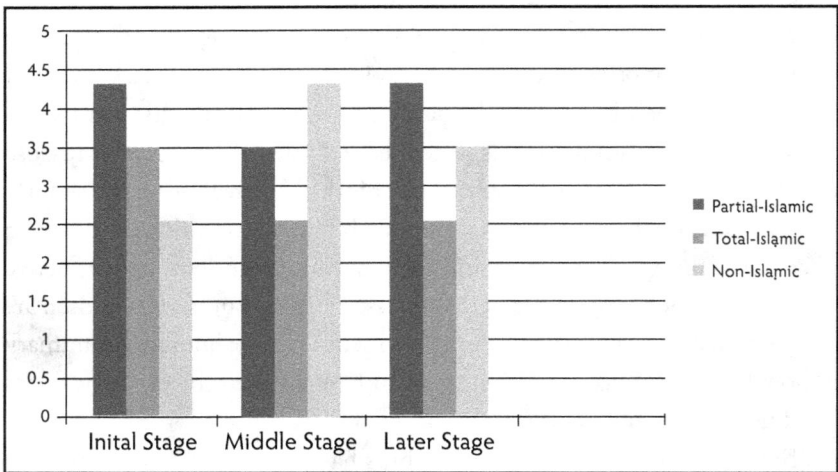

Diagram 25: Luo Tradition and Islam in the Three Stages of Luo-Muslim Funeral

Conclusion

This chapter has presented a description of the elements of the Luo traditional view that still exists in the contemporary Luo-Muslim perception. It was first divided into three sections. In the first section, the existence of Luo traditional views in their cultural perception of death was explained. This was done by further dividing the Luo-Muslim funeral into three stages: initial, middle and later stage. In each stage, the Luo traditional and Islamic elements in Luo-Muslim funeral beliefs and practices were compared and contrasted. The outcome of it was that in the initial stage, the domain of partial-Islamic element was rated the highest followed by total-Islamic element and non-Islamic element. That order of rating shows that it is Islamic rather than Luo traditional customs that are dominant in the initial stage of the Luo-Muslim funeral beliefs and practices. In the middle stage the order of the domains from the highest to the lowest are: non-Islamic element, partial-Islamic element and total-Islamic element. That order reveals that it is the elements in the Luo traditions that are most prevalent in the Luo-Muslim funeral. The most popular domain in the later stage is the partial-Islamic element, followed by the non-Islamic element. The last one is the domain of total-Islamic element. The general view is that Luo traditional elements are the most popular in the later stage.

The Luo traditions were again categorized into two groups: the old/former and the current/latter Luo traditions. The former Luo traditions are followed in the initial and later stages while the latter are mostly followed in the middle stage. The Luo Muslims who participate in Luo traditional rituals were classified into the three stages according to their age and gender. The initial and the later stages are represented by adult Muslims while the middle stage is the Muslim youths and children. With respect to gender, the initial stage consists of both men and women combined, while in the middle and later stages the men are more involved than the women. The former Luo customs that are practiced by the Luo-Muslim adults have little impact in the initial stage. The current Luo traditions that the Luo-Muslim youths and children follow, especially the male, have a moderate impact in the middle stage of the funeral. The Luo adult Muslims, especially female in particular, follow the Luo old traditions. The impact of these traditions is great in the later stage of the Luo-Muslim funeral beliefs and practices.

CHAPTER 6

The Effects of Luo Traditional View on Luo-Muslim Understanding of Death and Its Related Practices

The findings in the previous chapters (chs. 4 and 5) have revealed that the funeral beliefs and practices that the Luo Muslims follow contain some elements of the Luo traditions. These Luo traditions (both old and new) affect the Luo Muslims in different ways. The effects of the Luo traditions were looked at based on each stage (initial stage, middle stage and later stage) of the funeral of the Luo Muslims. In order to do this, the selective coding in the GTM (Grounded Theory Method) was utilized[1] (see methodology chapter). Through it, the Luo traditional concepts that the Luo Muslims have retained in each stage of their funerals were first identified. They were then classified into different categories in the three stages of the Luo-Muslim funeral. How Luo traditional views have affected the perception of the Luo Muslims on death and its related practices, the extent to which it has affected their perception of death, and the relationship between one category and the other in each stage of the Luo-Muslim funeral, were described.

The Influence of Luo Traditions in the Initial Stage of Luo-Muslim Funerals

Diagrams 19 and 24 above show the kind of influence that the Luo traditions have had on the Luo-Muslim perception of death and its related practices in the initial stage of their funeral funeral. In the findings, the

---

1. Corbin and Strauss, *Basics of Qualitative Research*, 116, 143

domain of partial-Islamic element has been shown to be the biggest followed by the domain of total-Islamic element. The domain of non-Islamic element appears last. This shows that the domain of non-Islamic-element is the one that the Luo traditions have had the least influence. Elements in the Luo traditions that have been been discussed in this section, and which are also contained in the initial stage of the Luo-Muslim funeral, include; loud wailing, issues of gender with regard to preparing and viewing the body of the deceased before it is taken to the graveyard to be buried. These Luo traditional elements have had great influence in the initial stage of the Luo-Muslim funeral. As it has been made clear in each section under this chapter, those Luo traditional elements have affected the way Luo Muslims view death and the rituals surrounding it.

The Effects of Luo Traditions on Luo-Muslim Perception of Mourning

As it has been discussed in the previous chapter, wailing or weeping because one has lost their loved one is not totally prohibited by the Luo Muslims. It is a form of mourning and is perceived as a very healthy way of expressing the pain in one's heart for having lost somebody special. According to the descriptions by Luo Muslims, the wailing or weeping happens when people have no words to say but only tears roll down the cheek because of their sorrow. These tears are commonly shed by women. Men may also weep or wail. However, in most cases as the informants explained, the way they express their sorrow is to enter into the house or home of the deceased. They remain quiet throughout the period they spend there. It is through this quietness that one may tell that they are in a mourning period. But they also get involved in running different chores that pertain to the funeral. Those duties include cutting firewood that is meant for cooking, ferrying big jerry cans of water in a bicycle, and voluntarily washing and preparing the body of the deceased for burial. The latter is carried by them if the deceased is of the same gender.

Perceptions of the Luo Muslims on loud wailing

It is the loud wailing together with the utterance of words in that process of mourning that is prohibited. Since this is mostly done by women, the majority of them are usually victimized by this prohibition. Whereas the

Luo Muslims see nothing wrong with wailing or weeping, they do, however, caution their people not to be so emotional to the extent that they can't control their tears. This is usually difficult. A few who follow this rule are most often seen covering their faces with a *leso* (in Swahili, meaning a piece of cloth that women tie round their waist) while crying. Sometimes they are assisted by their fellow women and taken to weep away from where the body is laid or where other mourners can see them. The Luo Muslims admit that it is hard to control weeping or crying by which one sheds a lot of tears and utters certain words. The researcher also witnessed this during the two burials that took place in Kendu Bay. Despite the prohibition, some Luo-Muslim women wailed a lot over their loved ones. This kind of wailing has its roots in the Luo tradition, which has apparently affected the Luo-Muslim understanding of death.

Loud wailing and uncontrollable shedding of tears are believed to affect the Luo Muslims in several ways. First, it elicits Allah's anger against those who practice it. This is said to be so because it was Prophet Muhammad who prohibited it. Even though the grounds under which he prohibited it for Arabian Muslims may be different from that of the Luo Muslims, it is still expected to be obeyed by Muslims all over the world. Failing to obey is like disobeying God himself. This disobedience meets the wrath of God. It is also in reference to this disobedience that some informants made claim that out of a thousand men in paradise there would be one woman. Another claim which they made was that out of a thousand women in hell there would be one man. All these claims are consequences that apply to women who cry loudly. This means that women are the most affected. The effect is a very negative one. Second, uncontrollable tears have effect on the deceased. Shedding a lot of tears is perceived to be like a burning coal on the body of the deceased. It makes the deceased too weak to carry on with their journey towards their destiny. This in turn limits their chances of being allowed by Allah to enter paradise. On the other hand, the person who wails very uncontrollably is also believed to be disadvantaged. The good deeds that they have been practicing since they were born are reduced into ashes by such a behavior. The prayers by other Muslims that seek the deceased's forgiveness may not be accepted by Allah. This, however, does not in any way suggest that the person who wails loudly won't be prayed for when they die. Luo

Muslims hold it as their duty to pray for their loved ones who have died irrespective of what kind of life they lived. It is left for Allah to decide since he is the only one who knows every detail of a person's life.

Loud wailing is a Luo traditional custom that is believed to make the dead and the ancestors happy. It is a sign that the deceased has a very close and loving relationship in the community. It is also a way of expressing the displeasure of the people about death. It is therefore very common to hear words like *ngane ne oyuag ahinya* (in Luo, meaing the deceased was thoroughly mourned). *Yuak mar nduru* (in Luo meaning, loud wailing), as some informants put it, cultivates a sense of belonging. It is a fulfilling ritual that one identifies with as being a part of the community. The heavy rain that pours during the funeral preparations or after the burial is believed to be the "blessings" (*gueth* in Luo) that God gives to the people because of their loud wailing. These blessings guarantee good harvest of crops. It also guarantees safety of the livestock since there is now plenty of grass and water for the animals to feed on.

The words mourners utter to the deceased while mourning

Loud crying and uttering of words go hand in hand. Although not many of them cry aloud like women do, they also say words such as: *mosna ngane* (in Luo, meaning greeting me so-and-so), *iweya gi nga?* (in Luo, meaning whom have you left me with?), *tho jajuok* (in Luo, meaning death is a witch) and *ngama noyuaga katho?* (in Luo, meaning who will mourn me when I die?). *Mosna ngane* is often uttered by men to their fellow deceased males. The greetings assume that where the deceased has gone is where others who died before him are. It is also assumed that they are alive in the different world where they are. The greetings are basically meant to strengthen the bond between the living and the dead. It is believed that once they get those greetings, they feel excited to know that they are still being remembered. The words, *iweya gi nga* are most often uttered by a widow who has lost her husband or a woman whose only son has died. This applies if the deceased was the breadwinner of the family. Both to the widow and the woman who has lost her son, those words imply that they are now left with somebody to take care of them. It also expresses how lonely they feel without the physical presence and the support of their loved ones. The words acknowledge that the future would be difficult without them. *Ngama noyuaga katho* (in Luo, meaning who will mourn me when I die?) may come from both genders. It is mostly from elderly people whose worry in life is about how they would be buried when they die. If their son that they have been looking up to dies before them, then they use those words to express their emotion.

A couple or a woman who has lost all her children may also utter those words. It is through loud wailing and uttering of those words that truly define the kind of a relationship that one had with the deceased. The explanation in the teachings of Islam that crying loudly and uttering such words cannot bring the deceased back to life is often ignored. The pain of losing a loved one together with the feeling to keep the Luo traditions is usually so overwhelming. Upon such Luo Muslims the effects are double in a positive way. First, they consider the pouring of their hearts through wailing loudly and shedding tears as quite relieving. This is psychological. Their actions also give them the opportunity to prove that they are Luo. This proof is so significant since it identifies them with the rest of the Luo community. It is by doing what is traditionally appropriate that one feels a sense of belonging to the community. The feeling of guilt and alienation that they sometime face from their fellow community members who are not Muslims is thus minimized. But the fact that some are against a loud wail and uttering of words while others are in support of them shows that there is inconsistency in what Luo Muslims follow. This lack of consistency makes it difficult for the Luo Muslims to support their claim that they are truly Muslims.

Significance of cultural meanings that Luo Muslims attach to loud wailing

It is also through the loud wailing that people come to know that somebody has died. This is considered as traditionally appropriate. No one could give an excuse that he has not been informed. At the same time, no blame is cast on the bereaved that they never informed people about what has happened. Loud wailing is therefore a form of communication that is still held necessary until today. If a widow fails to wail loudly when she has lost her husband, she is treated with a lot of suspicion. She is looked at as the one who has killed her husband. This explains why the wife is closely watched when her husband dies irrespective of his religion. Her behavior and actions beginning from the time her husband dies until after his burial is closely monitored. If she does not cry loudly for religious reasons, other relatives and friends who may also happen to be in the same religion are the very ones who would condemn her as a witch. Others may claim that the woman had no true love for the deceased. Some informants also remarked that by failing to cry loudly, the woman is simply not religious as she claims. By this they meant that a true religion such as the one they belong (Islam), has no hindrance to the traditions that have been followed for many generations. This statement shows that some Luo Muslims view Islam not as a religion that hinders them but as a vehicle through which they are able to comprehend their Luo traditional customs better.

Wailing loudly and uttering words are practices that still affect the Luo Muslims in Kendu Bay. Women in particular are more affected. The demand by Luo traditions on one hand and by Islam on the other hand confuses them. The former makes them unable to explain whether their loud wail is genuine or just out of fear. They do not seem clear if they even fulfill their Luo traditions. The latter makes them also uncertain about their identity as Muslims. But together with all these questions, to which they don't have answers, Luo-Muslim women, especially widows, find Islam to be more comforting than any other religion. The findings have revealed that wailing is a ritual that begins right from the time a loved one has passed on. This is therefore contrary to Ndisi's perspective that describes Luo women as crying at the top of their voices only after the burial of the deceased has taken place.[2]

The Effect of Luo Tradition on the Mixing of Gender in the Luo-Muslim Funeral

It is very common in some of the Luo-Muslim funerals to see men and women mixing and interacting with each other. This is very much the case following the news that somebody has died. Depending on where the person has died, there is always an influx of people streaming in to have a glance of the deceased. At that point there is very little thinking about who should go and who shouldn't go. Sometimes even children are found at the scene of the death. It is almost impossible to begin separating the people on the basis of gender even if the need to do so is there. The reason is that at the point of death what is important is the presence of people. Telling people of the opposite sex to move out of the house or any other place that the

2. Ndisi, *Study in the Economic*, 81.

deceased has been laid is simply interpreted as a cover up over something that people are not allowed to know. Some Luo Muslims find it difficult to contain this kind of a situation due to its prohibition in Islam. Rather than making a public announcement or pushing away people of the opposite sex, it is left to one's conscience to decide. The retreating of the people becomes more of an individual than corporate or collective affair.

Although it is a disgrace in Islam for people of the opposite sex to mix in a gathering such as funeral, the Luo Muslims view it differently. According to the informants, what they consider to be important is that the people who were close or knew the deceased have attended their funeral. This means that the Luo Muslims consider one's presence in the funeral, more important than the person's gender. The mixing of gender in Islam is also associated with impurity. The informants reported that Islam discourages the mixing on the ground that some women who are present may be having their monthly period. This is a state that requires seclusion. The impurity of one individual affects the whole group. This is regarded as a very serious matter that even Allah is not pleased with. It brings into question the mandate of the Islamic leaders. It also harbors hatred between the opposite sexes or between the people and their leaders who may be hard pressed to discipline them at a later time. But regardless of their awareness that there are consequences in the mixing of gender, the Luo Muslims still find themselves together as male and female. For them, they consider equality of male and female as Allah has made them (4:1) to be paramount. They also view the issue of impurity among women as something natural and personal. In other words, a woman has not control over her monthly periods. A woman's impurity is viewed as personal in the sense that it is shame to mention it in the public. It is like a pregnancy that even though people can see, they don't talk about it, lest something worse happen. According to some Luo Muslims, the death of a loved one is a public affair. It is what is considered to be a priority. This means that personal or private issues like the monthly period of a woman should not hinder her from coming to see the deceased.

Some informants also remarked that it is very difficult to avoid the mixing of both genders in a funeral. The reason is that the coming together of both male and female persons in a funeral has been dictated by the death of their loved one. Any person who was related to the deceased in one way or another, or lived in the neighborhood must come to the funeral. In that case, the mixing of both genders becomes a situational rather than an intentional matter. In a situational issue such as death, it is how first one responds upon hearing or witnessing the demise of a loved one that is important. Some of the people who also come to see the deceased are non-Luo Muslims. Their coming therefore has very little to do with religion. It has more to do with their relationship with the deceased. In such a situation where both Luo Muslims and non-Luo Muslims have come together, the rule in Islam that requires male persons to sit or stand separately from the female persons has litte effect. The mixing brings a sense of togetherness among the Luo Muslims. It also gives them a sense of identity as Luos. This implies that the Luo Muslims consider their identity as Luos to be more important than their identity as Muslims.

The Effect of Luo Tradition on Luo-Muslim Viewing of the Body

Another Luo traditional element that is found in the initial stage of the Luo-Muslim funeral practices is the viewing of the body. After washing, the body is put in a place where members of the public who are interested may queue and pay their last respect to the deceased. This practice of view-ing the body has several effects as far as the Luo-Muslim understanding of death and its related rituals are concerned. First, it is time consuming. As has been highlighted in other areas of the study, it is within Islam that the burial of the deceased is conducted as soon as possible. However, as many informants narrated, this is sometimes very unpractical. The process of viewing the body may take so long that the deceased ends up being buried very late in the evening. The delay obviously has a negative effect on the deceased since he would miss being interrogated by the angels, Nakir and Munkir. Missing this important step of one's life is so painful both to the deceased and the Muslim community in the sense that the individual may fail to enter paradise and the community feels guilty from causing that to happen. It is how one responds to the interrogative questions as posed to him by the two angels that determines the next step of his journey towards paradise (see table 1 in chapter 4).

The Muslim group that has caused the delay may also suffer the same consequences as individuals when they die. A record is kept that shall be used against them at the time of their demise. In such a situation as this where there are different demands from both Islam and Luo tradition, conflicts are unavoidable. The conflicts are also heightened by the fact that in any funeral in Kendu Bay, whether the person who has died is a Muslim or non-Muslim, people from different religious backgrounds are always represented. It is therefore not uncommon to hear people quarreling or arguing over time with each other. But, besides the long queue to view the deceased, which sometimes proves to be time consuming, there is also a challenge as to how to ensure that the rule about the gender is kept. There is usually a rush to view the body. It is a way of bidding goodbye to the deceased to which everyone feels obligated. The chances of separating the people and making them queue on the basis of their gender are usually very impractical. It is, by itself, time consuming. On the other hand, the idea of separating them infuses a feeling that they are immoral. The table below illustrates the different meanings that the Luo Muslims attribute to the gender issue in any gathering.

Table 8: The Concept of Mixing of Gender in the Luo-Muslim Funeral

	Luo Muslims	
Meanings Attached to Mixing of Gender	Islamic Perspective	Luo Traditional Perspective
	It is immoral to mix	It is immoral not to mix
	Not mixing reflects a true community of Muslims.	Mixing reflects a true community of Luo.

The mixing of gender during the viewing of the body

While the present discussion is focused on the mixing of gender in the Luo-Muslim funeral, the general principle behind it applies in any Luo-Muslim gathering. In reference to the above table, it is clear that Luo Muslims have both Islamic and Luo traditional perspectives with regard to meeting of the opposite sex in funeral. There is an inward tension that a Luo Muslim experiences. On one side he is pulled by the Islamic idea that it is immoral to mix, while on the other hand his Luo traditional heritage tells him that the mixing is healthy and it reflects harmonious living among the Luos. These issues are mind-throbbing; thinking that by meeting or gathering together with the opposite sex is immoral is in itself also viewed as immoral. This is the perspective that Luo tradition holds.

These bombarding experiences in the minds of the Luo Muslims have resulted in them living a life of convenience. It is a lifestyle that borders between Islamic and Luo traditional customs. This explains the reason why, even though it bothers them, most of the Luo-Muslim funerals are generally mixed. The intermingling is there in some areas while in others, both men and women separate and sit or carry out certain activities as different groups. The separation by gender is entirely a matter of convenience since it is dictated by the nature of the event or activities involved as Luo Muslims are cognizant of the environment in which they are. It is this understanding that makes it realistic to think of Luo Muslims as "ordinary Muslims."[3]

Talking to the deceased during the viewing of the body

Some people use the viewing of the body as an occasion to address or talk to the deceased. The talking that comes from women usually happens amidst the sobs. In some cases it is too loud while at other times it is just quiet whispers and the nodding of the head. While these are going on, the individual viewing the body fixes her eyes on the deceased. For some men, it may be occasioned by the outburst of some words such as *thuon* (in Luo, meaning, a warrior or a person of valor). The words used during this time of viewing the body are different from the ones that are used by those who trickle in immediately after they have heard that their loved one has passed on. In the former, the words are mainly in praise of the deceased, especially those that come from men. They are actually in praise of their fellow men. The words spoken in the latter are out of the shock of what has happened. Most of them are loud enough to be heard by those who are present.

Luo Muslims who utter the words of lamentations move or run slowly between where the deceased is laid and the gate. Although the content of these utterances point to what happened in the day-to-day life of a Luo Muslim in general, they have nonetheless provided what is very common among them as Muslims. Because of their faith in Islam, the Luo Muslims

---

3. According Kim, "'ordinariness' refers especially to the human condition that represents a general tendency of human mind before it is formulate or empowered by any ideology or theology through a deep and long intentional thinking process" (Kim, "Considering 'Ordinariness,'" 180).

sometimes lament quietly. Silent following is non-verbal. They also do it cautiously. In other words, they don't do those practices as openly as other non-Luo Muslims do. A good illustration is that instead of wailing loudly or uttering words, some people may simply stand and gaze at the deceased for a long time without saying anything. After seeing the body, some walk away with their faces down. However much as they would want to be self-composed and behave as if nothing much happened, their facial expression gives a different picture. It tells how distressed and sorrowful they are. Some informants remarked that while they are in that state of distress, the questions that they ask themselves quietly include: why did the deceased have to die? Who killed him? These questions together with the fact that some Luo Muslims feel unable to utter the words, *ina lilahi waina ileyi rajiun* (we are all from Allah and all of us must return to him) that Islam requires, is a clear indication that the Luo traditions have affected the way they view death.

Emotions during the viewing of the body

After the body has been washed and shrouded, it is carried out and placed in a place somewhere that allows for the public to view it. Many informants acknowledged that the viewing of the body is a practice that is not followed in Islam. The reason why Islam does not allow for the viewing of the body is because people's emotions are affected by it. Some people after seeing the dead body burst into tears that sometimes go out of control. Some people even collapse. Men in particular, express their emotions by remaining quite. It is for this reason that sometimes immediate family members are barred from viewing the body. Even though the informants admitted that some people have behaved indifferently to Islam after viewing the body of their loved one, the understanding of emotions involved is quite different. The Luo Muslims explained that showing emotions during the viewing of the body makes the deceased feel accepted and loved. It is also a way of showing the deceased that they will still be remembered. In other words, death has not completely cut-off the relationship between the deceased and the living.

Whereas in some other Muslim communities the viewing of the body that results into emotions is regarded as something bad to the deceased, the Luo Muslims take it as something good to the deceased. The view that some other Muslim communities hold about the emotions is an indication of the Islamic influence while the view by the Luo Muslims that emotions are good for the deceased shows influence from the Luo traditions. Those other Luo-Muslim communities that have been influenced by Islam tend to prohibit the viewing of the body while Luo Muslims allow it. In the Luo traditional thought, that the Luo Muslims represents, what is good for the deceased is also good for the bereaved. Unlike in Islam, the important thing in Luo traditions is to ensure the wellbeing for the living. This wellbeing is dependent on how the bereaved have behaved toward the deceased. Good behaviors that include showing emotions during the viewing of the body guarantee security for the family members and the relatives of the deceased. Describing emotions and the viewing of the body from a Luo traditional perspective implies that the focus of the Luo Muslims centers on the deceased themselves and not on their future destiny.

Effects that the viewing of the body has on Luo Muslims

The Luo Muslims who have witnessed and viewed many bodies of the deceased in the past talk more cautiously about death than the ones with little or no experience in the matter. The category of the mature Luo-Muslim adults is the one that weighs words before responding to the questions about death. They have lived long enough and have witnessed many people dying. Unlike them, the Luo-Muslim youths and children talk a lot about death. Their experiences are limited by their ages. The little talk by the mature Luo-Muslim adults is due to the fact that they see themselves closer to death than the youths and children. Every time they view the body, they are reminded about the reality of death and that their turn to die is much closer than others. While this is true, the viewing of the body has the overall purpose of instilling in the minds of everyone that death is a reality.

This consciousness is necessary since it makes the Luo-Muslim individuals devote their lives to God and in the service of fellow human beings. The ultimate purpose for their devotion and doing good deeds is such that they believe that by Allah's permission they may be allowed to enter paradise. For some, the viewing of the body reminds them of the futility of life. They therefore rededicate their lives to Allah and strive to use their resources for the good of others. This explains why social actions in which one provides for the less fortunate society is common among the Muslim communities. Alhough the Luo traditions have affected the perspective of Luo Muslims regarding death in this initial stage of their funeral, the effects become greater as one moves to both the middle and the later stages.

The Influence of Luo Traditions in the Middle Stage of a Luo-Muslim Funeral

Diagrams 9 and 13 indicate the extent to which Luo traditions have affected the Luo-Muslim funeral practices in the middle stage. The order of domains is that non-Islamic element comes first, followed by partial-Islamic element, and total-Islamic element comes last. This gives an indication that the majority of the Luo-Muslim funeral practices in the middle stage are basically Luo traditional in nature. As was discussed in chapter 5 (under the heading "Similarities and Differences in the Middle Stage"), this stage describes the procedures undertaken after the body has been shrouded and displayed for public viewing to the point where it is laid in the grave to rest. Besides the viewing of the body that has already been covered, there are other specific elements that are Luo traditional in nature in this stage. They include: the carrying of the body in a bier/casket, prayers, fundraising, and ancestral land burial.

Carrying the Body to the Graveside

When it comes to the carrying of the body to the burial site, Luo Muslims use a bier. This is a simple structure and rectangular in shape. It is made without nails. The simplicity by which the bier is made mainly follows the former Luo tradition. Carrying the body of the deceased using a *geneza* (in Swahili, meaning a bier) that is not made of nails remains a practice for the Muslims all over the world, but the cultural aspect of a particular context cannot be ignored. This is the case in Kendu Bay where the Luo Muslims have mainly adopted the way the carrying and disposing of the dead used to be done in the former Luo tradition. The body was simply wrapped from head to toe and transported to the burial site using a wooden structure joined together by using a papyrus and reeds.

Just as it was then, the bier that Luo Muslims use is economically less expensive. In fact, the bier is something that is made once. It is kept in the mosque and is removed to be used whenever there is a need. Such simplicity is also evident on *sanda* that is used to cover the *geneza*. It is usually white and gives the sense that the place for which the deceased is heading in the hereafter is a holy place. Making a bier available to transport the deceased to their final resting place is economically relieving especially to the less privileged people. This simple way of transporting the body of the deceased to the graveside incurs less expense. The little expenses that are involved have been one of the reasons that have made some Luos to convert to Islam.

Different preferences for the Luo-Muslim groups in disposal of the body

A group of the Luo Muslims, particularly Luo-Muslim adults, identify themselves with the former Luo traditional way of burying the dead. It is simple and less economical. The majority of Luo-Muslim youths on the other hand, prefer the modern way of Luo burial. This is where a casket that is modeled in a different fashion is used. It actually reflects what is common in contemporary way of carrying and disposing the dead by the Luo people. The liking of the Muslim youths over this modern Luo way of burial is due to three reasons. First, there is an argument that faith is a matter of the heart. In other words, one's belief in Allah and the good deeds they do are what count for them when they die. Whatever is done to the body such as putting it in a casket that is made of nails does not therefore affect where the soul goes.

Second, most of the Muslim youths live and work in urban centers. Most of their friends are also working class. The fact that they are working makes it easy for them to purchase very expensive coffins for the burial of their loved ones. Sometimes these loved ones are very close family members who were depending on them for their livelihood. Buying expensive items for the burial that includes a casket is a way to appreciate the role that the deceased has played in their life. But also, as some informants put it, some of the young people are Muslims by the virtue of their birth. Even though they have received Islamic teachings in *madras* in their tender ages, the influences from urban setting have made them open to other ideas and practices such as burying in a casket. Since the way the family wants their loved one to be attended to when they die is a very paramount practice among the Luo Muslims, the *imams* have no option but to allow a casket burial to take place. They are the ones, however, to conduct the burial. Their involvement in leading prayers for the deceased before his body is transported to the burial site is thus what may be said to make the funeral Islamic.

Putting the body in a casket made of nails is mostly common where the deceased is laid to rest in his home. It is here where many visitors from all walks of life stream in so as to pay their last respects to the deceased. The kind of the casket they are laid in may define their social status in life. In other words, the more expensive it is, the more the people may think of the deceased as coming from a financially well-to-do family. But this may not necessarily be so since part of the money used to purchase the coffin may have been contributed by relatives and other friends of the deceased. This is particularly so if the deceased died in a far distant place and their body is to be transported to their ancestral land for burial. Besides demonstrating economic stability, laying the body in an expensive casket also has a religious significance. People are drawn to do good deeds for the deceased with the hope that, when they too die, they will go to paradise as others do the same for them.

Perceptions of the Luo Muslims on the use of caskets to bury the dead

Burying in a casket affects the life of the Luo Muslims in several ways. First, it distorts the true teachings of Islam concerning what to use for burial. Second, it makes it very uncertain whether the deceased would get the chance to be interrogated. This is because the casket is usually closed while the deceased ought to be in a free place where he can respond to questions posed to him by the angels at his graveside. Third, casket burial, especially an expensive one, brings competition. Those who attend the burial of the deceased would wish to be buried in such an expensive casket. Such a wish implies that what matters is the way by which somebody has been buried and not the place where the deceased is going. But casket burial is both economically involving and time consuming. It takes quite a while to design and make the coffin that the family members or the relatives of the family have ordered. This in turn affects the timeline and the procedures of the funeral. Depending on where it has been ordered, a funeral that was supposed to take a maximum of three days may be delayed. Also, the money that some Luo Muslims believe should be spent in taking care of the immediate family of the deceased is channeled into something that rots in the soil.

Some of the Luo Muslims who are opposed to burying in a casket also argue that what is important is where the soul travels to. To them, therefore, it is not what others do for the deceased that counts but rather what the deceased did while still alive. This thinking makes it very valid to argue that there are two types of Luo Muslims. The first type consists of those who carry out the good deeds with a view to helping the deceased reach his destiny. The second group includes those who perform funeral rituals for their own benefits. The former emphasizes personal involvement in good deeds in order that by Allah's permission one may secure a place in paradise. On the other hand, the latter places their destiny as dependent on the good deeds they do to the deceased.

A person who belongs to the first type is dedicated and very active with good deeds throughout his life. His good deeds are mainly to other people who are less privileged in the society. He hopes that when he dies he may enter paradise. Another person of the second group is also dedicated to the Islamic faith. He carries out his good deeds as a sign of his dedication to his religion. He considers attending mosque prayers and giving generously towards the development of Islamic institutions and other people as part of his good deeds that Allah is pleased with. But his biggest contribution in good deeds is towards the deceased. It is here where he believes that the good he does to the deceased will earn him a place in paradise. Those good deeds include: contributing towards buying an expensive casket, getting new clothes/suits and shoes for the deceased, carrying the coffin to the graveyard and participating in the digging of the grave. Since entering paradise is the ultimate concern, he spares nothing in conducting funeral rituals that would be accredited to them as good deeds.

Perceptions of the Luo Muslims on good deeds

Table 9 gives a summary of how Luo Muslims are affected by their understanding of good deeds in relation to themselves and the deceased. They generally conduct the first type of good deeds with the common view of benefitting themselves. The benefits here are the envisioned rewards or entry into paradise that they would gain at the end of their journey on earth. But together with the good deeds, there is still no guarantee that the individual would enter paradise. The uncertainty of entry to heaven is in itself motivating. The person keeps on doing good deeds whenever he gets opportunity. He holds the belief that the more he does them the closer he gets to God. The column of the second type shows how Luo Muslims are different in terms of the two different types. The Luo Muslims of type 1 practice the good deeds "for" the deceased while those of type 2 carry them out "to" the deceased. The goods deeds "for" the deceased are done with the intention of helping the deceased to find favor in the eyes of Allah. The favor would enable them to enter paradise. The good deeds done "to" the deceased are meant to please the deceased. When the deceased is pleased, people's lives and the lives of their animals are secure.

Table 9: Luo-Muslim Perception of Good Deeds

Types of Luo Muslims Based on Good Deeds	Types of Good Deeds		The Reasons for the Doing of the Good Deeds
	Type 1 of Good Deeds	Type 2 of Good Deeds	
Type 1 of Luo Muslims	Good deeds done by the people who are alive to other fellow human beings or Islamic institutions	Good deeds done "for" the deceased by the people who are alive	To aid the deceased by Allah's permission to paradise
Type 2 of Luo Muslims		Good deeds done "to" the deceased by the people who are alive	1. To help the living to enter paradise when he or she dies. 2. To enhance security for the living

As have been explained in the previous chapter, these have a goal to benefit the deceased and the bereaved respectively. The deceased can receive benefits if people conduct their funeral rituals as quickly as possible. The faster they are done the better for them and the more smoothly they can travel on the journey. The individual carrying out the good deeds also hopes to benefit with a reward to heaven when they die. However, this is not always the primary focus for the person. The Luo Muslims of type 2 practice the good deeds to the deceased mainly for selfish reasons. They hope that the same would be done to them by others when they die. The good deeds are believed to offer security to the bereaved. The living would no longer be disturbed by spirits of the dead.

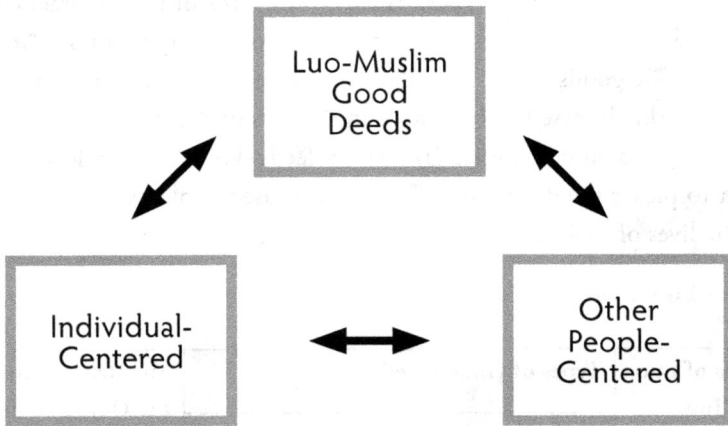

Diagram 26: Luo-Muslim Perceptions of Good Deeds on the Living and the Dead

Diagram 26 above illustrates how Luo Muslims view good deeds. The Luo Muslims of type 1 are individual-centered in two ways. First, when they are still living, their good deeds are done for their own benefit. When that very individual dies, or anybody else for that matter, it is the good deeds of the deceased that count. On the other hand, the Luo Muslims of type 2 are other-people centered. They get satisfaction from what they do to others. It is for this reason that they strive to do as many good deeds as possible for the deceased. They in turn expect that other people will do the same at their funeral when they die.

The Effect of Fundraising on the Luo-Muslim Funeral

A Luo traditional element that has increasingly become common in contemporary Luo-Muslim funerals is the fundraising. This usually takes place at the home where the deceased would be buried. This fundraising is essentially a later Luo traditional development (it falls under the category of new or latter Luo traditions). It is a later development because in the old Luo traditions, people's presence at the deceased's funeral was considered very vital. This fundraising is different from the one that is conducted before the body is transported back to its ancestral land (that is, if the deceased died away from their ancestral home). The first *harambee* (in Swahili, meaning fundraising) is especially carried out if the deceased dies in a far distant place.

Both Muslims and non-Muslim friends come together in order to raise funds that would be used to transport the body home and meet other funeral expenses. Besides collecting funds, *harambee* is also a platform that friendship between the people who are present and the deceased is renewed. Also, for a Muslim, the giving of money in such a function is part of the good deeds that contributes to a better life for the individual person in the hereafter. Unlike the first one, the second *harambee* is considered mandatory. It is the last tribute that one pays to the deceased before they are finally laid to rest. Even though the giving of money or any other assistance should be a secret affair of the individual as Islam teaches, the Luo Muslims do it differently.

In the second *harambee*, the master of ceremony announces in the hearing of everyone the amount of money each person has given in the funeral. This fundraising period is usually after the family members and other close relative of the deceased have eulogized the deceased. Depending on the social status that the deceased had before their death, the function of fundraising can sometimes be very long. The master of ceremony positions himself (it is always a male person who get delegated the responsibility to be the master of ceremony) on the dais where some dignitaries, relatives and the family members of the deceased have sat. The master of ceremony may either be a Muslim or a non-Muslim. Before inviting people to give, he has to mention all the good deeds that the deceased used to do. He also emphasizes the importance of giving in one's funeral. All these nice talks are meant to motivate people to give.

After giving a nice speech, the people are then called upon to start giving. They come in a single line. Both men and women queue together in a line. As the master of ceremony receives the money from each person, he calls them by name and announces the amount they have given. This public announcement is intentional. It's believed to instill a sense of fulfillment to the person who has given their money. This fulfillment is such that even if somebody had a bad relationship with the deceased before they died, this giving in public is believed to restore their relationship with the deceased. The giving in this case is like a cleansing ritual that when the dead "sees," it they withdraw the hate they had against the giver. Even if giving is purely out of one's love for the deceased and their family, the reason for giving is still centered on relationship between the giver and the deceased. In other words, the one who gives in a fundraising out of the love they have for the deceased does so in order to strengthen their relationship with the deceased. On the other hand, a person who gives their money towards the deceased does so as a way of renewing their relationship with the deceased. This implies that the Luo Muslims value relationships. The remark that Omar made that it is a person who dies but not one's relationship with the deceased, is a proof that keeping relationships with the dead are very significant to the Luo Muslims.[4]

Announcing to the public what one has given is not always the case in every Luo-Muslim funeral. In some funerals especially if most of the deceased's family members and relatives are Muslims, giving in *harambee* is not announced to the public. This kind of giving communicates non-verbally about one's liking for the deceased. It is also a sign of being in solidarity with the bereaved family. The reason why the giving is never announced is basically Islamic. It is in line with the belief that one's good deeds are their secrets between them and Allah. In some cases, the master of ceremony would whisper to the giver whether they would want their giving to be announced publicly. Some Luo Muslims would suggest that it should be announced while others would want it to remain secret. Apart from the good deeds, other areas that the Luo Muslims also consider as secrets include the deceased body parts, death, and hereafter.

Secrets (*weche mobuto/mopand*) in the Luo-Muslim Funeral

According to some informants, it is a taboo for a Luo person to show their private parts. Even if somebody has died, the first thing to be done is to cover them. If the deceased is a minor, any mature person, male or female can cover the deceased. But if the person who has died is a mature person, it is only the people of the same gender that can cover or wash the body. The people who do the washing are also not allowed to tell others what they have seen on the body of the deceased. The descriptions that the informants gave are exactly what they follow as Luo Muslims. This means that the Luo traditions have affected them. The Luo Muslims also consider death as a secret. According to them, it is a secret because it comes at a time when nobody

---

4. Omar, interview with author.

expects. Death is also a secret because it can strike any one; the rich, the poor, the young, and the old. Because death is a secret, people come from far and near to mourn with the bereaved. Their coming signifies that they would want others to attend their funeral when they die.

Looking at death as uncertain is something that originates from the Luo traditions. It is for this reason that some Luo Muslims even seek knowledge from *ajuaga* (in Luo, meaning a witchdoctor) as to why their loved one died. This they do despite what Islam teaches them that death is written on the forehead of every newborn baby. Although the Luo Muslims are aware that there is life in the hereafter – either paradise or hell, they hardly talk about them. Most of them would say that the deceased has gone to heaven (*polo* in Luo) without specifying where exactly they think the deceased has gone. This is also a view that has been adopted from the Luo traditions. As some informants put it, nobody knows what happens beyond death. They said that it is only *Nyasaye* (in Luo, meaning God) who knows. It is in this sense that the Luo Muslims talk of hereafter as a secret that only Allah knows. In other words, he alone knows who will go to paradise or hell. The diagram below gives a summary of what Luo Muslims consider as secrets in a funeral.

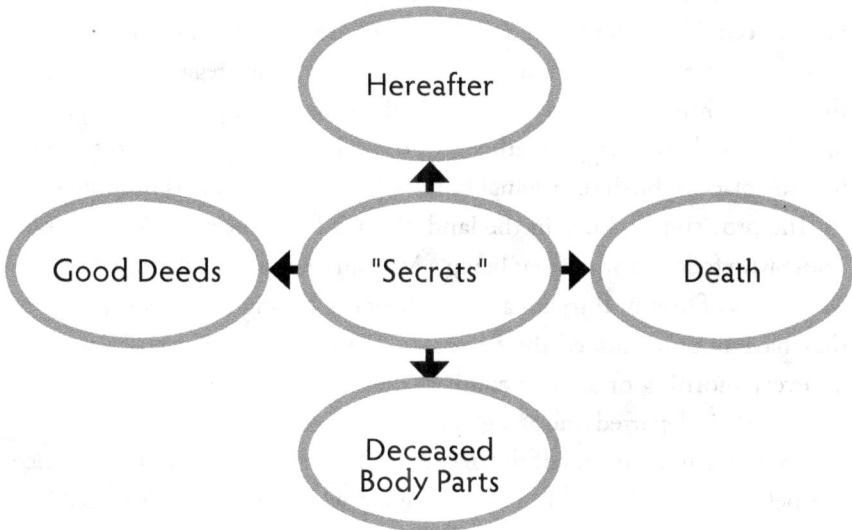

Diagram 27: "Secrets" in Luo-Muslim Funeral

The Luo-Muslims' View on Ancestral Land and Their Decisions Regarding Burial Site

Another Luo traditional practice that has affected the way Luo Muslims understand death and its related rituals is burial in the ancestral land. The story of the late S. M. Otieno that has been narrated in both the introductory and literature review chapters is all about where his remains should be disposed. Although many years have passed since he died, his story still lingers on and has been used by many scholars and ordinary people to illustrate how significant the ancestral land burial is to the Luo community. As it has been stated in the previous chapter, Luo Muslims can either bury their loved ones in the cemetery or at home. Burying in the cemetery is a practice that is generally followed by almost every Muslim community in the world. For some Luo Muslims in Kendu Bay, the presence of a cemetery has significantly reduced the worry of where to be buried when one dies. It is also for this reason that some Luo people have joined Islam. Their thinking has now shifted from being concerned about where their bodies would be laid to being concerned about where their souls would finally go to. The quarrelling or fighting over land that is very common in other places has been reduced. It has increased the awareness that death is real due to the presence of many graves that they see in their day-to-day life. This awareness has reduced the stigma that is associated with death. Although the cemetery is situated in Kendu Bay among the Luo, any Muslim regardless of where they come from can be buried there. This has made it possible for people of different clans to stay together without having the pressure to go back to one's place of birth or original home when sick or in crisis of some sort.

The provision to bury in the land of one's forefathers is also available. Those who follow it argue that being a Muslim does not hinder or take away one's roots of origin. Burying at home fosters a feeling in the bereaved that they have not abandoned the deceased. The fact that they can be waking up every morning or as they conduct their day-to-day businesses see the grave of their departed one at a glance is a consoling experience to them. It brings up fresh memories of the deceased. This memory is significant since it is believed to make the deceased feel good wherever he is mentioned in a conversation. Since he is very close to the ancestors, the way he feels produces results among the living. It can bring rain, plenty of harvests from the farms, or just the guarding or protecting of the family against other evil harms that may be directed against them by some unknown forces. Although a visit to the cemetery is encouraged, many Luo Muslims who stay in a distant town or city and buried their family members at home make frequent visits to their home. Even if they have not been home for a long time, they feel obligated to visit home often and see the place where their loved ones are resting. The grave even after many years becomes a historical site for them. Due to the rains that keep on carrying the grave soil away, they may plant a tree or plaster the grave with cement. It becomes a permanent mark that many generations will always keep in contact with.

Burying outside one's home or ancestral land is viewed as losing that person. It is also taken to mean that the deceased was not wanted during his lifetime. It is especially worse if the deceased is buried by their spouse away from the ancestral land. Many questions would linger in the minds of many people. Such questions include: Does the spouse have a home? Had they built a house there? Did the spouse love their partner? Did they kill their spouse? What is the spouse trying to hide that they bury the deceased away from home? These and many others have no easy answers. Knowing full well that these questions would come, some Luo Muslims today work very hard to build a house in the ancestral land. This also explains why very few Luo Muslims who have been born in Kendu Bay stay in the *miji* (homesteads). Most of the residents staying there are from other Luo clans whose parents moved and settled in Kendu Bay. Most of them came to do business with the Arab Muslims.

Home burial is also associated with land and inheritance of other property. The presence of one's grave gives their family members a guarantee to lay claim over their land and property. It is under this environment that the children of the deceased may also be taken care of. A home is perceived to be the place where proper funeral rituals that are in step with Luo tradition can be conducted. It is a place where the voices of the ancestors can be heard through the village elders. These voices cannot be ignored since they guide the community concerning the direction they should follow. This is particularly so following many mysterious deaths in the community. The Luo Muslims who see home burial as significant also argue that women whose husbands are buried at home or in the ancestral land have a stronger relationship with their husbands' relatives in that home and elsewhere than the ones whose husbands were buried in a cemetery or outside the ancestral land. Home burial therefore affects the relationship between the widow and her husband's other family members and relatives.

The same applies to *miji* where it was discovered that the majority of the widows who live there are those whose husbands were either buried in a cemetery in Kendu Bay or in the distant place they were staying before. The reason for this is that except for a few Luo-Muslim homes, the majority of the homes where Luo Muslims stay are also occupied by non-Luo Muslims. Due to differences in religion, a woman may recommend her Muslim husband to be buried in the cemetery. This may be against the wish of other family members of her late husband. But since according to Islam her wishes are what count, the decision to bury at the cemetery or outside the ancestral land are reluctantly given in to. However, the relationship between the widow and the rest of the family members would be strained. They will always be thinking that the widow not only knew what had killed the husband but also participated in his death. To them, that becomes the reason why she decides to bury her husband outside the home in a cemetery or ancestral land.

Due to the strained relationship, the widow may decide to go and stay in *miji* (homestead). This implies that at the death of the husband, a widow who encounters such an experience detaches herself from the relatives of her late husband and clings to the Muslim community where she has found refuge in the *miji*. The fact that even some Luo Muslims who are related to the widow's husband may disagree with her over her decision to bury her husband in the cemetery or outside the home shows how deep the tradition is. It does not only affect family relationships but also relationships between one religion and the other. However, while there is the evidence of strained relationship, some Luo-Muslim women are in support of burying the deceased at home. They get the opportunity to witness the burial of their deceased husbands, though at a distance. The fact that Luo-Muslim women are able to watch the burial procession even if it is from a distance is enough proof of the influence of Luo traditions.

The Influence of Luo Traditions in the Later Stage of Luo-Muslim Funerals

The activities that appear in the later stage of Luo-Muslim funeral include the feeding of mourners and the rituals pertaining to the widow. Widows are required to undergo some ritual practices. As shown in diagrams 23 and 24 of the previous section, the domain of partial-Islamic element is the biggest followed by the domain of non-Islamic element. The area of total-Islamic element is the least. The order signifies that many practices that the Luo Muslims follow in their later stage of the funeral are more Luo than Islamic in nature. The Luo traditions that they follow are former ones (see table 3). In terms of age and gender, it is the adult female Muslims who mostly follow them (see tables 4 and 5). The impact of these Luo traditions is described as great (see table 6).

The Effects of Luo Traditions on Luo-Muslim Practice of Feeding Mourners

Feeding mourners who attend the funeral affects the Luo Muslims in several ways. First, it is economically expensive. As many informants reported it is in a funeral where many people attend. Some of them may not be related to the deceased in any way. A funeral reaches its climax at the time of eating. Almost everyone who comes must eat before going on their way. In order to feed the large population that has come to bid their friend or relative goodbye, quite a number of animals and chickens are slaughtered. The expenses that go into this, including drinks, are always incurred by the family that has been bereaved. Sometimes they are forced to take loans due to the overwhelming number of mourners. The money collected during the fundraising may not be enough since some or most of it has to be paid for hospital bills and transporting the body to the ancestral land. Expenses for the funeral means that the bereaved family is left with very little to take care of themselves. This may be quite disturbing for the family, especially if the deceased was the sole breadwinner of the family. The support that they may be receiving from their fellow Muslims afterwards may not be anything close to what their loved one used to supply.

Besides facing financial challenges, feeding mourners is also emotionally involving. Organizing and coordinating in a way that ensures that everybody has eaten and is satisfied is always very problematic. The difficulty is also realized in the seating arrangements. The in-laws and other important guests may sit and be attended to separately from the rest of the people. This is done in order to avoid the embarrassment that is usually common with many people pushing each other in the queue to get themselves food. Some people may queue and eat several times in different serving points before a visitor gets his first share of the meal. Sometimes it is not that food is not enough but that it has been hidden by other people who would take it to their homes to feed their children. Controlling the crowd who follow those who are serving because they have never been served with food or because whatever they have been given is so little may also be overwhelming. These experiences make the heart of the bereaved more painful than the pain of losing a loved one. It may therefore take them a long period of time to come to terms with these double tragedies. The Luo traditions have long been adapted to an extent that people feel offended when they are not offered food at the funeral. It becomes a story that would remain in their memory as long as they live.

While food, or the absence of it, has some negative effects on both the bereaved and the mourners, the opposite is also true. Food is very symbolic. It marks the end of mourning or bereavement and opens up a new chapter of celebration. It is a social platform that is used by relatives and friends who may have stayed long without seeing each other. They get the opportunity to chat and to get to know how each other is doing. They also consider it as an occasion to catch up with one another over the events and issues that have transpired within the period that they have been away from each other. Eating of food and having fellowship with each other provide a forum in which people's minds shift from thinking about death to thinking about life beyond death. Food in this case symbolizes that life. It is for this reason that eating in most cases comes last in the funeral. But for the guests who may want to leave early, they are urged to eat even before the burial ends. Leaving without eating is a shameful thing to the bereaved. It is also taken to be embarrassment and a sign of disrespect to the deceased to see part of his "guests" (*wende* in Luo) walk away without eating. It is feared that he may react to this by causing some unpleasant incidences such as premature deaths of children and barrenness in the family. It is therefore first and foremost a concern for the immediate family to see that people have eaten in the funeral. They would do everything possible to ensure that mourners are fed. This explains why *harambee*, especially the first one, may not end soon in today's Luo society.

The sense of fear implies that the family provides food to mourners as a duty that is endured rather than enjoyed. But the idea that mourners are the guests of the deceased is also counteractive. It gives family members a sense of feeling privileged to serve food to a people who have come to mourn the one they are related to. They therefore consider themselves as also being mourned (*ubiro yuaga* in Luo). Food then becomes a token of appreciation to the mourners as well as a substance that replenishes the energy that they have lost in mourning. Mourning here is in the form of loud wailing and weeping. But one's presence and involvement in other areas of the funeral are also considered as part of mourning. Feeding mourners becomes exciting rather than an enduring experience. It is the family members who feel aggrieved if some mourners go away without eating. They feel as if they have been denied the opportunity to express how grateful they are to them.

As some informants explained, a Muslim is generally generous. Part of their generosity is in the act of giving food to people in their various occasions such as a funeral. It is therefore their joy to see as many people as possible eating at the funeral. They do this out of a belief that the more one gives the more they get and the closer they draw to Allah. Supplying food to mourners is something that many informants remarked that it is not common in Islam. In Islam, it is those who have come to mourn who are expected to carry food to the bereaved. This means that the feeding of mourners as Luo Muslims do today is an act that has originated from the Luo traditions. As it is in the Luo traditions, the feeding of mourners by the Luo Muslims signifies that the deceased was a very generous person. But besides showing that the deceased was generous, the Luo Muslims have attached religious meaning to the act of feeding mourners. It is part of the good deeds that is believed to be acceptable to Allah.

The Luo Muslims also believe that their relationship with each other is affected by the food they eat at the funeral. This emerges from a Luo traditional thinking that friends eat together while enemies don't. As a sign that one was in true friendship with the deceased they would not leave the funeral without eating. At the same time, it is when somebody declines to eat that people would begin to think about them suspiciously. This is especially so for a person who was very close to the deceased or lived in the neighborhood. The eating is therefore a way of avoiding any doubt about a person's relationship with the deceased. It is also a sign that the person has forgiven what the deceased owed him or he has paid back what he owed the deceased. He is now free and it is the eating that authenticates his freedom. A strong effect of Luo traditions on the feeding of mourners by the Luo Muslims is that it brings the relationship between the deceased and the mourners very close. Despite the religious effect, it is this relationship with the deceased that the Luo Muslims value most. An indication that they value the relationship is that they would keep on referring to the funeral of the deceased even after many years have elapsed. As they refer to it, they point to how the deceased was "escorted well" (*ne okow maber* in Luo). By this statement, they mean how mourners were taken good care of in the deceased burial.

The Effects of Luo Traditions on the Luo-Muslim View of Widow and Widowhood

As has been noted at the beginning of this chapter, the later stage of a Luo-Muslim funeral also contains rituals that apply to widows. These rituals affect their lives in different ways. First, the awareness by married and unmarried women that there are rituals that await them causes little surprise when later in life they encounter the loss of their husbands. This is mostly true with women who have been Muslims since they were born. They make little distinction between Islam and Luo traditions. Second, a combination of Luo traditional and Islamic rituals makes it very extensive. This discourages women and widows in particular. It causes them to think of death as a law that stresses or puts a lot of demand on them. It makes them feel that they carry two different but heavy loads: the load of losing a husband and that of being engaged in the elaborate cleansing rituals. This is more aggravating.

Third, the thinking that Islam shields the widows quickly fades away with the realization that Luo traditional rituals are practiced by the Luo Muslims. This is particularly true to the widows who joined Islam after their husbands have died. They get dismayed and demoralized with the discovery that they have been caught up with the practices they were running away from. They begin to relate to Islam as a religion that is no different from the old Luo customs or Christianity except in care-giving and material support they received. Fourth, the experiences and challenges that widows encounter in following Luo traditions as practicing Muslims have made some unmarried Muslim women decide to stay single the rest of their lives. But the pressure to marry as a way of limiting promiscuity in the community makes them get married anyhow. The cultural Luo practices on Luo-Muslim widows have made them live double lives. One foot is in Islam while the other is in Luo traditions. The fact that they follow Luo practices makes them feel less different from the rest of the Luo people. This belief implies that the difference between a true Luo and untrue one lies on whether one still follows the fundamental values of Luo tradition. This truth shows that it is the practicing of Luo traditions that defines who a Luo is. Being in a religion such as Islam or Christianity has therefore very little bearing on an individual's identity as a Luo.

The impure state by which widows find themselves after they have lost their husbands is also affected. Restriction to their movements immediately takes full effect without considering their ages as Islam teaches. The elderly widows who are supposed to enjoy some freedom of movement also find themselves being looked upon with suspicion. The chasm that develops between them and close relatives that they have been in good relationship with before their husbands die keeps them aloof. The choice to re-marry whoever they want is never an easy task especially for the young Muslim widows. Due to their age, they are still considered unable to make right choices over which man to marry. Husbands are therefore imposed on them through a traditional process. Apart from a soured relationship with the relatives, such widows find themselves in a dilemma over which religion to follow. The credibility of Islam as a religion that practices what it teaches is also thrown into doubt.

Continuity and Discontinuity of the Luo Traditional View of Death among Luo Muslims

As stated in the methodology chapter, this section utilizes Strauss and Corbin's interrogative pronouns such as the who, what, why, where, how, and when of death.[5] Through these interrogative pronouns, areas where similarities and differences lie between Islam and Luo traditional customs in the three stages of the Luo-Muslim funeral have been identified. Similarities speak of continuity while differences point to the discontinuity of the Luo traditional view in Luo-Muslim funeral beliefs and practices. Since the similarities and differences between Luo traditions and Islamic funeral customs has been discussed in response to the first part of research question 2 (RQ2), it is critical in this section is to describe what determines the continuity or discontinuity of the Luo traditional view of death among Luo Muslims in Kendu Bay. In every stage of Luo-Muslim funeral, therefore, the first task is to offer a brief description of their beliefs and practices. Second, is to identify past Luo funeral customs that Luo Muslims continue to follow and the factors that have caused them to follow those beliefs and practices.

Since the domains of the partial-Islamic and non-Islamic elements are where the similarity of both customs lies, they have been used to describe this aspect of continuity. Last, the beliefs and practices of the Luo traditions that the Luo Muslims no longer follow in their funerals and the factors that have caused them to stop have also been identified and explained. The domain of total-Islamic element points to the differences. It therefore clarifies aspects of discontinuity. The diagram below has been used as a reference point in describing how the aspects of continuity and discontinuity of Luo traditional views appear in the three stages of a Luo-Muslim funeral. But since there is an overlapping of some interrogative pronouns in different sub-categories, a separate diagram was used in each of the three stages of the Luo-Muslim funeral. It describes how each of the six interrogative pronouns (who, what, why, where, how, and when) defines the relationship between the main and the other sub-categories of death. It was here that the similarities and the differences that explain the aspects of continuity and discontinuity of Luo traditional view were drawn.

---

5. Corbin and Strauss, *Basics of Qualitative Research*, 123.

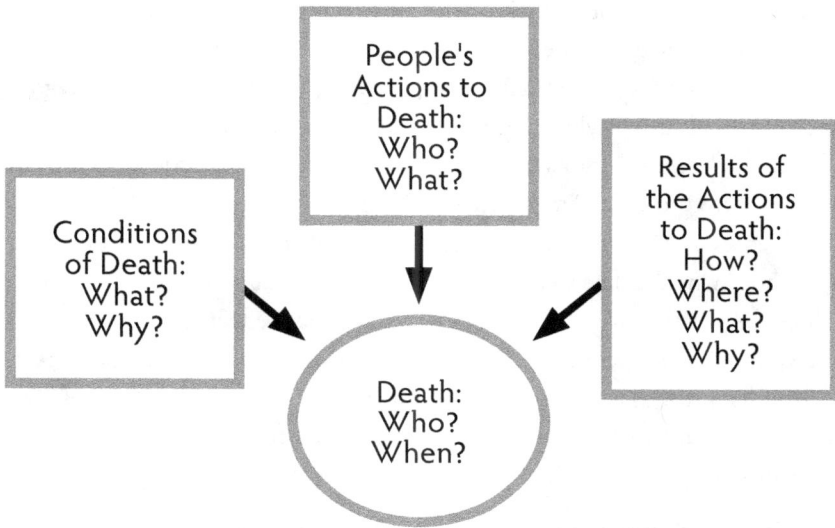

Diagram 28: A Reference Point for Continuity and Discontinuity of Luo Traditional View in Three Stages of Luo-Muslim Funeral

Initial Stage: Continuity or Discontinuity of Luo Traditional View of Death

As has been disclosed in the previous two sections of this study, both Luo traditional and Islamic elements are present in Luo-Muslim funeral beliefs and practices, though varied. This echoes what Rosander predicted that, as the Islamization process takes place, the line between Islam and the local custom would become clear.[6] The funeral context of Luo Muslims presents a case in which both Islamic and Luo indigenous customs can be compared and contrasted from each other. Interestingly though, and as Rosander has forecasted, the line between the two customs is clearer to the outsiders than the indigenous people who are practicing Muslims. However, this point of discussion is dealt with in the next chapter.

Both diagrams 19 and 24 in the previous section show that Islamic customs are more practiced than the Luo traditional ones in the initial stage of Luo-Muslim funeral. The implication to this is that the differences between

---

6. Rosander, "Islamization of 'Tradition,'" 6.

them outweigh their similarities. This further implies that it is discontinuity rather continuity that is the most prevalent in the initial stage. This profound truth is part of what diagram 28 above conveys. Death as the main category is the bedrock upon which other sub-categories or ligaments (Conditions of Death, People's Actions to Death, and Results of the Actions to Death) are connected to. The interrogative pronoun of "who" as it relates to death provides a description of the person who has died in terms of gender and age while "when" refers to the time of demise. But due to the interconnectedness between death and its sub-categories that reflect the behavior and the actions of the people, all of the six interrogative pronouns have been utilized as much as necessary at every stage of the Luo-Muslim funeral. The table below shows similarities and differences of Luo traditions in the initial stage of Luo-Muslim funeral.

Table 10: The Content of Luo Traditions at the Initial Stage of Luo-Muslim Funeral

Category/ Sub-Category	Inter-rogative Pronouns Applied	Descriptions	Luo-Muslim Funeral Beliefs and Practices	
			Similar to Luo Traditions	Different from Luo Traditions
Death	Who?	Deceased gender & age – as a determinant of who washes and shrouds.	No	Yes
	When?	Time of demise – other funeral functions center on it.	No	Yes
Conditions of Death	What?	Causalities of death – human or divine?	Yes	Yes
	Why?	Underlying reasons for death	Yes	Yes

People's Actions to Death	Who?	People factor in the initial stage in terms of:		
		• Numbers in attendance.	Yes	No
		• Numbers in *ghusl*	No	Yes
	What?	Ritual activities involved in washing and shrouding:		
		• Weeping/wailing	Yes	Yes
		• Gender & Age	No	Yes
Results of the Actions to Death	How?	Procedures for washing and shrouding	No	Yes
	Where?	Place where *ghusl* and shrouding are done	No	Yes
	What?	The materials used for the *ghusl* ritual	Yes	Yes
	Why?	The meaning/significance of rituals in the initial stage	Yes	Yes

Continuity and discontinuity in Luo-Muslim view of death and its related rituals

As reflected on the table above, all the six interrogative pronouns have been used in the main and the rest of the sub-categories to establish the similarities and the differences of Luo traditions in a Luo-Muslim funeral. The description column shows how they have been applied in the main and other sub-categories of death. Under the column of Luo-Muslim beliefs and practices, the level of Luo traditional view in the Luo-Muslim funeral customs has been compared and contrasted. Where similarities lie are represented by "Yes" while the differences are marked by "No." As shown on the table, the interrogative pronoun of "who" appears in the main category of death and in the sub-category of people's actions to death. It represents both the person participating in the rituals and the deceased on whose account the rituals are being conducted. It relates to age, gender, and number of people in attendance as well as in conducting the funeral activities in the initial stage. Ideally, the "who" as a person is in direct relationship with the other interrogative pronouns: when, what, why, where, and how. This shows that the different categories as well as the three stages of Luo-Muslim funeral relate with each other. The relationship that they share thus implies that it is also impossible to classify Luo funeral beliefs and practices as independent entities of Luo traditional and Islamic customs.

As the "Yes" and "No" reflect on the table, it is evident that areas of similarities in the main category of death and its sub-categories of people's actions to death are fewer than the differences. This implies that discontinuity is more prevalent than the continuity in these two categories. The interrogative pronoun of "what" appears in the sub-categories of conditions of death, people's actions to death, and the results of the actions to death. It points to causality and the circumstances that may have led to the death of an individual. It also describes the rituals that are undertaken in this stage such as weeping, wailing, and the material used for washing and shrouding. All these are observed in relation to gender and age of the persons ("who") involved.

As the diagram shows, most of what Luo Muslims believe and practice during their funeral service are similar but at the same time different from the Luo traditional view except in gender and age. Those areas are represented by "Yes" in both columns of "similar to" and "different from." Those areas of similarities and differences lie in the form and meaning that the Luo Muslims have attached to them. The "Yes" on both sides gives a sense of continuity and discontinuity in part. Since the Luo customs practiced in this initial stage are of the former Luo traditions, the aspect of continuity is due to the need to continue with Luo practices that are in line with the Islamic practice. But the part of discontinuity implies that some Luo old practices have been modified while others that are not in line with Islam have been discarded. It is in these areas that show the evidence of continuity and discontinuity that make the basis of argument in the next chapter.

Continuity and discontinuity in conditions and the results of the actions to death

The interrogative pronoun of "why" is found in both sub-categories of conditions of death and results of the actions to death. It describes the underlying reasons that could have led to one's demise as well as providing meaning or significance to the rituals undertaken at the initial stage. The "Yes" answer in the sub-category of conditions of death shows that the way Luo Muslims seek answers to death is similar to yet different from the way it is sought traditionally among the Luo people. Death is explained in part as divinely caused. This divine perspective of death is in step with what Islam teaches. It reflects the kind of belief some Luo Muslims have. But it is also different because some Luo Muslims also believe that human causality may be involved in one's death. This is particularly so because of the complaints about the evil eye or tongue that is common among them. This belief is, however, perceived very quietly since it is against Islamic faith to accuse someone of being responsible for such vices. The evidence of discontinuity however is strong. This is perceived to be so through the words from the majority of adult Muslims. They glorify Allah in death. This means that death starts and ends with him. However, the quietness by which some Luo Muslims talk about human causality is enough proof that the practice is still being followed secretly.

The "Yes" for both the similarity and the difference shows that the meaning or significance that the rituals have under the sub-category of results of the actions to death carries both the aspect of continuity and discontinuity. In other words, some meanings or significances are Luo traditional while others are Islamic. But as it has been pointed out, it is not easy to draw a line between what is continued and what is not continued. The interrogative pronoun of "where" surfaces on the sub-category of results of the actions to death. It points to a place where *ghusl* and shrouding are done. The "No" and "Yes" answers indicate that it is an area where discontinuity has prevailed. The reason for this is that in most cases the Luo Muslims conduct the rituals of *ghusl* and shrouding in the mosque. This applies even in a situation where the burial is expected to take place at the deceased's home. However, the home washing of the body is also allowed though in a limited sense. The reason why it is preferred to be done at the mosque is to avoid the disruption of the people conducting the ritual. But also by the virtue of being a holy place, the deceased is believed to benefit more since Allah's presence is with him.

Just like in the "where," the "how" also has the "No" and "Yes" as the answers that point to discontinuity of Luo traditional view. The procedures that it stands for are much related to the place where the *ghusl* takes place. The essence of time as represented by the interrogative pronoun "when" is taken with a lot of seriousness among the Luo Muslims. Being a component in the main category, it affects the activities at every stage of the funeral. The "No" and "Yes" answers that it refers to makes it clear that it carries the element of discontinuity. This is made visible through the swiftness by which death messages are relayed and the immediate commencement of *ghusl* ritual. The ultimate goal is to bury the deceased as fast as possible. Even if for some reasons there is a delay, the maximum it should take is three days. But transporting the body to be buried in the ancestral land may sometimes be delayed. The body is kept in the mortuary while fundraising is conducted to cater for the hospital bills and other expenses. This, however, is usually very minimal.

Except for the interrogative pronouns of "what" and "why" that contain a mix of continuity and discontinuity, all the others represented in the main and sub-categories point to the discontinuity. The few of the Luo traditions that are still followed in this initial stage are former Luo traditions (see table 3). They are mainly carried out by adult Muslims of male and female gender (see tables 4 and 5). They are, however, of little impact at this initial stage of the Luo-Muslim beliefs and practices (see table 6). The picture being depicted is that what the Luo Muslim believes and practices in the initial stage of their funerals has very little in common with the Luo traditions. In other words, they follow them minimally. Factors that promote continuity and discontinuity in each stage of the Luo-Muslim funeral are dealt with at the end of the third stage.

Middle Stage: Continuity or Discontinuity of Luo Traditional View of Death

Diagrams 20 and 24 give a summary of the extent to which Luo traditional view has affected the Luo-Muslim understanding of death and its related rituals. The order of domain that puts the non-Islamic element as the leading followed by the partial-Islamic element and finally the total-Islamic element is clear evidence that the middle stage of the Luo-Muslim funeral has a lot of Luo traditional elements compared to the Islamic ones. This section, just as in the previous one, identifies funeral beliefs and practices that the Luo Muslims continue or have discontinued from their past Luo background.

Table 11: The Content of Luo Traditions at the Middle Stage of Luo-Muslim Funeral

Category/ Sub-Category	Interrogative Pronouns Applied	Descriptions	Luo-Muslim Funeral Beliefs and Practices	
			Similar to Luo Traditions	Different from Luo Traditions
Death	Who?	Gender – bier carriers and burying the deceased	Yes	No
	When?	Time for viewing and transporting the body to grave	No	Yes
Conditions of Death	What?	N/A	N/A	N/A
	Why?	N/A	N/A	N/A
People's Actions to Death	Who?	People factor in the middle stage in terms of: • Mourners in attendance.	Yes	No
		• Numbers and Gender	Yes	Yes
	What?	Ritual activities involved: • Prayers for deceased and saints	Yes	No
		• Grave burial	Yes	No

Results of the Actions to Death	How?	Procedures in burial	Yes	Yes
	Where?	Area and position of burial	Yes	Yes
	What?	The items used for burial	Yes	No
	Why?	The meaning/significance of rituals in the middle stage	Yes	Yes

Continuity and discontinuity in the Luo-Muslim view of death and its related rituals

Funeral beliefs and practices that are followed in the middle stage range from shrouding to the laying of the body in the grave. In the above table, the interrogative pronoun of "who," appears in both the main category of death and the sub-category of people's actions to death. It shows that the practice of carrying the bier by Luo Muslims and the way they bury is similar to the Luo traditions. Similarity is in the sense that carrying of a bier or a casket and laying the dead in the grave are taken to be men's responsibility. The fact that Luo men have been responsible in burying the dead means that Islam has not brought anything different. It is shows that there is continuity. But there is continuity and discontinuity with regard to numbers and gender. This is represented by the "Yes" answer on both sides of "similar to" and "different from" as indicated on the table. Continuity is based on gender and mourners in attendance while discontinuity is with reference to numbers.

The gender here refers to male. As it has been pointed out, it is men who dig the grave and transport the *geneza* that carries the remains of the deceased to the burial site. They then lay it to rest in the grave. The men who perform these duties in this middle stage are mostly youths. This stage is usually characterized by many mourners who want to pay their last respect to the deceased or just have a glimpse of him before the burial procession begins. In such occasions the crowd is always a mixed one. Both male and female interact together. There is no difference with the Luo tradition in this. Just like the other areas of Luo-Muslim funeral rituals where the number counts, the male persons who enter the grave in order to bury the dead are usually restricted to three. This is Islamic and it is in contrast to the Luo traditions where, even though men are the ones responsible, the number that does the burial is unlimited. The difference is therefore an indication of discontinuity

Continuity and discontinuity in conditions, people's actions and results of actions to death

Conditions of death, people's actions to death, and results of the actions to death are all sub-categories that are identified with the interrogative pronoun of "what." As pointed out in the diagram under the sub-category of conditions of death, the use of "what" that describes the circumstances leading to death is not applicable (N/A) at this middle stage. The reason is that it is at the beginning (initial stage) when news about one's demise is received with different reactions. Some may cry loudly as they utter words while others may just be at a shock over the incidence. People may gather in small groups and ask each other quietly about the circumstances that have caused death, especially if it is a mysterious one. Some would simply be praising Allah (*Allah akbar*) while others sink in deep thoughts. Depending on which side of the divide one belongs to, the cause of death can either be attributed to Allah or to a fellow human being. With time there is acceptance of what has happened. The weeping or loud crying that may happen during the time the body is viewed as it gets prepared to be transported to the graveside has very little to do with remembering the circumstances of death. The weeping or loud crying has all to do with facing the reality that the loved one has truly died.

But under the category of people's actions to death, there is both "Yes" and "No" in areas of prayers for deceased and other saints as well as in the grave burial. The "Yes" and "No" answers signify that there is continuity of Luo traditional beliefs and practices over those areas of Luo-Muslim funeral. Although its mode or form may be different, prayers are generally accepted and viewed as significant in the life of every individual. The Luo traditional prayers for the deceased are usually directed to the ancestors. The view here is that they pray to their forefathers who died a long time ago, who in turn take their prayers to God. They essentially believe in God and the ancestors as his intermediaries. The fact that prophet Muhammad and Abraham and their families are also prayed for while praying for the deceased provides some similarities. They too are considered as ancestors. The difference is that they are not prayed to but rather prayed for.

There is similarity in the grave burial in the sense that it is a burial that takes place rather than disposing the body by other means such as throwing it into a forest or river. Under the sub-category of results of the actions to death, there is "Yes" and "No" over the items used for burial. Other items for burial such as *sanda* and the bier (though Luo Muslims prefer to use the one made without nails) are the same, but the one with most similarity is the soil. After the dead is laid in the grave, the soil is returned back. Besides cultural reasons associated to it, covering the body with the soil prevents bad smell that could otherwise affect people.

Just as it is with the interrogative pronoun "what," so it is with "why" in the sub-category of conditions of death. It is not applicable because the underlying cause for death, whether human or divine is something that is less considered in the middle stage of the funeral. But in the sub-category of the results of the actions to death, the "why" is used to point to the meaning or significance of the rituals conducted in the middle stage. The fact that they are similar to and different from the Luo traditions as represented by "Yes" on both sides shows both the aspect of continuity and discontinuity. The rituals include the viewing of the body that sometimes is done in the initial stage, observing silence while carrying the bier to the graveyard and the throwing of soil on the grave by family members before the rest of the soil is returned to the grave. The discontinuity part is mostly on the aspect of scooping and throwing soil on the grave. Due to Islamic influence it is done by male relatives since women in most cases are not allowed to come close to the grave, especially if the burial takes place at the cemetery.

The interrogative pronoun, "where" has also been utilized under sub-category of results of the actions to death. It speaks of an area and the position of burial. Here too the practice by Luo Muslims is similar to and different from the Luo traditional perspective. The similarity that points to continuity is evidenced by the fact that Luo Muslims allow the burial of the deceased to take place in their home. This is done in response to the wishes of the family but also in keeping with the tradition of the Luo.[7] With regard to the position of burial, the head of the deceased must face somewhere. Though not completely the same, the position where the head

---

7. The need to be identified as a Luo person makes it possible.

faces argues for continuity. The burials conducted in the cemetery strictly reflect the requirement in Islam that the body should face Mecca (Kaaba) whereas the ones conducted at home may be done culturally in line with Luo tradition. Those differences point to an element of discontinuity. The body of the deceased, however, is laid on its side based on gender. A male is laid to sleep on his right hand while a female sleeps on her left hand.

The right side represents a position of authority while the left side signifies weakness. Men are therefore viewed as possessing authority, for instance, as the head of the home, while women are regarded as weak. The weakness is a physical and emotional one. The laying of the deceased on their sides is continuity. It is a practice that has been passed on to the Luo people for many generations. It is also similar to the "how" of burial, as found in the same sub-category of results of the actions of death. It spells out the procedures followed in laying the dead to rest in the grave. The procedure that is followed is that there must be some people inside the dug grave who would receive the body. It is basically the same with the exception of the number of male persons that should be in the grave. That slight difference is what argues for discontinuity. The interrogative pronoun of "when" as it applies in the main category of death is the backbone of other sub-categories. It conveys the element of time. All the rituals in the initial and the middle stages are done with a view to burying the deceased within twenty-four hours. It is an area where discontinuity stands as represented by "Yes" and "No" answers. But just as it has been explained in the initial stage, the possibility of going beyond the twenty-four hour period cannot miss.

All of the six interrogative pronouns except one as used in the main and the sub-categories of death hold descriptions of continuity. The one that points to discontinuity is the interrogative pronoun of "when." This implies that the majority of funeral beliefs and practices of the Luo Muslims in the middle stage are Luo traditional in nature. But, since those who are involved in this stage of Luo-Muslim funeral beliefs and practices are mostly youths and children (see table 4), they tend to follow the current or latter Luo traditional practices than the former (see table 3) that are associated with the adult Muslims. It is the male youths and children who are very involved in this stage (see table 5). The impact of this continuity of Luo traditions is, however, moderate in the funeral beliefs and practices that the Luo Muslims follow (see table 6).

Table 12: The Content of Luo Traditions at the Later Stage of Luo-Muslim Funeral

Category/ Sub-Category	Inter-rogative Pronouns Applied	Descriptions	Luo-Muslim Funeral Beliefs and Practices	
			Similar to Luo Traditions	Different from Luo Traditions
Death	Who?	Gender and age of the deceased buried	Yes	No
	When?	Memories of the deceased	Yes	No
Conditions of Death	What?	N/A	N/A	N/A
	Why?	N/A	N/A	N/A
People's Actions to Death	Who?	People factor in the later stage in: • Feeding	Yes	No
		• Ritual practitioner	Yes	No
	What?	Rituals or activities involved: • Eating by mourners	Yes	No
		• Rituals by widows and their behavior	Yes	No
Results of the Actions to Death	How?	Procedures in 'iddah of widows	Yes	Yes
	Where?	Place where widows stay	Yes	Yes
	What?	The widow's wear	Yes	No
	Why?	The meaning/significance of rituals in the later stage	Yes	Yes

Later Stage: Continuity or Discontinuity of the Luo Traditional View of Death

The information that is shown on diagrams 9 and 12 presents the partial-Islamic element as leading in scores. The non-Islamic element comes second while the total-Islamic element is third. This order of sequence signifies that the Luo traditions are more common in the later stage of Luo-Muslim funeral than the Islamic beliefs and practices. As noted in the previous sections, the rituals or activities that are predominant in the later stage are the feeding of mourners and those that are exercised on widows. These activities are what take place after the burial. From time to time people get to visit the cemetery and other places where their fellow Muslims have been buried. The places to visit do not necessarily have to be where one's own family member or relative has been buried. Just like in the previous two sections, Strauss and Corbin's coding paradigm as well as their interrogative pronouns[8] have been utilized. The goal is to help identify customs in Luo-Muslim funeral where there are aspects of continuity and discontinuity of the Luo traditions. The following table provides the details of the activities and the outcomes involved.

Continuity and discontinuity in the Luo-Muslim view of death in relation to people's actions

The "who" in the main category of death is different from the "who" of the sub-category of people's actions to death. The former is in relation to the deceased while the latter refers to the individuals who participate in the activities that come after death. The gender and the age of the deceased are very important. They determine whether it is the woman who should carry out the rituals. If the deceased is a married man, then his wife would automatically enter into 'iddah (widowhood) period. The husband is taken to be of age by the virtue of being married. This implies that one's age, especially for a man, is determined by whether or not he is married. Being married elevates him to a status of *jaduong* or *wuon pacho* (which literally means in Luo, an elder or the owner of the house or home). So, in the view of Luo Muslims' age factor for a man is pegged not so much on the number of years one has lived but on whether he is married. In this scenario, a person who is advanced in years and not yet married is regarded as a child. A younger man who is married is more respected than him. But due to the stigma and mistrust that being unmarried brings to an individual, most of them get

---

8. Corbin and Strauss, *Basics of Qualitative Research*, 99, 123.

married generally early in life. However, physical challenges like blindness as is in Saidi's case[9] may make someone to take long before getting married.

The second interrogative pronoun of "who" that lies under the sub-category of people's actions to death, describes the individuals participating in eating and widowhood rituals. The former is usually a big group comprising of both genders. The latter is what is determined by the interrogative pronoun of "who" that is found in the main category of death. All the answers that are conveyed as shown in both the main category and the sub-category of peoples' actions to death are "Yes" and "No." This implies that in both categories there is the evidence of continuity. This continuity is because of the gender in the main category of death that determines the gender in the sub-category of death. It is also with respect to eating since this is a practice the Luo people have carried on with. But just like in other areas, the aspect of discontinuity cannot be ruled out. It is found in the details regarding the rituals that the Luo-Muslim widow follows. Some of it is continued while others are Islamic.

Continuity and discontinuity of the Luo-Muslim view of death in relation to actions and results

Under the sub-category of conditions of death, the interrogative pronoun "what" is not applicable. This is because people have finally submitted to Allah's will for taking the deceased's life. There could still, however, be questions in their minds regarding the circumstances that led to the person's death. Rather than speaking out, they ponder them in their hearts. In the sub-category of people's action to death, it is the food that mourners eat and the behavior of the widow that the interrogative pronoun of "what" describes. Just like in Luo tradition, the Luo Muslims provide a lot of food to the mourners. The meaning they attach to this is also similar. After burying the widow's husband, her behavior is closely watched. Due to the loss that is still very fresh in her memory, she is expected to avoid talking too much or intermingling freely with other people. The way to be detached from these activities is to stay indoors most of the time. Even though she may not be told directly, going out and sharing light moments with people is construed as being disrespectful to the deceased. These are beliefs and

---

9. Saidi, interview with author.

practices that are very familiar in the Luo traditional context. They therefore demonstrate continuity.

The "Yes" and "No" that the interrogative pronoun of "what" points to under the sub-category of results of the actions to death also shows the evidence of continuity. The widow's clothes, whether in the former or latter Luo traditions is often black or any material that is close to black. It signifies that she is in a mourning period. It is by this practice of the same by Luo-Muslim widows that leads to the conclusion that they still follow Luo traditions. However, it is the *'iddah* period that is fixed at four months and ten days that makes the difference. This difference, although negligible, highlights the fact that it is almost impossible to talk of continuity of the Luo traditions in Luo-Muslim funeral beliefs and practices without considering the element of discontinuity. The same truth applies where discontinuity is predominant.

The interrogative pronoun of "where" has been applied in the sub-category of the results of the actions to death as a pointer to the place where the Luo-Muslim widow stays. This place of stay is similar to and yet different from the Luo tradition. The similarity is mostly common during her period of *'iddah*. She confines herself to her late husband's home. It is after the *'iddah* period where the difference with regard to her place of stay lies. Depending on the decision she makes as to whether to remain single or to re-marry, she has the option to continue staying in her late husband's home. She may also decide to re-locate to *miji* where other Luo Muslims are residing or move to stay at the home of her new husband or re-locate to a completely new place. But even in areas where there are differences, the Luo traditions still surface.

The same sub-category of the results of the actions to death has also utilized the interrogative pronoun of "why." It describes the meaning/significance of rituals in the later stage of Luo-Muslim funeral as being similar to and different from the Luo tradition. The food that the Luo Muslims provide during the funeral has similar religious, economic and social significance to the Luo traditions. There is, however, some slight differences on the rituals pertaining to the widow as have been described. Similarity points to continuity while the difference signifies discontinuity. They are, however, not in the same proportion. The interrogative pronoun of "how" has also been used under the sub-category of results of the actions to death to describe procedures that the Luo-Muslim widows undergo during *'iddah* period. The "Yes" answer on both sides of the Luo-Muslim funeral beliefs and practices signify the presence of both continuity and discontinuity. The procedures in *'iddah* that include a period of seclusion, the wearing of a black cloth, and the issue of re-marriage are all related to *chola/okola* of the Luo tradition. They are areas where continuity of the Luo traditions is evident. But the length of the period that *'iddah* takes, the decision to re-marry, and the place to settle after getting re-married are somehow different. The difference is what shows discontinuity.

The interrogative pronoun of "when" points to the memories that the Luo Muslims have concerning their loved ones after being buried. Both genders are affected by the memory of the deceased, though not in the same way. The widows who decide not to remarry have longer memories of their departed husbands than those who settle into another marriage shortly after they have buried their husbands. This quick remarriage is due to the loneliness that the widows encounter. The decision to stay without getting remarried is due to a healthy and strong relationship that a widow had with her spouse before his demise. Such a widow is convinced that having a relationship as she had with her late husband may not be possible in a marriage with another husband. The ones who have remarried settle and get occupied with the affairs of their new family. They therefore lose the memories of their loved ones so fast. It is only when the new marriage fails to function properly that their minds flash back to the good life they used to enjoy with their late husbands.

The answers of "Yes" and "No" confirm that the memories of the Luo Muslims concerning their dead ones have their roots in the Luo traditions. They have therefore been continued. The continuity that is evident in this later stage of Luo-Muslim funeral identifies more with the former Luo traditions (see table 3). It is the adult Muslims but particularly of the female gender that are most involved (see tables 4 and 5). The involvement of the adult Muslims is because these traditions are linked with old life. They are more attractive to them than the Muslim youths or children. The impact that the continuity of Luo traditions has brought in Luo-Muslim funeral beliefs and practices is described as great. Although there are spots of discontinuity,

continuity characterizes most aspects of Luo-Muslim beliefs and practices in their later stage of the funeral. The table below gives a summary of continuity and discontinuity of Luo traditions and how best they have been described in each stage of the Luo-Muslim funeral.

Table 13: Continuity and Discontinuity in the Three Stages of Luo-Muslim Funeral

Stages in Luo-Muslim Funeral	Description
Initial Stage	Discontinuity with Minimal Continuity
Middle Stage	Continuity with Minimal Discontinuity
Later Stage	Continuity with Minimal Discontinuity

Continuity and Discontinuity in the Three Stages of Luo-Muslim Funeral

As the table demonstrates, it is in the initial stage of the Luo-Muslim funeral that shows strong elements of discontinuity. Continuity is minimal. The middle and the later stages show the opposite. They have very strong elements of continuity but minimal in the aspect of discontinuity. The discovery that the Luo Muslims follow Luo traditions in some areas of their funeral while in other areas they have abandoned them is quite insightful. First, it contradicts the position that some scholars such as Odaga and Ogutu have held for many years.[10] They see no change in Luo funeral practices despite the influence of Christianity or Islam. Their view of the lack of change implies that, despite being Muslims or Christians, the Luo people have maintained solely their old funeral beliefs and practices. On the other hand, the argument by Olupona that Christianity and Islam have filtered and changed the people from traditional beliefs and practices gives the impression that religion has swept away traditional customs.[11] However, the case of the Luo-Muslim funerals in Kendu Bay presents the two sides of the coin. It acknowledges that there is change in some areas while other areas have remained unchanged.

---

10. Odaga, *Luo Oral Literature*, 39–40; Ogutu, "African Perception," 104.
11. Olupona, "Major Issues in the Study," 26.

Continuity of the Luo traditions may be attributed to many factors. First, it is as a result of the wishes that the family of the deceased give. Throughout the Luo-Muslim funeral, the wishes of the immediate family of the deceased are taken seriously. Some of their family members are Muslims while others are not. But regardless of their religious affiliation, they are consulted in every step of the funeral. It is through their wishes that the burial may be delayed to a few more days. This applies when there are some members of the family that are still abroad. It is only when they come that the burial may proceed. At times the delay is because the family members and relatives are still raising funds to meet funeral expenses. The delay may also occur in order not to make the deceased feel that he is unloved.[12] The family may also ask for their loved one to be buried in the home instead of the cemetery. The use of an expensive casket that is made by nails is sometimes allowed. Sometimes it is the Luo Muslims themselves who either ask or grant these wishes. The fact that they are involved in the decision making and in ensuring that the family values are respected, give proof of continuity.

The perception that the Luo people have about ancestral land has been one of the factors that has greatly affected the way they live in different parts of the country. The issue has more to do with the ancestral spirits than the land itself. The feeling to be close to the graves of their forefathers is what causes the attraction to home. The concept that they have about doing things as a community and not as an individual also contributes to the thinking about the ancestral land. This practice is common in a funeral meeting where the decision of the majority, especially that of the elders in the group, will carry the day. It is a *taboo*, so it is believed, to go against the wishes of the elders. The practicality of this is also evident in Luo politics where following (*luwo* in Luo) majority's decision is practiced. The seeing of vehicles transporting dead bodies of the Luo Muslims back to the ancestral home for burial is therefore not unfamiliar.

Another contributing factor is linked to human dignity. Dignity for a Luo, as Luo Muslims explained it, includes a healthy lifestyle and a deserving and befitting burial. The former consists of financial resources that make one's life comfortable while the latter is about providing plenty of food and

---

12. The belief here is that the more days the deceased take before buried the more he feels that he is loved and cared for.

drinks to the guests who attend the burial. The latter requires an environment that is conducive and can host many people and many burial activities. This disqualifies the cemetery and other burial outside the home. It is when people are able to attend one's burial in their home or in the home where they have built a house that they feel that they have accorded the deceased a proper burial. Burying outside the home or in a cemetery is equated with throwing away the body in a forest. This is shameful and amounts to lowering not only the dignity of the deceased but also that of his family members and relatives. It becomes a talk that may go on for a long time. The need to preserve one's dignity after he dies is the reason why many Luo people in the recent past have been putting up homes in their ancestral land. It is believed that the deceased is as dignified as the place where he comes from. It is not viewed as a dignified act to bury outside one's home. These deep-seated thoughts from the Luo Muslims go beyond what a non-Luo Muslim knows. They help to advance the argument that some Luo Muslims have continued to follow the past traditions of their forefathers.

The need to have a sense of belonging is another factor that has caused continuity. There is a feeling among some Luo Muslims that unless they follow Luo traditions they have no full recognition as members of the Luo community. This experience is worsened by the way other Luo people look down upon them. The comparison to the effect that Christianity allows Luo traditions to thrive has also worsened the matter. This is very ironic since in other places in Kendu Bay, it is the Luo Muslims who get accused by Christians of following the customs of Luo tradition. In order to minimize such accusations and perceptions from both within and from other people, and in order not to be isolated and thus lose one's identity from the wider community of Luo, reverting into Luo traditional practices has been justified among some Luo Muslims. Even though Islam has significantly transformed many lives of its followers, some are still skeptical about Islam. They are in Islam and yet the fear of abandoning traditional rituals such as *ter* (wife inheritance) has a strong grip on them. They therefore follow some of these traditions secretly so as not to be seen as the root causes of *chira* (in Luo, meaning curses) in the community.

Scarcity of land in Kendu Bay is one of the factors that have contributed to the discontinuity of some Luo funeral traditions. For instance, some

Luo Muslims who have very little or no piece of land were found to prefer a cemetery over the home burial. They argue that cemetery is a place where any Muslim can be buried while burial at home or in one's ancestral land is sometimes never guaranteed. The reason why it may not be automatic to be buried at home or in the ancestral land, especially for the deceased who has been living away from home for long, is that some people whom he may be related to could be staying on the piece of land that he was entitled to. Staying away for many years without coming home sometimes makes people assume that the person had already died and was buried in the city. This is particularly so with the news that the person has converted to Islam or Christianity.

When one converts into either of the two religions, they are said to be lost (*olal*). Coming home to settle on one's piece of land now becomes very difficult. Religion in this sense is perceived to make their culture lost to people. In other words, they ignore their cultural roots in the name of religion. But even if one manages to get a place, it might still be too small to contain all his family members, let alone the space to be buried. The issue of where one would be buried is a great concern for many Luo people regardless of one's religious affiliation. The scarcity of land therefore makes it imperative for them to think of other alternatives. One of the options is to join Islam. For those who have been active Muslims elsewhere and have come to settle at home, they may simply continue with the Muslim group that is on the ground. Others, especially those who have relational or land related problems, may decide to settle on one of the Luo-Muslim *miji* in Kendu Bay. By identifying with the rest of Luo-Muslim community, their burial at the cemetery when they die is assured. Cemetery burial signifies that they have discontinued the way Luo traditional burial is conducted.

In his study among the Yoruba people of Nigeria, Gilliland observes: "If Islam has a strong influence where there was once an active ancestor cult, the practices that center on the dead will be modified to fit the Muslim pattern."[13] This is true to the Luo Muslims in Kendu Bay in some aspects. Their participation in ancestor-related customs has been the basis upon which continuity has been explained. But it is also true that they have altered

---

13. Gilliland, *African Religion Meets Islam*, 106.

some of the funeral practices of Luo traditions in order to match with the Muslim way of life. It is this alteration, which is very deliberate, that gives a sense of discontinuity. As pointed out by Gilliland, this adjustment is very deliberate. It is a way of making a very clear distinction between what is Islamic and what is traditional. But the essence of modifying a custom in order to gain relevance may simply be a contextualization issue. In that case, there is nothing much that has been carried forward or discarded in the new lifestyle.

The majority of the Kenyan population consists of youths. According to the findings that are represented in tables 3 to 5, they are the group that is very active in the middle stage of the Luo-Muslim funeral. They follow current or latter rather than the former or old Luo traditions. This has some implications. First, to follow latter Luo traditions that are contemporary in standards implies that some former or old Luo traditions have become extinct. This however has a lesser impact compared to the great impact in the later stage of adult Muslims (see table 6). The latter follow the old or former Luo traditions. Also, the search for education and better living environments has led some Muslim youths to move and settle in urban centers. By interacting and relating with their non-Muslim peers, they have come to develop a mindset that tends to look down upon anything that is traditional. Their religious orientation also informs their thinking. As a result, they have consciously or unconsciously discontinued both the former and, to some degree, the latter Luo traditional funeral beliefs and practices.

Conclusion

This chapter was centered on how Luo traditional view has affected the Luo-Muslim understanding of death and its related practices. The same procedure in which funeral beliefs and practices are divided into the three stages was followed. The various Luo traditional elements were reviewed in their respective domains. In the initial stage that begins from the time the news of one's death is heard and ends with the shrouding of the body, the elements that are commonly practiced are Islamic in nature. It is therefore an area where Luo traditions have made little effect. The middle stage begins from the shrouding of the body to burial in the grave. Young people are mostly involved at this stage. The impact of Luo traditions is moderate.

The later stage has two main functions: rituals involving widows and the feeding of mourners. It is an area where Luo traditions have a great impact.

The last section of this chapter looks at the aspects of continuity and discontinuity of Luo traditions in Luo-Muslim funeral beliefs and practices. The researcher has utilized the following method for his data analysis: Strauss and Corbin's six interrogative pronouns, namely, who, how, what, when, where, and why as well as their coding paradigm that focuses on the following elements: the conditions or situations in which phenomenon occurs, the actions or interactions of the people in response to what is happening in the situations, and the consequences or results of the actions taken or inaction.[14] Those areas point to the similarities and the differences that the Luo-Muslim funeral beliefs and practices have with the Luo traditions. The area of similarities was represented by the "Yes" answer. It signifies continuity while a funeral element that is different from the Luo tradition points to discontinuity.

---

14. Corbin and Strauss, *Basics of Qualitative Research*, 99, 123.

CHAPTER 7

The Synthetic Conceptualization of Death among the Contemporary Luo Muslims in Kendu Bay

Introduction

The previous sections have dealt with the influence of Islam and the elements of Luo traditional views that still exist in the contemporary Luo-Muslim perceptions of death. The fact that the Luo Muslims still follow certain aspects of Luo traditions in their funeral practices is an indication of the mixing between Luo traditional and Islamic customs. This study was meant to accomplish three things. First, it seeks to describe the nature of the mixing between Islamic and Luo traditional funeral customs. Second, it aims to describe the kind of experiences that the contemporary Luo Muslims encounter in their understanding of death and its related practices as a result of the mixing of both customs. Lastly, it offers an understanding of how Luo-Muslims' experiences in mixing Islam and Luo traditional customs explain their conceptualization of death.

This chapter responds to research question 3 (RQ3). It deals with the relationship between the official Islam (as derived from the textual study) and the actual experiences among Luo Muslims relating to death (as were encountered during the field research) in Kendu Bay. In order to provide an adequate description of the synthetic nature of the Luo-Muslim perception of death, Kim's concept of the Domain of Total Synthesis, DTS[1] and Conn's

---

1. Kim, *Islam among the Swahili*, 58–68.

Ultimate Synthesis[2] were utilized (see Methodology chapter). Kim's DTS, which he represents by letter "D," is a product of the mingling and the fusion of the other three domains.[3] It is this "Domain of Total Synthesis" that is relevant to this study. Just like Kim's DTS, Conn's concept of Ultimate Synthesis is the outcome of the interaction between Islam and African culture. This interaction is on equal terms in which both cultures gain and lose at the same time. Kim and Conn's concepts provide the understanding of the nature of Islam among the coastal people of East Africa. The use of terms such as *mila* and *dini* (especially by Kim) are therefore very applicable within that context. But while retaining some of their terms like "Synthesis" and "Domain," other terms that fit the local context of Luo Islam in Kendu Bay have been introduced. Apart from the terms, a diagram as shown below has also been drawn. It shows experiences and relationships that a Luo Muslim in Kendu Bay has. The diagram has been developed from both Kim's DTS and Conn's Ultimate Synthesis. The diagram summarizes the Luo-Muslim experiences in Kendu Bay and their dynamic relationships as a crucial foundation to their understanding of death.

Religio-Cultural Characteristics and Themes Underlying Luo-Muslim Views of Death

As highlighted in the previous chapters and as demonstrated by the above diagram, Islam has had a considerable influence on the funeral beliefs and practices of the Luo Muslims in Kendu Bay. While this is true, other areas in the Luo-Muslim understanding of death have partially or totally not been affected by Islam. The extent to which Islam has affected the funeral beliefs and practices of the Luo Muslims was the basis upon which the domains of total-Islamic, partial-Islamic and non-Islamic element were coined (see chapter 4). These three domains signify that there is continuity and discontinuity of the Luo traditional elements in the funeral beliefs and practices of the Luo Muslims in Kendu Bay. This was covered in chapters 5 and 6.

---

2. Conn, "Islam in East Africa," 80.

3. Domain A: Integration of *Dini* (Official Islam) and *Mila* (Traditions); Domain B: Integration of *Mila* and Other Popular Islamic Practices and Domain C: Integration of *Dini* and Other Popular Islamic Practices (Kim, *Islam among the Swahili*, 60–66).

The same chapters also underlined the factors that have contributed to the aspects of continuity and discontinuity. These two aspects are the basis upon which the study in this section has been built. It describes the kind of a lifestyle that the Luo Muslims have acquired as a result of mixing Islamic and Luo traditional customs in their funerals.

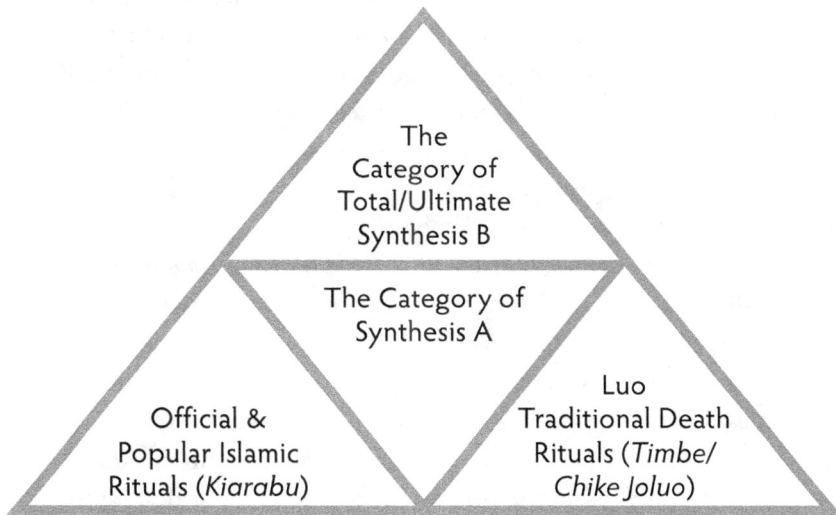

The
Category of
Total/Ultimate
Synthesis B

The Category of
Synthesis A

Official &
Popular Islamic
Rituals (*Kiarabu*)

Luo
Traditional Death
Rituals (*Timbe/
Chike Joluo*)

Diagram 29: Luo-Muslim Experiences and Relationships in Kendu Bay

Diagram 29 above shows how Islam and Luo traditions have mixed with each other into a single whole. They have integrated to the highest level of total or ultimate synthesis. On the extreme left of the diagram is the domain of official and popular Islam. Unlike Kim's figure of internal aspects of Swahili Islam where he puts official and popular Islam into two different categories respectively[4] here they have been combined. The reason for combining them into a single domain is based on the informants' description of their beliefs and practices. They said that their customs are what other Muslims follow in different parts of the world. This means that those customs are universal in nature according to them. They also explained that some of their customs originated from the Arab world. These, however,

---

4. Kim, *Islam among the Swahili*, 59.

may not necessarily be universal. The single term which they often used in describing their beliefs and practices was *Kiarabu* (meaning Arab lifestyle in Swahili). It denotes the cultural elements that are familiar to the Arabian world. These were specifically noted in the Luo-Muslim references to the beliefs and practices as contained in both the Qur'an and the Ḥadīth. Examples include the performance of *ghusl* ritual, the terms such as *almaut, almarhum* and *almarham* that refer to death, male and female deceased respectively, the odd number of people who do *ghusl* and burial ritual, and the laying of the dead in the grave with their head facing Mecca. The application of *Ijma* and *Qiyas* and the rituals that were often quoted from the Ḥadīth that highlight what should be done in areas where the Qur'an is silent are also other examples. This domain contains what may be described as the domain of dogmatic and non-dogmatic elements.[5]

On the extreme right of diagram 29 is the domain of *timbe* or *chike Joluo* (Luo traditional rituals). This is an area where in the life of a Luo Muslim, Luo-traditional elements that relate to death have been identified. Examples include *nduru* (meaning loud wailing for the deceased in Luo), *chiwo* or *golo neno* (meaning eulogy in Luo) and *tero* or *lako* (meaning cohabiting with the widow in Luo). These elements represent the domain of non-Islamic element as highlighted in the previous two chapters. But despite the fact that both Islamic and Luo traditional elements are distinct from each other, they have nevertheless been integrated. The two levels of integration are represented by the "Category of Synthesis A" and the "Category of Total or Ultimate Synthesis B" (diagram 28). The "Category of Synthesis A" is the immediate level that provides the outcome of the mixing of *Kiarabu* and *Timbe* or *Chike Joluo*. The interaction has resulted into some elements from both Islam and Luo traditions being fused into a single whole. This is contained in the "Category of Total Synthesis B."

The "Category of Synthesis A" contains elements of Islam and Luo traditions that can still be distinguished. However, in the "Category of Total Synthesis B," the elements have been fused together into a single whole. The

---

5. Kim explains: "'Official Islam' stands for the fundamental Islamic dogmas and practices such as six basic beliefs and five duties, which are to be observed by all Muslim members in the society. 'Other Popular Islamic Practices' refers to non-dogmatic practices such as Sufi *tariqa*, saints' worship, and Arabic magic and astrology" (Kim, *Islam among the Swahili*, 59).

two categories are the basis upon which the experiences of the Luo Muslims regarding their understanding of death and its related practices have been described. The descriptions point to the nature of Luo Islam that the Luo Muslims in Kendu Bay have adopted in each stage of the Luo-Muslim funeral. Whereas the mixing of both Luo traditional and Islamic elements vary from one stage of the Luo-Muslim funeral to the other, it is generally not possible to separate Islamic elements from the Luo traditions. The elements from both Islam and Luo traditions have been integrated into one another. The integration of elements from both sides has produced what has been referred to in the chapter as "Luo Islam."[6] In this Luo Islam, several cultural characteristics and themes have emerged that help to explain how Luo Muslims in Kendu Bay conceptualize death.[7]

Inter- and Intra-Triangular Relationships in the Three Stages of the Luo-Muslim Funeral

The "Category of Synthesis A" (see diagram 28) is the point at which official and popular Islamic (*Kiarabu*), and Luo traditional (*chike/Tmbe Joluo*) elements have met together. The meeting together of those elements has been possible in all the three (initial, middle and later) stages of the Luo-Muslim funeral (see chs. 5 and 6). Each stage is characterized by the domains of total-Islamic, partial-Islamic and non-Islamic elements (see ch. 5). The domains are, however, in different proportions of each stage of the funeral. For example, in the initial stage, the domain of partial-Islamic elements rates the biggest. It is followed in that order by the domain of total-Islamic elements and non-Islamic elements. In the middle stage, non-Islamic elements come first followed by partial-Islamic elements and total-Islamic elements. In the middle stage, the domain of partial-Islamic elements is the most dominant. It is followed by total-Islamic elements and non-Islamic elements. The diagram below is a summary of the existing relationships between the three stages of the Luo-Muslim funeral and their domains.

---

6. "Luo Islam" is the Luo-Muslim expression of Islam within the local context of Kendu Bay.

7. Spradly defines a cultural theme as "any principle recurrent in a number of domains, tacit or explicit, and serving as a relationship among subsystems of cultural meaning" (Spradley, *Participant Observation*, 141).

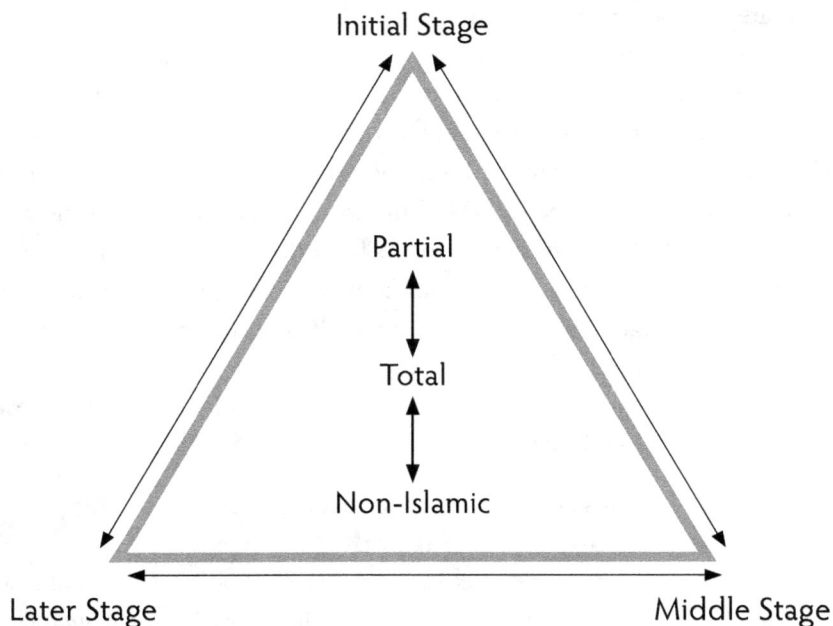

Initial Stage

Partial

Total

Non-Islamic

Later Stage   Middle Stage

Diagram 30: Relationships between Stages of Luo-Muslim Funeral and Their Domains

The term "inter-triangular relationships" has been used to refer to the correlation between one stage of the Luo-Muslim funeral to the other while "intra-" refers to the relationship within each stage of the Luo-Muslim funeral. The inter- and intra-relationships are represented by the double-arrows on each side of the triangle (see diagram 30). The triangle represents a complete life of the Luo-Muslim in relation to their experiences in death. Each side of the triangle signifies the closeness in the inter- and intra-relationships. The closeness is such that one cannot fully understand the perceptions Luo Muslims have on death by isolating one stage of the domain from the others. Such isolating is like removing one part of the triangle. If it is removed, the triangle becomes weak and also loses its identity. The three sides of the triangle with each side bearing the label of each of the three stages of the Luo-Muslim funeral define who the Luo Muslims are. The closeness between inter- and intra-relationships in the three stages is due to the fact that both Islamic and Luo traditional elements in Luo-Muslim funerals have been synthesized into a single whole (as represented under the "Category of Total or Ultimate Synthesis B"). The inter- and intra-relationship between one stage of the Luo-Muslim funeral and the other is one that follows "a cyclic pattern."[8] The cyclic pattern relationship means that there is uniformity from one stage of the funeral to the other. This uniformity is characterized by the kind of people involved and the type of funeral rituals they do. The participation of the people and the kind of rituals that they do during the funeral may further be classified on the basis of gender and age, social relations, and religio-cultural identity.

Regarding gender and age, the attendance and the participation of Luo Muslims in their funeral are both voluntary and involuntary. According to Kraft, involuntary participation or association in "gender-age-based groups" is "limited to those of our sex and age."[9] Voluntary participation, on the other hand, is not tied to the same gender and age.[10] Both voluntary and involuntary participation run across the three stages of the Luo-Muslim funeral, though in different proportions. In the initial stage, the washing and the shrouding of the deceased are done by the people of the same gender as the deceased. It thus points to involuntary participation. But since there are instances where a person of the opposite sex may perform *ghusl* and the shrouding to the body of the deceased (see chapters 4 and 5), both voluntary and involuntary participations are inseparable.

In the middle stage of the funeral, there is a mix of voluntary and involuntary participation. Both genders, young and old alike, are involved in the viewing of the body. In the washing, shrouding and the viewing of the body, voluntary or involuntary participation is determined by the gender of the deceased. However, the people who transport and bury the body are not determined by the gender of the deceased. These are solely the work of male persons who in most cases are youths. In the later stage, both male and female persons of all ages participate voluntarily in the eating of food. The same mixing is also apparent when it comes to providing support to

---

8. According to Spradley, ethnographer follows a cyclic rather than a linear pattern (Spradley, *Participant Observation*, 26).

9. Kraft, *Anthropology for Christian Witness*, 337–338.

10. This is the researcher's interpretation. It is based on Kraft's definition of the term, "involuntary."

the bereaved. In other words, the bereaved can receive material or any other support from any gender. The voluntarily and involuntary participation presents a contrast between Luo traditional and Islamic customs. Voluntary participation by the Luo-Muslim in a funeral is based on social relations. In other words, it seeks to identify with the deceased, the people who have been bereaved and the Luo community. Voluntary participation shows evidence of both Islam and Luo traditional elements. Such elements are, however, very limited in involuntary participation.

Limiting participation to gender and age is a characteristic that shows that involuntary participation is predominantly Islamic. Voluntary and involuntary participation in the three stages of the Luo-Muslim funeral represents a state of conflict in the mind of a Luo-Muslim. This religio-cultural conflict is a "push and pull"[11] conflict. On one hand, the voluntary participation pushes a Luo-Muslim towards Luo traditions. On the other hand, involuntary participation pulls a Luo-Muslim away from Luo traditions to Islam. The "push and pull" conflict, however, varies from one stage to the other. In the initial stage, the "pull" conflict is stronger than the "push" conflict. This is based on the fact that the Islamic elements are predominant. In the middle and later stages, the "push" is stronger than the "pull" conflict. This is because the Luo traditional elements are predominant in both stages.

The fact that Luo Muslims identify themselves as Muslims without denying their Luo ethnic identity implies that there is a creative balance in their religio-cultural experiences of death. The balance is not of dualism in which they divorce their religious life as Muslims from their Luo traditional life, but rather it is of synthesis. In other words, they have integrated together both Islamic and Luo traditional elements into one whole. This synthesis is inadvertent or unintentional. This implies that the Luo Muslims do not think of their actions or behaviors as either Islamic or Luo traditional. On the other hand, the concept of dualism represents an advertent or intentional actions or behaviors. Just as in theology, dualism[12] creates conflicts between two opposing powers. Understanding the Luo Muslims from a dualistic

---

11. Researcher's own terms.

12. Grudem, states: "The problem with dualism is that it indicates an eternal conflict between God and the evil aspects of the material universe" (Wayne Grudem, *Systematic Theology: An Introduction to Biblical Doctrine* [Leicester: Inter-Varsity Press, 1994], 269).

perspective would therefore signify that the conflicts between Islamic and Luo traditional elements in their experiences on death are both irresolvable and irreversible. The transition from one stage of the funeral to the other, however, comes with minimal difficulty. This smooth transition is synthetic. It shows that the experiences that the Luo Muslims have on death are not two coins with two separate entities (dualism) but rather one coin with two distinct entities (synthesis).

The Divine and Human Causality of Death

Kraft defines causality as "the process by which some person, quality, power, or agency brings about something else."[13] Death is one of the major misfortunes in life that just like any other society in the world, Luo Muslims seek answers. It is by explaining the cause of death that meaning is given.[14] Their analytical model, which includes, (1) Adversity, (2) A belief system to explain it, (3) Diagnosing the cause using this system, and (4) Selecting a remedy and application, of dealing with misfortune was found useful in understanding and explaining the experiences the Luo Muslims have on death. They identify death as a misfortune or adversity. However, their belief system offers different explanations as to the cause and occurrence of death. On one hand they attribute the cause of death to human agency while on the other hand they view it as caused by divine or supernatural being. A third category that Kraft calls "naturalistic causality"[15] is lacking in the Luo-Muslim understanding of death. He has, however, put human beings under the category of naturalistic causality. But the human causality that is in the minds of the Luo Muslims is different from the naturalistic causality. The latter, as Kraft's explains, centers its "approach and primary concerns on human effort and ability to handle life's vagaries through science."[16] Naturalistic causality expresses Western rather than African thinking. It therefore offers very little answers to the misfortune of death that the Luo Muslims are faced with.

Divine causality is centered on Allah while human causality is centered on human beings and the spirits of the dead (*juogi* in Luo). The understanding

---

13. Charles Howard Kraft, *Worldview for Christian Witness* (Pasadena, CA: William Carey Library, 2008), 124.

14. Hiebert, Shaw, and Tiénou, *Understanding Folk Religion*, 117.

15. Kraft, *Worldview for Christian Witness*, 246.

16. Kraft, 246.

of death from both divine and human causalities imply a Luo-Muslim view of death from two perspectives – Islamic and Luo traditional. The two are, however, synthesized into one whole. They are therefore inseparable. The elements that point to divine causality include: making references to the Qur'an and the Ḥadīth about death, the words, *ina lilahi waina ileyi rajiun* (meaning in Arabic, "we have come from Allah and we will go back to him") that are uttered at the time somebody dies, the *dhikr* (remembrance of death) that is done by visiting the graves of the dead, and prayers that are directed to Allah. Characteristics that point to human causality include: loud wailing and uttering of words while wailing, seeking help from *ajuoga* (witchdoctor) in order to know who has caused death, and finally, ancestor veneration. The Luo Muslims have combined all these elements into their belief system. The combination may best be described as "systems causality."[17] The variables in the systems causality affect each other.[18] This systems causality implies that in the mind of Luo Muslims, death is perceived to be caused by multiple sources rather than one single source.

The systems causality is very different from the linear causality.[19] Their differences lie in the sense that in the linear causality the variables affect each other without themselves being affected. It is hierarchical in nature – supposing that Allah gives the power to human beings who in turn cause death. But both of them are also similar, and these two are simultaneously found in the Luo-Muslim view of death. Luo Muslims understand death as being caused by both Allah and human agents. The oscillation between the divine and human causality of death provides values that explain the experiences that the Luo Muslims have on death. These values have been viewed in the following sections by using the third and fourth items of the explanatory process in the analytical model presented by Hiebert, Shaw, and Tiénou.[20] The third item is to diagnose the cause using this system, while the fourth deals with selecting a remedy and applying it.

---

17. Paul G. Hiebert, *Transforming Worldviews: An Anthropological Understanding of How People Change* (Grand Rapids, MI: Baker Academic, 2008), 76.

18. Hiebert explains "systems causality" as: "A can cause B and C, but B and C can also cause/affect A" (Hiebert, *Transforming Worldviews*, 76).

19. In linear causality, "A causes B, which causes C" (Hiebert, *Transforming Worldviews*, 76).

20. Hiebert, Shaw, and Tiénou, *Understanding Folk Religion*, 141.

Acceptance and fear of death

The values of acceptance and fear play out in the mind of a Luo Muslim. The belief system among the Luo Muslims points to death as caused by Allah and human agents. The divine causality is centered on their Islamic belief system. In this belief system, Allah is perceived as the ultimate cause of death. He, however, uses means such as sicknesses, accidents, and other natural catastrophes. The cause of death through these means has very little to do with the mistakes or evils that human beings have committed. Rather, it is viewed to rely on what Allah has already set or decreed for every person before they were born. It is in this sense that the Luo Muslims talk of death as something that Allah has written on the forehead of every person before they are born. This knowledge makes the Luo Muslims conscious of the fact that death is inevitable. The remedy then is to accept it. One way they show this acceptance of death is by uttering words, *ina lilahi waina ileyi rajiun* (we have come from Allah and we will go back to him).

The terms the Luo Muslims use to describe the state of the deceased such as *onindo* (meaning in Luo "he or she has slept") and *odhi wuoth* (meaning in Luo "he or she has travelled") also bear some level of acceptance. The terms imply that death is a transition. The concepts of *nindo* (meaning sleeping in Luo) and *wuoth* (meaning journey in Luo) have two meanings – one is Luo traditional while the other is Islamic. In a Luo traditional sense, *nindo* and *wuoth* carry the meaning that the spirit of the dead is still with the people. But from Islamic perspective, the Luo Muslims understand *nindo* and *wuoth* as referring to the future state of the deceased's existence. In Luo traditions, therefore, death is a transition that makes a person become closer to the living while in Islamic, death is a transition that sends a person away from the living. In other words, the deceased is viewed to be closer to Allah than the human beings who are still living. In Luo Islam, therefore, the dead is perceived to be far yet still near to the people. This contention of being far yet near, on one hand, pushes the Luo Muslims to stay close to Allah. This they do through their participation in funeral activities. The activities they do to the deceased are part of the good deeds that they believe Allah uses to judge the dead. On the other hand, the far and yet near concept makes them do the funeral rituals as a way of keeping their contact with the dead.

While the Luo Muslims accept death, they also fear it. This fear is not based on the ultimate cause (divine causality) of death but on the agents or intermediate (human causality) cause. In the ultimate cause level, Allah is invisible. His actions or thoughts are therefore not known. The Luo Muslims are, however, less perturbed by what they don't see. Their thinking and behavior are mostly affected by what they see. The intermediate cause level therefore makes more meanings to the Luo Muslims than does the ultimate cause level. The realm of intermediate cause level includes *juogi* (meaning witches in Luo) and *sihoho* (meaning evil eye in Luo). These are practices whose effects are real in the minds of Luo Muslims. The effects include deaths that come after a short illness or no illness at all, loss of life through accidents and disappearance of a person who after being searched is found dead with some body parts missing. These are deaths that Luo Muslims believe are abnormal or bad. Their occurrences are linked to some bad feelings or bad relationships that other people might have had toward the deceased.

These deaths may be described as horizontal rather than vertical in nature. Death is horizontal in the sense that it affects relationships between people, and it is also vertical because it affects the relationship between people and Allah. What affects the relationship between people is most feared than the relationship with Allah. This fear is based on what is visible (human beings) as compared to what is invisible (Allah). The human causality of death is centered on the visible or human relations while divine causality is centered on the invisible reality of death. The bad deaths that fall under the category of human causality and relate to the visible human relationships are in the level that Kraft calls the "deep level."[21] By describing deep level as invisible, it implies that the deaths under human causality are considered bad only in the minds of the Luo Muslims. In other words, the way they behave or react to death is completely different from the way they think. Their behaviors, which in many cases are verbal, express their loyalty to Allah as the one who gives and takes life. These behaviors point to the divine causality of death. Since they are visible, they function at the "surface level."[22]

---

21. Kraft describes deep level as "patterned/structured assumptions (including values and commitments)."

22. Surface level consists of behaviors that are "patterned or structured and usually habitual. They are often visible" (Kraft, *Worldview for Christian Witness*, 12–14).

In summary, deaths that Luo Muslims view as normal are categorized as of divine causality, vertical in nature, of surface level (visible), and verbal. On the other hand, deaths that are associated with fear are believed to be connected to human causality. Other characteristics include: being horizontal in nature, of deep level (invisible), verbal, and nonverbal. The acceptance of death as caused by Allah is at the surface level. It is usually expressed at the initial stage of the funeral. This behavior, however, changes with time. The value in the Luo Muslims that may not be easily noticed at the time of the funeral is fear. This fear is imbedded in the deep level and is usually associated with human causality. While there is some degree of acceptance of death, the fear of death has the strongest impact in the life of a Luo Muslim. It is "habitual"[23] in the sense that it affects the way Luo Muslims relate with each other and the way they view life. The belief by the Luo Muslims that the past is part of the present makes libation, visiting the graves of the dead and the veneration of the ancestors a reality that may continue for many generations. Since these practices are hardly condemned by local Islamic officials, doing them is a means of maintaining equilibrium between the value of acceptance and the value of fear of death. Maintaining a balance between acceptance and fear of death is the point at which a Luo Muslim derives their security. This security is necessary for a peaceful co-existence with Allah, fellow human beings and the world of the spirits.

The physical presence for relationships

Another important value that stands out in the divine and human causalities of death is physical presence. By physical presence the researcher means the actual attendance that one makes to the home of the deceased. It represents three different levels of relationship: (1) Relationship between the living and the deceased (immediate relationship); (2) Relationship between the living and the living (communal relationship); (3) Relationship between the living and the living dead/ancestors (long-term relationship). The concept of relationships is very common in both African and Arab Muslim societies. In Africa, the concept of relationships is conveyed in what Mbiti describes as "I am because we are."[24] By this statement, Mbiti highlights the need for

---

23. Kraft, *Worldview for Christian Witness*, 412–413.
24. Mbiti, *African Religions and Philosophy*, 2–10.

community existence. In other words, what affects one person also affects the rest of the people. Mbiti's statement centers on relationships. In the Arab Muslim world, the concept of *umma* (meaning community in Arabic) is similar to Mbiti's. It is a concept that encourages group existence and participation by all the Muslims in the world. Mbiti's concept and the *umma* of Muslims are very much familiar to the Luo Muslims in Kendu Bay.

The concept "I am because we are" has been the foundation upon which Luos have built for many years. It may not therefore be accurate to say that Islam has totally affected the way Luo Muslims view relationships. On the other hand, it may also not be accurate to say that Luo traditions have totally changed the perspective of the Luo Muslims regarding relationships. While it is important to recognize that neither Luo traditions nor Islam has totally affected how Luo Muslims view relationships, it is also fair to recognize that the Luo-Muslim perspective of relationships has some elements from both Islam and Luo traditions. These elements have been synthesized in a way that is not possible to separate. The total synthesis has produced the kind of Islam that Luo Muslims hold today. The extent to which the various elements from both Islam and Luo traditions have been synthesized is reflected in the three levels of relationships.

In the immediate relationship, the living views the dead as their relative. Although there is no doubt that some people who come physically in the home of the deceased are not related to them by blood, it is such a sense as "I have lost part of my body" that drives them to come. They have experiences that are similar to the loss of part of their physical body. They feel pain, sorrow and empathy. These feelings are expressed even by the people who are alleged to have been enemies with the deceased. By coming physically to the home of the deceased, they affirm that their relationship with the deceased is more permanent than death itself. In the second level of relationship, the physical presence of mourners signifies that it is not only the immediate family and relatives of the deceased who have been affected by their death but the entire community. The people themselves may have been enemies or strangers to each other. The demise of the deceased whom they have come to witness becomes a platform on which they view each other as friends and as a people of the same family. It is believed that the deceased causes them to center their focus on what unites them rather than on the things that divide them.

In the third level, relationship between the living and the living dead/ancestors is considered as a long-term relationship. This relationship is very significant because it is in this third level together with the first level of relationships that many elements from Islam and Luo traditions have mixed together. In the first level, making one's physical appearance in the home of the deceased as a way to please them is a Luo traditional element. But if one's physical presence and their participation in the funeral activities in the initial stage are meant to assist the deceased, then the motive is Islamic. However, these elements in the mind of a Luo Muslim are blended to a complete synthesis. The blending into a single whole makes it difficult to separate Islamic and Luo traditional elements from each other. They exist alongside each other like a thread that when pulled affects others. It is almost impossible to pull one without pulling the other. In this case, it is the behavior and not merely the physical presence of a Luo Muslim that shows if it is Islam or Luo tradition that has affected them most.

In the third level, the relationship between the living and the living-dead/ancestors suggests that it is the Luo traditions that cause a person to be physically present at the home of the deceased. Describing this relationship in the third level as long-term actually indicates that it has been there for a long time. It emphasizes that such a relationship would go on for a long period of time. It is therefore not expected that the value that the Luo Muslims attach to their living dead and the ancestors would disappear soon. The perception in the Luo-Muslim cosmology that the living dead and the ancestors stay close to God is the reason why they would want to continue relating with them. This relationship is expressed by one's physical presence. The physical presence of many at the deceased home symbolizes a smooth transition of the deceased into the next world. It is part of *kopo* (meaning "to escort" in Luo) that Luo Muslims do for the deceased. This is part of the reasons why many people would not want to fail to attend the funeral of the deceased. Even if they are not able to come immediately due to the distance, they try by all means to come before the burial takes place. Apart from relationships, the physical presence of Luo Muslims in the home of the deceased also carries the sense of identity.

Luo-Muslim Identity Based on Relationships

While relationships may be regarded as personal, which touches on one individual and the other, identity is both personal and communal. Identity is the lenses through which a Luo Muslim sees themself and the world around them. It provides them with a sense of security and belonging. Mbiti's expression, "I am because we are,"[25] also denotes the idea of identity. Mbiti's concept of identity as derived from his expression emphasizes the significance of an individual belonging to a group. The Luo Muslims in Kendu Bay identify themselves in four levels of identity: (1) Personal level; (2) Family level (3) Religious level; and (4) Ethnic level.

Personal, family, and religious identities

In the personal level, a Luo Muslim recognizes that they are a human being. They also recognizes that they are different from the other individuals. The desire to pursue education for a better living standard in the future is very strong in the personal level. At the family level, a Luo Muslim identifies themself with their parents, siblings and other extended family members. In a family, its members identify each other as brothers, sisters, cousins, uncles, and so forth. The family name such as Otieno or Adoyo is transferred from one generation to another. The religious level signifies a sense of belonging by the virtue of being in the religion of Islam. The lives of members under the religious level are regulated by the belief of the religion. Examples among the Luo Muslims in Kendu Bay include attending mosque prayers, teachings in *madras*, circumcision, observing fast (*sawm* in Arabic) in the month of Ramadan, and attending wedding ceremonies.

Ethnic identity

Whereas all those different levels of identity are important, the one that mostly informs the way Luo Muslims view death in all the stages of funerals is their identity at the ethnic level. There is a relationship between one level of identity and the other. Identity at the ethnic level affects other levels of identity as well. The physical presence that people make to the home of the deceased upon hearing the demise of their loved one is due to the influence that they have received in the ethnic level. Identity in the ethnic level is

---

25. Mbiti, 2–10.

centered on the recognition that the person who has died is a Luo. In other words, at death one's sense of belonging to their tribe as a Luo becomes more important than their religious identity. For example, the informants could say *wadhi eyik mar ngatwa* (we are going to the burial ceremony of our own in Luo) instead of saying *wadhi eyik mar jalembwa* (we are going to the burial of someone we are in the same religion with). It is for this reason that both Luo Muslims and non-Luo Muslims come physically to the home of the deceased to witness what has happened. It is also on the strength of one's ethnic identity as a Luo and not on a religious ground that makes them close their business, or postpone their journey, or seek permission from their place of work in order to come to the deceased home.

The fact that Luo Muslims and even non-Luo Muslims come together to mourn the deceased without thinking or asking which religion the deceased belonged to implies that their identity at the ethnic level is stronger than their identity at the religious level. Second, the coming together and the participation of Luo Muslims and non-Luo Muslims in the funeral of the deceased shows that being a Muslim does not deny someone a sense of belonging to their tribe or ethnicity as a Luo. Third, identity at the ethnic level has made Luo Muslims to center their interests on what benefits a group rather than an individual. In other words, they are more of group-centered than individual-centered. This explains why their main concern, even as they reflect on the death of their loved one, is not so much about the destiny of the deceased but about the family members and other dependents that have been left. Their concern for the family of the deceased and not for the deceased themself has some elements from both Islam and Luo traditions (especially the former or old traditions). As have been noted in the previous three chapters, examples that show the importance of ethnicity over religious identity include weeping or wailing for the deceased. Both Luo Muslims and non-Luo Muslims wail for the dead alike. The carrying of coffin to the graveyard is also done by both Luo-Muslim and non-Luo-Muslim men alike.

As it has been discussed in the previous finding chapters, taking care of the family of the deceased was a common practice in old Luo traditions. This was possible due to their strong sense of identity in the ethnic level. Since the Arab Muslims who transmitted Islam to Luos had the same sense of identity (*umma*), the integration of both Islam and Luo old traditions was very fast. The contemporary Luo Muslims have continued with the same practices. The same practice, however, is very minimal among contemporary non-Luo Muslims. Changes in the economy are the main reasons why the non-Luo Muslims in Kendu Bay tend to be more individualistic. Some Luos have converted to Islam because of the care they were accorded by the Luo Muslims after they lost their loved ones. Last, the coming of both Luo Muslims and non-Luo Muslims to the home of the deceased implies that death is taken to be a public rather than a private affair. Death has a larger gathering than any other religious ceremony. It brings together both Christians and Muslims. In the Luo context, it brings together individuals, families, relatives, friends and clans. All these different groups are united by their identity in the ethnic level. This implies that there is a minimal distinction between a Luo Muslim as a religious person and a Luo Muslim as an ethnic person. The conflicts between Islamic and Luo traditional elements that they encounter in their understanding of death are very minimal. With this information in mind, it is suffice to say that when a Luo Muslim identifies themselves as a Muslim, they do so without losing their ethnic identity.

Person, Activity, and Time Orientation

By using Kraft's person, activity and space orientation,[26] the life and the experiences of the Luo Muslims on death revolve around three core areas: Person, Activity, and Time. These three terms are interwoven together in such a way that one cannot be understood without the other. The person factor consists of individuals who play different roles in the funeral. As was shown in the previous finding chapters, the person factor is grouped according to the age and gender as adults, youths and children, male and female. Based on religion, the person factor may be grouped as Luo Muslims and non-Luo Muslims. In relation to the deceased, the person factor may be categorized as family members, relatives and friends. The activity factor is composed of all the rituals in the initial, middle and later stages of the Luo-Muslim funeral (see chapter 4 and 5). Funeral rituals explain how belief systems are applied in the day-to-day life. The element of time is in relation to the past, present, and future. In other words, it focuses on how the Luo Muslims relate the past, present, and future with the death of the

---

26. Kraft, *Worldview for Christian Witness*, 231–237.

deceased. The three terms represent different perceptions or values that the Luo Muslims attach to death. They explain the experiences that the Luo Muslims have as centering on the events, group rather than individual and on the bereaved and the deceased.

Luo-Muslims' concept of time: event-oriented

In the time/event-oriented perception, a comparison is made between the value that Luo Muslims place on time and the events of the funeral. Examples that show that Luo Muslims value time include the rituals of washing and shrouding the body (see chapters 4 and 5). These activities are done within the shortest time possible. They are done quickly with the view of burying the dead within twenty-four hours. The 'iddah (seclusion of the widow) period, which usually takes four months and ten days, is also an indication that the Luo Muslims value time. In the writings of many scholars such as Sharif, Raje, and Halevi the value of time in Muslim burials have been emphasized.[27] They show that Muslims place high value on time when it comes to burying their loved ones. Placing high value on time is also common in other societies such as in North America. As Hiebert explains, North Americans view time as something that is "scarce and should be saved, for it can be wasted and lost."[28] This view of time is "linear."[29] The writings by many scholars give little suggestion that quick burials among the Muslims are based on their linear understanding of time. Their writings nevertheless portray the hasty burial as something that is universal among the Muslim communities who live in different parts of the world. The case of the Luo Muslims does not, however, reflect this universalism.

As Hiebert puts, "This emphasis on time is quite foreign to peoples of nonindustrial cultures. Work is not tied to time, but to the immediate task to be done."[30] The Luo Muslims are among the non-industrial culture whose immediate concern in life is not on the quality of time but rather on the task – the funeral arrangements of the deceased. The task or the events of

---

27. Sharif, Herklots and Crooke, *Islam in India*, 90–91; Raje, *Death and Beyond*, vol. 26, 40; Halevi, "Wailing for the Dead," 159.

28. Hiebert, *Anthropological Insights for Missionaries*, 130.

29. Hiebert describes time as linear in the sense that "it has a beginning and an end" (Hiebert, *Anthropological Insights for Missionaries*, 131).

30. Hiebert, *Anthropological Insights for Missionaries*, 130.

the funeral therefore become a priority over time. Time for the Luo Muslims may be described by what Hiebert refers to as "episodic and discontinuous."[31] This simply means that they read their time not based on the clock but on the events of the funeral.[32] Putting priority on the event rather than on time is a quality that characterizes the Luo-Muslim funeral. This is shown by extending the period of burial to three days rather than just limiting it to twenty-four hours. The need to extend the period of burial is usually based on the wishes of the family of the deceased. The family members of the deceased may be Luo Muslims or non-Luo Muslims. The fact that they are consulted first before washing, shrouding, and burying the body means that Luo Muslims greatly value and respect the wishes of the immediate family. Placing priority on the family of the deceased regardless of whether they are Muslims or not also signifies that on matters to do with relation-ships, affinity in the family is stronger that religious affiliation. The wishes of the family that allow them to bury their loved one on the third day rather than within twenty-four hours are usually event-oriented. They are meant to allow for more time for other family members and relatives who live in distant places to attend the funeral. The wishes are also for the purpose of conducting fundraising to meet funeral expenses (see chapter 5).

Future orientation

Kraft's statement that "not infrequently the worldview focus is on the qual-ity of an event rather than on the quantity of time"[33] describes the kind of orientation that the Luo Muslims have on time and event. This means that it is the event that determines the amount of time rather than the time de-termining the quantity of an event. Time in this sense is cyclic rather than linear. Hiebert describes linear time as pointing to the future while cyclic time points to the past.[34] The future has to do with the future state of the soul – either in paradise or hell. As shown in the previous chapters, cleaning and wrapping the body in *sanda* (white sheet), the reading of the Qur'an and prayers by the *imams* in the funeral, and *nika* (wedding) marriages of

---

31. Hiebert, 131.

32. Hiebert refers to events such as "births, marriages, and deaths as ritual time" (Hiebert, *Anthropological Insights for Missionaries*, 131).

33. Kraft, *Worldview for Christian Witness*, 207.

34. Hiebert, *Anthropological Insights for Missionaries*, 131–132.

the widows have one thing in common. They are future-oriented. In other words, they are "purity rituals" that are part of moral requirements in Islam. They are the standards that represent or define the future existence of the person. Those funeral rituals that are future-oriented basically represent Islamic mindset that the Luo Muslims have.

Past orientation

Past-orientation that Luo Muslims represent is characterized by what Kearney calls "ancestor worship, filial piety, a strong sense of family, traditional, and almost compulsive concern with record keeping and history."[35] According to Mbiti, the traditional African thought focuses on the past, not the future. He illustrates this by dividing time into three.[36] The mythical past, the recent past, and the present, as Mbiti describes, are all similar characteristics that define the Luo-Muslim view of time. The mythical past is represented by their beliefs in the ancestors. Burying the deceased in their place of birth or ancestral land is a practice that the Luo Muslims still follow. Ancestors, as shown in chapters 1 and 2, are viewed in a traditional sense, as part of the Luo community cycle. Paying respect or honoring the ancestors by burying the deceased in ancestral land is based on the belief among the Luo Muslims that it is the body that dies and not the relationship. Good relationship is kept among those who are still alive. Even if somebody dies, their relationship with the living is still intact. The relationship that the living has with the dead is viewed to be stronger than the relationship the one has with their fellow living human beings. The difference is the belief that the dead are in the invisible realm. They are not only superior but also are able to control the affairs of the living. Contacts with them are therefore very important. Points of contact include graves and other human beings.

Mbiti classifies ancestors as occupying the realm of the recent past (see Mbiti's second division in footnote 36). However, in Luo Muslims, this realm is occupied by the living dead. These living dead are fondly remembered especially by the contemporary Luo Muslims. They are remembered, for

---

35. Michael Kearney, *World View* (Novato, CA: Chandler & Sharp, 1984), 97.

36. Mbiti's three division of time are: "(1) the mythical past, a long period during which the great tribal events took place; (2) the recent past, a relatively short period during which those ancestors who are still remembered lived; and (3) the present, which includes the immediate past and the immediate future" (Mbiti, *African Religions and Philosophy*, 15–28).

example, by recognizing the children the deceased bore as his children. This is even after the widow has been re-married. The immediate past and the immediate future in Mbiti's third division (see footnote 36) are centered on the deceased who has just died. The deceased is remembered based on the meaningful contributions that they have made. This may be in building a mosque or educating a child from a poor family. The remembrance is based on the events surrounding the life of the deceased. It is in this sense that somebody's date of birth or the exact time they died may not be remembered as much as the events surrounding their death and the way they had impacted the community.

Future-past orientation

While there is a sense in which elements in the Luo-Muslim funeral represent future or past orientation, they can hardly be divided. The gap between the linear and cyclic concepts of time is very minimal in the minds of the Luo Muslims. As they do funeral rituals, their minds center on the future without ignoring the past or the present. They, however, tend to lean on the past more than on the future. The emphasis that Luo Muslims place on the past more than on the future means that the past has more value to them than the future. The value that they attach to the place in which they bury their dead illustrates how their minds oscillate between the future and past orientations. The Luo-Muslims' concept of time has some relationships to their concept of space as illustrated below.

1. The place of burial: cemetery and homestead

The burial ceremonies for Salama and Muhammad in Kendu Bay were done differently. Salama was buried in the cemetery while Muhammad was laid to rest in his homestead (see chapters 4, 5, and 6). Just like in other rituals, it is family members who choose where to bury their loved one – whether in the cemetery or in the homestead of the deceased. The freedom that the family of the deceased has in choosing either to bury their loved one in the cemetery or in their homestead is an indication that the Luo Islam is not strictly orthodox or ideological Islam. It is a hybrid comprising of elements in Islam and Luo traditions. The concept of homestead burial as opposed to cemetery as *Kiarabu* Islam (the Islam that Muslim Arabs brought in Kendu Bay) requires is an example that distinguishes Luo Islam from Islam that other communities practice. Cemetery burial is basically Islamic. In other words, it conforms to the belief in Islam about where a Muslim should be buried.

From a *Kiarabu* perspective (see diagram 29), the creation of a cemetery is meant to help Luo Muslims have less worry concerning where they will be buried. Having less worry makes a Luo Muslim able to concentrate on doing good deeds that would cause them to enter paradise. The entry into paradise, however, depends on Allah's will. While it is true that Luo Muslims follow this *Kiarabu* style of burial, they have at the same time modified it. The modification has been done in a way that makes a cemetery perceived not only as a place where the deceased is interrogated by the angels, Munkir and Nakir, and then sets off for their next journey, but also as a "home"[37] for the deceased. The concept of "home" is basically Luo traditional. By following *Kiarabu* without neglecting their Luo traditional understanding of a cemetery, the Luo Muslims have thus produced a local Islam that is relevant to them. For the Luo Muslims, the presence of a cemetery answers the question related to the future (future existence in the hereafter). Homestead burial on the other hand ensures that contacts with the ancestral spirits are kept (the past). But the family's choice to bury their loved ones in the cemetery or in the homestead does not negate the thinking of the Luo Muslims on death as centering on both future and past. This thinking is maintained by their periodic visits to the graves in the cemetery or in the homestead.

From the perspective that Kim calls official Islam or orthodox Islam,[38] the presence of a grave reminds a Luo Muslim that life on earth is short and temporal. This reminder of the temporal state of the world is meant to cause a Luo Muslim to spend their time to the maximum in doing good deeds. But on the other hand, the "ordinariness"[39] in a Luo Muslim makes

---

37. A "home" also connotes a feeling of being comfortable or having less worry. Cemetery is the point where the living makes contacts with the deceased, the living dead and the ancestors. According to some informants, these contacts prompt healthy relationships between the living and the dead.

38. According to Kim, "'Official Islam' stands for the fundamental Islamic dogmas and practices, such as six basic beliefs and five duties, which are to be observed by all Muslim members in the society" (Kim, *Islam among the Swahili*, 61); see also Kim, "Considering 'Ordinariness,'" 185.

39. Kim, "Considering 'Ordinariness,'" 180.

them think of a grave as a source of "power."[40] This thinking is due to the belief that the spirits in the invisible world (the deceased, the living, and the ancestors) use the grave as a contact point. Following official Islamic and Luo traditions at the same time has produced what Kim calls "the discrepancies that occur between the ordinary dimension of life and the Islamic ideal"[41] in the life of a Luo Muslim. But the synthesizing process has minimized the difference between what is Islam and what are Luo traditions in the mind of a Luo Muslim. This minimal difference is almost inseparable. It has thus produced a behavior among the Luo Muslims in which on one hand the grave is viewed as a symbol of the life to come, while on the other hand it is seen as the seat or the contact point for the spirits. These two perspectives represent two sides of the same coin.

2. The place of burial: land

At the root of burying the deceased in the cemetery or in homestead lies the issue of land. The mixing of Islamic and Luo traditional elements is the result of what Kim calls human "ordinariness"[42] in the mind of a Luo Muslim. They therefore view life from an ordinary perspective.[43] This ordinariness manifests itself especially relating to the place for burial (graveyard) and the grave itself. These two elements point to the importance of land. Due to the ordinary lifestyle that a Luo Muslim has acquired, their greatest concern does not lie on where they will go when they die but where they will be buried. In other words, a Luo Muslim considers the place where their soul goes after death (paradise or hell) as less important compared to the place where they would be buried or where their body would be laid when they die. This explains why Luo Muslims place very high value on land. The importance of land as a burial ground is associated with the belief in ancestral spirits. To

---

40. "Power" denotes to a superior insight or "baraka" (blessings) as Kim (in "Considering 'Ordinariness,'" 180, and *Islam among the Swahili*, 57) calls it. A Luo Muslim believes that they receive it as a result of keeping contact with the spirits of the dead. Power can also be in a form of security or protection from sickness or calamities that one receives from the spirits of the dead.

41. Kim, "Considering 'Ordinariness,'" 179.

42. Kim, 180.

43. Kim defines an ordinary person as "someone who thinks, acts, and does all cultural things as a truly human being . . . *He or she* feels his/her needs and seeks for solutions (or "baraka") from varied sources of power that are deemed helpful in coping with life challenges" (Kim, "Considering 'Ordinariness,'" 180, italics are the researcher's).

use the words of Hiebert, Luo Muslims consider land as "sacred and more important than time."[44] Being buried in the ancestral land signifies that the person has not lost their Luo traditional roots. To a Luo, losing one's cultural roots is like losing life.[45] The land, as Hiebert reports, "ties people to their ancestors, culture heroes, and gods in a way that time never can."[46] The importance of land cannot therefore be overemphasized.

From an economic perspective, land is the resource that is believed to determine the amount of wealth one has.[47] Land is a source of wealth in the sense that it is transferred from one generation to another. It is because of this transfer of land from one generation to another that it is called ancestral land. An ancestral land can only be transferred to family members and relatives, and not sold. The selling or lack of land does not only imply that one has little or no wealth to transfer to their children but also that they have no place to be buried. Lack of a place to be buried is a source of worry for many Luos in Kendu Bay. In the past, the population of Luos in Kendu Bay was very small. The Arab Muslims who came were given vast pieces of land within the vicinity of Kendu Bay. They were given land by the virtue of being married to Luo women. They thus became "relatives."[48] The Arab Muslims designated a place as a cemetery where they could bury their dead ones. The increase of population in Kendu Bay has made the land become very scarce. As a result of this scarcity, many Luos are increasingly getting worried about where they would be buried. The most affected are the Luo adults who tend to think that they are growing old and very soon they would die. It is because of this worry that some Luos have converted to Islam. Seeing that they have a cemetery or a place they would be buried when they die has given the Luo Muslims more comfort and relief than the mere thinking about their final destiny.

---

44. Hiebert, *Anthropological Insights for Missionaries*, 133.

45. Life here signifies the benefits that a person receives as a member of a Luo ethnic community. Such benefits include helping one another in difficult times such as death.

46. Hiebert, *Anthropological Insights for Missionaries*, 133.

47. In the Luo traditional society, it was the male person who would own land. The new constitution in Kenya, however, gives the right for a female person to inherit or own land.

48. Luos consider a relative also as someone who is related to them by marriage. They may not necessarily be a Luo. Arab Muslims are such an example.

The group orientation: significance of ethnic identity

The Luo Muslims are seen through the eyes of what Kraft calls "Groupism-Individualism."[49] Two sets of characteristics that Kraft identifies in this orientation are "dependency-independency and security-freedom."[50] Among the Luo Muslims, the group/individual orientation is a perception that highlights the kind of participation they have in the funeral. In all the three (initial, middle, and later) stages of the Luo-Muslim funeral, the groupism rather individualism is manifest. Examples include physical presence at the funeral, washing and shrouding, carrying the bier to the grave, burial, cooking and eating of food after burial, and the support accorded to the widow (see the previous three chapters findings). The group is both close and distant. The close-group consists of family members, relatives and neighbors. They are both Muslims and non-Muslims. The distant-group includes friends, colleagues and fellow tribe-mates. In some areas of the Luo-Muslim funeral, the requirements for the group are specific while in other areas they are general. For example, the washing and shrouding requires an odd number of participants, who are of the same gender as the deceased. The same rule applies to those who transport and bury the body. They are always men. But viewing the body, praying for the bereaved and giving support to them, the requirement is unlimited.

Characteristics that Hiebert identifies in a group include: "collective interest, corporate responsibility and decisions."[51] The concept of group-centeredness among the Luo Muslims holds similar characteristics. There is a sense of collective interest. For example, in weeping or wailing, it is hardly a one person affair. The same case applies in transporting the bier to the graveyard. Collective interest goes hand in hand with a corporate responsibility. Decisions centering on burials are usually made by family members of the deceased. Where they are unable, they refer to *imams*. The *imams* in turn consult with each other before deciding on the way forward. This group-oriented perception is not independent but dependent. In other words, as Hiebert puts, "people do not see themselves as autonomous, but as

---

49. Kraft, *Worldview for Christian Witness*, 233.
50. Kraft, 234.
51. Hiebert, *Transforming Worldviews*, 64.

members of the groups to which they belong."[52] Seeing oneself as belonging
to a group brings a sense of security. Conducting funeral rituals as a group
and not as an individual instills a sense of identity at the ethnic level. This
ethnic identity is an experience that, as Fishman remarks, is viewed as "being
the 'bone of their bone, flesh of their flesh, and blood of their blood."[53] The
statement implies there is commitment within the ethnic group. This ethnic
commitment among the Luo Muslims is expressed in different ways such as
keeping secrets, respect, morality, hospitability, and ineffability.

Keeping secrets, respect, and morality
The keeping of secrets or being confidential is part of the reason why the
washing and shrouding is done by the people of the same gender as the deceased. Washing and shrouding as a group also reminds each group member
that they need each other. Respect is accorded to all people regardless of age,
status, and gender. It is for this reason that everyone who dies is washed and
shrouded by *sanda*. The dead are shown respect by not talking ill about them
and by attending their burial ceremony. The *imams* are also respected. They
are consulted in decision-making. They are the pillars and authority figures
who give religious instructions and guidance to the Luo Muslims in Kendu
Bay. They are also the link between the community of the Luo Muslims and
the civil or government authority.

Morality or maintaining proper behaviors is a value that Luo Muslims
cherish. It ensures not only the purity of Islam as a religious institution but
also the purity of a Muslim as a person. One area in which morality is emphasized is widowhood. Instead of cohabiting, the Luo Muslims encourage
their widows (especially the young ones) to re-marry through a wedding
(*nika*). Re-marriage is allowed as a way of bringing about or regulating
proper behavior. Although the concept of *nika* is Islamic, it has some Luo
traditional elements. The concept of *nika* has modified the new or latter Luo
traditional *ter* (wife inheritance through cohabitation). It recognizes that
widows (especially the young ones) are still active sexually. *Nika* provides a
legal framework in which sexual needs of the widow can be met. It reduces

---

52. Hiebert, *Anthropological Insights for Missionaries*, 122.
53. Joshua Fishman, "Ethnicity as Being, Doing, and Knowing," in *Ethnicity*, eds. John
Hutchinson and Anthony D. Smith (New York, NY: Oxford University Press, 1996), 63.

the level of immorality that could otherwise be an embarrassment to the
Luo-Muslim community as a religious community.

Hospitality

Hospitality is very foundational in Luo Islam. As noted in chapters 4 and
5, it is the family of the deceased that provide food to the mourners. The
family feels offended if somebody goes away without eating. The hospitality
is accorded to the widow and her children. Hospitality is in terms of providing material or financial support to them. Such hospitality is an attempt
to "behave as ancestors behaved."[54] This behavior is generational. In other
words, it has been passed from one generation to another. The concept of
a woman as *chiwa* (meaning "our wife" in Luo) explains why a widow and
her children are offered support. *Chiwa* as a concept brings the sense of
identity and relationship.

The concept signifies that a woman does not only belong to her husband
but also to the community. She identifies with the community where she is
married. By the virtue of her marriage, she becomes a relative to that community. This implies that when her husband dies, the community takes care
of her and her children. The concept of *chiwa* was commonly practiced in
the old or former Luo traditions. The Luo Muslims who practice it have
therefore borrowed from the old Luo traditions rather than the new or current Luo traditions. The old Luo traditions that the current Luo Muslims
identify are centered on offering material help to the widow and her children.
It has very little to do with cohabiting with the widow as is common in the
new or latter Luo traditions.

The relationships between the bereaved and the deceased

The bereaved/deceased-centeredness is a perception that explains why rituals
such as *ghusl* and shrouding are done. The mind of a Luo Muslim seems to
oscillate between doing rituals for the sake of the deceased and doing rituals
for the sake of the bereaved. Doing rituals for the sake of the deceased implies
that the rituals are offered as assistance to the deceased as they move to their
next life. The washing, which is sometimes done twice, and the shrouding
of the body with *sanda* (white sheet), are the assistances that the deceased

---

54. Fishman, "Ethnicity as Being," 65.

receives. Looking at these helps that the deceased is offered from an Islamic perspective, it is evident that they are done with the future of the deceased in mind. In other words, the assistance is meant to create an environment that would allow the deceased to transit into the next life without difficulty. This perspective in Islam implies that the living (bereaved) also play a role in shaping the destiny of the deceased. Since the Luo Muslims believe that Allah will reward them based on their good deeds, they perform funeral rituals with this hope in mind.

Importance of emotions

The general atmosphere in a Luo Muslim is usually characterized by emotions. Showing emotions are what Luo Muslims call "proper mourning." Shedding tears, viewing the body, and eating food that has been cooked on behalf of the deceased are the "signs"[55] that explain how the Luo Muslims understand their experiences at the death of their loved one. Emotions are expressed by tears. They are very subjective, but they also reflect the objective reality of death. The viewing of the body induces emotions. This viewing is driven by the perception that the body is good. This perception is based on the belief by the Luo Muslims that everything that Allah has created is good (see chapter 6). The body is viewed as part of Allah's creation. According to this view, the good that Allah has created is something that cannot be terminated by death. One of the reasons why the Luo Muslims wash and shroud the body of the deceased is due to the recognition that the body is good. In the Luo-Muslim thinking, the body represents the whole person (*ngane* in Luo). Whenever they are describing the death of their loved one, they simply say that the person has rested (*oyweyo* in Luo). In their minds, they are aware that the soul has departed from the body, but in their emotions it is as if the body and the soul are still together. It is due to their feelings at the emotional level that sometimes cause some of them to talk to the dead while viewing the body. A true relationship between one Luo Muslim and the other is found at the emotional level. A Luo Muslim has few problems viewing the body of the deceased. This is partly because of their feelings at

---

55. Hiebert describes "signs" in three different ways: "(1) Signs point to objective reality. This include sentences, (2) Signs such as words, are cultural constructs that shape the way people see the world, and (3) Signs point to external realities and evoke subjective images in the mind" (Hiebert, *Transforming Worldviews*, 37).

the emotional level that their relationship with the deceased has not been affected by death. It is also due to their belief that the body is good.

For a Luo Muslim, seeing is a very special element in a relationship. Just as those who are in a good relationship want to see each other more often, so a Luo Muslim wants to see the body of the deceased. The viewing of the body helps a Luo Muslim to retain the memory of the deceased for a long time. This is necessary because one's relationship with the deceased is something that is expected to continue beyond death. The viewing of the body displays some conflict in understanding gender between Islam and Luo traditions. This conflict comes from the fact that both men and women queue together as they view the body. This mixing together of both genders is contrary to the Islamic norm. The fact that both men and women can queue together in the viewing does not minimize their Islamic belief. Rather, it simply shows that in a death situation how a Luo Muslim feels (emotion) is more important than the knowledge they have in their mind (cognition). However, their awareness about death and the emotions they express cannot totally be separated from each other. In fact, emotions/feelings, knowledge and values are what Hiebert calls "three basic dimensions of culture."[56] They are like a tapestry into which so many threads are woven. Pulling one thread of emotions is not possible without affecting the other threads of knowledge or values.

The Luo Muslims also perform funeral rituals with the bereaved in mind. The goal here is to please the deceased, and in a broader sense, to please the living dead and the ancestors. The washing and the shrouding include dressing the body with suits, shoes and expensive clothes. It also includes placing the body in a coffin that is made of nails. These practices are non-Islamic. They are Luo traditional (especially current or latter Luo traditions). These activities are believed to make the deceased happy[57] and by extension the living dead and the ancestors. It is by making the deceased, the living dead, and the ancestors happy that Luo Muslims also feel happy. This happiness (*mor* in Luo) for a Luo Muslim means that the family and the relatives of

---

56. Hiebert, *Anthropological Insights for Missionaries*, 30.

57. The Luo Muslims describes happiness (*mor*) as the absence of bad or tormenting dreams and calamities, getting plenty of rain thus great harvest of crops and plenty of grass for livestock, and harmonious social relations between members of the community.

the deceased are secure. It also means that the land would be very produc-
tive and that there would be less barrenness among women. The more the
deceased, the living dead, and the ancestors are made happy, the happier
the bereaved feels and the more secure in their day-to-day living. Some
degree of "happiness" is also attained in bereavement. This happiness is not
the absence of pain but a sense of feeling that others are in solidarity with
them in bereavement. This "affection," which Fishman describes as "great
emotional strength of ethnic bonds"[58] keeps the Luo Muslims together in
good times and also in bad times.

Ethnic solidarity

As was explained in chapter 5, the Luo traditions regard the children who
the deceased bore and the ones born in new marriage as belonging to the
dead husband. But by making a distinction that the children born in the
former marriage belong to the dead husband while the ones born in the
new marriage belong to the new husband, Luo Muslims have made it clear
that they follow Islam without neglecting Luo traditions. The freedom that
is bestowed upon the widow to re-marry a husband of her choice without
being forced to cohabit with a stranger and the overwhelming support that
she receives from the community are very significant. They signify that for
a Luo Muslim a woman's sense of identity and her relationship with the
community do not end with the death of her husband. They also signify
that the interest of a Luo Muslim centers on the bereaved more than on the
deceased. This freedom and the support that widows receive have been the
cause for some of them to convert to Islam.

Since a Luo Muslim wants happiness, it means that they would keep on
doing these forms of rituals throughout their life. This then implies that
there would be no such a time when Luo Muslims would be considered to
have completely abandoned Luo traditions. Seeking happiness in terms of
what they do to the deceased also implies that Luo Muslims regard what they
do (practices) to be more important than what they believe (orthodoxy).
The deceased/bereaved-centered perception contains some levels of contradictions between Islam and Luo traditions in the mind of a Luo Muslim.
The conflict or contradiction is based on their allegiance to Islam or Luo

---

58. Fishman, "Ethnicity as Being," 65.

traditions. In the cognitive level, the mind of a Luo Muslim functions in a way that sorts and separates Islamic and Luo traditional elements from each other. In their emotional level, however, they behave as if the elements in both Islam and Luo traditions have been synthesized together. The mixing produces a kind of allegiance that shows compromise between Islam and Luo traditions. This compromise is such that the values that Luo Muslims place on the deceased are almost close or identical to the values they place on the bereaved. These values border on Islam and Luo traditions.

The Luo-Muslim Conceptualization of Death as Reflected in Funeral Rituals

The experiences that the Luo Muslims have on death are a hybrid or intersection between Islam and Luo traditions. This mixing has affected every stage (initial, middle, and later) of their funerals. The Luo traditions, both of the old and the current, have also affected the adult Luo Muslims, the youths, and children differently. The blend between Islamic and Luo traditions have made Luo Muslims to respond to the misfortune of death with mixed reactions. In some parts, their behaviors show partial or complete acceptance of both Islam and Luo traditions while in other parts there is partial or complete rejection of either Islam or Luo traditions. These responses include conformity, accommodation, and adoption to both Islam and Luo traditions into their belief system. They are all a result of the processing that goes on in the minds of the Luo Muslims. This mental or psychological processing is centered on different concepts such as "familiar and unfamiliar," "give and take"and "*luwo*" (follow). These different concepts are also somehow related to each other.

The Mental Processing of Familiar and Unfamiliar Elements Regarding Death

The funeral beliefs and practices from both Luo traditions and Islam that the Luo Muslims follow have created a state of imbalance in their minds. Their mind is in a state of conflict. This conflict centers on allegiance. On one hand, they want to be closer to Allah when they die; on the other hand, they want to get closer to the living. The person who is still alive also wants to do good deeds that are pleasing to Allah with the view of entering paradise when they die. At the same time, on the other hand, they still want to keep relating with the ancestors and other living dead. In order to resolve this inner inconsistency, the Luo-Muslim mind isolates and selects cultural elements. This process of isolating and selecting begins with what is familiar and then moves to what is unfamiliar or foreign. The word "familiar" here speaks of the cultural context in which a person has been raised up. Examples include the cultural elements that were passed on to the current Luo Muslims by their forefathers. Horton describes what the forefathers have passed on as "the cults of the dead."[59] He points out that these cults are coordinated by the group that is familiar to these cults but highly unlikely to be adopted by individuals and groups outside this social context.[60] Since the majority of the Luo Muslims are familiar with the cults of the dead, they have easily adopted them. This adoption is due to the filtering process in which the mind isolates and selects ideas and then expresses them in ways that are convenient.

This isolation and selection process is carried out through the Luo-Muslim enculturation[61] with the knowledge that *Kiarabu* Islam has instilled in the minds of the Luo Muslims. Through the process of enculturation, cultural values and behaviors are passed on to a person at their early stages of life. Their perception of life including the way they respond to the misfortune of death is informed by how they have been socialized or brought up in life. This socialization or enculturation is sometimes diachronic[62] in nature. In diachronic, personal, biographical and cosmic stories are the narratives that give meaning to life. According to Hiebert, "stories are based on both imaginative and rational analysis and deal with the complexities of human experience that cannot be probed by the rational mind alone; they include contradictions, compromise, conflict, and crisis."[63]

---

59. Horton, "Tradition and Modernity Revisited," 40.

60. Horton, 40.

61. Enculturation is "the process by which individuals acquire the knowledge, skills, attitudes, and values that enable them to become more or less functioning members of their society" (Kraft, *Anthropology for Christian Witness*, 40).

62. "Diachronic" refers to meanings people give about life or death based on the stories. These stories may be biographical, group history, or cosmic drama (Hiebert, Shaw and Tiénou, *Understanding Folk Religion*, 112–117 cf. Hiebert, *Transforming Worldviews*, 27–28, 65–68).

63. Hiebert, *Transforming Worldviews*, 66.

The Luo Muslims are a people who have been socialized in both *Kiarabu* Islam (Islam that Arab Muslims passed to the Luo Muslims) and Luo traditions. Enculturation in Luo traditions means that the values such as respect and fear that the Luo Muslims bestow on the ancestors are embedded in their subconscious mind. They are part of the stories that are very familiar to the Luo Muslims. They are filtered in the mind and then expressed outwardly. Most of these expressions are usually done unintentionally and unconsciously. In other words, the Luo Muslims do not think of their behaviors and actions as centering on Luo traditions. The knowledge of Islam that has been instilled in some of them from childhood while others in their later years of life also affects the way they behave or act. They utter the words, *ina lilahi waina ileyi rajiun* (we are all from Allah and all of us must return to him), when their loved one dies, and this is their expression of their allegiance to Allah. Before making the pronouncement, their minds first select and adopt what is convenient for the moment. In situations where Islamic and Luo traditional elements interact at almost equal terms, the processing in the mind reaches a level where compromise is settled. This compromise means that paying allegiance to Allah and Islamic beliefs and practices is stressed but at the same time Luo traditions are also accommodated.

The Concept of *Luwo* (to Follow) and the Naturalization Process of Give-and-Take in the Luo-Muslim View of Death

In chapter 1 of this book, *luwo* is the term from which the word *Luo* has been derived. Ongong'a uses it to refer to the way Luos used to follow each other in groups in search of better pasturage.[64] He uses the term *luwo* in a geographical sense. Ogot, however, extends its scope by indicating that the term also applies to the customs of burial.[65] Ogot sees the term *luwo* from a cultural perspective. It is this cultural perception of *luwo* that has mostly affected the lifestyle of the Luos including the Luo Muslims in Kendu Bay. In a broader sense, the term *luwo* relates to ethnic identity. This ethnic identity, however, is not deliberate. It is an unconscious act of the will that senses the need to belong to or identify with the larger Luo community.

---

64. Ongong'a, *Life and Death*, 7.
65. Ogot, *History of the Southern Luo*, 108–112.

This feeling is in-group. In other words, the whole group rallies together whenever there is a threat or misfortune such as death. This sense of ethnic identity is founded on the values and the norms that the forefathers of the Luos had set. These values and the norms are passed on from one generation to another. The terms such as *taboo* (*chira* in Luo) and *juogi* (spirits) are very familiar to the Luo Muslims. *Chira* is the punishment that *juogi* impose on those who have deviated from the norms or the behaviors that they have set for the community. Deviation is in the sense of leaving the Luo traditions. This belief in *chira* and *juogi* is associated with human causality of death. As explained in the previous section, it is the human rather than the divine causality of death that Luo Muslims are most afraid of.

The fear of death is an element that is centered in the minds of the Luo Muslims. It controls the way they behave or act in the funeral. Whenever death occurs, the mind aligns itself to the rules and the norms that the forefathers have passed to the community. This implies that the chances of doing Luo traditional rituals are higher than the chances of doing rituals that are Islamic. The remarks by Mbiti that beneath the new changes lies the subconscious mind of *zamani* (the past) and that this tribal life is only dormant, not dead,[66] explains why it is so hard for the Luo Muslims to completely abandon Luo traditions. This difficulty is based on what Ongong'a describes as "the collective consciousness, the social personality or relationship of the deceased with the living."[67] Collective consciousness means a uniform response or a feeling that is geared towards the same situation. It is a mental process that pushes an individual to identify or align with what the group does. It is centered on the group rather than an individual. Wailing, for example, results from the sense to identify with the group. Failure to weep or wail as others do is to betray what Munday calls "the emotions of joy at a death."[68] Such a person not only risks being accused of sorcery (*jajuok*) but also of being isolated. To be isolated or to be accused as *jajuok* is an experience that causes mental torture to the individual. These are worse than death itself. In order to minimize such a torture, the mind goes into the process of eliminating what is recent and choosing what is original. It then

---

66. Mbiti, *African Religions and Philosophy*, 22.
67. Ongong'a, "River-Lake Luo Phenomenon," 227.
68. Munday, *Luyia Response to Death*, 249.

conforms or harmonizes with the latter. The recent is the *Kiarabu* Islam that was passed to the Luo Muslims in the later periods. The original is the Luo traditions. They are foundation upon which Luos perceive their identity.

The fear of not following (*luwo*) Luo traditions is not only linked to death but also to the future wellbeing of the family of the deceased. For example, the insistence that a widow must undergo a "cleansing ritual" by sleeping with another man is done with the future wellbeing of the family in mind. It is feared that if the cleansing ritual of a widow is not done, other misfortunes such as barrenness, mental sicknesses, and staying unmarried or disintegration of the family may occur. The mixing of Islam and Luo traditional elements has, however, modified the practice of widow cleansing. Instead of cohabiting with the widow, the *nika* (wedding) marriage has been introduced. The idea of wedding gives a Luo Muslim a sense of feeling that they are committed to their religious obligations. The reason why *nika* is encouraged is to preserve the morality of the Luo-Muslim community. It is also done with the view of meeting the material needs of the widow and her children. The idea of *nika* is very much identical with the old Luo traditions. Unlike the current Luo traditions, the former Luo traditions emphasized the provision of material support to take care of the widow and her children without necessarily cohabiting with her. The old Luo traditions have therefore been diffused into Islam. This diffusion is on the basis of what can be called the naturalization process of give-and-take.

Accepting Luo traditions in Islam is a naturalization process. According to Kwenda, "naturalization does not mean taking away anything but rather, giving something a new release on life and a new way of being."[69] This idea of naturalization means that widow inheritance especially as understood within the context of old Luo traditions has not been abandoned or taken away. Rather, it has been re-defined based on the religious conviction. The same naturalization process applies to the understanding that the Luo Muslims have on death. While the understanding tends to lean more on human causality, the aspect of divine causality has not in any way been minimized. This is seen in the description of death as a journey or a passage. As Ongong'a

---

69. Kwenda, "Jekhanke of Senegambia," 294.

also remarks,[70] it is this perception of death as a journey that makes the Luo Muslims think that there must be a continuation of life after death. The belief in life after death is not something new to the Luo Muslims. It is embedded in the Luo traditional thinking of the Luo Muslims. Naturalization has led to the situation in which the elements in Islam and Luo traditions co-exist with each other despite their differences. This co-existence is a deliberate act of the will in which the difference is ignored, and concentration is made on what is common. The common elements in both Islam and Luo traditions are more evident in the three stages (initial, middle, later) of the Luo-Muslim funeral than their differences. The commonality implies that it is the mix of both Islam and Luo traditions that gives a Luo Muslim their identity.

Conclusion

This chapter has centered on describing the synthetic conceptualization of death among the contemporary Luo Muslims living in Kendu Bay. The descriptions have been viewed under two different subheadings. The first part has explored the religio-cultural characteristics and themes that underlie the Luo-Muslim conceptualization of death. The second part describes how the Luo Muslims conceptualize death in their funeral rituals. Under the first subheading, it was discovered that due to the mixing of both Luo traditions and Islamic practices the Luo understanding of death is not uniform. There is inter and intra relationships in the three (initial, middle and later) stages of the Luo-Muslim funeral. Death is explained from both the perspective of divine and human causality. On one hand, there is acceptance and on the other hand there is fear of death. The death of a Luo-Muslim affects both Luo Muslims and non-Luo Muslims. Their attendance of the funeral is therefore on the basis of their ethnic rather than religious affiliation. The relationship between the living and the deceased never ceases at death. It is in the account of this relationship that Luo Muslims provide hospitality to everyone who attends the funeral and to the immediate family of the deceased. It is also due to the relationship that the deceased is buried in the ancestral land.

---

70. Ongong'a, "River-Lake Luo Phenomenon," 227.

Death is never understood solely from the Islamic or Luo-traditional perspective. It is understood as a mixture of both Islam and Luo traditions. The mixing has happened unconsciously. In other words, Luo Muslims have seldom taken notice that their actions are Islamic or Luo traditional. The people simply think of themselves as Muslims. They hardly recognize their beliefs and practices as representing either Islamic or Luo traditions. The mixing of both customs produces a conflict in terms of what one should believe and practice. Such a conflict is, however, moderate in some areas of the funeral while it is high in others. The moderation is mainly due to the fact that the elements in both Islamic and Luo traditions are very close to each other. In such cases, it becomes almost impossible to separate the two. A place where this moderation seems to be represented is in the initial stage. The turning up of the people in large numbers at this stage of the funeral cannot be easily regarded as either Islamic or Luo-traditional. The same is true with the ritual of weeping where someone wails loudly.

On the other hand, the conflict is high where the Islamic customs are completely incompatible with the Luo traditional ones. In such cases, it is clear that the Luo Muslims give their allegiance to their Luo traditions. The middle and the later stages of the funeral are areas where high conflicts are common. Some rituals that the Luo-Muslim widows engage in have a high concentration of Luo traditional elements. Despite these differences, Luo Muslims describe their feelings as purely Islamic. But they do so without ignoring or denying that the Luo traditions have influenced them. Their descriptions are based on how their minds process death. In processing, the mind begins with the familiar cultural elements and moves to the unfamiliar elements. The concept of *luwo* (follow) and the naturalization process of "take-and-give" have been identified in the processing of death. The processing, however, contains conflicts between Islam and Luo traditions. Due to the conflict, death is explained as inevitable but at the same time as something that is not accidental. Celebrating the death of an individual in the form of eating food provides a positive view of death. It shows that despite the pain that people experience in losing their loved ones, they eventually come into terms with the reality of death. They therefore accept it. However, for some, the search for people that have caused it or for the reason why the deceased died always remains unresolved. It is for this reason that they visit witchdoctors with a view to finding solution to their problem.

CHAPTER 8

Conclusions

In this chapter, a summary of the findings has been provided. The implications and recommendations to the church, mission organizations, and the field of academia have also been proposed. Finally, recommendations for further studies have been made. In the overall summary, the researcher has investigated the impact that the Luo traditional view has on the contemporary Luo-Muslim conceptualization of death in Kendu Bay. The so-called "classical approaches in Islamic studies"[1] has provided very little information concerning the experiences that the Luo Muslims have pertaining to death and its surrounding rituals. As a result of the little knowledge, differentiating Islam from a Luo-Muslim life has been difficult. The lack of knowledge on how Islam has been affected by the local culture has often led to the view that Islam is a single and unified entity whose beliefs and practices are the same throughout the world. Whereas it is true that Luo Muslims have been affected by Islam in the way they view and do their funeral rituals, they have also been influenced by Luo traditions. In order to assess the extent to which Islam and Luo traditions have integrated and affected each other, the study was divided into four parts.

In the first part, the kind of Islamic teachings on death that the Luo Muslims in Kendu Bay follow were identified and described. The way Islamic teachings have informed the contemporary Luo-Muslim view of death in Kendu Bay was also explained. In the second part, the Luo-traditional cultural elements around death that the contemporary Luo Muslims still observe were ascertained. The study also described how the contemporary Luo Muslims explain the existence of Luo traditional elements in their cultural

---

1. Kim, "Considering 'Ordinariness,'" 178.

perception of death. In the third part, the researcher also discussed how the Luo traditional view has affected the Luo-Muslim understanding of death and its related practices. In this third part, factors that determine the continuity and the discontinuity of the Luo traditional view of death among the Luo Muslims was also identified. In the fourth part, analysis was made concerning the synthetic conceptualization of death among the contemporary Luo Muslims in Kendu Bay. This fourth part was divided into two sub-sections. The first sub-section covered the religio-cultural characteristics and themes underlying Luo-Muslim view of death. On the second sub-section, analysis was made centering on the Luo-Muslim conceptualization of death in funeral rituals.

Different methodologies were utilized. They were aimed at developing some theoretical frameworks. These theoretical frameworks were useful in building a theory that not only describe but also give an understanding concerning the impact that Luo traditional view has on the contemporary Luo-Muslim understanding of death within the context of Kendu Bay. Kim's STA[2] was one of the major methodologies that was utilized. It provided a systematic order through which this whole study was approached. In using the first part of Kim's approach (philological), a textual study concerning aspects of death in Islam was reviewed. These aspects of death were traced from the perspective of Shafi'ite's School of Law, which is followed by the Luo Muslims in Kendu Bay. The Shafi'ite's School of Law emphasizes the application of both the Qur'an and Ḥadīth into its various cultural practices. Therefore the researcher reviewed how both the scriptures have informed the perspectives of Luo Muslims with regard to death and funeral practices. It was also through the study of Shafi'ite's School of Law that the Three Step Order of Law (TSOL) was appropriated. Besides the Qur'an and Ḥadīth, the TSOL adds other components such as *Ijma* and *Qiyas* in order of their importance. They are part of what is emphasized in the Shafi'ite's School of Law.

The second part of Kim's STA focuses on ethnographic research. In order to generate information in the field research that help to understand the day-to-day experiences that the Luo Muslims have on death, Spradley's

---

2. Kim, 183.

ethnographic interviews and participant observations methods were administered.[3] A total of sixty-five Muslim informants were interviewed. The category of the informants consisted of adults, youths, and children. With the help of a research assistant, the interviews were conducted both on the one-to-one basis and focus groups. The questions that were administered to the informants were open-ended questions. Besides the interviews, observations were made in two different funeral functions. The period that the research lasted was four months (May to August, 2015).

The Kim's third stage of STA (interdisciplinary) was applied in analyzing all the collected data. It was done with an aim of identifying cultural categories, domains, and the meanings that the Luo Muslims in Kendu Bay have given to death. The collected data was analyzed using a theory that was formulated from Strauss and Corbin's Grounded Theory Methods (GTM)[4] and Spradley's Developmental Research Sequence (DRS).[5] Other methodologies that the researcher utilized toward building his own theory on the synthetic nature of the funeral beliefs and practices of the Luo Muslims included Gilliland's immediacy and futuristic view,[6] Conn's Ultimate Synthesis,[7] and Kim's Domain of Total Synthesis.[8]

Summary of Findings

This section gives a summary of findings based on the research questions (see chapter 1). These research questions were dealt with throughout the varoious chapters' findings. The first research question, which is chapter 4's findings, is centered on how Islam has influenced the Luo traditional view of death among the Luo Muslims in Kendu Bay. The Islamic teachings on death that the Luo Muslims follow have influenced the way they view death. These teachings are provided in mosques and *madras*, through other Islamic institutions of learning, and during funeral services. The teachings cover the

---

3. Spradley, *The Ethnographic Interview*; Spradley, *Participant Observation*.

4. Corbin and Strauss, *Basics of Qualitative Research*; Strauss and Corbin, "Grounded Theory Methodology."

5. Spradley, *The Ethnographic Interview*; Spradley, *Participant Observation*

6. Gilliland, *African Traditional Religion*.

7. Conn, "Islam in East Africa."

8. Kim, *Islam among the Swahili*.

beliefs and practices that a Luo Muslim is expected to follow immediately from the time they hear the news or witnesses the demise of a fellow Muslim to the period after the burial. The Luo Muslims follow the Shafiʻite's School of Law. They are Shafiʻite Muslims. The influence of Islam has caused the Luo Muslims to view death as a transition to the life in the hereafter. They talk of paradise and hell as the two places where the dead go depending on one's deeds and the will of Allah.

Islam has also affected the way Luo Muslims respond to the news of death and the rituals surrounding it. Some simply shed tears without wailing loudly. Others wail loudly. The fact that they are not condemned for wailing or weeping implies that Islam is accommodative to the Luo traditions despite its strong theology. The requirement that those who wash the body should be of odd number and of the same gender, and the burying of the body within twenty-four hours, are all indicators that indeed Islam has influenced the Luo Muslims. However, the fact that the consent of the immediate family of the deceased is sought before preparing and burying the body, and the fact that the family is granted permission to bury their loved one at a later day (but not more than three days), show that Islam is flexible and easily adjust itself to the Luo traditional customs. The requirement that a Luo-Muslim widow who wishes to remarry must do the Islamic wedding (*nika*) also gives the sense of Islamic influence. Although it is evident that Islam has changed the way Luo Muslims view death, some Luo traditional elements are still being followed.

In chapter 5, a description of the Luo traditional view that still exists in the contemporary Luo-Muslim perception of death has been conducted. The funeral service of the Luo Muslims was divided into three stages: the initial, middle, and later stages. In the initial stage, Islamic elements are dominant compared to Luo traditional elements. In the middle and the later stages, the Luo traditional elements are the most popular. Those three stages of the Luo-Muslim funeral were described as the domain of total-Islamic element, non-Islamic element, and partial-Islamic element respectively. The domains were described based on the elements that are predominant in each stage of the Luo-Muslim funeral. Different groups of the informants responded differently to the Luo traditions in their different stages of the funeral. For instance, Luo-Muslim adults follow old or former Luo traditions in the initial and later stages of their funeral. Those old Luo traditions have a very minimal impact in the initial while in the later stage the impact is great. The Luo-Muslim youths and children follow current or latter Luo traditions in the middle stage of the funeral. They have a moderate impact. Going by their age, Luo-Muslim adults are the most in the initial and the later stages while youths and children are the most in the middle stage. When grouped according to gender, both men and women are found in the initial stage. But men dominate the middle stage while in the later stage women are the majority.

Chapter 6 describes how Luo traditional view has affected the understanding the Luo Muslims have on death and its related practices. In the initial stage, most of the practices are Islamic in nature. The effects of Luo traditions are therefore very minimal. The most active participants in the middle stage are the Luo-Muslim youths and children. They assist in the cooking and carrying the body (male youths) to the graveside. The impact of Luo traditions is moderate. The later stage centers on widows and the feeding of mourners. The impact of Luo traditions is great at this stage. The last section of this chapter describes continuity and discontinuity of Luo traditions in Luo-Muslim funeral beliefs and practices. The descriptions were given based on Strauss and Corbin's six interrogative pronouns of who, how, what, when, where, and why.[9] Each interrogative pronoun was used to assess the conditions or situations under which death occurs, the actions or interactions of the Luo Muslims in their response to death, and the consequences or results of the actions or inaction they take. The answers from the interrogative pronouns highlighted where similarities and differences lie between the funeral beliefs and practices of the Luo Muslims and the Luo traditions. Areas of similarities were represented by the answer "Yes." They signify that there is continuity. The funeral elements that are different from the Luo traditions point to discontinuity.

The last chapter's findings highlights the synthetic nature of the contemporary Luo-Muslim conceptualization of death in Kendu Bay. In other words, the chapter describes the experiences that the Luo Muslims have on death as a result of mixing Islamic and Luo traditional elements. The chapter is an evaluation that touches on what has been described from the previous

---

9. Corbin and Strauss, *Basics of Qualitative Research*, 99, 123.

chapters' findings. The description that death carries both divine and human causalities implies that Luo Muslims understand death as partly Islamic and partly Luo-traditional. The fact that they hardly notice that their actions are either Islamic or Luo traditional implies that the mix between the two traditions are inseparable. The mixing of Islamic and Luo traditional elements produces some conflicts in the minds of Luo Muslims. These conflicts are demonstrated by their actions and behaviors. They, however, vary from one stage of the funeral to the other. In some of their experiences, the conflicts are moderate. The moderation is due to the closeness that Islamic and Luo traditional elements have with each other. The elements are so close that it becomes almost impossible to separate them. Conflicts are high when Islamic elements are completely incompatible with the Luo traditional ones. Such incompatibility is due to what Gilliland describes as "non-negotiable ethos."[10] At the point where elements are incompatible, Luo Muslims seem to regress toward their Luo traditions. The middle and the later stages of the funeral are areas where high conflicts are common. Some rituals in which the Luo-Muslim widows engage have a high concentration of Luo traditional elements. In view of the conflicts that the mixing of Islamic and Luo traditional elements have produced, the Luo Islam that Luo Muslims hold is not strictly Islamic nor is it entirely Luo-traditional. They identify themselves as Muslims, but at the same time they do not deny their roots in Luo traditions.

Implications and Recommendations to Different Stakeholders

An investigation into the impact that Luo traditional view has had on the contemporary Luo-Muslim conceptualization of death in Kendu Bay has brought forth a new understanding of the cultural experiences of the Luo Muslims on death and its related rituals. This understanding makes some significant contributions to the church, mission organizations, seminaries, and other institutions of higher learning. A meaningful understanding of the experiences that ordinary Luo Muslims have on death and its related rituals have far reaching implications. The pastors, missionaries and other church

---

10. Gilliland, *African Religion Meets Islam*, 28.

workers who are engaged in the cross-cultural ministry in Muslim contexts would see the need to devise relevant approaches and programs that not only appreciate local culture but also respond to the felt-needs of the people. Second, the meaningful understanding of the experiences of the ordinary Muslims causes the missionaries and other church workers to respect the culture of the local people. It is this respect to their local culture that would in turn make the Luo Muslims in Kendu Bay open up for dialogue with the missionaries and other cross-cultural workers in their midst.

The understanding of cultural experiences that the Luo Muslims have on death and its related rituals also increases the knowledge of Islam as a religion that is not only centered on ideological issues but also on the ordinary life of the Muslim people. Centering on real life experiences of the Muslim as a person rather than just on their faith and ideologies is very significant. It would help theologians, anthropological researchers, and other scholars in institutions of higher learning to produce effective training manuals, discipleship programs, and curricula for the churches, seminaries, and other cross-cultural mission organizations in Africa and beyond. The produced materials should be theologically sound, contextual, and relevant to the felt-needs of the people in their own cultural milieu. The chapters' findings have revealed some important aspects of the real life experiences of the ordinary Luo Muslims. These aspects, which include the present/past versus future orientation, the bereaved/deceased-centeredness, time/event-orientation, and the Muslim-centeredness, are what define the Luo Islam that Luo Muslims have created through their experiences. These aspects are the foundations upon which pastors, theologians, missionaries, researchers, and scholars in various fields can build their researches and ministries to meet varied felt-needs of the people cross-culturally.

Missiological Implications

As it has been described in chapter 7, it is clear that Luo Muslims are oriented to their present and past without neglecting the future. The discovery that both Luo Muslims and non-Luo Muslims make their physical presence felt at the home of the deceased immediately they hear the news of death is also very important. In fact, their physical presence is felt throughout the period the funeral takes place. The physical presence of the people and their stay in the funeral until the end is a practice that Luos have followed for a long time. This means that despite being in Islam, the Luo Muslims still keep the traditions of their forefathers. Rather than having what Kraft calls "negative attitude toward that custom,"[11] pastors, missionaries and other church workers should seek to understand the values that the Luo Muslims attach to their past. The past is tied to their relationship with the ancestors. It is through this relationship that a Luo Muslim first identifies himself or herself as a Luo then Muslim second. This realization sets the order by which a Luo Muslim should be approached. They should be approached as a people who are familiar with their past orientation. Approaching or engaging them simply on religious ground without acknowledging their ethnic identity gives them the feeling of being alienated from the wider Luo ethnic group.

Knowing the importance of the present and the past more than the future, the Christian workers should introduce to people like Luo Muslims and even to converts from Muslim backgrounds teachings that touch on here-and-now. Such teachings include, for example, how to take care of one's physical body and to help each other in times of need based on God's common grace and general revelation through nature and history. Taking care of one's body is not limited to proper feeding. It also involves the need to avoid indulging in immoral acts or behaviors. The description of Paul that the body is the temple of the Holy Spirit (see 1 Cor 6:18–20) implies that there is connection between the body and the soul. In other words, as a person takes care of their body, they are also mindful of their soul. When Christians demonstrate their objection to the misconception that the body and the soul are two unrelated different entities, it will attract Luo Muslims to the Christian message, being mindful of both the body and the soul. The viewing of the body will no longer be taken just as the practice of a traditional custom but regarded as a practice that helps the viewers to relate with the spiritual aspect of their existence.

What Luo Muslims see affects them more than what they hear. Just as it has been explained, the seeing induces emotions. Showing emotions authenticates that one is in solidarity with the bereaved in mourning. Emotions are part of the life experiences of the Luo Muslims. While others simply shed tears as they mourn the deceased, others may outburst in tears. In whichever

---

11. Kraft, *Anthropology for Christian Witness*, 4.

form they mourn, the important thing is to create an environment where people can express their emotions without being looked down upon. As Hiebert affirms, "emotions play an important part in human relationships."[12] They are the mechanism by which people identify with each other in difficulties that they experience. As Hiebert also puts it, "missionaries should keep the three dimensions[13] of culture in mind in their work, for the gospel has to do with all of them."[14] This means that there is need to be sensitive to the people's experiences in their lives. This sensitivity would help a missionary to know a right cultural dimension to apply to the people for whom they work. They should apply the right cultural dimension without ignoring the other two dimensions (see footnote 13). The sensitivity also means that a missionary or any other type of church workers would try their best to discern what cultural elements cause their local hosts to feel excited. For the Luo Muslims, it is what they see that excites them. They are similar to the Hindu villagers in South India as Hiebert writes: "They soon became tired with preaching but stayed half the night to see a drama to its end."[15] Sensitivity requires that one is mindful of, and applies, what is relevant to that particular culture in which they work.

Theological Implications

For such a culture as Luo Muslims', a theology that focuses not only on the future but also on the present and the past realities needs to be developed. Such a theology should address human predicaments like sicknesses, accidents, calamities, and other misfortunes in life from biblical perspectives. The Luo Muslims offer an explanation to their human predicaments that lead to death from a human rather than divine perspective. In other words, they center sufferings or the means through which death comes on human causality. The whole issue of suffering and death as Luo Muslims understand should be addressed by first looking at their perception of evil. According to Dau, the African worldview does not "tolerate suffering and

---

12. Hiebert, *Anthropological Insights for Missionaries*, 33.

13. The three dimensions are: "cognitive (knowledge, logic and wisdom), affective (feelings and aesthetics), and evaluative (values and allegiance)" (Hiebert, *Anthropological Insights for Missionaries*, 31, parentheses are the researcher's).

14. Hiebert, *Anthropological Insights for Missionaries*, 34.

15. Hiebert, 32.

evil or fatalistically accept them, but recognize them as realities deserving of unqualified resistance and rejection."[16] This perception of suffering and evil as bearing human causality is very active in the minds of the Luo Muslims. They tend to reject or resist the human cause of death by visiting witchdoctors for answers. Therefore, a comprehensive theology that also examines other root causes of suffering and evil, such as natural calamities and human effects by sin, needs to be developed.

There is need to apply a contextualized critical theology. As Hiebert suggests, this theology is a process in which "old beliefs and customs are neither rejected not accepted without examination in the light of biblical norms."[17] The four steps of carrying out contextualized critical theology as Hiebert suggests are very appropriate and applicable procedures in conducting discipleship training for converts who come from Muslim backgrounds.[18] The concern for the Luo Muslims about where they would be buried more than where their soul would go when they die suggests that the land and belief in the ancestors are important to them. The Old Testament has many examples that show how important land was to God's people. Land was the promise that God gave to Abraham (Gen 12:1–4). His descendants were to occupy the land of Canaan (Gen 17:7–8). When Sarah died, Abraham bought a piece of land among the Hittites so that he could bury his wife (Gen 23:7–16). In generations later, when the Israelites left Egypt and went to live in the land that they were promised (Exod 6:2–8). The promise of land was God's covenant with his people that defined how close their relationship was.

In the New Testament, many references are given as direct quotes of the promises that God made with his people in the Old Testament. As Burge remarks: "Land is potent not simply because it represents geography we may own, but because it represents a place where we are rooted and can

---

16. Isaiah Majok Dau, *Suffering and God: A Theological Reflection on the War in Sudan* (Nairobi, Kenya: Paulines Publications Africa, 2003), 158.

17. Hiebert, *Anthropological Insights for Missionaries*, 186.

18. "(1) An individual or church must recognize the need to deal biblically with all areas of life, (2) local church leaders and the missionaries must lead the congregation in *uncritically* gathering and analyzing the traditional customs associated with the question at hand, (3) The pastor or missionary should lead the church in a Bible study related to the question under consideration, and (4) The congregation to evaluate critically their past customs in the light of their new biblical understandings and make a decision regarding their use" (Hiebert, *Anthropological Insihgts for Missionaries*, 187; italics are the author's).

understand who we are."[19] Burge's statement highlights the significance of land as a resource that gives a person a sense of identity and belonging to their culture. This sense of identity and belonging is not complete unless one is buried in their ancestral land. Churches that are planted cross-culturally should be encouraged to develop teachings that point to the importance of land. They should also be in the frontline in purchasing and dedicating some portions of their land as places for the burial of their members. By doing so, they would be addressing the worry that many Luo Muslims have about where to be buried when they die. Since the concern over where one would be buried when they die is related to their wish to stay close to the ancestors, a theology that centers on Christ as the greatest ancestor is necessary.[20] This Christology is a contextualized theology in which Jesus is presented to the Luo Muslims by using metaphors and typologies that apply to their ancestors. Such metaphors and typologies include: Jesus as the healer, Jesus as traditional healer, Jesus as ancestor, and Jesus as the mediator.[21] Using those images that Luo Muslims are familiar with would make them feel close to Jesus. Their understanding of Jesus as the greatest ancestor would make them re-direct to him their worries and questions for which they hardly find answers from their religious traditions.

Recommendations for Actions

As been highlighted in the previous chapter, the beliefs of the Luo Muslims in death and the different activities that they do in their funerals contain critical elements that are very significant toward the understanding of the kind of Islam that Luo Muslims follow. These elements include: their orientation to the past and present rather than the future, doing the rituals with the bereaved and deceased in mind, being event-centered, making distinctions between Islam and a Muslim. It is hoped that by focusing on these key elements, difference stakeholders such as churches, mission organizations,

---

19. Gary M. Burge, *Jesus and the Land: The New Testament Challenge to "Holy Land" Theology* (London: SPCK; Grand Rapids, MI: Baker Academic, 2010), ix.

20. Peter T. N. Nyende, "Jesus the Greatest Ancestor: A Typology-Based Theological Interpretation of Hebrews' Christology in Africa" (PhD thesis, Edinburgh, 2006); Diane B. Stinton, *Jesus of Africa: Voices of Contemporary African Christology* (Nairobi, Kenya: Paulines Publications Africa, 2004).

21. See Nyende, "Jesus the Greatest Ancestor," 183, 204; Stinton, *Jesus of Africa*, 80–129, 130–162.

theological and non-theological institutions, and the government would develop relevant policies, guidelines and structures for the better understanding of the Luo Muslims in Kendu Bay.

Paying due diligence to the past and present orientation of the Luo Muslims

As explained in chapter 7, the Luo Muslims are more past and present-oriented than future-oriented. Their past and present versus future orientation is similar to Gilliland's concepts of "immediacy or here-and-now quality of indigenous religion."[22] The present/past versus future orientation is a disposition that shows that the ordinary life experiences of the Luo Muslims are centered on the present and the past more than on the future. In other words, it is the present reality that they can feel and identify with, which appeals most to them. The component of the past also suggests that the past (Luo traditions) that has been passed to the Luo Muslims by their forefathers give more meanings to their present life than their future life. The missionaries and other people working among the Luo Muslims should therefore provide lessons and opportunities that allow the Luo Muslims to remind themselves of their Luo traditional heritage. The government, through the ministry of education, culture, and social service should also encourage and support schools and other institutions of higher learning in develop ing curriculum that centers on traditional values, beliefs and practices among different communities in Kenya.

As it has also been explained in the previous chapters, it is not only the physical presence that brings fulfillment to a Luo Muslim but also the seeing or the viewing of the body. It is the seeing of the body of the deceased and not just the hearing that is significant to a Luo Muslim. When they see the body of the deceased, their emotions are induced. Once emotions have been induced, a person may cry or just remain silent. Being in this state of emotion symbolizes that a person is united together with the family of the deceased in grieve and sorrow. The body that they can see represents the now or the present. The soul of the deceased represents the future. The present for a Luo Muslim is a sphere that covers what is visible. The death of a person is therefore a visible reality. This visible reality calls for immediate actions and

---

22. Gilliland, *African Religion Meets Islam*, 25.

responses. The actions and responses include asking questions such as who or what has caused the death of their loved one. The missionaries and other church workers should not ignore or take lightly these questions. Unless they are addressed, visiting witchdoctors and fortunetellers in order to get answers to their problems is inevitable. Besides teaching in the church, the Christian community should use funeral as an occasion to teach biblical truth about death and the destiny of the deceased. Such teachings should be done over and over again. They minimize the thinking that someone else has caused the death of a loved one.

The past is also important to a Luo Muslim. The past is centered on the living dead and the ancestors. The graves symbolize the past. Where the graves of their forefathers are located therefore becomes important. It is in this sense that the demand to bury the deceased in their ancestral land has persisted. The church, and missionaries, should give full support to this custom. It is a sure way of identifying with the local people. As it has also been mentioned in the previous chapter, a Luo Muslim is more concerned with where they will be buried than where their soul will go when they die. The importance that is attached to land suggests that Luo Muslims are more centered on the present and the past than the future life. The future lies in the hands of Allah. It is therefore very uncertain and unpredictable. This uncertainty means that a Luo Muslim faces the future with lots of fear. Sound biblical teachings that are based on the character and the nature of God are therefore necessary.

The knowledge that God is transcendent and immanent should inspire confidence in the heart of a Luo-Muslim convert that their future is secure. The worry in a Luo Muslim that is not so much of death but of the means by which death comes in another area that needs to be addressed. The means through which death comes is centered on human while the cause of death is believed to be divine. Centering on the means of death more than on death itself implies that it is human causality rather than divine causality that Luo Muslims are most afraid. This fear can be lessened by explaining that no human being holds the power of death except God. Examples from the Bible and from life experiences where God has brought deliverance to people who have been subjected to fear could be encouraging.

Developing a caring attitude towards the bereaved and the deceased

Another aspect in the experiences of the Luo Muslims that show tension between Islamic and Luo traditions is the bereaved/deceased-centeredness. In this aspect, the Luo-Muslim funeral rituals are meant to serve two purposes. First, the rituals are performed for the sake of the wellbeing of the bereaved. The bereaved here are not limited only to the immediate family of the deceased but also including their relatives. The wellbeing of the bereaved include good health for both human beings and their animals, protection from bad dreams and any other forms of harassment by evil spirits (*juogi* in Luo), plenty of rain, and good harvest of crops. The funeral rituals are also regarded by Luo Muslims as performed "to" the deceased (see chapter 4). The rituals that are centered on the deceased were described in chapter 4 as Luo-Muslim funeral rituals "for" the deceased. In other words, these rituals that are done "for" the deceased are meant to make the deceased feel comfortable thus quickening their journey to their final destiny. As pointed out in chapters 4–7, all the funeral rituals that Luo Muslims conduct have both the bereaved and the deceased in mind. The Luo Islam that the experiences of the Luo Muslims have produced is one that centers on the bereaved without ignoring the deceased. The understanding of this dual perspective in which Luo Muslims pay attention to the needs of the bereaved while at the same time providing necessary support to the deceased is very significant. For this reason, the cross-cultural missionaries and church workers should consider these cultural meanings and values in developing ministry approaches, and they must deal relevantly with issues related to both the bereaved and the deceased.

The aspect of bereaved/deceased-centeredness indicates a religio-cultural dimension in the experience of the Luo Muslims that focuses on relationships. For the Luo Muslims, the relational experience takes place between living people and between the living and the dead. The relationship is intertwined into a single whole. Discussions in chapter 4 to chapter 7 provide many evidences that the Luo Muslims are very relational. These evidences include the attendance of the funeral by many people who travel far and near, the active participation in the funeral activities until the deceased is buried, the material and emotional support to the widow and her children, and shedding tears during mourning. Cross-cultural missionaries and other types of church workers should realize the Luo-Muslim value of relationship. It is this sense of relationship that makes the funeral function a public event rather than private.

The "people factors"[23] are manifest in Luo Islam. So, for example, if a missionary or any outside church worker insists on limiting the number of people attending the funeral, it may be interpreted as a disapproval of the people with whom the Christian worker has come to share the love of Christ. The public participation is very. The announcement about the death of the deceased should reach even the family members, relative and friends who live abroad. The people should also be allowed to do the funeral rituals as their culture requires except for the issues that contradict the Bible. In dealing with issues that contradict the Bible, wisdom is required. It is through attending and interacting with Luo Muslims in their funerals that the missionaries would be able to identify funeral rituals that are contrary to the Bible. Bible lessons should then be developed that addresses the felt-needs of Christians from Luo-Muslim backgrounds. In a funeral where a Luo-Muslim woman has lost her husband, Christian communities led by their leaders should be on the forefront in mobilizing and encouraging their members to offer emotional and material support to the widow and her children. It is through this support that the widow would feel attracted to the Christian community. The church should follow the examples of Jesus who first met the physical needs of the people before meeting their spiritual needs (Matt 9:36–38; John 6:1–14). Meeting the physical needs of the people became a platform on which Jesus preached and met their spiritual need. The many funeral rituals that the Luo Muslims do with a view to securing the well-being of the bereaved are important lessons that Christians should learn. One of the lessons is that the Christian community should learn from the Luo-Muslim funeral rituals how to make efforts to meet the needs of the bereaved with the love of Christ. Showing the love of Christ by caring for the bereaved provides an opportunity not only to share the gospel with the family whose loved one has died but also to explain the meaning of death and the eternal destiny of the dead.

---

23. Kraft, *Worldview for Christian Witness*, 39–41.

Being event-oriented

As described in the finding chapters, the Luo-Muslim concept of time is more event-oriented. Their focus in life is more centered on event. For a Luo Muslim, time is measured based on event. In other words, the time for any activity to begin is not measured by a clock but by the event itself. Kraft describes such a cultural behavior as focusing on "the quality of an event rather than on the quantity of 'time consumed' by the event."[24] He explains it further that "those people are simply more concerned with what is happening – be that a conversation or a public meeting – than with how long it goes on."[25] The Luo-Muslim funeral is such an example of a public forum where their interest lies in the happenings and the various rituals they do than in the time taken to do those activities. The events in a Luo-Muslim funeral include fundraising before and during the burial and waiting for the arrival of family members and relatives of the deceased from abroad before their body can be buried. These are very important events that explain why sometimes, instead of burying the deceased immediately as Islam requires, the Luo Muslims may take up to three days.

Just like the Luo Muslims, most communities in Africa are more event-oriented Understanding this type of time/event concept among the Luo Muslims is very helpful especially for the missionaries who come from the West. Kraft explains the difficulties that a Western missionary may encounter if they fail to understand the worldview of the hosting people: "Differences in assumptions concerning time can underlie the most frustrating experiences for the cross-cultural worker."[26] Understanding that the Luo Muslims are more event-oriented in their funeral practices will also reduce the bias that Muslims throughout the world bury their dead ones almost immediately. This generalization of funeral practices in Islam as being the same in different parts of the world has mainly relied on the historical and theological accounts of Islamic funeral rather than anthropological study about Muslims. The historical and theological accounts are based mostly on the beliefs and practices of the Arabian people in the pre-Islamic and early Islamic period. These historical and theological approaches spread to the rest of the world

---

24. Kraft, 207.
25. Kraft, 207.
26. Kraft, 208.

including Africa and influenced people's thoughts about death and funeral. For this reason, it is required that the cross-cultural missionaries and other scholars in institutions of higher learning should conduct a profound anthropological research so that they can comprehend the changing dynamics of Islam through its contact with the local cultures. Focusing on the event of the funeral rather than on the time implies that a cross-cultural worker would exercise patience by allowing the local people to do their funeral rituals in the way that best suits them. A cross-cultural worker should also apply the same patience when it comes to church meetings and discipleship.

Differentiating between a Muslim and Islam

While it is sometimes almost impossible to separate a person from their beliefs and practices, a study on Luo Muslims has shown that this is necessary. There is not only the need to understand the difference between the Muslim and Islam but also between one Muslim and another. The failure to recognize the difference between one Muslim and another often leads to lumping all Muslims into one group of people, such as "a violent people in fundamentalist spirit."[27] If one fails to understand the difference between the Muslim and Islam, this will also lead to over-generalizing that Muslims practice the same kind of Islam across the whole Muslim world. The kind of Islam that is mostly associated with is ideological in nature. If, however, one studies "Muslims' ordinary life experiences,"[28] it would help them to understand that Islam is shaped by the culture in which it exists. Islam can be understood in light of the day-to-day issues that affect the lives of Muslims, such as sicknesses, calamities, death, and other misfortunes. Their concern in life seems to have little in common with the ideological aspect of Islam. Many scholars have concentrated in writing books and journals that center on the political and social aspects of Islam without considering the cultural experiences of ordinary Muslims. Missionaries who only comprehend the ideological part of Islam have found it very difficult to relate with or appreciate the customs of local Muslims. Lack of understanding of "how ordinary Muslims understand, view, interpret, and live their religion in daily life"[29] has

---

27. Kim, "Considering 'Ordinariness,'" 179.
28. Kim, 179.
29. Kim, 179.

made many missionaries still live in what Hiebert calls "the tourist stage"[30] even after working and living amongst them for many years.

Understanding the difference between one Muslim and the other

As the findings have revealed, Luo Muslims understand and practice Islam differently from each other. They are also affected differently by the Luo traditions. For instance, in chapter 5, it is the Luo-Muslim adults who are affected by the old or former Luo traditions in the initial and later stages while the Luo-Muslim youths and children are affected by the current or latter Luo traditions in the middle stage of their funerals. Their understanding of and participation in the funeral rituals in those three stages of the funeral are also different due to their age and gender. In other words, the ways that Luo traditions affect them are different, and the differences in their age and gender also require different approaches in dealing with Luo Muslims missiologically or even in anthropologically. It is almost impossible to generalize Luo traditions as one and the same entity.

The fact that most of the youths and children are being affected by the latter Luo traditions more than the former means that in generation to come some of the old or former Luo traditions will become obsolete. It also implies that in the coming generations the current Luo traditions would be transformed and understood differently. It is therefore paramount for the researchers in various academic fields to keep on doing research with the view to bringing new knowledge that is relevant and applicable within the time and period of that particular generation in existence. The remarks by Braswell[31] that Muslims may be united in their beliefs and pillars of their religion but different from each other by politics, legal interpretations, theological positions, and cultural variations make it necessary to understand the experiences of Muslims as different from each other.

---

30. Hiebert describes "The Tourist Stage" as a cycle of culture shock in which a missionary "live in hotels, with other missionaries, or in homes not too different from what we [they] are used to, and we [they] associate with nationals who can speak our [their] language and are gracious to us [them] as foreigners" (Hiebert, *Antrhopological Insights for Missionaries*, 74).

31. George W. Braswell, *What You Need to Know about Islam and Muslims* (Nashville: B & H, 2000), 60.

Understanding the difference between a Muslim and Islam

Apart from differentiating one Muslim from another, there is also need to differentiate between the Muslim and Islam. The beliefs and practices that Luo Muslims do in their initial, middle, and later stages of the funeral as shown in the finding chapters demonstrate that they have embraced Islam without losing their ethnic identity as Luos. To say it differently, Luo Muslims are deeply Islamic, but their Islamic faith has modified their religious systems instead of eradicating their Luo traditional view of death. This fact implies that a Luo Muslim identifies themself both ethnically and religiously. But their ethnic identity as a Luo is greater compared to their religious identity. This is in line with Gilliland's remarks: "When the African worldview is being observed with respect to change, it is always the primary culture which has the greatest amount of influence upon the emergence of the new."[32]

The relationship between the Luo Muslim as a person and the religion of Islam that they follow may be described as mutual accommodation. This is the same thing that Braswell describes: "When Islam crosses cultures, it may accommodate to certain values of the culture or that culture may add some of its values to its interpretation of Islam."[33] Going by Braswell's remarks and by the experiences that have been witnessed among the Luo Muslims, it is almost impossible to understand the kind of Islam that a particular community follows without considering the cultural values that have been added to it. But since cultures are diverse and different from each other, the kind of Islam that one community follows is different from the Islam that another community follows. This apparent difference makes it inevitable for missionary workers, especially those who keep on changing from one context to the other, to view every Islam as different from each other. Understanding that one type of Islam is different from another one would help a missionary to develop new strategies that are useful and relevant to the local context in which they work.

The way people behave or respond to issues affecting them in their day-to-day life experiences may or may not be determined by the religion that they follow. This fact also applies to the Luo Muslims. As many of their

32. Gilliland, *African Religion Meets Islam*, 32.
33. Braswell, *What You Need to Know*, 61.

cultural experiences have little in common with the religion of Islam that they follow the effort to understand their life experiences calls for a profound ethnographic research. As Kraft remarks, "doing research in libraries and in the laboratories as has been traditional for scholars"[34] has not been very fruitful in understanding the behaviors of the people in a particular context. It is the understanding of people's cultural behaviors that may in turn lead to a better understanding of their religion. A field research is therefore necessary for Christian cross-cultural workers as Kraft explains.[35] All types of Christian workers including missionaries and even non-Christian workers should view a Muslim person primarily as a fellow human being that God has created in his own image (Gen 1:27). It is when a Muslim is recognized as a fellow human being that they can be treated with the respect that they deserve. It is in the spirit of mutual respect for each other that a serious dialogue between Christians and Muslims can take place. Some Muslims like Luo Muslims are born in Muslim families while others convert to Islam in their later stages of life. The mutual respect recognizes that it may not be one's choice to be in the religion. But even if they follow Islam by choice, the "complicated issues pertaining to the Islamic world,"[36] as Kim refers to, should not be labeled on all the Muslims as being responsible. The failure to see the difference between the Muslim and the religion of Islam leads to a prejudice and makes one become judgmental. While the debate on whether Africans have been Islamized or Islam has been Africanized may take a long time to be resolved, the findings on the perception of death and its surrounding rituals have revealed that the kind of Islam that the Luo Muslims follow is "Africanized Islam."[37]

---

34. Kraft, *Anthropology for Christian Witness*, 12.

35. Kraft says that "field research is appropriate in order to find out what the world is like from their [local cultural] point of view. It is also profitable for discovering what felt-needs they [people in the local culture] have, which have not been solved by their cultural practices. Lastly, through field research, the gospel can be communicated in ways that are meaningful to them from their point of view and in relations to their needs" (Kraft, *Anthropology for Christian Witness*, 12, brackets are the researcher's).

36. Kim, "Considering 'Ordinariness,'" 179. Although Kim does not explain what are the "complicated issues in the Islamic world," they include sucidal bombing, the killing of many innocent people in the name of religion, and the like.

37. By this term, the researcher means a kind of Islam that has mixed both African cultures (Luo traditions) and Islamic elements into a single whole. This single whole is both

Recommendations for Further Studies

The findings have revealed the Luo-Muslim experiences pertaining to death and their understanding of it. Through the findings some significant themes are disclosed. They include present/past versus future orientation, the bereaved/deceased-centeredness, time/event orientation, and the Muslim/Islam-centeredness. These themes will be useful for missiological and anthropological research tools, and theological discourses can also be built upon them. However, while the research into the beliefs and practices of Luo Muslims in their funeral ceremonies in Kendu Bay has revealed what is helpful to the church, missions, and academia, there are a lot of issues that still require further studies. The first one is the issue of Christian-Muslim relations. As it has been discovered, a funeral is a very important event not only to the Luo Muslims but also to the non-Luo Muslims in Kendu Bay. The majority of those in Kendu Bay who are non-Luo Muslims are Christians from different denominations. The death of a loved one in the community brings the two religious groups together. They not only attend but also participate in the various functions of the funeral. They also provide necessary supports to the bereaved family despite their different religious boundaries. While this is recommendable, there is need to explore ways in which Christians and Muslims can actively engage and enhance their relationship with each other even in the times when there is no funeral. Mutual relationship that is built in the spirit of trust and sincerity to each other would minimize tensions and blame games that sometimes characterize both sides of the religious divide.

Second, as the former Luo traditions affect Luo-Muslim adults and the latter Luo traditions affect the Luo-Muslim youths and children, the understanding of death and its surrounding rituals among the contemporary Luo Muslims would be different from one generation to the other. Due to the changing of times, the current research may not be relevant in interpreting the Luo Islam in the next coming generation in Kendu Bay. In other words, different Luo-Muslim generations would require a new research into their understanding of death and related rituals. This should be done with a view

---

different from and similar to Islam and Luo traditions. The contents of Luo Islam as an Africanized Islam are inseparable.

to establishing the kind of Luo traditions that affect them in different times. Lastly, a research into the relevance of power encounter ministry among the Luo Muslims in Kendu Bay would be necessary. The need for a further research into this area stems from the fact that the supernatural world of ordinary Luo Muslims is real. According to Love, "Folk Muslims confess Allah but worship spirits. They are more concerned with magic than they are about Muhammad."[38]

The major concern that Luo Muslims have about their life is centered more on the day-to-day issues than the future life after their death. The issues are what Musk describes as "huge needs"[39] such as natural calamities and different kinds of sicknesses. Love explains power encounter as "the demonstration of God's power over Satan (primarily in healing and exorcism) and it plays essential role in reaching folk Muslims."[40] The ministry of power encounter would be very helpful to the missionaries who work cross-culturally. They require it as "part of building up the church"[41] among the people group that they work with. A research into the existing demonic activities among the Luo Muslims in Kendu Bay should be pursued with theological approaches. However, as Keith and Sarah comment, "'the powers,' with which the Christian must contend, are not only spirits but human institutions, be they commercial, religious legal, or governmental."[42] In other words, apart from just looking into how spirits affect the personal lives of the ordinary Luo Muslims, there is also need to study how their beliefs in spirits affect their public participation and engagement in businesses, politics, and other spheres of life.

---

38. Rick Love, "Power Encounter among Folk Muslims," in *Encountering the World of Islam*, eds. Keith E. Swartley and Sarah E. Holmes (Waynesboro, GA: Authentic, 2005), 209.

39. Musk, *Unseen Face of Islam*, 247–248.

40. Love, "Power Encounter," 211.

41. Love, 214.

42. Keith E. Swartley and Sarah E. Holmes, *Encountering the World of Islam* (Littleton, CO: BottomLine Media, 2014).

Ethnographic Research Questions

The following are the open end questions that would guide the researcher while interacting with some of his informants during the interview sessions. They are designed in such a way as to respond to the Research Questions in the subject area of study. While interviews with the informants were necessary, the researcher also adopted participant observation method in situations where necessary in order to compliment the ideas that the interviews generated.

Research Question 1: How has Islam influenced the contemporary Luo-Muslim view of death?

(a) What is the Islamic teaching on death that Luo Muslims in Kendu Bay follow?

1. What is your name?
2. How did you come to live here in Kendu Bay?
3. When did you become a Muslim?
4. How long have you been a Muslim?
5. How old are you now?
6. What is your social status?
7. How did you become a Muslim?
8. From which religion are you originally from?
9. How would you describe your new experience as a Muslim?
10. What activities are you involved with as a Muslim?
11. What Islamic teachings are you provided with about death?
12. How do the teachings of Islam about death relate with the Muslims' belief in God?
13. Which place do these teachings about death take place?

14. Who usually provide these teachings about death?
15. What are the Islamic teachings that you are provided with about death?

(b) How does the Islamic teaching in Kendu Bay inform the contemporary Luo-Muslim view of death?

1. What happens when someone dies in Islam?
2. How do the Luo Muslims react to the news about death?
3. What do the Luo Muslims belief to bring about the death of an individual?
4. How do the people deal with the problem of death?
5. What are the activities which are carried out from the time somebody dies to the time his or her body is buried?
6. What other activities are carried out after burial?
7. Which category of people is involved in the various activities surrounding death?
8. What determine the category of people who should be involved in the various activities surrounding death?
9. What are the materials/tools/equipment being used during mourning, burial and after burial?
10. What are the significances of those equipments/tools?
11. Who attends funeral ceremonies?
12. What do they bring when they are coming for the funeral?

Research Question 2: What are the elements of Luo traditional view that still exist in the contemporary Luo-Muslim perception of death?

(a) How do the contemporary Luo Muslims explain the existence of Luo traditional view in their cultural perception of death?

1. What are the beliefs and practices of death that the Luo Muslims are following today?
2. What are the challenges that the Luo Muslims are facing in following those beliefs and practices of death?
3. What are the beliefs and practices of the Luo traditions that the Luo Muslims are still practicing during funerals?
4. What makes the Luo Muslims believe and practice their former Luo customs of death?

(b) How does the primal worldview affect the Luo-Muslim understanding of death and its related practices?

1. How do the Luo Muslims understand death and its related practices?
2. How does the Luo-Muslim understanding of death different from the Luo traditional one?
3. What are the effects of the Luo traditional beliefs and practices on the Luo-Muslims' view of death?
4. How do the Luo Muslims respond to the effects of Luo traditional beliefs and practices surrounding death?

(c) What determines continuity or discontinuity of the Luo traditional view of death among Luo Muslims in the Kendu Bay context?

1. How would you describe the Luo-Muslim beliefs and practices concerning death?
2. What are the beliefs and practices of the Luo traditions that the Luo Muslims are continuing to observe in death situations?
3. What are the beliefs and practices of the Luo traditions that the Luo Muslims are no longer following as far as death is concerned?
4. What factors have caused the Luo Muslims to continue with the beliefs and practices of the Luo traditions concerning death?
5. What factors have caused the Luo Muslims to stop following the beliefs and practices of the Luo traditions on death?

Research Question 3: How can we best describe the synthetic conceptualization of death among contemporary Luo Muslims in Kendu Bay?

(a) What are the religio-cultural characteristics and themes underlying Luo-Muslim view of death?

1. What is now the Luo-Muslim understanding of death and its related practices as a result of mixing both Luo and Muslim customs?
2. How have the Luo Muslims mixed their Luo and Muslim customs of death and its related practices?
3. What has been the result of mixing both Luo and Muslim customs regarding death and its related practices?
4. How do the Luo Muslims describe their feeling towards the mixing of both Luo and Muslim customs concerning death?

(b) How do the Luo Muslims conceptualize death in their funeral rituals?
1. How do the Luo Muslims explain death?
2. To what extent have the Luo traditional and Muslim's view of death affected the Luo-Muslim understanding of death?
3. How do the Luo Muslims explain the effects of the Luo and Muslim customs of death and other related practices surrounding it?

A History of Luo in Kenya and Their Contact with Islam

Several authors such as Ogot, Ongon'ga Adede, Perrin-Jassy and Crazzolara have provided a general account of the Luo migration into Kenya. Other scholars including Ochieng and Ndisi also agree that the Luo were originally living in Bahr-el-Ghazal province of the Republic of Sudan.[1] P'Bitek and Cohen both refer to Sudan, the original home of the Luo people as "cradle land."[2] But while the meaning they attach to this term "cradle" may be uncertain, the dictionary defines it as something "delicate." Perhaps this points to the fragile situation of war that the Luo people fought as they moved out of Sudan. But Ndisi also adds: "The Nilotes at this time (while in Sudan) were known as Lwoo and later, when the group went to Kenya and settled around Lake Victoria, they changed their name to Luo."[3]

This change of name, as Ndisi explains, may not necessarily be pointing to anything significant but nevertheless it explains the difference that exists among various Luo (*Lwoo*) groups. In fact, this difference is also apparent in their dialects. For instance, the dialect of Kenyan Luos is different from that of the Ugandan or Sudanese Luos. This difference might have been attributed by their geographical setting. Ochieng outlines this setting by pointing that the Luos of Kenya are "a section of the three *Jii*-speaking groups, the other two being the Jiaang (or Dinka) and the Naath (or Nuer) who are still living

---

1. Ochieng', *People around the Lake*, 3; Ndisi, *Study in the Economic*, 7.
2. p'Bitek, *Religion of the Central Luo*, 8; Cohen, "River-Lake Nilotes," 135.
3. Ndisi, *Study in the Economic*, 7.

in the Sudan."[4] The Luo of Sudan and those of Uganda have some slight differences in their dialects. But this dissimilarity of dialect is also evident among the various Luo groups of Kenya. The division of Kenyan Luos into "Joka-Jok, Joka-Owiny, Joka-Omoloa nd Joka-Suba,"[5] and their settlement in various geographical areas must have caused this disparity. Sometimes environment affects the worldview of the people. It is therefore not surprising to find that the Luo community in Kenya are performing their funeral rituals differently from each other depending on the kind of environment they are located.

The Kenyan Coast and Mumias have also played a very critical role in the spread of Islam among the Luos especially in Kendu Bay. The possibility that Luos had interaction with Muslims from the Coast though not directly is found in what Sperling describes as trading in the "hinterland."[6] What he implies is that the Coastal Arabs were in trading business with the interior people. Part of the interior communities that Sperling could be referring to as trading partners with the Coastal Arabs is the Mumias people. Trimingham confirms this claim when he argues that: "The inhabitants of Mumias trading settlement are Muslims (Arabs, Somalis, Nubis, and some local converts). Islam is strong among the native population of Wanga and Maragoli. Some were converted whilst serving on the army or as porters and Swahili influence was felt from the end of the last (nineteenth) century."[7] But as to how Luos got in touch with Islam in this part of Mumias since there is no mention of them by Trimingham is something that can only be implied by looking at what Richards says: "Early traders through what was first called by Arabs and Swahili traders Kavirondo and is now known as Nyanza Province are all united on some aspects of the country."[8] This, assertion, however, may not directly link the Luos with the Coastal people but rather through their contact with the Muslims in Mumias.

---

4. Ochieng', *People around the Lake*, 3.

5. Johnson Nganga Mbugua and Mary N. Getui, *Funeral Rites Reformation for Any African Ethnic Community Based on the Proposed New Funeral Practices for the Agikuyu.* (Eugene, OR: Wipf & Stock, 2006), 450; Ochieng', *History of the Kadimo Chiefdom*, 29; Ochieng', *People around the Lake*, 4, 6.

6. Sperling, " Coastal Hinterland," 273.

7. Trimingham, *Islam in East Africa*, 27–28.

8. Richards, *Fifty Years in Nyanza*, 6.

Concerning the spread of Islam into the interior parts of the Coast, Sperling argues that: "by the end of the nineteenth century, most Africans in the immediate coastal hinterland had experienced the impact of Islam in one way or another."[9] The penetration of Islam into the interior part of Kenya must have come later. The later date is considered based on Pouwels's claim: "by 1500 and as early as 1200, Islam had become the majority religion of the Coastal people."[10] Marriage to the local people by Arab Muslims has been suggested as one of the tings that took place during the penetration of Islam at the Coast and in the interior parts of Kenya.[11] Apart from explaining why Arab Muslims intemarried with the local women, Were et. al mention the learning of language as another outcome of Islam's penetration: "Muslims learned the language of the people they lived among and, because they brought few or none of their own women with them, they married into African families."[12]

But whereas it is difficult to explain why it took so long for Islam to penetrate into the interior amidst the claim of intermarriages, the presence of Islam in Mumias today cannot be denied. Said traces the history of Islam in Mumias dating back to the period between 1870 and 1885, just before the Kenya-Uganda Railways was constructed.[13] According to him, Sharif Hassan Abdallah from Pangani was the first to spearhead the trade caravans into Mumias, the seat of the Wanga tribes whose paramount Chief, Nabongo Mumia, dramatically embraced Islam during one of the Idd festivals. He then adopted the Muslim name of Muhammad Mumia. Soon many members of his cabinet, his three brothers (Kadima, Mulama, and Murunga) and others were inspired and accepted Islam as their faith. Sharif Hassan got encouraged and sent more missionaries to different areas in Western Kenya and Uganda.[14] While writing on the same aspect on how Islam entered Mumias, Ogot, also record that the Arab-Swahili) caravans penetrated Kenya's territory for trade and by 1857 – that is during the reign of Shiundu – had probably begun to

---

9. Sperling, "Coastal Hinterland," 284.

10. Pouwels, "East African Coast," 251.

11. Trimingham, *Islam in East Africa*, 4, 10.

12. Were, Kipkorir, and Ayiemba, *South Nyanza District*, 2.

13. Said, "Outline History of Islam."

14. Said, 21.

appear in Wanga and by 1868, their presence was certainly there. By 1870, the Arab-Swahili routes through "Maasailand" were established. Thereafter, their presence continued, and Kwa Sundu became a regular resting and refreshing point for caravans traveling between the Coast and the interior.[15]

Both Said and Ogot highlight two important periods by which Islam got its way into Mumias. It is evident from their writings that Islam was a religion that was not strange to both King Nabongo of Wanga and Shiundu. Although both Said and Ogot have not said anything about whether Mumia and Shiundu were related or not, the perspective of Osogo is quite clear on this matter. He says: "Shiundu was the father of Nabongo Mumia."[16] In highliting some significant contribution that the presence of Islam has made in Mumias, Osogo, narrates that Thomson, accompanied by a fellow European named Martin, arrived at Mumia's court on 2 December, 1883. Thomson's men were mainly Swahilis from the Coast and it is interesting to note that they had no difficulty in being understood by Mumia and his senior officials as they had had contacts with Swahili and Baluchi slave traders who had been visiting Kwa-Shiundu (the place of the father to Mumia) by way of Uganda for the previous thirty-five years.[17]

Osogo's claim that Shiundu (father to King Nabongo Mumia) and his son Mumia had many wives from South Nyanza[18] shows that Luos and Luhyas are related by marriage. His mention of South Nyanza is very pivotal since it is the place Kendu Bay is located. It is due to their intermarriages that Ochieng speaks of the present Luos as "not a 'pure race.'"[19] He also claims that the Luo people were not the original inhabitants of Nyanza.[20] He clarifies that the people of Nyanza were very successive: Hunters – Southern Cushites – Bantu – Luo.[21] The Luo as he claims, came and fought out all these other people giving them a label, *mwache* – meaning "barbarians."[22]

---

15. Ogot, *History of the Luo-Speaking Peoples*, 612–613.

16. Osogo, *Nabongo Mumia of the Baluyia*, 6.

17. Osogo, 9.

18. Osogo, 6.

19. Ochieng', *A History of the Kadimo Chiefdom of Yimbo in Western Kenya*, 27.

20. Ochieng', *Outline History of Nyanza*, x; Ochieng', *History of the Kadimo Chiefdom*, 27; Ochieng', *People around the Lake*, 3.

21. Ochieng', *People around the Lake*, 3.

22. Ochieng', *History of the Kadimo Chiefdom*, 27.

This perspective about the Luo and their settlement in Nyanza is also captured by Ogot who in his observation rules that: "Strictly speaking, the history of the Kenya Luo begins only with their settlement in Nyanza, between
1490 and 1517, because prior to that there was no single nationality called
Jo-Luo.[23] Putting those dates as the possible period in which the Luo people
settled in Nyanza makes a lot of sense in understanding the argument that
supports Chushites and Bantu as the occupiers of Nyanza prior to Luo.

But although Ogot speaks of Nyanza in general as having been occupied
by the Kenyan Luo within those dates he has mentioned, Ochieng makes a
specific reference to South Nyanza:

> [F]rom about 1730 the Luo began to arrive in South Nyanza.
> As more and more of them came in, the lack of space in
> which they could graze their cattle caused more migrations,
> ever southwards. By 1900 the Luo had not only established
> themselves firmly in the present-day South Nyanza, but they
> had also taken up land in the Maraa and Musoma Districts of
> present-day Tanzania.[24]

His mention of Luo in Tanzania is part of the history that has seen Luos
spreading to many other different parts of East Africa since their exit
from Sudan.

It is claimed that there were intermarriages with these other communities
that Luo were referring to *mwache* (foreigners) during their settlement in
parts of Nyanza. These *mwache* according to Ochieng were mainly Bantus
who were too weak to fight during the Luo invasion into Nyanza.[25] In fact,
through these intermarriages, Ochieng suggests that a number of Luo clans
are still known as the descendents of ladies from foreign groups.[26] In Homa
Bay District (now County), for example, there is a large group of Luo who
are called Kanyamwa. Their ancestor is generally regarded as Chwanya.
He married several Luo and *mwa* (foreign) wives. Kanyamwa people now
reside in Homa Bay. They are the offspring of one of the foreign ladies who

---

23. Ogot, *History of the Luo-Speaking Peoples*, 485.
24. Ochieng', *People around the Lake*, 90.
25. Ochieng', 3.
26. Ochieng', 3.

was married to Chwanya. Kendu Bay is now part of Homa Bay County. Ochieng traces Chwanya from Joka-Jok (one of the Luo groups that moved into Kenya). He observes that from Joka-Jok, came Ramogi Ajwang'. He had two sons, Odongo and Jok. Jok son of Ramogi beget Imbo and Mumbo. Mumbo (son of Ramogi) beget Alego and Chwanya. The family of Chwanya later formed the Joka-Chwanya of South Nyanza.[27]

Ochieng' has highlighted the fact that the Luo people intermarried with Samia group.[28] From his assertion, Both Samia and Yimbo were the two important Bantu settlements in Nyanza before the arrival of the Luo.[29] Samia is today part of the wider Luhya community but have very close cultural ties with the Luo due to intermarriages. But closely linked with Samia are the Bugwe. In fact, Ogot describes this Bugwe people as Samia-Bugwe. The Bagwe (Bugwe) were originally the inhabitants of Samia-Bugwe. They were defeated by the Jok' Owiny (part of the Luo group who settled in different parts of Nyanza) and accepted to be ruled by them. The Bagwe are known to the Luos as Otewe.[30]

The above history points to a possible conclusion that Bagwe, which were part of Samia were among the Bantu communities that the Luo people intermarried with. While tracing the movement of Islam in South Nyanza and Kendu Bay in particular, Said reports that: "In about 1905, the first Arab, Nasser bin Ali, reached Wangwe in South Nyanza where he carried on with his trade in hides and skins. He then decided to migrate to Kendu Bay where he arrived about 1909."[31] Wangwe is a location in South Nyanza though different from Kendu Bay. The assumption here is that Wangwe, Bugwe and Bagwe that have appeared commonly used in different places are referring to the same place. Bagwe according to Osogo is a name signifying that they are a people from the "East (*bugwe* in Luo)."[32] The discussion points to the fact that the current residents of South Nyanza and in particular Kendu Bay

---

27. Ochieng', *Outline History of Nyanza*, 23–24.

28. Ochieng', *People around the Lake: Luo*, 3.

29. Ochieng', 3.

30. Ogot, *History of the Luo-Speaking Peoples*, 507–508.

31. Said, "Outline History of Islam," 21.

32. John N. B. Osogo, *A History of the Baluyia*. (Nairobi; New York: Oxford University Press, 1966), 103, 104.

are not "pure" Luo. They have been affected by the Islam from Sudan and by their relationship with the Luhya. Both Luo and Luhya cultures are close and significant to each other that Ochieng remarkes: "It must be regretted that any work which discusses the Lake Region of Kenya and leaves out the Abaluyia must be considered largely artificial, for the history of origin, migrations and evolution of the Nyanza people very much connects them with the history of origin, migrations and evolution of the Abaluyia."[33] The origin of the Luos cannot therefore be looked without understanding the kind of relationship they share with Luhyas.

---

33. Ochieng', *Outline History of Nyanza*, x.

The History and the Development of Islam in Kendu Bay

A lot of studies have been conducted regarding Kendu Bay. However, it is still not clear when Luo settled in Kendu Bay. But from what Ochieng discusses about the Luo migration into South Nyanza, it is possible to get a clue. He explains that:

> [F]rom about 1730 the Luo began to arrive in South Nyanza. As more and more of them came in, the lack of space in which they could graze their cattle caused more migrations, ever southwards. By 1900 the Luo had not only established themselves firmly in the present-day South Nyanza, but they had also taken up land in the Maraa and Musoma Districts of present-day Tanzania.[1]

Since Kendu Bay is part of South Nyanza, one can only estimate that their establishment into Kendu Bay came around that time. Other writings by Ogot[2] also propose similar date concerning the arrival of the Luo in Nyanza. From that the understanding of when Luo settled in Kendu Bay can be approximated.

Giving both geographical and historical perspective of South Nyanza in general, Were, Kipkorir and Ayiemba, observe: "South Nyanza is a frontier district which is bordered by the Republic of Tanzania to the South and the Republic of Uganda across the lake (Lake Victoria) to the west."[3] They

---

1. Ochieng', *People around the Lake*, 90.
2. Ogot, *History of the Southern Luo*, 2009.
3. Were, Kipkorir, and Ayiemba, *South Nyanza District*, 1.

also present various communities that live in South Nyanza: "The people of south Nyanza belong to two main groups, Bantu (Abakuria, Abasuba, Luhya-Kanyamgao and Suna locations) and Nilotic (Luo)."[4] The presence of these two main groups co-existing with each other in South Nyanza raises the possibility of intermarriages between them. In fact, Were, Kipkorir and Ayiemba describe South Nyanza as a "cultural melting point." They em-phasize that various cultures live together, each contributing to the general development of the area.[5] The Bantus are alleged to have been the first to live in South Nyanza. Ochieng confirms this by adding that: "It would appear that among the earliest invaders of South Nyanza were a Bantu-speaking people who were a splinter group from the Abawanga, the progenitors of the future ruling Abashitsetse of the Wanga kingdom."[6] By describing this Wanga splinter group as early occupants of South Nyanza, Ochieng is not only confirming that there were intermarriages between the Wanga with the Luos but also a possible trend that witnessed the penetration of Islam into some parts of South Nyanza including Kendu Bay.

Kendu Bay is one of the fastest growing towns in Kenya. Its population is predominantly Islamic. According to Adede, the name "Kindu" (often written as "Kendu") originated from the small river which was flowing between the two small hills in *Kotieno Magumba* sub-location. The word *kind* in dholuo means, "between," hence the word *kind* was pronounced *kindu* which became the name of the present day Kendu Bay town.[7] The interaction of Kendu Bay with Islam dates back to early twentieth century. Exchange of commodities in trade was mainly the way Arab Muslims got acess to Kendu Bay as Adede explains: "When the Arabs came, they found the people of Karachuonyo (Kendu Bay) growing crops like groundnuts, cotton, peas and beans. The Arabs brought khaki materials, blankets, bead sheets and other ornaments."[8] The commercial exchange between the Luos and the Arab Muslims in Kendu Bay did not only lead to the development

---

4. Were, Kipkorir, and Ayiemba, 8–16.
5. Were, Kipkorir, and Ayiemba, 16.
6. Ochieng', *An Outline History of Nyanza up to 1914*, 33.
7. Adede, Luo Origins.
8. Adede, 45; cf. Ochieng', *Outline History of Nyanza*, 86.

of the town but also led to many local people converting to Islam.[9] This conversion must have been possible through intermarriages as Said puts:

> It is noteworthy that most Arabs who settled at Kendu Bay had no wives. As time went on, most of them married the local women, e.g. Nasser bin Ali married a Nubian girl from Kisii, and Nasser bin Bukheith was married to a Luo girl. Such spirit of real integration was one of the factors which contributed to the earlier conversion of the local people into Islam, which teaches human equality. Local people like Ramadhan Nyalianga and Islem Ododo were converted to Islam in about 1910, exactly four years after Christianity had had a footing in that area. From here Islam expanded into other areas, like Oyugis, Homa Bay, Migori, Sakwa, Awendo, Sondo, Suna, Marindi, etc.[10]

The issue of intermarriages within South Nyanza was a very complex one. It did not only involve marriages with the Bantu but also with the Arab Muslims who had found their way into the region. The current population of Kendu Bay, which is now predominantly Muslims, explains the extent to which intermarriages reached. According to Said, the Muslim presence in Nyanza is a growing one: "Islam continued to gain converts, and today its [her] followers number several thousands in Nyanza province's districts of Kisumu, Siaya, Homa Bay, Kisii and Nyamira."[11] However, this steady growth as Said claims contradicts the observation which Hauge has made: "There are only a few Moslems among the Luo, most of them in Kisumu, and very few in Kendu Bay and Homa Bay."[12] Although the the current total population of Luo Muslims living in Kendu Bay is not known,[13] they are widespread in the area. The coming of Islam in Kendu Bay has witnessed a significant impact not only in trade but also the cultural aspect of the Luos. One such vital area which is believed to have been affected by Islam is the

---

9. Adede, Luo Origins.

10. Said, "Outline History of Islam," 21–22.

11. Said, 23.

12. Hans-Egil Hauge, *Luo Religion and Folklore* (Oslo, Norway: Scandinavian University Books, 1974), 19.

13. The next census in Kenya will be done in 2019.

Luo traditional customs surrounding the passing on of their loved ones. Such traditions have been held by Luos for decades. They have been the center of conflict with Christianity that views them as traditions whose time has past. Some Christian communities in Kendu Bay have therefore insisted that they should be abondoned. According to Akrong and Azumah, the call to abondon African traditions is not something new in Christian history:

> Collectively, African Traditional Religions were considered as a "backward and childlike sort of religion" with little or nothing that could be considered as high ideals. Not only were ATRs considered worthless, they were inimical to Christian teaching and values. In extreme cases, overzealous missionaries embarked on physical destruction of traditional shrines and artifacts to prove that these were not worthy of worship.[14]

The looking down upon the Luo traditions by the missionaries is one of the reasons that have made some Christians in Kendu Bay to leave the church and join Islam or African Independent Churches (AICs). Some of those who have remained in Christianity still find themselves reverting to the customs of their ancestors. The description that South Nyanza is a "cultural melting point"[15] means that even though some Luos in Kendu Bay have embraced Islam, their cultural traditional beliefs and practices have not completely disappeared. It is therefore very difficult to separate their traditions from the Islam that they follow. The difficulty in seperating their traditions from their belief in Islam further makes it almost impossible to give true identity of who the Luo Muslims are. It is in this sense that Were, Kipkorir and Ayiemba write: "As in many African societies, one cannot say that the Luo belong to such and such a *dini* or individually apprehended religion. Their religious beliefs and observances are part and parcel of everyday life."[16] The kind of identity that Luo Muslims have acquired as a result of their contact with Islam is therefore very special and distinctive.

---

14. Akrong, "Hermeneutical and Theological Resources," 69.
15. Were, Kipkorir, and Ayiemba, *South Nyanza District*, 16.
16. Were, Kipkorir, and Ayiemba, 19.

Relationships in *Ijma, Jumia* and *Ijumma*

This *ijma* as Rashid explained is derived from the root word, *ijuma* (Swahili word: *kusanyika* "gathering").[1] It is from this word that Friday (*ijumma*) is also derived. *Ijumma* is the busiest day of the week for the majority of the Muslims since they must gather (*kusanyika*) in a mosque for prayers and *hotuba* (in Swahili, meaning, sermons) from their leaders. Exception to this Friday prayer is given to those who are traveling, women in their monthly period and the nursing mothers. *Ijma* is convened in order to give an opinion in a case where both Muhammad and Allah have been silent. This silence is in fact in reference to both the Ḥadīth and the Qur'an.

Rashid pointed to some areas where *ijma* applies.[2] He indicated that it applies in situations where there is no clear direction from the Qur'an and the Ḥadīth and yet tough decisions have to be made. Such areas include: security matters such as *al-Shabaab* (in Arabic, meaning, the youths. In this case, it refers to those who are engaged in killing other human beings), *muhadhara* (in Arabic, meaning open debates in the public places) and matters involving the death of a Muslim who has been living among Christians. In matters of security, *al-Shabaab* has not only posed challenge to non-Muslims but also to other Muslim communities as well. Since most of them claim to be Muslims, consensus is required in order to provide a guideline of how to handle the situation. *Muhadhara* also need consensus if it is deemed necessary as a way of defending or providing answers to issues that are theologically controversial. This mostly borders between Christians and Muslims. *Ijma* is used to help sort out death issues. This applies in a

---

1. Rashid, interview with author.
2. Rashid, interview with author.

situation where a Muslim dies in an area which is dominated by Christians or they are the only Muslim in that family. The non-Muslim family or that Christian dominated community may be granted the permission to bury the deceased Muslim. The granting of the permission must however come by consensus from the other Muslim leaders who may be staying far away.

Ijma is also conducted in an incidence where a mother insists that she must bury her son in a coffin made by nails. Since this is a practice that Islam does not allow, she may be permitted to do so through a consensus agreement. Consensus is also necessary in a situation where a Muslim dies and his Christian family wants more days for mourning them before they are buried according to Islamic customs. This request calls for consensus since it exceeds the twenty-four hour period as been set in Islam for the burial of a Muslim. The request for extension of time whether it is for the burial of a Muslim whose family members are Muslims or non-Muslims is usually made due to two reasons. First, the family members of the deceased may want their other members who are far away to also attend the funeral. This might take quite some time depending on where those family members stay. The request to delay burial may also be placed in case the family members want more time to raise burial expenses. Such a request is mostly common from a non-Christian family where their loved one who has died is a Muslim. They may want to wait until they gather enough resources to enable them give their loved one a nice send-off. This nice send-off involves great celebrations in eating and drinking in the funeral. Since it is a custom that is not very common in Islam, consensus is required to reach a decision.

Relationship between *'Iddah* and *Talāq* (Divorce) in Islam

Just like in several African cultures, widows in Islam go through many rituals than the rest of the family members and relatives of the deceased. Following the demise of her husband, a widow begins a period of *'iddah*.[1] The same *'iddah* also applies in divorce cases. The *'iddah* of divorce is a three month period where a husband checks his wife for three things before dissolving the marriage. First, she is checked to ascertain whether she was pregnant with her husband's child. If she is found to be expectant, then she would be given time until the child is born. She then lives with the child until they are of age. The husband is, however, responsible to provide for the up-keeps of that child. Second, three month period is given with the hope that the issues that were threatening to disolve the marriage would be settled. Three months (*'iddat* in Arabic), is also a period where after the separation had taken place with no formal divorce and the husband discovers that his wife is still a virgin or has not slept with any man since they separated (they may still be leaving under the same roof), he may if he so wishes change his mind and get back to his wife. The decision to divorce fully lies on the husband. However, there are also some cases where a woman may seek for divorce.

Uttering careless words is not only prohibited against the deceased but also against one's spouse. A statement like, "you are like the back of my mother," are abusive (meaning that the husband lives with his mother instead of his wife).*Ijoga* (in Luo, meaning, you are a nuisance) is another unkind

---

1. *'iddah* (in Luo it is referred to as *chola*), which is usually four months and ten days, refers to a period in which a widow goes through a moment of mourning for her husband. This period is characterized by a number of ritual activities.

word that when a spouse uses against each other, may be the ground to seek
for divorce (ṭalāq). But the decision for the wife to divorce her husband who
has spoken those unkind words may be revised if he agrees to fast for two
months consecutively and promises that he would stay together with his wife.
He may also be required to feed sixty *maskin/kafara* (poor or needy people).
Fulfilling those requirments is viewed as a form of repentance (*tawba* in
Arabic) to which, according to Rashid, if one fails, the wrath of God would
be upon him.[2] The same penalties apply to the wife also. Other reasons
which were given as a source of divorce include: (1) a wife not giving birth,
(2) a husband who cannot provide for his family. It is wrong in Islam for a
wife to be the one providing for the family unless it is out of mutual understanding, (4) when both spouse are in agreement that they should dissolve
the marriage. This may come after realizing that they are not compatible with
each other, (5) a woman is uncomfortable with marriage (*khu* in Arabic).
This may be as a result of pressure from parents/relatives or hatred from
the family that she is married. (6) Forced marriage. This was explained as
marriage between an adult man and a girl who is still under age. Here, the
researcher was interested to know whether Muhammad's marriage to his
many wives of which some of them were still pretty too young could be
classified as forced marriage. The response he got was that in Muhammad's
case, his marriage was like a gift to him. He also married many wives in
order to end wars and be friendly to other communities. Concerning the
question of age, the informants pointed out that the moment one reaches
adolescent stage and has gained some knowledge formally or informally, that
person is considered ready for marriage. Knowledge is given priority due to
the belief that any learned person has simply inherited it from the prophet
and the messengers in Islam. However, the issue of marrying somebody who
is below eighteen years of age even if she is schooling is today viewed as
unconstitutional in Kenya. It is in this sense that forced marriage is treated
as a basis for divorce.

The seventh reason for divorce as was mentioned by the informants is
sex outside marriage. This has to be proved by some witnesses. For a man, it
must have four witnesses while for a woman it is two witnesses. Due to the

---

2. Rashid, interview with author.

differences in terms of witnesses, it implies that it is twice as hard to prove that a man has engaged in extra marital affairs as it is for a woman. Lastly, denouncing Islam is also a reason for divorce. The fact that one is divorced if they leave Islam means that converting to it is easier than leaving. In fact, as Siraj put it, "converting somebody to Islam brings a greater gift; it is a way of increasing the number."[3] The three types of divorce that were highlighted include: Kadhi court order (*Bain* in Arabic), consent of the wife (*khula* in Arabic) and consent of the husband (*rajaa* in Arabic). The husband can seek for divorce on the grounds that his wife does not give birth, he is uncomfortable with her or her character is not good.

The issue of divorce as has been discussed is supported in the Qur'an (65:2–12; 2:224–237). Those scriptures show that God hates divorce. But while this is true, it is also very clear from both the Qur'an and the experience of a Luo Muslim that a man has more options than a woman in matters of divorce. In other words, the reasons given to a man as a basis of divorce outweigh those of the woman. If this is so, then the question as to how equality between men and women is explained in Islam becomes very critical. The informants pointed out that the divorce is considered permanent after a husband has issued a third *ṭalāq*. This means that there are three *ṭalāq* that are required to dissolve the marriage completely. But in a situation where a husband dies after he has pronounced *ṭalāq* twice only, that divorce period ends and the widow now begins an *'iddah* of death. It is here that both *'iddah* of divorce and the *'iddah* of death are found to be related to each other. Their similarity is based on the fact that they both give details about what women usually face during that period.

---

3. Siraj, interview with author.

Bibliography

Interviews

Abdallah, Onyango. Interview with author, Kendu Bay. 23 May 2015.
Abdul, Rehman. Interview with author, Kendu Bay. 15 June 2015.
Aboo, Shaban. Interview with author, Kendu Bay. 25 August 2015.
Ahmad, Omar. Interview with author, Kendu Bay. 22 May 2015.
Ahmed, Aware. Interview with author, Kendu Bay. 15 June 2015.
Aisha, Shamar. Interview with author, Kendu Bay. 18 June 2015.
Azis, Odero. Interview with author, Kendu Bay. 15 August 2015.
Bruck, Said. Interview with author, Kendu Bay. 17 May 2015.
Hakim, Abuor. Interview with author, Kendu Bay. 3 July 2015.
Hasan, Nabil. Interview with author, Kendu Bay. 16 May 2015.
Hisham, Zakaria. Interview with author, Kendu Bay. 7 June 2015.
Ikbar, Nabil. Interview with author, Kendu Bay. 18 June 2015.
Jimila, Saidi. Interview with author, Kendu Bay. 13 June 2015.
Mariam, Abubakri. Interview with author, Kendu Bay. 24 May 2015.
Omar, Oginga. Interview with author, Kendu Bay. 3 May 2015.
Ramsam, Shaban. Interview with author, Kendu Bay. 20 July 2015.
Rashid, Alamin. Interview with author, Kendu Bay. 2 August 2015.
Razia, Apiyo. Interview with author, Kendu Bay. 3 August 2015.
Rehema, Jamar. Interview with author, Kendu Bay. 5 August 2015.
Rukia, Adhiambo. Interview with author, Kendu Bay. 14 May 2015.
Saidi, Idi Simba. Interview with author, Kendu Bay. 16 May 2015.
Saleh, Okello. Interview with author, Kendu Bay. 6 June 2015.
Sarah, Abdallah. Interview with author, Kendu Bay. 9 May 2015.
Shaban, Otieno. Interview with author, Kendu Bay. August 2015.
Siraj, Omar. Interview with author, Kendu Bay. August 2015.
Swaleh, Suedi. Interview with author, Kendu Bay. 15 July 2015.
Swedi, Karim. Interview with author, Kendu Bay. 28 May 2015.
Tatu, Amina. Interview with author, Kendu Bay. 5 May 2015.

Zachariah, Juma. Interview with author, Kendu Bay. 22 July 2015.
Zainab, Hamed. Interview with author, Kendu Bay. 26 June 2015.
Zarika, Akinyi. Interview with author, Kendu Bay. 11 June 2015.
Zuhura, Juma. Interview with author, Kendu Bay. 29 May 2015.

Primary Resources

Abū Sulaymān, 'AbdulḤamīd. *The Qur'anic Worldview: A Springboard for Cultural Reform*. Virginia, USA: International Institute of Islamic Thought, 2013.

Abu-Lughod, Lila. "Islam and Gendered Discourse on Death." *International Journal of Middle East Studies* 25, no. 2 (May 1993): 187–205.

Achieng, Jane. *Paul Mboya's Luo Kitgi Gi Timbegi*. Nairobi, Kenya: Atai Joint, 2001.

Adede, George W. Otieno. *Luo Origin and Politics: Emergence of Nilotic Luo in 1000 AD and After*. Nairobi: Gramowa, 2010.

Afe, Adogame. "Practitioners of Indigenous Religions of Africa and the African Diaspora." In *Religion in Focus: New Approaches to Tradition and Contemporary Practices*, edited by Graham Harvey, 75–99. London: Equinox, 2009.

Aguilar, Mario I. "African Conversion from a World Religion: Religious Diversification by the Waso Boorana in Kenya." *Africa: Journal of the International African Institute* 65, no. 4 (1995): 525–544.

Akrong, Abraham. "Hermeneutical and Theological Resources in African Traditional Religions for Christian Muslims in Africa." In *The African Christian and Islam*, edited by John Azumah, and Lamin Sanneh, 65–84. Carlisle: Langham Monographs, 2013.

Allen, J. W. T. *The Customs of the Swahili People: The Desturi Za Waswahili of Mtoro Bin Mwinyi Bakari and Other Swahili Persons*. Berkeley, CA: University of California Press, 1981.

Armour, Rollin. *Islam, Christianity, and the West: A Troubled History*. Faith Meets Faith Series. Maryknoll, NY: Orbis Books, 2002.

el-Aswad, el-Sayed. "Death Rituals In Rural Egyptian Society: A Symbolic Study." *Urban Anthropology and Studies of Cultural Systems and World Economic Development* 16, no. 2 (1987): 205–241.

———. *Muslim Worldviews and Everyday Lives*. Lanham, MD: AltaMira, 2012.

Ayoub, Mahmoud. *Islam: Faith And History*. New York: Oneworld, 2004. Accessed 17 July 2018, http://rbdigital.oneclickdigital.com.

Ayubi, Shabeen, and Mohyuddin Sakina. "Muslims in Kenya: An Overview." *Institute of Muslim Minority Affairs Journal* 15, no. 1–2 (1994): 144–156.

Bah, Alpha Mahmoud. *Glimpses of Life after Death: A Collection of Hadiths on the Transition from This Life to the Hereafter, the Entrance to Paradise or Hell.* London: Ta-Ha, 2001.

Beattie, John. *Other Cultures.* London: Routledge; Kegan Paul, 1966.

Bediako, Kwame. *Theology and Identity: The Impact of Culture upon Christian Thought in the Second Century and in Modern Africa.* Oxford: Regnum Books, 1992.

Behera, M. C. *Tribal Religion: Change and Continuity.* New Delhi: Commonwealth Publishers, 2000.

Bennett, Clinton. *Understanding Christian-Muslim Relations.* New York: Continuum, 2008.

Bhatti, Harvinder Singh. *Folk Religion Change and Continuity.* New Delhi: Rawat Publications, 2000.

Bīlī, 'Utmān Sayyid Aḥmad Ismā'īl al-. *Some Aspects of Islam in Africa.* Reading: Ithaca, 2008.

p'Bitek, Okot. *Religion of the Central Luo.* Nairobi: East African Literature Bureau, 1971.

Black, John. "Death and Bereavement: The Customs of Hindus, Sikhs and Moslems." *Bereavement Care* 10, no. 1 (1991): 6–8.

Booth, Newell S. "Time and Change in African Traditional Thought." *Journal of Religion in Africa* 7, no. 2 (1975): 81–91.

Branch, Daniel. "The Search for the Remains of D'iddahn Kimathi: The Politics of Death and Memorialization in Post-Colonial Kenya." *Past and Present* 206, no. 5 (n.d): 301–320.

Braswell, George W. *Islam: Its Prophet, Peoples, Politics, and Power.* Nashville, TN: Broadman & Holman, 1996.

———. *What You Need to Know about Islam and Muslims.* Nashville: B & H, 2000.

Braukämper, Ulrich. "Aspects of Religious Syncretism in Southern Ethiopia." *Journal of religion in Africa* 22, no. 3 (1992): 194–207.

Brodeur, Patrice C. "From Postmodernism to 'Glocalism': Toward a Theoretical Undertanding of Contemporary Arab Muslim Constructions of Religious Others." In *Globalization and the Muslim World: Culture, Religion, and Modernity,* edited by Birgit Schäbler and Leif Stenberg, 188–205. Syracuse, NY: Syracuse University Press, 2004.

Broom, Leonard. "Acculturation: An Exploratory Formulation." *American Anthropologist* 56, no. 6 (1954): 973–1000.

Bunger, Robert Louis. *Islamization among the Upper Pokomo.* Syracuse, NY: Eastern African Studies Program, 1973.

Burge, Gary M. *Jesus and the Land: The New Testament Challenge to "Holy Land" Theology.* London: SPCK; Grand Rapids, MI: Baker Academic, 2010.

Carr, Melissa S. *Who Are the Muslims?: Where Muslims Live, and How They Are Governed*. Broomall, PA: Mason Crest, 2004.

Clarke, Peter. "Religion in the Service of Politics and Service in the Politics of Religion." 4 (1993): 35–42. Accessed at the Bodleian Library, Oxford.

Cohen, David William, and E. S. Atieno Odhiambo. *Burying SM: The Politics of Knowledge and Sociology of Power in Africa*. Social history of Africa. Nairobi: East African Educational Publishers, 1992.

———. "The River-Lake Nilotes from the Fifteenth to the Nineteenth Century." In *Zamani: A Survey of East African History*, edited by B. A. Ogot, 135–149. Nairobi, Kenya: Longman Kenya, 1974.

Conn, Harvie M. "Islam in East Africa: An Overview." *Islamic Studies* 17, no. 2 (1978): 75–91.

Corbin, Juliet M., and Anselm L. Strauss. *Basics of Qualitative Research: Techniques and Procedures for Developing Grounded Theory*, 4th ed. Thousands Oaks, CA: Sage, 1998.

———. *Basics of Qualitative Research: Techniques and Procedures for Developing Grounded Theory*. Newbury Park, CA: Sage, 1990.

Crazzolara, Pasquale. *The Lwoo. Part I: Lwoo Migrations*. Verona: Instituto Missioni Africane, 1950.

Creswell, John W. *Research Design: Qualitative, Quantitative, and Mixed Methods Approaches*. Thousands Oaks, CA: Sage, 2003.

———. *Research Design: Qualitative and Quantitative Approaches*. Thousands Oaks, CA: Sage, 1994.

Dau, Isaiah Majok. *Suffering and God: A Theological Reflection on the War in Sudan*. Nairobi, Kenya: Paulines Publications Africa, 2003.

Dessing, Nathalia Maria. *Rituals of Birth, Circumcision, Marriage, and Death among Muslims in the Netherlands*. Leuven: Peeters, 2001.

Diene, Doudou, and Jean Burrell. "A Dynamic Continuity between Traditions." *Diogenes* 47, no. 187 (1999): 11–19.

van Doren, John W. "Death African Style: The Case of S. M. Otieno." *The American Journal of Comparative Law* 36, no. 2 (1988): 329–350.

Dubisch, Jill. "Death and Social Change in Greece." *Anthropological Quarterly* 62, no. 4 (1989): 189–200.

Durkheim, Emile, and Joseph Ward Swain. *The Elementary Forms of Religious Life*. Stilwell: Neeland Media LLC, 2013.

Egan, Sean, ed. "SM Otieno: Kenya's Unique Burial Saga." *Daily Nation Newspaper*. Nairobi, 1987.

Elliston, Edgar J. *Introduction to Missiological Research Design*. Pasadena, CA: William Carey Library, 2011.

Faloloa, Toyin. "The Spread of Islam and Christianity and Their Impact on Religious Pluralism in Africa." *Dialogue & Alliance* 2, no. 4 (1988): 5–18.

Faulkner, Mark R. J. *Overtly Muslim, Covertly Boni: Competing Calls of Religious Allegiance on the Kenyan Coast*. Studies of Religion in Africa 29. Leiden: Brill, 2006.

Fishman, Joshua. "Ethnicity as Being, Doing, and Knowing." In *Ethnicity*, edited by John Hutchinson and Anthony D. Smith, 63–69. New York, NY: Oxford University Press, 1996.

Fontana, Andrea, and James H. Frey. "The Interviews: From Structured Questions to Negotiated Text." In *Handbook of Qualitative Research*. 2nd ed., edited by Norman K. Denzin and Yvonna S. Lincoln, 645–672. Thousands Oaks, CA: Sage, 2000.

Fosarelli, Patricia D. *Prayers & Rituals at a Time of Illness & Dying: The Practices of Five World*. West Conshohocken, PA: Templeton, 2008.

Geertz, Clifford. *The Interpretation of Cultures*. New York: Basic books, 1973.

———. *Islam Observed: Religious Development in Morocco and Indonesia*. Chicago: University of Chicago Press, 1971.

Ghazzālī, Abu Hamid Muhammad ibn Muhammad, and Timothy Winter. *The Remembrance of Death and the Afterlife: Book XL of the Revival of the Religious Sciences, Iḥyā' 'ulūm al-dīn = Kitāb Dhikr al-mawt wa-mā ba'dahu*. Cambridge, UK: The Islamic Text Society, 1989.

Gilliland, Dean S. *African Religion Meets Islam: Religious Change in Northern Nigeria*. Lanham; London: University Press of America, 1986.

———. *African Traditional Religion in Transition: The Influence of Islam on African Traditional Religion in North Nigeria*. Ann Arbor, MI: Univ. Microfilms, 1972.

Ginena, Karim, and Azhar Hamid. *Foundations of Shari'ah Governance of Islamic Banks*. Chichester, West Sussex: Wiley, 2015.

Glaser, Barney G. *Basics of Grounded Theory Analysis: Emergence vs Forcing*. Mill Valley, CA: Sociology Press, 1992.

Glasse, Cyril. *The New Encyclopedia of Islam. Revised Edition of the Concise Encyclopedia of Islam*. New York: Altamira, 2001.

Goddard, Hugh. *A History of Christian-Muslim Relations*. Chicago, IL: New Amsterdam Books, 2000.

Goldziher, Ignaz. *Introduction to Theology and Law*. Princeton, NJ: Princeton University Press, 1981.

———. "On the Veneration of the Dead in Paganism and Islam." In *Muslim Studies*. Vol. 1, edited by S. M. Stern, translated by C. R. Barber and S. M. Stern, 209–238. London: Allen & Urwin, 1967.

Granqvist, Hilma. *Muslim Death and Burial: Arab Customs and Traditions Studied in a Village in Jordan*. Helsinki: Societas Scientiarum Fennica, 1965.

Greste, Peter. "Kenya Defends Tribal Census Figures." *BBC News, Africa*, 31 August 2010, https://www.bbc.co.uk/news/world-africa-11143914.

Grudem, Wayne. *Systematic Theology: An Introduction to Biblical Doctrine.* Leicester: Inter-Varsity Press, 1994.

Gunga, Samson O. "The Politics of Widowhood and Re-Marriage among the Luo of Kenya." *Thought and Practice: A Journal of the Philosophical Association of Kenya* 1, no. 1 (2009): 161–174.

Halevi, L. *Muhammad's Grave: Death Rites and the Making of Islamic Society.* New York: Columbia University Press, 2007.

———. "Wailing for the Dead: The Role of Women in Early Islamic Funerals." *Past and Present* 183, no. 1 (2004): 3–39.

Hauge, Hans-Egil. *Luo Religion and Folklore.* Oslo, Norway: Scandinavian University Books, 1974.

Hedayat, Kamyar. "When the Spirit Leaves: Childhood Death, Grieving, and Bereavement in Islam." *Journal of Palliative Medicine* 9, no. 6 (2006): 1282–1291.

Hertz, Robert. *Death and the Right Hand.* London: Free Press, 1960.

———. *Death and the Right Hand.* 2nd ed. London: Routledge, 2004.

Hiebert, Paul G. *Anthropological Insights for Missionaries.* Grand Rapids, MI: Baker Books, 1985.

———. *Transforming Worldviews: An Anthropological Understanding of How People Change.* Grand Rapids, MI: Baker Academic, 2008.

Hiebert, Paul G., Robert Daniel Shaw, and Tite Tiénou. *Understanding Folk Religion a Christian Response to Popular Beliefs and Practices.* Grand Rapids, MI: Baker Books, 1999.

Holt, P. M., Ann K. S. Lambton, and Bernard Lewis. *The Cambridge History of Islam. Vol. 2B: Islamic Society and Civilization.* Cambridge: Cambridge University Press, 1970.

Horton, Robin. "Tradition and Modernity Revisited." In *Rationality and Relativism*, edited by Martin Hollis and Steven Lukes, 201–260. Oxford: Basil Blackwell, 1982.

Hoskins, Edward J. *A Muslim's Mind: What Every Christian Needs to Know about the Islamic Traditions.* Colorado Springs, CO: Dawson Media, 2012.

Hussain, Zamir. *A Gift for the Bereaved Parent: A Remedy for Grief from the Islamic Perspective Using Quotes from the Qur'an and Ahadith.* London: Ta-Ha, 2010.

'Aṭṭās, 'Abd Allāh ibn 'Alawī, and Badawî Mostafâ. *The Lives of Man: A Sufi Master Explains the Human States: Before Life, in the World, and after Death.* Louisville, KY: Fons Vitae, 1997.

Islam, Khawaja Muhammad. *The Spectacle of Death: Including Glimpses of Life beyond the Grave.* Delhi, India: Adam, 1992.

———. *The Spectacle of Death: The Scene of Death and What Happens after Death.* Delhi, India: Adam, 2001.

Jaya Kumar, G. Stanley. *Tribals from Tradition to Transition: A Study of Yanadi Tribe of Andhra Pradesh*. New Delhi: M D Publications, 1995.

Jenkins, Philip. *The Lost History of Christianity: The Thousand-Year Golden Age of the Church in the Middle East, Africa, and Asia – and How it Died*. New York: HarperOne, 2011.

Jindra, Michael. *Funerals in Africa: Explorations of a Social Phenomenon*. Oxford: Berghahn Books, 2011.

Jonker, Gerdien. "The Many Facets of Islam: Death, Dying and Disposal between Orthodox Rule and Historical Convention." In *Death and Bereavement across Cultures*, 147–165. London: Routledge, 2000.

Kaniki, Martin Hoza Y. *The Impact of Islam on African Societies*. Dar es Salaam: University of Dar es Salaam, 1974.

Kasozi, A. B. K. *The Spread of Islam in Uganda*. Nairobi: Oxford University Press, 1986.

Kassatly, Huda. "Local Traditions and Islamic Tradition: The Dynamics of a Conflict Seen Through the Study of a Specific Case: Funeral Rites in a Shi'ite Village in South Lebanon." *Islam and Christian-Muslim Relations* 2, no. 1 (1991): 23–41.

Kato, B. H. *African Cultural Revolution and the Christian Faith*. Jos, Nigeria: Challenge Publications, 1976.

———. *Theological Pitfalls in Africa*. Kisumu, Kenya: Evangel, 1975.

Kearney, Michael. *World View*. Novato, CA: Chandler & Sharp, 1984.

Kennedy, John G. *Nubian Ceremonial Life: Studies in Islamic Syncretism and Cultural Change*. Cairo, Egypt: American University in Cairo Press; Berkley, CA: University of California Press, 1978.

Kenya National Bureau of Statistics. *The 2009 Kenyan Population and Housing Census*. Nairobi: Kenya National Bureau of Statistics, 2010.

Khan, A. S. *Muslim Culture and Traditions: Information Pack*. Belfast: Al-Nisa Association NI, 2006.

Kilonzo, Susan. "The Ahmadiyya Muslim Community and Peace Building in Kisumu District, Kenya." *Journal of Peace Building and Development* 6, no. 1 (2011): 80–85.

Kimathi, Wambui. "A Strategic Seclusion–Yet Again! The 1997 General Elections in Luo Nyanza." In *Out of the Count: The 1997 General Elections and Prospects for Democracy in Kenya*, edited by Marcel Rutten, Alamin Mazrui and Francois Grignon, 495–511. Kampala: Fountain, 2001.

Kim, Caleb Chul-Soo. "Considering 'Ordinariness' in Studying Muslim Cultural and Discipleship." In *Discipleship in the 21st Century Mission*, edited by Timothy Park and Steve K. Eom, 177–192. Kyunggi, Korea: East West Center for MRD, 2014.

———. *Islam among the Swahili in East Africa*. 2nd ed. Nairobi: Acton, 2016.

Kirby, Jon. "Cultural Change and Religion: Conversion in West Africa." In *Experience and Expression*, edited by Thomas D. Blakely, Walter E. A. van Beek and Dennis L. Thomson, 57–72. London: James Currey, 1994.

Kisiara, Richard. "Some Sociopolitical Aspects of Luo Funerals." *Anthropos* 93, no. 1/3 (1998): 127–136.

Klass, Dennis. "Continuing Bonds in the Resolution of Grief in Japan and North America." *American Behavioral Scientist* 44, no. 5 (2001): 742–764.

Klass, Dennis, Phyllis R. Silverman, and Steven L. Nickman. *Continuing Bonds: New Understandings of Grief.* Washington, DC: Taylor & Francis, 1996.

Kraft, Charles H. *Anthropology for Christian Witness.* Maryknoll, NY: Orbis, 1996.

———. *Worldview for Christian Witness.* Pasadena, CA: William Carey Library, 2008.

Kwenda, C. V. "The Jekhanke of Senegambia: A Study in Religious Naturalization." *Encounter* 53, no. 3 (1994): 287–300.

Kyewalyanga, Francis-Xavier Sserufusa. *Traditional Religion, Custom and Christianity in Uganda: As Illustrated by the Ganda with Some References to Other African Cultures and Islam.* Freiburg: Krause, 1976.

Lalande, Kathleen M., and George A. Bonanno. "Culture and Continuing Bonds: A Prospective Comparison of Bereavement in the United States and the People's Republic of China." *Death Studies* 30, no. 4 (2006): 303–324.

Lawson, E. Thomas. *Religions of Africa.* New York, NY: Harper & Row, 1984.

LeCompte, Margaret Diane, and Jean J. Schensul. *Designing & Conducting Ethnographic Research: An Introduction.* 2nd ed. Lanham: AltaMira Press, 2010.

Levine, Ellen. "Jewish Views and Customs on Death." In *Death and Bereavement Across Cultures*, edited by Colin Murray Parks, Pittu Luangani and Bill Young, 98–130. London; New York: Routledge, 2000.

Levtzion, Nehemia, Michel Abitbol, and Amos Nadan. *Islam in Africa and the Middle East: Studies on Conversion and Renewal.* Aldershot; Burlington, VT: Ashgate/Variorum, 2007.

Lewis, I. M. *Islam in Tropical Africa.* 2nd ed. London: International African Institute, 1980.

———. "Sufism in Somaliland a Study in Tribal Islam." *BSOAS* 17, no. 3 (1955): 581–602.

Loimeier, Roman. *Muslim Societies in Africa: A Historical Anthropology.* Bloomington, IN: Indiana University Press, 2013.

Love, Rick. "Power Encounter among Folk Muslims." In *Encountering the World of Islam*, edited by Keith E. Swartley and Sarah E. Holmes, 209–215. Waynesboro, GA: Authentic, 2005.

Lowry, Joseph E. *Early Islamic Legal Theory: The Risāla of Muḥammad Ibn Idrīs Al-Shāfiʿī*. Studies in Islamic Law and Society. Leiden: Brill, 2007.

Lybarger, Loren. "The Demise of Adam in the Qisas al-Anbiyā: The Symbolic Politics of Death and Re-Burial in the Islamic 'Stories of the Prophets.'" *NU Numen* 55, no. 5 (2008): 497–535.

MacKenzie, Peter R. *Inter-Religious Encounters in West Africa: Samuel Ajayi Crowther's Attitude to African Traditional Religion and Islam*. Leicester: Blackfriars, 1976.

Madidi, Abdur Rahman. *The Spread of Islam in Southern Africa and Its Impact on Society: A Geographical Perspective*. 3rd ed. South Africa: University of Stellenbosch, 2003.

Mardini, Souran. *Islam: Worldly Life and the Hereafter*. Istanbul: Murat Center, 2013.

Marranci, Gabriele. *The Anthropology of Islam*. Oxford; New York: Berg, 2008.

Mazrui, Ali A. "African Islam and Competitive Religion: Between Revivalism and Expansion." *Third World Quarterly* 10, no. 2 (1988): 499–518.

———. "Islam between Ethnicity and Economics: The Dialectics of Africa's Experience." In *Africa, Islam and Development: Islam and Development in Africa: African Islam, African Development*, edited by Thomas Salter and Kenneth King, 15–49. Edinburgh: University of Edinburgh, 2000.

Mbiti, John S. *African Religions and Philosophy*. New York: Praeger, 1969.

———. *Concepts of God in Africa*. Nairobi, Kenya: Acton, 2012.

———. *Introduction to African Religion*. 2nd ed. Nairobi, Kenya: East African Educational Publishers, 1975.

Mbugua, Johnson Nganga, and Mary N. Getui. *Funeral Rites Reformation for Any African Ethnic Community Based on the Proposed New Funeral Practices for the Agikuyu*. Eugene: Wipf & Stock, 2006.

Mugenda, Olive M., and Abel G. Mugenda. *Research Methods: Quantitative and Qualitative Approaches*. Nairobi: Acts Press, 1999.

Munday, E. J. "The Luyia Response to Death: A Case Study from Wanga, Western Kenya." PhD diss., University of Oxford, 1983.

Musa, Aisha Y. "Al-Shafi'i, the Hadith, and the Concept of the Duality of Revelation." *Islamic studies* 46, no. 2 (2007): 163–197.

Musk, Bill A. *The Unseen Face of Islam Sharing the Gospel with Ordinary Muslims at Street Level*. London: Monarch, 2004.

Nagel, Tilman. *The History of Islamic Theology: From Muhammad to the Present*. Princeton, NJ: Markus Wiener, 1999.

Nanji, Azim. "Beginnings & Encounters: Islam in East African Contexts." In *Religion in Africa: Experience and Expression*, edited by Thomas D. Blakely, Walter E. A. Van Beek, and Dennis L. Thomson, 47–72. London: James Currey, 1994.

Ndisi, John W. *A Study in the Economic and Social Life of the Luo of Kenya.* Uppsala, Sweden: Uppsala, 1974.

Nyambega, Gisesa. "Controversy Stalks Wambui Otieno Even in Death." *Standard Newspaper Kenya*, May 19 2013, https://www.standardmedia. co.ke/article/2000083940/controversy-stalks-wambui-otieno-even-in-death.

Nyaundi, Nehemiah M. *Religion and Social Change: A Sociological Study of Seventh-Day Adventism in Kenya.* Lund, Sweden: Lund University Press, 1993.

Nyende, Peter T. N. "Jesus the Greatest Ancestor: A Typology-Based Theological Interpretation of Hebrews' Christology in Africa." PhD thesis, Edinburgh University, 2006.

Ochieng', William R. *A History of the Kadimo Chiefdom of Yimbo in Western Kenya.* Nairobi: East African Literature Bureau, 1975.

———. *An Outline History of Nyanza up to 1914.* Kampula: East African literature Bureau, 1974.

———. *People around the Lake.* London: Evans Brothers, 1985.

Ocholla-Ayayo, A. B. C. "Death and Burial: An Anthropological Perspective." In *The S.M. Otieno Case: Death and Burial in Modern Kenya*, edited by J. B. Ojwang and J. N. K. Mugambi, 30–39. Nairobi: Nairobi University Press, 1989.

Odaga, Asenath. *The Luo Oral Literature and Educational Values of its Narratives.* Kisumu, Kenya: Lake, 2011.

Oduyoye, Mercy Amba. *Hearing and Knowing: Theological Reflections on Christianity in Africa.* Eugene, OR: Wipf & Stock, 1986.

Ogbuagu, Stella C. "The Changing Perception of Death and Burial: A Look at the Nigerian Obituaries." *Anthropologica* 31, no. 1 (1989): 85–101.

Ogot, Bethwell A. *A History of the Luo-Speaking Peoples of Eastern Africa.* Kisumu: Anyange, 2009.

———. *History of the Southern Luo.* Nairobi: East African Publishing House, 1967.

Ogutu, Gilbert E. M. "Eschatology: An African Perception." In *Immortality and Human Destiny: A Variety of Views*, edited by Geddes MacGregor, 102–111. New York, NY: Paragon House, 1985.

———. *Ker Jaramogi is Dead: Who Shall Lead My People? : Reflections on Past, Present, and Future Luo Thought and Practice.* Kisumu, Kenya: Palwa Research Services, 1995.

Olaleye-Oruene, Taiwo O. "The Yoruba's Cultural Perspective of Death with Special Reference to Twins." *Twin Research* 5, no. 3 (2002): 154–155.

Olupona, Jacob K. "Major Issues in the Study of African Traditional Religion." In *African Traditional Religions in Contemporary Society*, 25–33. St. Paul, MN: Paragon House, 1991.

Ongong'a, Jude J. *Life and Death: A Christian–Luo Dialogue.* Eldoret, Kenya: Gaba Publications, AMECEA Pastoral Institute, 1983.

———. "The River-Lake Luo Phenomenon of Death." In *Rites of Passage in Contemporary Africa: Interaction between Christian and African Traditional Religions,* edited by James L. Cox, 224–239. Cardiff: Cardiff Academic Press, 1998.

Onyango-Ogutu, Benedict, and Adrian A. Roscoe. *Keep My Words: Luo Oral Literature.* Nairobi: East African Educational Publishers, 1974.

Odhiambo, Lawrence Oseje. *A Study of the Influence of Islam on the Traditional Death, and Burial Rites of the Luo Community in Kendu Bay: Implications for Christian Witness.* Nairobi: NEGEST, 2009.

O'Shaughnessy, Thomas J. *Muhammad's Thoughts on Death A Thematic Study of the Qur'anic Data.* Leiden: Brill, 1969.

Osiro, Rebecca. "Women's Views on the Role of Kadhi's Courts." In *Sharia in Africa Today,* edited by J. A. Chesworth and F. Kogelmann, 195–212. Leiden Brill, 2015.

Osogo, John N. B. *A History of the Baluyia.* Nairobi; New York: Oxford University Press, 1966.

———. *Nabongo Mumia of the Baluyia.* Nairobi: East African Literature Bureau, 1969.

Parkin, David J. *The Cultural Definition of Political Response: Lineal Destiny among the Luo.* London: Academic Press, 1978.

Parrinder, Geoffrey. *African Traditional Religion.* New York: Harper & Row, 1962.

———. *Religion in Africa.* New York: Praeger, 1969.

Parshall, Phil. *New Paths in Muslim Evangelism: Evangelical Approaches to Contextualization.* Grand Rapids, MI: Baker Books, 1980.

Patton, Michael Quinn. *Qualitative Research & Evaluation Methods: Integrating Theory and Practice.* Thousands Oaks, CA: Sage, 2002.

Perrin-Jassy, Marie France. *Basic Community in the African Churches.* Maryknoll, NY: Orbis Books, 1973.

Peters, F. E. *Islam: A Guide for Jews and Christians.* Princeton: Princeton University Press, 2003.

Pobee, John S., and Emmanuel H. Mends. "Social Change and African Traditional Religion." *Sociological Analysis* 38, no. 1 (1977): 1–12.

Pouwels, Randall L. "The East African Coast, C. 790 to 1900 C.E." In *The History of Islam in Africa,* edited by Nehemia Levtzion and Randall L. Pouwels, 251–266. London: James Currey, 2000.

Prince, Ruth. "Christian Salvation and Luo Tradition: Arguments of Faith in a Time of Death in Western Kenya." In *Aids and Religions Practice in Africa,* edited by Felicitas Beeker and P. Wenzel Geissler, 49–83. Netherlands: IDC, 2009.

Qadri, Anwar Ahmad. *A Sunni Shafi'i Law Code.* New Delhi: Islamic Book Service, 1997.

Quinn, Charlotte. *Mandingo Kingdoms of the Senegambia Traditionalism, Islam, and European Expansion.* London: Longman, 1972.

Qurṭubī, Muḥammad ibn Aḥmad, Reda Bedeir, and Khadija Ford. *An authentic selection of Imam al-Qurṭubī's At-Tadhkirah fi aḥwālil-mawtá wal-ākhirah = in remembrance of the affairs of the dead and doomsday.* Egypt: Dar-Al Manarah, 2004.

Raje, Ismail. *Death and Beyond.* Vol. 26. Bradford: Jamea Publications, 1998.

Rapport, Nigel, and Joanna Overing. *Social and Cultural Anthropology: The Key Concepts.* 2nd ed. New York, NY: Routledge, 2007.

Richards, Elizabeth. *Fifty Years in Nyanza: 1906–1956 : The History of the C.M.S. and the Anglican Church in Nyanza Province, Kenya.* Maseno, Kenya: Nyanza Jubilee Committee, 1956.

Riday, Muhammad Abdalla. *Masahaba kumi waliobashiriwa pepo.* Mombasa, Kenya: Adam Traders, 1993.

Rippin, Andrew, and Jan Knappert, eds. *Textual Sources for the Study of Islam.* Chicago: University of Chicago Press, 1990.

Robinson, David. *Muslim Societies in African History.* Cambridge: Cambridge University Press, 2004.

Rosander, Eva Evers. "The Islamization of 'Tradition' and 'Modernity.'" In *African Islam and Islam in Africa: Encounters between Sufis and Islamists,* edited by Eva Evers Rosander and David Westerlund, 1–27. London: Hurst & Company, 1997.

Said, Ahmed Salim. "An Outline History of Islam in Nyanza Province." In *Islam in Kenya Proceedings of the National Seminar on Contemporary Islam in Kenya,* edited by Mohammad Bakari and Saad S. Yahya, 19–39. Nairobi: Mewa Publications, 1995.

Sanneh, Lamin O. *The Crown and the Turban: Muslims and West African Pluralism.* Boulder, CO: Westview press, 1997.

van Santen, Josepha C. M. *They Leave Their Jars Behind: The Conversion of Mafa Women to Islam (North Cameroon).* Leiden: VENA, 1993.

Schlee, Günther, and Abdullahi A. Shongolo. *Islam and Ethnicity in Northern Kenya and Southern Ethiopia.* Rochester, NY: Boydell & Brewer, 2012.

Schwartz, Nancy L. "Active Dead or Alive: Some Kenyan Views about the Agency of Luo and Luyia Women Pre- and Post-Mortem." *Journal of Religion in Africa* 30, no. 4 (2000): 433–467.

Seedat, Noorjehan bint Faqir. *What to Do When a Muslim Dies.* London: Ta-Ha, 2004.

Sesi, Stephen Mutuku. "Prayer among the Digo Muslims of Kenya and Its Implications for Christian Witness." PhD thesis, Fuller Theological Seminary. Pasadena, CA: Fuller Theological Seminary, 2003.

Sharif, Ja'far, G. A. Herklots, and William Crooke. *Islam in India or the Qanun-i-Islam; the Customs of the Musalmans of India; Comprising a Full and Exact Account of Their Various Rites and Ceremonies from the Moment of Birth to the Hour of Death*. London: Curzon, 1972.

Sharkey, Heather J. "Sudan." In *Muslim Cultures: A Reference Guide*, edited by Kathryn Coughin, 177–185. London: Greenwood, 2006.

Shiino, Wakana. "Death and Rituals among the Luo in South Nyanza." *African Study Monographs* 18, no. 3/4 (1997): 213–228.

Shipton, Parker MacDonald. "Debts and Trespasses: Land, Mortgages, and the Ancestors in Western Kenya." *Journal of the International African Institute* 62, no. 3 (1992): 357–388.

———. *Mortgaging the Ancestors Ideologies of Attachment in Africa*. London: Yale University Press, 2009.

von Sicard, S. "Malagasy Islam: Tracing the History and Cultural Influences of Islam in Madagascar." *Journal of Muslim Minority Affairs* 31, no. 1 (2011): 101–112.

Siddiqi, Abdul Hamid. *Sahih Muslim: Arabic-English*. Vol. 1. New Delhi: Idara Isha'at-e-Diniya, 1983.

———. *Sahih Muslim: Arabic-English*. Vol. 3. New Delhi: Idara Isha'at-e-Diniya, 2007.

Silverman, David. *Doing Qualitative Research*. London: Sage, 2005.

Smith, Jane Idleman, and Yvonne Yazbeck Haddad. *The Islamic Understanding of Death and Resurrection*. Oxford: Oxford University Press, 2002.

Sperling, David. "The Coastal Hinterland and Interior of East Africa." In *The History of Islam in Africa*, edited by Nehemia Levtzion, and Randall L. Pouwels, 273–297. UK: James Currey, 2000.

Spradley, James P. *The Ethnographic Interview*. Orlando, FL: Holt, Rinehart & Winston, 1979.

———. *Participant Observation*. Orlando, FL: Holt, Rinehart & Winston, 1980.

Stamp, Patricia. "Burying Otieno: The Politics of Gender and Ethnicity in Kenya." *Journal of Women in Culture and Society* 16, no. 4 (1991): 808–845.

Stensson, Jonas. "Muslims Have Instructions: HIV/AIDS, Modernity and Islamic Religious Education in Kisumu, Kenya." In *Aids and Religious Practice in Africa*, edited by Felicitas Beeker and P. Wenzel Geissler, 189–219. Leiden: Brill, 2009.

Stewart, Charles. "Syncretism and Its Synonyms: Reflections on Cultural Mixture." *Diacritics* 29, no. 3 (1999): 40–62.

Stinton, Diane B. *Jesus of Africa: Voices of Contemporary African Christology.* Nairobi, Kenya: Paulines Publications Africa, 2004.

Strauss, Anselm Leonard, and Juliet M Corbin. "Grounded Theory Methodology." In *Handbook of Qualitative Research*, edited by N. K. Denzin and Y. S. Lincoln, 272–285. Thousand Oaks, CA: Sage, 1994.

Swartley, Keith E., and Sarah E. Holmes. *Encountering the World of Islam.* Littleton, CO: BottomLine Media, 2014.

Tayob, Abdulkader. *Islam: A Short Introduction: Signs, Symbols and Values.* Oxford: Oneworld, 1999.

Trimingham, J. S. *A History of Islam in West Africa.* London: Edinburgh House Press, 1962.

———. *The Influence of Islam upon Africa.* 2nd ed. London: Longman, 1986.

———. *Islam in East Africa.* Oxford: Clarendon, 1964.

Vannaprasœt Chaveewan, Phīrayot Rāhimmūlā, and Mānop Čhitphūsā. *The Traditions Influencing the Social Integration between the Thai Buddhists and the Thai Muslims.* Translated by Prachitr Mahahing and Kate Ratanajarana. Pattani, Thailand: Faculty of Humanities and Social Sciences and Center for Southern Thailand Studies, Prince of Songkhla University, 1986.

Venhorst, Claudia, et al. "Islamic Ritual Experts in a Migration Context: Motivation and Authority in the Ritual Cleansing of the Deceased." *Mortality* 18, no. 3 (2013): 235–250.

Walls, Andrew F. *The Cross-Cultural Process in Christian History Studies in the Transmission and Appropriation of Faith.* Maryknoll, NY: Orbis Books, 2002.

———. *The Missionary Movement in Christian History Studies in the Transmission of Faith.* Maryknoll, NY: Orbis Books, 1996.

Watt, William Montgomery. *Islamic Fundamentalism and Modernity.* New York, NY: Routledge, 1999.

———. *Islamic Philosophy and Theology.* Edinburgh: Edinburgh University Press, 1985.

Were, Gideon S., Ben E. Kipkorir, and Elias O. Ayiemba. *South Nyanza District: Socio-Cultural Profile.* Nairobi: Institute of African Studies, 1986.

Whisson, M. G., and J. M. Lonsdale. "The Case of Jason Gor and Fourteen Others: A Luo Succession Dispute in Historical Perspective." *Africa: Journal of the International African Institute* 45, no. 1 (1975): 50–66.

Whitehouse, Harvey. *Modes of Religiosity: A Cognitive Theory of Religious Transmission.* Oxford: AltaMira Press, 2004.

Yannoulatos, Anastasios. "Christian Awareness of Primal World-Views." In *Mission Trends No. 5: Faith Meets Faith*, edited by Gerald H. Anderson and Thomas F. Stransky, 249–257. Grand Rapids, MI: Eerdmans, 1981.

Langham
PARTNERSHIP

Langham Literature, with its publishing work, is a ministry of Langham Partnership.

Langham Partnership is a global fellowship working in pursuit of the vision God entrusted to its founder John Stott –

to facilitate the growth of the church in maturity and Christ-likeness through raising the standards of biblical preaching and teaching.

Our vision is to see churches in the majority world equipped for mission and growing to maturity in Christ through the ministry of pastors and leaders who believe, teach and live by the Word of God.

Our mission is to strengthen the ministry of the Word of God through:
• nurturing national movements for biblical preaching
• fostering the creation and distribution of evangelical literature
• enhancing evangelical theological education
especially in countries where churches are under-resourced.

Our ministry

Langham Preaching partners with national leaders to nurture indigenous biblical preaching movements for pastors and lay preachers all around the world. With the support of a team of trainers from many countries, a multi-level programme of seminars provides practical training, and is followed by a programme for training local facilitators. Local preachers' groups and national and regional networks ensure continuity and ongoing development, seeking to build vigorous movements committed to Bible exposition.

Langham Literature provides majority world preachers, scholars and seminary libraries with evangelical books and electronic resources through publishing and distribution, grants and discounts. The programme also fosters the creation of indigenous evangelical books in many languages, through writer's grants, strengthening local evangelical publishing houses, and investment in major regional literature projects, such as one volume Bible commentaries like the *Africa Bible Commentary* and the *South Asia Bible Commentary*.

Langham Scholars provides financial support for evangelical doctoral students from the majority world so that, when they return home, they may train pastors and other Christian leaders with sound, biblical and theological teaching. This programme equips those who equip others. Langham Scholars also works in partnership with majority world seminaries in strengthening evangelical theological education. A growing number of Langham Scholars study in high quality doctoral programmes in the majority world itself. As well as teaching the next generation of pastors, graduated Langham Scholars exercise significant influence through their writing and leadership.

To learn more about Langham Partnership and the work we do visit **langham.org**

www.ingramcontent.com/pod-product-compliance
Lightning Source LLC
Chambersburg PA
CBHW050624280326
41932CB00015B/2508

* 9 7 8 1 7 8 3 6 8 5 4 3 1 *